Football in the Republic of Ireland

– a statistical record 1921 to 2021

Michael Robinson

INTRODUCTION

This book features a statistical history of football in Ireland from 1921 when the country gained independence from the United Kingdom and became the Irish Free State. The Football Association of Ireland was founded in 1921 together with the Free State Football League. When, in 1949, the country again changed its name to the Republic of Ireland, the Free State Football League became known as the League of Ireland.

In addition to the results of all League matches and Final League tables, a list of the top goalscorers and results of the latter stages of the national Cup competition are also included. The club names are listed in the following format: Club Name (Home Town/City/Village).

In the League of Ireland, if teams finished level on points, the placings were decided on goal average until 1976. After 1976, goal difference decided placings. The exception to this rule is if two or more teams are level on points at the top of the League. In this case, the championship is decided by a play-off.

In an attempt to ensure accuracy, the information has been checked and collated. However, if any errors are found, readers are invited to notify Soccer Books care of the address below and, if possible, provide the corrected information.

British Library Cataloguing in Publication Data

A catalogue record for this book is available from the British Library

ISBN 978-1-86223-454-3

Copyright © 2021, SOCCER BOOKS LIMITED. (01472 696226)   www.soccer-books.co.uk
72 St. Peter's Avenue, Cleethorpes, N.E. Lincolnshire, DN35 8HU, United Kingdom

All rights are reserved. No part of this publication may be reproduced, stored in a retrieval system or transmitted, in any form or by any means, electronic, mechanical, photocopying, recording, or otherwise, without the prior written permission of Soccer Books Limited.

Printed by 4Edge Limited.

1921-22

Free State Football League Division "A" 1921-22	Bohemian FC	Dublin United FC	Frankfort FC	Jacobs AFC	Olympia FC	St. James's Gate FC	Shelbourne FC	Y.M.C.A.
Bohemian FC	■	4-2	0-0	2-0	1-0	1-2	2-0	5-0
Dublin United FC	2-5	■	6-0	3-1	0-3	0-2	1-2	3-2
Frankfort FC	1-3	5-0	■	3-0	3-3	2-1	0-4	4-4
Jacobs AFC	1-3	4-0	4-1	■	2-1	0-0	1-4	3-1
Olympia FC	1-3	2-0	1-1	2-2	■	0-4	1-1	2-1
St. James's Gate AFC	1-0	5-1	2-0	4-2	0-1	■	4-1	2-0
Shelbourne FC	2-1	2-3	3-1	1-1	3-1	0-2	■	4-1
Y.M.C.A.	1-5	2-4	1-1	2-2	0-2	0-2	2-4	■

	Division "A"	Pd	Wn	Dw	Ls	GF	GA	Pts	
1.	ST. JAMES'S GATE AFC (DUBLIN)	14	11	1	2	31	8	23	
2.	Bohemian FC (Dublin)	14	10	1	3	35	13	21	
3.	Shelbourne FC (Dublin)	14	8	2	4	31	21	18	
4.	Olympia FC (Dublin)	14	5	4	5	20	21	14	
5.	Jacobs AFC (Dublin)	14	4	4	6	23	27	12	
6.	Frankfort FC (Dublin)	14	3	5	6	22	32	11	#
7.	Dublin United FC (Dublin)	14	5	-	9	25	39	10	
8.	Y.M.C.A (Dublin)	14	-	3	11	17	43	3	#
		112	46	20	46	204	204	112	

Top goal-scorers 1921-22

1) Jack KELLY (St. James's Gate AFC) 11
2) Patrick SMITH (Jacobs AFC) 10
3) E. POLLOCK (Bohemian FC) 9

\# Frankfort FC (Dublin) and Y.M.C.A. (Dublin) were not re-elected to the league for next season.
Elected: Athlone Town AFC (Athlone), Dublin Pioneers FC (Dublin), Midland Athletic FC (Dublin), Rathmines Athletic FC (Dublin), Shamrock Rovers FC (Dublin), Shelbourne United FC (Dublin)
The league was extended to 12 clubs for next season

FAI Cup FAI Cup Final   (Dalymount Park, Dublin – 17/03/1922 – 15,000)

ST. JAMES'S GATE AFC (DUBLIN)	1-1	Shamrock Rovers FC (Dublin)
Kelly	*(H.T. 1-0)*	*Campbell*

St James's Gate: Coleman, Murphy, Kavanagh, McKay, Heaney, Carter, Carey, Kelly, Duncan, Dowdall, Gargan.
Shamrock Rovers: Nagle, Kelly, Warren, Glen, Byrne, Birthistle, Campbell, Cowzer, Flood, Fullam, Doyle.

Final Replay   (Dalymount Park, Dublin – 08/04/1922 – 10,000)

ST. JAMES'S GATE AFC (DUBLIN)	1-0	Shamrock Rovers FC (Dublin)
Kelly	*(H.T. 1-0)*	

St James's Gate: Coleman, Murphy, Kavanagh, McKay, Heaney, O'Shea, Carey, Kelly, Duncan, Dowdall, Gargan.
Shamrock Rovers: Nagle, Kelly, Warren, Glen, Byrne, Birthistle, Campbell, Cowzer, Flood, Fullam, Doyle.

Semi-Finals

St. James's Gate AFC (Dublin)	0-0, 2-1	Shelbourne FC (Dublin)
Shamrock Rovers FC (Dublin)	1-0	Bohemian FC (Dublin)

Quarter-Finals

Bohemian FC (Dublin)	7-1	Athlone Town AFC (Athlone)
Shamrock Rovers FC (Dublin)	5-1	Dublin United FC (Dublin)

St. James's Gate AFC (Dublin) and Shelbourne FC (Dublin) both received byes

1922-23

Free State Football League Division "A" 1922-23	Athlone Town FC	Bohemian FC	Dublin United FC	Jacobs AFC	Midland Athletic FC	Olympia FC	Dublin Pioneers FC	Rathmines Athletic FC	St. James's Gate AFC	Shamrock Rovers FC	Shelbourne FC	Shelbourne United FC
Athlone Town AFC	■	2-1	6-1	2-1	2-1	4-0	5-0	4-2	1-3	0-1	0-0	3-3
Bohemian FC	2-0	■	7-1	1-1	4-0	8-0	7-0	4-1	2-2	0-2	1-4	1-0
Dublin United FC	0-4	0-6	■	2-2	2-2	3-3	2-3	6-1	1-0	1-7	0-6	4-2
Jacobs AFC	1-2	1-4	2-1	■	8-0	0-0	2-2	5-2	2-0	2-4	1-1	1-2
Midland Athletic FC	0-4	2-6	3-2	1-0	■	2-1	2-3	5-3	1-4	1-3	0-3	1-0
Olympia FC		1-1	1-0	1-3	1-4	■	0-0	2-1	0-1	0-6	0-3	0-4
Dublin Pioneers FC	1-2	1-2	3-1	2-0	4-0	1-1	■	2-1	1-5	1-5	0-9	5-1
Rathmines Athletic FC	2-0	1-4	-:+	0-0	1-2	1-0	0-4	■	1-7	1-5	0-6	1-2
St. James's Gate AFC	4-1	1-5	4-1	3-1	4-1	1-1	5-2	2-0	■	1-1	0-2	1-2
Shamrock Rovers FC	4-2	2-0	3-1	2-2	9-1	6-0	4-1	3-1	2-1	■	0-0	0-1
Shelbourne FC	3-1	1-1	3-0	0-1	3-0	6-0	7-0	5-0	3-0	2-7	■	4-0
Shelbourne United FC	3-1	0-5	2-1	2-2	1-1	2-1	4-2	6-1	4-0	0-1	2-1	■

	Division "A"	Pd	Wn	Dw	Ls	GF	GA	Pts	
1.	SHAMROCK ROVERS FC (DUBLIN)	22	18	3	1	77	19	39	
2.	Shelbourne FC (Dublin)	22	15	4	3	72	14	34	
3.	Bohemian FC (Dublin)	22	14	4	4	72	23	32	
4.	Shelbourne United FC (Dublin)	22	12	3	7	43	37	27	
5.	St. James's Gate AFC (Dublin)	22	11	3	8	49	35	25	
6.	Athlone Town AFC (Athlone)	22	11	3	8	46	33	25	
7.	Jacobs AFC (Dublin)	22	6	8	6	38	34	20	
8.	Dublin Pioneers FC (Dublin)	22	8	3	11	38	65	19	
9.	Midland Athletic FC (Dublin)	22	7	2	13	30	68	16	
10.	Dublin United FC (Dublin)	22	4	3	15	30	70	11	#
11.	Olympia FC (Dublin)	22	2	7	13	13	57	11	#
12.	Rathmines Athletic FC (Dublin)	22	2	1	19	21	74	5	##
		264	110	44	110	529	529	264	

Top goal-scorers 1922-23

1)	Robert FULLAM	(Shamrock Rovers FC)	27
2)	Ralph ARDIFF	(Shelbourne FC)	26
3)	Stephen DOYLE	(Shelbourne FC)	14
	Patrick DUNCAN	(St. James's Gate AFC)	14
	Christy ROBINSON	(Bohemian FC)	14

Rathmines Athletic FC resigned from the league after 21 games. Their last match was awarded to Dublin United FC with a 0-0 scoreline registered (shown in the table as -:+).

* The Olympia FC v Athlone Town AFC match was not played. The FA awarded 1 point to each team and the match was recorded as a draw.

\# Dublin United FC (Dublin) and Olympia FC (Dublin) were not re-elected to the league for next season.

Elected: Brooklyn FC (Dublin)

The league was reduced to 10 clubs for next season

FAI Cup Final   (Dalymount Park, Dublin – 17/03/1923 – 14,000)

ALTON UNITED FC (BELFAST)	1-0	Shelbourne FC (Dublin)
McSherry	(H.T. 0-0)	

Alton United: Maginnis, McNeill, Bell, Devlin, Brennan, Loughran, McSherry, Duffy, Ward, Russell, McCann.
Shelbourne: Walsh, Kavanagh, Connolly, Delaney, Harris, Foley, Brierley, Doyle, Harvey, Wilson, Ardiff.

Semi-Finals

Alton United FC (Belfast)	4-2	Fordsons FC (Cork)
Shelbourne FC (Dublin)	2-0	Jacobs AFC (Dublin)

Quarter-Finals

Dublin United FC (Dublin)	2-3	Fordsons FC (Cork)
St. James's Gate AFC (Dublin)	1-2	Shelbourne FC (Dublin)
Shamrock Rovers FC (Dublin)	1-2	Jacobs AFC (Dublin)
Shelbourne United FC (Dublin)	1-1, 0-2	Alton United FC (Belfast)

1923-24

Free State Football League Division "A" 1923-24	Athlone Town FC	Bohemian FC	Brooklyn FC	Jacobs AFC	Midland Athletic FC	Dublin Pioneers FC	St. James's Gate AFC	Shamrock Rovers FC	Shelbourne FC	Shelbourne United FC
Athlone Town AFC	■	0-1	4-1	3-1	6-0	3-0	3-2	1-2	2-3	0-0
Bohemian FC	4-1	■	3-1	2-1	4-0	3-2	2-1	4-1	2-0	5-0
Brooklyn FC	0-2	0-2	■	1-1	1-0	0-2	0-1	1-3	1-3	1-3
Jacobs AFC	1-2	1-2	3-0	■	7-1	1-0	2-1	2-1	2-1	1-0
Midland Athletic FC	0-2	2-4	0-3	1-6	■	1-0	0-3	2-4	0-6	2-6
Dublin Pioneers FC	1-1	1-7	0-6	1-2	1-4	■	2-6	2-1	1-7	1-3
St. James's Gate AFC	4-0	1-3	2-0	1-1	2-0	5-0	■	2-0	3-6	1-1
Shamrock Rovers FC	3-3	2-0	1-1	1-2	3-0	5-1	2-3	■	2-2	0-2
Shelbourne FC	0-0	5-2	5-1	3-1	2-0	2-0	2-0	3-2	■	4-0
Shelbourne United FC	1-1	1-6	2-5	0-1	2-0	3-0	3-0	1-2	2-1	■

	Division "A"	Pd	Wn	Dw	Ls	GF	GA	Pts	
1.	BOHEMIAN FC (DUBLIN)	18	16	-	2	56	20	32	
2.	Shelbourne FC (Dublin)	18	13	2	3	55	21	28	
3.	Jacobs AFC (Dublin)	18	11	2	5	36	21	24	
4.	Athlone Town AFC (Athlone)	18	8	5	5	34	24	21	
5.	St. James's Gate AFC (Dublin)	18	9	2	7	38	27	20	
6.	Shelbourne United FC (Dublin)	18	8	3	7	30	31	19	
7.	Shamrock Rovers FC (Dublin)	18	7	3	8	35	32	17	
8.	Brooklyn FC (Dublin)	18	4	2	12	23	37	10	
9.	Dublin Pioneers FC (Dublin)	18	2	1	15	15	60	5	
10.	Midland Athletic FC (Dublin)	18	2	-	16	13	62	4	#
		180	80	20	80	335	335	180	

Top goal-scorers 1923-24

1) Dave ROBERTS   (Bohemian FC)   20
2) Christy ROBINSON   (Bohemian FC)   12
   Frank RUSHE   (Shelbourne FC)   12

\# Midland Athletic FC (Dublin) were not re-elected to the league for next season.

Elected: Bray Unknowns FC (Bray)

FAI Cup Final   (Dalymount Park, Dublin – 17/03/1924 – 18,000)

ATHLONE TOWN AFC (ATHLONE)   1-0   Fordsons FC (Cork)
Hannon   *(H.T. 1-0)*

Athlone Town: O'Reilly, Monaghan, Hope, Judge, Dykes, Muldoon, Lyster, Hannon, Sweeney, Collins, Ghent.
Fordsons: O'Hagan, O'Mahoney, Miller, Maher, O'Sullivan, Barry, Hunter, Pinkney, Malpas, Buckley, Collins.

Semi-Finals

Athlone Town AFC (Athlone)	0-0, 2-0	Bohemian FC (Dublin)
Fordsons FC (Cork)	4-0	St. James's Gate AFC (Dublin)

Quarter-Finals

Bray Unknowns FC (Bray)	0-1	Bohemian FC (Dublin)
Jacobs AFC (Dublin)	0-2	Fordsons FC (Cork)
St. James's Gate AFC (Dublin)	2-1	Shelbourne United FC (Dublin)
Shelbourne FC (Dublin)	0-2	Athlone Town AFC (Athlone)

1924-25

Free State Football League Division "A" 1924-25	Athlone Town FC	Bohemian FC	Bray Unknowns FC	Brooklyn FC	Fordsons FC	Jacobs AFC	Dublin Pioneers FC	St. James's Gate AFC	Shamrock Rovers FC	Shelbourne FC
Athlone Town AFC	■	-:+	1-1	0-0	1-0	0-3	1-0	3-2	0-5	0-3
Bohemian FC	+:-	■	1-1	5-1	4-0	5-0	0-0	3-3	1-1	2-2
Bray Unknowns FC	3-1	0-2	■	4-3	1-3	1-4	3-5	0-1	0-3	2-3
Brooklyn FC	0-1	0-4	1-0	■	0-3	3-1	3-0	2-2	2-6	0-2
Fordsons FC	2-1	0-3	3-1	3-3	■	3-0	3-1	4-1	0-6	2-0
Jacobs AFC	1-1	1-2	3-2	6-2	2-0	■	4-1	2-0	1-4	1-3
Dublin Pioneers FC	1-3	0-6	1-2	1-2	1-5	1-6	■	5-3	1-7	1-6
St. James's Gate AFC	1-1	0-1	0-0	5-1	3-2	2-0	1-0	■	2-2	1-7
Shamrock Rovers FC	6-0	1-1	6-0	6-1	3-0	3-0	5-1	0-0	■	1-1
Shelbourne FC	4-1	1-0	3-0	8-0	1-2	2-1	5-1	3-3	1-2	■

Division "A"	Pd	Wn	Dw	Ls	GF	GA	Pts	
1. SHAMROCK ROVERS FC (DUBLIN)	18	13	5	-	67	12	31	
2. Bohemian FC (Dublin)	18	11	6	1	40	11	28	*
3. Shelbourne FC (Dublin)	18	12	3	3	55	20	27	
4. Fordsons FC (Cork)	18	10	1	7	35	32	21	**
5. Jacobs AFC (Dublin)	18	8	1	9	36	35	17	
6. St. James's Gate AFC (Dublin)	18	5	7	6	30	36	17	
7. Athlone Town AFC (Athlone)	18	5	4	9	15	32	14	*
8. Brooklyn FC (Dublin)	18	4	3	11	24	57	11	#
9. Bray Unknowns FC (Bray)	18	3	3	12	21	44	9	
10. Dublin Pioneers FC (Dublin)	18	2	1	15	21	65	5	
	180	73	34	73	344	344	180	

Top goal-scorers 1924-25

1) Billy FARRELL   (Shamrock Rovers FC)   25
2) Robert FULLAM   (Shamrock Rovers FC)   20
3) Eddie BROOKS   (Bohemian FC)   14

** Shelbourne United FC (Dublin) withdrew from the league on 07 September 1924, the day after the competition officially started. Their place was awarded to Fordsons FC (Cork).

* Athlone Town AFC – Bohemian FC matches were not played, both matches were awarded to Bohemian FC (shown above as +:- and -:+ with no goals registered).

Brooklyn FC (Dublin) were not re-elected to the league for next season.

Elected: Brideville FC (Dublin)

FAI Cup Final   (Dalymount Park, Dublin – 17/03/1925 – 23,000)

SHAMROCK ROVERS FC (DUBLIN)	2-1	Shelbourne FC (Dublin)
Fullam, Flood	*(H.T. 1-0)*	*Glen o.g.*

Shamrock Rovers: O'Reilly, Kirkland, Malone, Glen, Doyle, Marlow, Jordan, Fullam, Farrell, Flood, Fagan.
Shelbourne: Walsh, Daly, Kavanagh, Kelly, Harris, Foley, Laxton, Cowzer, Doran, Mulvanney, Wilson.

Semi-Finals

Shamrock Rovers FC (Dublin)	2-1	Bray Unknowns FC (Bray)
Shelbourne FC (Dublin)	4-0	Athlone Town AFC (Athlone)

Quarter-Finals

Bray Unknowns FC (Bray)	4-0	Dublin Pioneers FC (Dublin)
Brooklyn FC (Dublin)	0-4	Shelbourne FC (Dublin)
Drumcondra AFC (Dublin)	0-2	Athlone Town AFC (Athlone)
St. James's Gate AFC (Dublin)	0-1	Shamrock Rovers FC (Dublin)

1925-26

Free State Football League Division "A" 1925-26	Athlone Town	Bohemian FC	Bray Unknowns	Brideville FC	Fordsons FC	Jacobs AFC	Dublin Pioneers	St. James's Gate	Shamrock Rovers	Shelbourne FC
Athlone Town AFC	■	1-2	2-3	3-0	2-5	4-2	4-3	5-1	1-5	1-4
Bohemian FC	6-3	■	7-2	6-0	0-2	2-2	4-1	1-1	1-4	0-2
Bray Unknowns FC	3-5	2-6	■	7-1	1-1	2-5	3-1	1-3	1-1	0-5
Brideville FC	3-3	2-1	1-0	■	3-2	4-1	4-3	3-2	1-4	2-3
Fordsons FC	6-5	0-2	3-2	6-2	■	4-0	8-2	3-1	0-2	5-1
Jacobs AFC	4-1	3-1	1-1	4-4	1-2	■	2-0	4-2	1-4	0-8
Dublin Pioneers FC	1-2	0-4	1-3	2-1	0-7	3-5	■	2-4	0-5	0-8
St. James's Gate AFC	2-3	1-4	4-2	2-2	0-2	0-2	3-0	■	3-3	1-4
Shamrock Rovers FC	3-0	0-2	5-0	2-1	3-0	4-1	10-2	3-2	■	2-2
Shelbourne FC	3-1	2-1	3-1	2-2	4-2	2-2	5-0	4-1	3-2	■

	Division "A"	Pd	Wn	Dw	Ls	GF	GA	Pts	
1.	SHELBOURNE FC (DUBLIN)	18	14	3	1	65	23	31	
2.	Shamrock Rovers FC (Dublin)	18	13	3	2	62	21	29	
3.	Fordsons FC (Cork)	18	12	1	5	58	31	27	*
4.	Bohemian FC (Dublin)	18	10	2	6	50	28	20	*
5.	Jacobs AFC (Dublin)	18	7	4	7	40	48	18	
6.	Brideville FC (Dublin)	18	6	4	8	36	53	16	
7.	Athlone Town AFC (Athlone)	18	7	1	10	46	56	15	
8.	St. James's gate AFC (Dublin)	18	4	3	11	33	48	11	
9.	Bray Unknowns FC (Bray)	18	4	3	11	34	55	11	
10.	Dublin Pioneers FC (Dublin)	18	1	-	17	21	82	2	#
		180	78	24	78	445	445	180	

Top goal-scorers 1925-26

1) Billy FARRELL   (Shamrock Rovers FC)   24
2) John SIMPSON   (Shelbourne FC)   18
3) Jim SWEENEY   (Athlone Town AFC)   17

* Bohemian FC (Dublin) were "fined" 2 points which were awarded to Fordsons FC (Cork).
\# Dublin Pioneers FC (Dublin) were not re-elected for the next season.   Elected: Dundalk FC (Dundalk)

FAI Cup Final   (Dalymount Park, Dublin – 17/03/1926 – 25,000)

FORDSONS FC (CORK)	3-2	Shamrock Rovers FC (Dublin)
Barry 2, Roberts	*(H.T. 1-2)*	*Farrell, Fagan*

Fordsons: O'Hagan, Baylor, Carabine, Connolly, Sullivan, Collins, McKinney, Kelly, Roberts, Buckle, Barry.
Shamrock Rovers: O'Reilly, Malone, Kirkland, Glen, Doyle, Marlow, Jordan, Flood, Farrell, Fullam, Fagan.

Semi-Finals

Fordsons FC (Cork)	4-1	Bray Unknowns FC (Bray)
Shamrock Rovers FC (Dublin)	0-0, 3-0	Jacobs AFC (Dublin)

Quarter-Finals

Athlone Town AFC (Athlone)	2-3	Fordsons FC (Cork)
Jacobs AFC (Dublin)	1-1, 4-2	Lindon FC (Dublin)

Bray Unknowns FC (Bray) and Shamrock Rovers FC (Dublin) both received byes

1926-27

Free State Football League Division "A" 1926-27	Athlone Town AFC	Bohemian FC	Bray Unknowns FC	Brideville FC	Dundalk FC	Fordsons FC	Jacobs AFC	St. James's Gate AFC	Shamrock Rovers FC	Shelbourne FC
Athlone Town AFC	■	3-3	5-1	5-0	3-1	2-2	5-2	0-3	2-5	2-4
Bohemian FC	3-1	■	3-1	1-0	4-2	2-1	4-0	3-0	1-2	3-2
Bray Unknowns FC	2-5	2-0	■	4-2	2-1	3-2	3-0	4-2	3-6	1-2
Brideville FC	0-0	0-0	3-3	■	4-3	2-1	2-3	1-2	1-2	1-3
Dundalk FC	2-3	1-1	4-1	1-1	■	4-2	3-0	1-1	0-5	0-2
Fordsons FC	2-1	1-1	4-1	4-2	2-1	■	3-1	3-1	0-0	1-3
Jacobs AFC	1-1	0-2	4-3	2-2	1-1	1-0	■	4-2	0-3	0-4
St. James's Gate AFC	5-2	1-2	3-1	2-0	2-2	1-3	0-2	■	1-5	2-8
Shamrock Rovers FC	6-0	4-0	3-2	0-0	3-3	4-2	3-0	3-2	■	3-3
Shelbourne FC	1-1	3-3	9-0	3-1	3-0	2-1	6-2	5-0	0-3	■

	Division "A"	Pd	Wn	Dw	Ls	GF	GA	Pts
1.	SHAMROCK ROVERS FC (DUBLIN)	18	14	4	-	60	20	32
2.	Shelbourne FC (Dublin)	18	13	3	2	63	24	29
3.	Bohemian FC (Dublin)	18	10	5	3	36	24	25
4.	Fordsons FC (Cork)	18	7	3	8	34	32	17
5.	Athlone Town AFC (Athlone)	18	6	5	7	41	43	17
6.	Bray Unknowns FC (Bray)	18	6	1	11	37	58	13
7.	Jacobs AFC (Dublin)	18	5	3	10	23	47	13
8.	Dundalk FC (Dundalk)	18	3	6	9	30	40	12
9.	St. James's Gate AFC (Dublin)	18	5	2	11	30	49	12
10.	Brideville FC (Dublin)	18	2	6	10	22	39	10
		180	71	38	71	376	376	180

Top goal-scorers 1926-27

1) David BYRNE (Shamrock Rovers FC) 17
   John McMILLAN (Shelbourne FC) 17
3) Eddie BROOKS (Athlone Town AFC) 14
   Robert FULLAM (Shamrock Rovers FC) 14

FAI Cup Final   (Dalymount Park, Dublin – 17/03/1927 – 25,000)

DRUMCONDRA AFC (DUBLIN)   1-1   Brideville FC (Dublin)
McCarney   (H.T. 1-0)   McCarthy

Drumcondra: Cleary, Keogh, Moore, Coyle, Grace, Maxwell, Fleming, Swan, McCarney, Cullen, Murray.
Brideville: Gamblin, Lennox, Siney, Donovan, Armstrong, Fox, Murtagh, Maguire, Watters, O'Brien, McCarthy.

Final Replay   (Shelbourne Park – 09/04/1927 – 10,000)

DRUMCONDRA AFC (DUBLIN)   1-0   Brideville FC (Dublin)
Murray   (H.T. 0-0)

Drumcondra: Cleary, Keogh, Moore, Coyle, Grace, Maxwell, Fleming, Swan, McCarney, Cullen, Murray.
Brideville: Gamblin, Lennox, Siney, Donovan, Armstrong, Fox, Murtagh, Maguire, Watters, O'Brien, McCarthy.

Semi-Finals

Brideville FC (Dublin)	2-0	Shelbourne FC (Dublin)
Drumcondra AFC (Dublin)	3-1	Bohemian FC (Dublin)

Quarter-Finals

Bray Unknowns FC (Bray)	1-5	Shelbourne FC (Dublin)
Fordsons FC (Cork)	2-3	Bohemian FC (Dublin)

Brideville FC (Dublin) and Drumcondra AFC (Dublin) both received byes

1927-28

Free State Football League Division "A" 1927-28	Athlone Town	Bohemian FC	Bray Unknowns	Brideville FC	Dundalk FC	Fordsons FC	Jacobs AFC	St. James's Gt.	Shamrock Rov.	Shelbourne FC
Athlone Town AFC		1-2	2-1	2-5	2-5	0-2	2-1	0-0	0-4	2-7
Bohemian FC	2-1		5-1	4-2	2-0	4-0	2-0	5-1	3-2	2-3
Bray Unknowns FC	4-2	1-5		1-3	3-7	2-5	0-0	1-3	2-5	0-4
Brideville FC	3-1	1-4	2-2		1-4	4-2	3-2	4-2	0-0	1-2
Dundalk FC	1-0	1-4	3-1	2-1		2-3	2-0	4-1	3-3	2-4
Fordsons FC	5-0	2-0	5-2	1-1	2-2		4-2	5-0	2-2	2-1
Jacobs AFC	4-1	1-4	3-3	1-1	0-3	2-2		0-0	1-3	0-7
St. James's Gate AFC	3-1	2-3	3-3	2-5	2-1	2-1	1-2		1-1	3-1
Shamrock Rovers FC	3-1	0-0	5-0	0-0	5-0	2-0	3-1	2-1		1-1
Shelbourne FC	9-1	1-2	8-2	1-0	2-2	6-3	5-0	3-1	2-0	

	Division "A"	Pd	Wn	Dw	Ls	GF	GA	Pts	
1.	BOHEMIAN FC (DUBLIN)	18	15	1	2	53	20	31	
2.	Shelbourne FC (Dublin)	18	13	2	3	67	24	28	
3.	Shamrock Rovers FC (Dublin)	18	9	7	2	41	18	25	
4.	Fordsons FC (Cork)	18	9	4	5	46	34	22	
5.	Dundalk FC (Dundalk)	18	9	3	6	44	36	21	
6.	Brideville FC (Dublin)	18	7	5	6	37	33	19	
7.	St. James's Gate AFC (Dublin)	18	5	4	9	28	42	14	
8.	Jacobs AFC (Dublin)	18	2	5	11	20	46	9	
9.	Bray Unknowns FC (Bray)	18	1	4	13	29	70	6	
10.	Athlone Town FC (Athlone)	18	2	1	15	19	61	5	#
		180	72	36	72	384	384	180	

Top goal-scorers 1927-28

1) Charles HEINEMANN   (Fordsons FC)   24
2) Sammy McILVENNY   (Shelbourne FC)   22
3) John McMILLAN   (Shelbourne FC)   17

\# Athlone Town AFC (Athlone) were not re-elected for the next season.   Elected: Drumcondra AFC (Dublin)

FAI Cup Final   (Dalymount Park, Dublin – 17/03/1928 – 25,000)

BOHEMIAN FC (DUBLIN)	2-1	Drumcondra AFC (Dublin)
White, Dennis	*(H.T. 1-1)*	*Keogh*

Bohemian: Cannon, J. Robinson, McCarthy, McIlroy, McMahon, Thomas, Bermingham, Dennis, White, C. Robinson, Kavanagh.

Drumcondra: O'Callaghan, Kelly, Moore, Coyle, Grace, Maxwell, Doyle, Swan, McCarney, Keogh, Murray.

Semi-Finals

Bohemian FC (Dublin)	1-1, 0-0, 4-1	Shelbourne FC (Dublin)
Fordsons FC (Cork)	0-3	Drumcondra AFC (Dublin)

Quarter-Finals

Bohemian FC (Dublin)	5-0	St. James's Gate AFC (Dublin)
Bray Unknowns FC (Bray)	2-2, 1-4	Drumcondra AFC (Dublin)
Fordsons FC (Cork)	4-0	Jacobs AFC (Dublin)
Shelbourne FC (Dublin)	3-1	Dundalk FC (Dundalk)

1928-29

Free State Football League Division "A" 1928-29	Bohemian FC	Bray Unknowns FC	Brideville FC	Drumcondra AFC	Dundalk FC	Fordsons FC	Jacobs AFC	St. James's Gate AFC	Shamrock Rovers FC	Shelbourne FC
Bohemian FC	■	6-2	3-0	3-2	6-0	5-2	6-1	2-2	2-1	2-1
Bray Unknowns FC	1-2	■	2-4	0-3	0-3	0-1	4-4	1-4	1-1	1-2
Brideville FC	2-6	2-2	■	0-3	1-3	3-2	1-1	3-9	1-4	0-4
Drumcondra AFC	0-1	2-2	2-5	■	2-1	3-2	5-1	0-0	1-1	0-1
Dundalk FC	1-2	5-1	4-2	3-0	■	3-3	5-1	3-2	2-2	1-4
Fordsons FC	0-3	1-3	3-0	1-2	1-1	■	0-0	5-1	1-2	0-1
Jacobs AFC	3-7	3-0	0-0	0-0	4-3	1-2	■	2-2	2-3	1-2
St. James's Gate AFC	0-2	1-3	1-2	2-3	4-2	1-2	2-1	■	0-4	2-2
Shamrock Rovers FC	2-2	11-0	4-2	4-0	5-2	6-1	3-1	3-4	■	2-4
Shelbourne FC	3-1	3-1	4-0	4-0	4-1	1-0	3-0	4-0	2-0	■

	Division "A"	Pd	Wn	Dw	Ls	GF	GA	Pts
1.	SHELBOURNE FC (DUBLIN)	18	16	1	1	49	12	33
2.	Bohemian FC (Dublin)	18	15	2	1	61	23	32
3.	Shamrock Rovers FC (Dublin)	18	10	4	4	58	28	24
4.	Drumcondra AFC (Dublin)	18	7	4	7	28	31	18
5.	Dundalk FC (Dundalk)	18	7	3	8	43	44	17
6.	St. James's Gate AFC (Dublin)	18	5	4	9	37	44	14
7.	Fordsons FC (Cork)	18	5	3	10	27	36	13
8.	Brideville FC (Dublin)	18	4	3	11	28	57	11
9.	Jacobs AFC (Dublin)	18	2	6	10	26	48	10
10.	Bray Unknowns FC (Bray)	18	2	4	12	24	58	8
		180	73	34	73	381	381	180

Top goal-scorers 1928-29

1)	Eddie CARROLL	(Dundalk FC)	17
2)	David BYRNE	(Shelbourne FC)	15
	Billy DENNIS	(Bohemian FC)	15

FAI Cup Final (Dalymount Park, Dublin – 18/02/1929 – 22,000)

SHAMROCK ROVERS FC (DUBLIN)	0-0	Bohemian FC (Dublin)

Shamrock Rovers: O'Reilly, Maguire, Burke, Glen, Caulfield, Marlow, Golding, Flood, Sloan, Fullam, Sherwin.

Bohemian: Cannon. M.O'Kane, McCarthy, P.O'Kane, McMahon, Morton, Bermingham, Dennis, White, Horlacher, Kavanagh.

Final Replay   (Shelbourne Park – 06/04/1929 – 15,000)

SHAMROCK ROVERS FC (DUBLIN)   3-0   Bohemian FC (Dublin)

Flood 2, Fullam   *(H.T. 1-0)*

Shamrock Rovers: O'Reilly, Maguire, Burke, Glen, Caulfield, Marlow, Golding, Flood, Sloan, Fullam, Campbell.
Bohemian: Cannon. M.O'Kane, McCarthy, P.O'Kane, McMahon, Morton, Bermingham, Dennis, White, Horlacher, Kavanagh.

Semi-Finals

Bohemian FC (Dublin)	2-0	Drumcondra AFC (Dublin)
Shamrock Rovers FC (Dublin)	3-0	Dundalk FC (Dundalk)

Quarter-Finals

Bohemian FC (Dublin)	2-2, 4-2	Jacobs AFC (Dublin)
Drumcondra AFC (Dublin)	3-1	Cork Bohemians FC (Cork)
Dundalk FC (Dundalk)	6-2	Bray Unknowns FC (Bray)
Shamrock Rovers FC (Dublin)	4-0	Richmond United FC (Dublin)

1929-30

Free State Football League Division "A" 1929-30	Bohemian FC	Bray Unknowns FC	Brideville FC	Drumcondra AFC	Dundalk FC	Fordsons FC	Jacobs AFC	St. James's Gate AFC	Shamrock Rovers FC	Shelbourne FC
Bohemian FC	■	3-0	3-1	4-1	2-1	5-0	4-3	2-0	5-1	2-1
Bray Unknowns FC	0-1	■	3-1	3-3	2-2	3-3	5-1	4-1	0-1	1-3
Brideville FC	0-0	3-2	■	1-2	3-2	1-0	3-1	2-1	2-2	1-6
Drumcondra AFC	3-3	4-2	3-0	■	0-4	0-1	1-1	3-0	0-4	1-4
Dundalk FC	1-3	3-0	3-3	1-1	■	2-3	2-1	3-2	0-2	2-4
Fordsons FC	3-1	1-1	3-1	2-0	0-1	■	4-1	1-2	1-1	2-1
Jacobs AFC	1-8	3-3	2-4	0-1	2-8	2-7	■	0-8	1-3	2-3
St. James's Gate AFC	0-4	2-4	0-2	2-2	5-2	3-0	0-0	■	1-4	3-4
Shamrock Rovers FC	0-1	7-1	2-3	2-0	2-1	4-1	3-1	1-0	■	2-3
Shelbourne FC	2-0	6-0	4-3	3-1	1-0	4-1	9-1	0-0	1-3	■

	Division "A"	Pd	Wn	Dw	Ls	GF	GA	Pts	
1.	BOHEMIAN FC (DUBLIN)	18	14	2	2	51	18	30	
2.	Shelbourne FC (Dublin)	18	14	1	3	59	25	29	
3.	Shamrock Rovers FC (Dublin)	18	12	2	4	44	22	26	
4.	Fordsons FC (Cork)	18	8	3	7	33	33	19	*
5.	Brideville FC (Dublin)	18	8	3	7	34	39	19	
6.	Dundalk FC (Dundalk)	18	6	3	9	38	36	15	
7.	Drumcondra AFC (Dublin)	18	5	5	8	26	37	15	
8.	Bray Unknowns FC (Bray)	18	4	5	9	34	48	13	
9.	St. James's Gate AFC (Dublin)	18	4	3	11	30	38	11	
10.	Jacobs AFC (Dublin)	18	-	3	15	23	76	3	
		180	75	30	75	372	372	180	

Top goal-scorers 1929-30

1) Johnny LEDWIDGE   (Shelbourne FC)   16
2) Stephen McCARTHY   (Bohemian FC)   13
3) David BYRNE   (Shamrock Rovers FC)   11
   Fred HORLACHER   (Bohemian FC)   11

Elected: Dolphin FC (Dublin), Waterford AFC (Waterford)

The league was extended to 12 clubs for next season

* Fordsons FC (Cork) changed their club name to Cork FC (Cork) prior to the start of next season.

FAI Cup Final (Dalymount Park, Dublin – 17/03/1930 – 17,000)

SHAMROCK ROVERS FC (DUBLIN)   1-0   Brideville FC (Dublin)
Byrne   (H.T. 0-0)

Shamrock Rovers: O'Reilly, Cervi, Burke, Glen, Caulfield, Marlow, Flood, Sloan, Byrne, Fullam, Golding.
Brideville: O'Callaghan, Kenny, Bermingham, O'Reilly, Fox, Charles, Smith, Gaskins, Blair, Reid, O'Brien.

Semi-Finals

Brideville FC (Dublin)	2-1	Dundalk FC (Dundalk)
Fordsons FC (Cork)	2-2, 0-3	Shamrock Rovers FC (Dublin)

Quarter-Finals

Brideville FC (Dublin)	1-1, 2-2, 5-1	Dolphin FC (Dublin)
Dundalk FC (Dundalk)	5-0	Glasnevin FC (Dublin)
Fordsons FC (Cork)	1-0	Bohemian FC (Dublin)
Shamrock Rovers FC (Dublin)	4-2	St. James's Gate FC (Dublin)

1930-31

Free State Football League Division "A" 1930-31	Bohemian FC	Bray Unknowns	Brideville FC	Cork FC	Dolphin FC	Drumcondra AFC	Dundalk FC	Jacobs AFC	St. James's Gate	Shamrock Rovers	Shelbourne FC	Waterford AFC
Bohemian FC	■	3-2	2-4	2-1	2-2	1-1	3-1	0-1	1-1	5-2	1-2	3-1
Bray Unknowns FC	3-2	■	3-1	1-1	0-0	3-0	2-2	2-0	1-2	4-2	2-3	2-3
Brideville FC	0-3	4-2	■	1-1	2-4	3-1	1-1	2-1	1-1	2-2	0-3	3-0
Cork FC	1-0	2-1	2-3	■	2-4	2-1	3-1	2-1	6-1	3-1	1-4	4-1
Dolphin FC	1-2	1-3	1-4	6-1	■	3-1	2-2	4-2	0-3	2-4	0-2	3-2
Drumcondra AFC	2-2	0-1	2-5	3-3	2-3	■	1-3	0-0	3-2	2-1	0-2	2-1
Dundalk FC	2-2	4-2	5-1	1-4	4-3	1-4	■	7-1	4-1	6-0	3-3	7-3
Jacobs AFC	1-2	2-2	1-3	1-4	0-1	1-3	1-5	■	2-4	3-5	1-4	2-3
St. James's Gate AFC	0-1	1-2	1-1	3-7	1-4	2-2	1-2	1-0	■	0-4	1-0	3-1
Shamrock Rovers FC	3-3	4-1	4-4	3-1	2-2	4-3	1-2	7-0	2-1	■	1-0	1-2
Shelbourne FC	1-1	5-0	3-1	3-0	1-2	2-0	1-1	7-0	1-4	2-0	■	2-2
Waterford AFC	0-4	3-2	1-3	3-4	1-3	4-0	3-0	4-0	3-2	1-1	1-1	■

	Division "A"	Pd	Wn	Dw	Ls	GF	GA	Pts
1.	SHELBOURNE FC (DUBLIN)	22	13	5	4	52	22	31
2.	Dundalk FC (Dundalk)	22	11	6	5	64	43	28
3.	Bohemian FC (Dublin)	22	10	7	5	45	32	27
4.	Cork FC (Cork)	22	12	3	7	55	45	27
5.	Dolphin FC (Dublin)	22	11	4	7	51	43	26
6.	Brideville FC (Dublin)	22	10	6	6	49	44	26
7.	Shamrock Rovers FC (Dublin)	22	9	5	8	54	49	23
8.	Bray Unknowns FC (Bray)	22	8	4	10	41	45	20
9.	Waterford AFC (Waterford)	22	8	3	11	43	52	19
10.	St. James's Gate AFC (Dublin)	22	7	4	11	36	48	18
11.	Drumcondra AFC (Dublin)	22	5	5	12	33	49	15
12.	Jacobs AFC (Dublin)	22	1	2	19	21	72	4
		264	105	54	105	544	544	264

Top goal-scorers 1930-31

1) Alexander HAIR   (Shelbourne FC)   29
2) Johnny BLAIR   (Cork FC)   21
   David BYRNE   (Shamrock Rovers FC)   21
   Owen McNALLY   (Bray Unknowns FC)   21

FAI Cup Final   (Dalymount Park, Dublin – 18/04/1931 – 20,000)

SHAMROCK ROVERS FC (DUBLIN)   1-1   Dundalk FC (Dundalk)
Moore   *(H.T. 0-1)*   *McCourt*

Shamrock Rovers: Behan, Cervi, Burke, Glen, Caulfield, Kinsella, Delaney, Moore, Byrne, Flood, Golding.
Dundalk: McMullen, McKeon, McDiarmuid, Slowey, Reid, Johnstone, McCourt, McCahill, Firth, Hirst, Donnelly.

Final Replay   (Dalymount Park, Dublin – 09/05/1931 – 10,000)

SHAMROCK ROVERS FC (DUBLIN)   1-0   Dundalk FC (Dundalk)
Moore   *(H.T. 1-0)*

Shamrock Rovers: O'Reilly, Cervi, Burke, Glen, Caulfield, Kinsella, Fullam, Moore, Byrne, Flood, Golding.
Dundalk: McMullen, McKeon, McDiarmuid, Slowey, Reid, Johnstone, McCourt, McCahill, Firth, Hirst, Donnelly.

Semi-Finals

Dundalk FC (Dundalk)	1-1, 3-1	Dolphin FC (Dublin)
Shamrock Rovers FC (Dublin)	3-0	Bohemian FC (Dublin)

Quarter-Finals

Bohemian FC (Dublin)	5-1	Edenville FC (Dublin)
Dundalk FC (Dundalk)	3-1	Cork Bohemians FC (Cork)
Shamrock Rovers FC (Dublin)	5-1	Bray Unknowns FC (Bray)
Waterford AFC (Waterford)	2-3	Dolphin FC (Dublin)

1931-32

Free State Football League Division "A" 1931-32	Bohemian FC	Bray Unknowns FC	Brideville FC	Cork FC	Dolphin FC	Drumcondra AFC	Dundalk FC	Jacobs AFC	St. James's Gate AFC	Shamrock Rovers FC	Shelbourne FC	Waterford AFC
Bohemian FC		1-1	5-1	1-0	3-2	2-3	3-2	5-1	3-2	2-3	2-1	0-1
Bray Unknowns FC	1-0		3-2	2-2	4-8	3-1	2-2	1-1	5-1	2-2	3-1	3-4
Brideville FC	1-2	1-2		1-1	3-1	1-1	2-1	3-0	1-0	1-5	3-5	1-0
Cork FC	1-2	6-2	4-0		1-1	2-0	1-1	7-0	4-1	2-2	1-0	2-2
Dolphin FC	2-1	3-1	3-0	3-3		4-1	2-4	6-0	3-2	0-1	1-1	2-4
Drumcondra AFC	1-1	2-1	1-1	3-2	0-6		2-4	2-1	3-1	0-0	1-3	3-4
Dundalk FC	1-1	5-0	3-2	0-2	2-1	2-1		9-0	2-0	5-2	2-2	3-3
Jacobs AFC	1-2	1-2	2-1	0-6	1-6	0-1	0-5		1-4	0-8	1-1	2-3
St. James's Gate AFC	1-3	1-5	0-1	1-1	1-4	4-3	1-0	2-2		1-4	2-3	1-0
Shamrock Rovers FC	2-0	4-0	4-0	2-2	3-4	3-2	1-2	3-0	3-0		4-3	8-2
Shelbourne FC	2-4	2-0	1-0	0-2	3-2	1-1	2-1	4-0	4-1	2-2		1-0
Waterford AFC	5-0	1-2	3-1	3-5	5-1	2-1	1-0	9-1	7-0	4-4	1-1	

	Division "A"	Pd	Wn	Dw	Ls	GF	GA	Pts	
1.	SHAMROCK ROVERS FC (DUBLIN)	22	13	6	3	70	34	32	
2.	Cork FC (Cork)	22	10	9	3	57	27	29	
3.	Waterford AFC (Waterford)	22	12	4	6	64	42	28	#
4.	Dundalk FC (Dundalk)	22	11	5	6	56	31	27	
5.	Bohemian FC (Dublin)	22	12	3	7	43	35	27	
6.	Shelbourne FC (Dublin)	22	10	6	6	43	34	26	
7.	Dolphin FC (Dublin)	22	11	3	8	65	44	25	
8.	Bray Unknowns FC (Bray)	22	9	5	8	45	51	23	
9.	Drumcondra AFC (Dublin)	22	6	5	11	33	48	17	
10.	Brideville FC (Dublin)	22	6	3	13	27	47	15	#
11.	St. James's Gate AFC (Dublin)	22	4	2	16	27	62	10	
12.	Jacobs AFC (Dublin)	22	1	3	18	15	90	5	#
		264	105	54	105	545	545	264	

Top goal-scorers 1931-32

1) Pearson FERGUSON   (Cork FC)   21
   Jack FORSTER   (Waterford AFC)   21
3) Patrick MOORE   (Shamrock Rovers FC)   18
   Jimmy SHIELS   (Dolphin FC)   18

Note: Jacobs AFC 1-1 Shelbourne FC was abandoned but the result at time of abandonment was allowed to stand.

\# Brideville FC (Dublin) and Jacobs AFC (Dublin) were not re-elected to the league for next season.

Waterford AFC (Waterford) resigned from the league prior to the start of next season.

Elected: Cork Bohemians FC (Cork)

The league was reduced to 10 clubs for next season

FAI Cup Final   (Dalymount Park, Dublin – 17/04/1932 – 32,000)

SHAMROCK ROVERS FC (DUBLIN)   1-0   Dolphin FC (Dublin)
Moore   (H.T. 0-0)

Shamrock Rovers: McCarthy, Daly, Burke, Glen, Matthews, Kinsella, Flood, Byrne, Moore, McMillan, Smith.
Dolphin: Power, Nesbitt, Doyle, Robinson, Kelly, Watt, Stevenson, Shields, Somers, Paterson, (Unknown).

Semi-Finals

Dolphin FC (Dublin)	3-1	Shelbourne FC (Dublin)
Shamrock Rovers FC (Dublin)	3-2	Bohemian FC (Dublin)

Quarter-Finals

Bohemian FC (Dublin)	2-0	Drumcondra AFC (Dublin)
Dolphin FC (Dublin)	3-2	Cork FC (Cork)
Shamrock Rovers FC (Dublin)	4-2	Edenville FC (Dublin)
Shelbourne FC (Dublin)	4-2	Waterford AFC (Waterford)

1932-33

Free State Football League Division "A" 1932-33	Bohemian FC	Bray Unknowns FC	Cork FC	Cork Bohemians FC	Dolphin FC	Drumcondra AFC	Dundalk FC	St. James's Gate AFC	Shamrock Rovers FC	Shelbourne FC
Bohemian FC		1-1	4-1	0-0	1-0	1-0	0-4	3-2	2-3	0-4
Bray Unknowns FC	0-0		3-0	1-0	2-2	3-3	1-1	2-1	3-2	1-1
Cork FC	2-0	2-1		3-0	3-0	4-3	2-5	4-1	3-1	1-2
Cork Bohemians FC	3-1	3-4	1-2		2-5	4-2	0-1	4-2	1-4	4-3
Dolphin FC	2-0	1-1	1-1	2-0		0-0	0-2	0-3	5-2	3-1
Drumcondra AFC	2-2	0-1	1-3	3-3	2-1		1-3	1-2	0-2	0-1
Dundalk FC	4-2	2-1	1-0	1-1	5-2	2-1		4-2	0-2	3-0
St. James's Gate AFC	6-5	2-1	1-2	1-1	4-1	3-1	2-3		1-3	2-5
Shamrock Rovers FC	2-2	6-2	5-1	1-1	4-2	5-1	2-1	1-3		3-2
Shelbourne FC	4-0	2-1	5-1	2-2	6-1	3-1	2-2	0-1	2-0	

	Division "A"	Pd	Wn	Dw	Ls	GF	GA	Pts
1.	DUNDALK FC (DUNDALK)	18	13	3	2	44	21	29
2.	Shamrock Rovers FC (Dublin)	18	11	2	5	48	32	24
3.	Shelbourne FC (Dublin)	18	10	3	5	45	26	23
4.	Cork FC (Cork)	18	10	1	7	35	35	21
5.	Bray Unknowns FC (Bray)	18	6	7	5	29	29	19
6.	St. James's Gate AFC (Dublin)	18	8	1	9	39	41	17
7.	Cork Bohemians FC (Cork)	18	4	6	8	30	38	14
8.	Dolphin FC (Dublin)	18	5	4	9	28	39	14
9.	Bohemian FC (Dublin)	18	4	5	9	24	40	13
10.	Drumcondra AFC (Dublin)	18	1	4	13	22	43	6
		180	72	36	72	344	344	180

Top goal-scorers 1932-33

1) George EBBS   (St. James's Gate AFC)   20
2) Tommy DOYLE   (Shamrock Rovers FC)   17
3) Jimmy RORRISON   (Cork FC)   16

FAI Cup Final   (Dalymount Park, Dublin – 17/03/1933 – 22,000)

SHAMROCK ROVERS FC (DUBLIN)   3-3, 3-0   Dolphin FC (Dublin)
Byrne, Buchanan, Matthews pen.   (H.T. 1-2)   *Lennox 2 pens., Fallon*

Shamrock Rovers: McCarthy, Gaskins, Burke, Glen, Matthews, Kinsella, Daly, Flood, Byrne, Buchanan, Smith.
Dolphin: Slater, Lennox, Doyle, Watt, Kelly, Kendrick, Bermingham, Weldon, McCarney, Somers, Fallon.

Final Replay   (Dalymount Park, Dublin – 26/03/1933 – 18,000)

SHAMROCK ROVERS FC (DUBLIN)   3-0   Dolphin FC (Dublin)
Daly 2, Byrne   (H.T. 2-0)

Shamrock Rovers: McCarthy, Gaskins, Burke, Glen, Matthews, Kinsella, Daly, Flood, Byrne, Buchanan, Smith.
Dolphin: Slater, Lennox, Doyle, Watt, Kelly, Kendrick, Reid, Weldon, McCarney, Somers, Fallon.

Semi-Finals

Dolphin FC (Dublin)	1-0	Shelbourne FC (Dublin)
Shamrock Rovers FC (Dublin)	3-1	Bohemian FC (Dublin)

Quarter-Finals

Bohemian FC (Dublin)	7-1	Cork Bohemians FC (Cork)
Cork FC (Cork)	1-1, 0-3	Shamrock Rovers FC (Dublin)
Dolphin FC (Dublin)	2-1	Drumcondra AFC (Dublin)
Shelbourne FC (Dublin)	5-2	Sligo Rovers FC (Sligo)

1933-34

Free State Football League Division "A" 1933-34	Bohemian FC	Bray Unknowns FC	Cork FC	Cork Bohemians FC	Dolphin FC	Drumcondra AFC	Dundalk FC	St. James's Gate AFC	Shamrock Rovers FC	Shelbourne FC
Bohemian FC	■	3-1	1-4	4-3	1-1	1-1	2-2	2-2	1-0	2-0
Bray Unknowns FC	1-0	■	3-4	+:-	0-3	1-1	5-3	1-4	3-2	3-2
Cork FC	3-3	4-2	■	4-1	4-1	2-1	4-0	3-1	3-0	0-0
Cork Bohemians FC	1-3	2-0	1-4	■	2-0	1-3	1-1	0-0	1-2	1-1
Dolphin FC	0-2	4-1	0-0	3-0	■	1-0	3-0	0-1	0-1	2-0
Drumcondra AFC	0-2	3-0	3-0	3-1	2-2	■	0-1	3-2	1-2	1-1
Dundalk FC	0-1	5-2	2-1	3-0	4-1	2-0	■	3-0	2-0	2-0
St. James's Gate AFC	0-1	1-2	3-1	3-3	0-1	3-4	2-1	■	1-2	1-2
Shamrock Rovers FC	2-3	2-1	2-2	4-0	2-1	1-0	2-2	3-1	■	0-0
Shelbourne FC	2-6	1-0	2-4	3-0	1-0	5-1	1-0	0-1	1-1	■

	Division "A"	Pd	Wn	Dw	Ls	GF	GA	Pts	
1.	BOHEMIAN FC (DUBLIN)	18	11	5	2	38	23	27	
2.	Cork FC (Cork)	18	11	4	3	47	26	26	
3.	Shamrock Rovers FC (Dublin)	18	9	4	5	28	23	22	
4.	Dundalk FC (Dundalk)	18	9	3	6	33	25	21	
5.	Dolphin FC (Dublin)	18	7	3	8	23	21	17	
6.	Shelbourne FC (Dublin)	18	6	5	7	22	25	17	#
7.	Drumcondra AFC (Dublin)	18	6	4	8	27	28	16	
8.	St. James's Gate AFC (Dublin)	18	5	3	10	26	32	13	
9.	Bray Unknowns FC (Bray)	18	6	1	11	26	44	13	
10.	Cork Bohemians FC (Cork)	18	2	4	12	18	41	8	#
		180	72	36	72	288	288	180	

Top goal-scorers 1933-34

1) Alf RIGBY   (St. James's Gate AFC)   13
2) Ray ROGERS   (Bohemian FC)   12
3) Billy MERRY   (Drumcondra AFC)   11
   Timothy O'KEEFE   (Cork FC)   11

Note: Bray Unknowns FC v Cork Bohemians FC was not played, the points were awarded to Bray (shown as +:-)

\# Shelbourne FC (Dublin) resigned from the I.F.S. Shield on 23/03/1934 and Cork Bohemian FC (Cork) resigned on 22/04/1934 from the same competition. Neither club participated in the league or shield for next season.

Elected: Sligo Rovers FC (Sligo), Waterford AFC (Waterford)

FAI Cup Final   (Dalymount Park, Dublin – 17/03/1934 – 21,000)

CORK FC (CORK)	2-1	St. James's Gate AFC (Dublin)
O'Keeffe, Kelso	(H.T. 1-1)	Comerford

Cork: Foley, Hogg, Burke, Lennon, Chatton, Connolly, Buckle, Haddow, Kelso, Paton, O'Keeffe.
St James's Gate: Pidgeon, Hoey, Moylan, Simpson, Lennon, Murray, Kennedy, Comerford, Rigby, Dowdall, Geoghegan.

Semi-Finals

Cork FC (Cork)	2-2, 1-1, 2-1	Dundalk FC (Dundalk)
St. James's Gate AFC (Dublin)	1-0	Dolphin FC (Dublin)

Quarter-Finals

Cork FC (Cork)	1-1, 2-0	Bray Unknowns FC (Bray)
Drumcondra AFC (Dublin)	0-2	St. James's Gate AFC (Dublin)
Dundalk FC (Dundalk)	1-0	Bohemian FC (Dublin)
Queen's Park FC (Dublin)	1-1, 0-1	Dolphin FC (Dublin)

1934-35

Free State Football League Division "A" 1934-35	Bohemian FC	Bray Unknowns FC	Cork FC	Dolphin FC	Drumcondra AFC	Dundalk FC	St. James's Gate AFC	Shamrock Rovers FC	Sligo Rovers FC	Waterford AFC
Bohemian FC	■	5-3	4-1	0-4	2-2	2-3	3-1	1-1	1-2	4-0
Bray Unknowns FC	0-4	■	4-3	1-1	2-0	4-2	3-6	2-2	3-1	3-5
Cork FC	6-2	3-5	■	1-2	1-2	2-2	0-1	3-1	1-1	2-2
Dolphin FC	1-2	6-1	3-1	■	5-1	2-0	2-4	2-1	3-0	3-2
Drumcondra AFC	1-0	1-2	4-1	0-0	■	0-4	0-2	2-1	1-3	1-1
Dundalk FC	5-1	3-2	0-1	2-2	4-3	■	1-3	0-0	4-2	2-1
St. James's Gate AFC	3-2	1-0	4-2	2-2	1-1	3-1	■	1-3	1-4	5-4
Shamrock Rovers FC	2-5	3-1	1-1	0-2	2-1	3-1	0-2	■	2-2	3-2
Sligo Rovers FC	0-2	2-2	5-1	0-1	4-0	1-1	2-3	4-1	■	8-2
Waterford AFC	1-4	8-1	3-0	3-7	4-2	0-2	3-3	1-1	1-3	■

	Division "A"	Pd	Wn	Dw	Ls	GF	GA	Pts
1.	DOLPHIN FC (DUBLIN)	18	12	4	2	48	21	28
2.	St. James's Gate AFC (Dublin)	18	12	3	3	46	33	27
3.	Sligo Rovers FC (Sligo)	18	8	4	6	44	30	20
4.	Bohemian FC (Dublin)	18	9	2	7	44	36	20
5.	Dundalk FC (Dundalk)	18	8	4	6	37	32	20
6.	Shamrock Rovers FC (Dublin)	18	5	6	7	27	33	16
7.	Bray Unknowns FC (Bray)	18	6	3	9	39	56	15
8.	Waterford AFC (Waterford)	18	4	4	10	43	54	12
9.	Drumcondra AFC (Dublin)	18	4	4	10	22	39	12
10.	Cork FC (Cork)	18	3	4	11	30	46	10
		180	71	38	71	380	380	180

Top goal-scorers 1934-35

1) Alf RIGBY   (St. James's Gate AFC)   17
2) Charles McDAID   (Sligo Rovers FC)   16
3) Walter WALSH   (Waterford AFC)   13

Elected: Brideville FC (Dublin), Reds United FC (Dublin)

The League was extended to 12 clubs for next season
Note: Reds United FC (Dublin) were founded in 1935 by members of Shelbourne FC (Dublin) who resigned from The League in March 1934 after a dispute with the League of Ireland, and who were currently playing in the A.U.L. (Junior League).

FAI Cup Final   (Dalymount Park, Dublin – 14/04/1935 – 22,000)

BOHEMIAN FC (DUBLIN)   4-3   Dundalk FC (Dundalk)
Jordan 2, Horlacher, Menton   *(H.T. 4-2)*   *O'Neill, McCourt, Godwin*

Bohemian: Cannon, Morris, McGuire, O'Kane, Andrew, Maguire, Menton, Farrell, Ellis, Horlacher, Jordan.
Dundalk: McMahon, Powell, Richards, G.Godwin, T.Godwin, Hirst, Mills, Donnelly, O'Neill, McCourt, Gaughran.

Semi-Finals

Bohemian FC (Dublin)	1-1, 2-1	Dolphin FC (Dublin)
Dundalk FC (Dundalk)	2-0	Sligo Rovers FC (Sligo)

Quarter-Finals

Bohemian FC (Dublin)	5-2	Waterford AFC (Waterford)
Distillery FC (Dublin)	1-2	Dundalk FC (Dundalk)
Drumcondra AFC (Dublin)	0-2	Dolphin FC (Dublin)
Sligo Rovers FC (Sligo)	5-1	Cork FC (Cork)

1935-36

Free State Football League Division "A" 1935-36	Bohemian FC	Bray Unknowns FC	Brideville FC	Cork FC	Dolphin FC	Drumcondra AFC	Dundalk FC	Reds United FC	St. James's Gate AFC	Shamrock Rovers FC	Sligo Rovers FC	Waterford AFC
Bohemian FC	■	8-2	5-0	4-1	2-3	3-0	2-0	6-1	4-1	5-2	7-0	5-3
Bray Unknowns FC	1-2	■	1-2	3-4	1-3	0-4	3-2	0-2	0-4	1-4	2-5	0-3
Brideville FC	0-2	7-0	■	0-2	4-4	3-5	2-1	2-4	3-3	2-5	1-0	1-2
Cork FC	1-1	4-1	4-1	■	3-3	4-0	3-1	0-2	2-1	4-2	3-3	3-0
Dolphin FC	1-2	4-0	6-0	2-5	■	2-1	4-1	3-1	3-2	4-0	2-1	2-2
Drumcondra AFC	2-2	6-1	3-2	2-1	1-2	■	2-1	6-4	0-5	1-2	0-3	3-1
Dundalk FC	0-2	5-0	2-1	3-2	3-1	0-4	■	2-0	0-1	1-1	4-0	5-1
Reds United FC	2-3	5-0	2-1	2-1	1-4	4-1	1-1	■	3-2	3-2	3-2	0-2
St. James's Gate AFC	0-1	5-1	1-1	2-3	2-3	1-0	2-4	4-0	■	0-3	5-3	5-0
Shamrock Rovers FC	3-2	9-3	3-1	2-3	1-6	1-1	5-6	1-3	2-0	■	3-5	4-1
Sligo Rovers FC	2-0	2-0	3-1	2-4	1-3	4-1	1-0	1-2	5-0	1-2	■	2-2
Waterford AFC	2-5	9-3	6-0	1-4	4-1	7-2	1-1	3-0	1-1	5-4	2-2	■

	Division "A"	Pd	Wn	Dw	Ls	GF	GA	Pts	
1.	BOHEMIAN FC (DUBLIN)	22	17	2	3	73	27	36	
2.	Dolphin FC (Dublin)	22	15	3	4	66	38	33	
3.	Cork FC (Cork)	22	14	3	5	61	38	31	
4.	Reds United FC (Dublin)	22	12	1	9	45	47	25	#
5.	Waterford AFC (Waterford)	22	9	5	8	58	53	23	
6.	Shamrock Rovers FC (Dublin)	22	10	2	10	61	58	22	
7.	Dundalk FC (Dundalk)	22	9	3	10	43	39	21	
8.	Sligo Rovers FC (Sligo)	22	9	3	10	48	47	21	
9.	Drumcondra AFC (Dublin)	22	9	2	11	45	53	20	
10.	St. James's Gate AFC (Dublin)	22	8	3	11	47	42	19	
11.	Brideville FC (Dublin)	22	4	3	15	35	64	11	
12.	Bray Unknowns FC (Bray)	22	1	-	21	23	99	2	
		264	117	30	117	605	605	264	

Top goal-scorers 1935-36

1) Jimmy TURNBULL   (Cork FC)   37
2) Ray ROGERS   (Dolphin FC)   23
3) William OUCHTERLONIE   (Reds United FC)   20

* Due to the success and support given to Shelbourne FC (Dublin) in the A.U.L., the dispute between them and the League of Ireland was resolved and the club was invited to return to league membership. As a result of this decision Reds United FC (Dublin) (run by some members of Shelbourne FC) resigned from the league and disbanded.

Elected: Shelbourne FC (Dublin)

FAI Cup Final   (Dalymount Park, Dublin – 19/04/1936 – 30,946)

SHAMROCK ROVERS FC (DUBLIN)   2-1   Cork FC (Cork)
Moore, Reid   (H.T. 0-0)   *Turnbull*

Shamrock Rovers: Behan, Williams, Gaskins, Glen, Blake, Kinsella, M.Byrne, Moore, Reid, Ward, Dunne.
Cork: Harrington, Foy, Wade, Williams, Little, Connolly, O'Reilly, King, Turnbull, Madden, Percy.

Semi-Finals

| Cork FC (Cork) | 5-2 | Drumcondra AFC (Dublin) |
| Shamrock Rovers FC (Dublin) | 2-2, 2-1 | Dundalk FC (Dundalk) |

Quarter-Finals

Bohemian FC (Dublin)	1-1, 2-3	Cork FC (Cork)
Drumcondra AFC (Dublin)	1-1, 1-1, 3-2	Sligo Rovers FC (Sligo)
Dundalk FC (Dundalk)	2-1	Reds United FC (Dublin)
Shamrock Rovers FC (Dublin)	5-1	Brideville FC (Dublin)

1936-37

Free State Football League Division "A" 1936-37	Bohemian	Bray	Brideville FC	Cork FC	Dolphin FC	Drumcondra	Dundalk FC	St. James's	Shamrock R.	Shelbourne	Sligo Rovers	Waterford
Bohemian FC		4-0	2-0	1-4	5-2	3-2	2-1	1-0	2-5	2-2	3-4	3-1
Bray Unknowns FC	3-3		2-0	3-1	1-0	0-1	1-3	0-0	0-0	2-1	0-5	2-1
Brideville FC	2-4	0-1		2-3	3-4	2-1	1-2	2-2	2-0	2-0	2-1	2-4
Cork FC	4-2	1-2	3-3		8-2	1-2	2-2	1-0	3-2	1-1	3-4	2-3
Dolphin FC	2-5	1-4	1-0	2-0		3-4	2-0	3-3	2-2	2-1	1-1	2-3
Drumcondra AFC	3-2	2-2	1-1	3-1	0-0		2-0	0-2	3-2	2-5	1-3	1-4
Dundalk FC	3-2	2-0	4-2	7-2	0-1	3-1		2-2	3-1	2-2	1-1	2-0
St. James's Gate AFC	7-2	6-1	6-0	3-4	4-2	1-3	0-2		7-0	6-0	0-4	2-3
Shamrock Rovers FC	3-0	1-3	0-1	4-2	4-0	4-2	4-1	4-4		3-2	1-6	1-3
Shelbourne FC	3-1	4-1	0-2	6-2	2-0	5-2	2-1	1-2	5-2		0-2	7-1
Sligo Rovers FC	1-2	3-0	4-1	3-1	9-0	2-3	2-0	4-2	2-0	2-0		3-0
Waterford AFC	4-3	0-2	6-2	3-1	0-1	1-2	2-0	2-4	2-3	8-2	8-2	

	Division "A"	Pd	Wn	Dw	Ls	GF	GA	Pts	
1.	SLIGO ROVERS FC (SLIGO)	22	16	2	4	68	30	34	
2.	Dundalk FC (Dundalk)	22	10	4	8	41	34	24	
3.	Waterford AFC (Waterford)	22	12	-	10	59	49	24	
4.	Bray Unknowns FC (Bray)	22	10	4	8	30	39	24	
5.	St. James's Gate AFC (Dublin)	22	9	5	8	63	43	23	
6.	Drumcondra AFC (Dublin)	22	10	3	9	41	47	23	
7.	Bohemian FC (Dublin)	22	10	2	10	54	56	22	
8.	Shelbourne FC (Dublin)	22	9	3	10	53	48	21	
9.	Shamrock Rovers FC (Dublin)	22	8	3	11	46	55	19	
10.	Dolphin FC (Dublin)	22	7	4	11	33	59	18	#
11.	Cork FC (Cork)	22	7	3	12	51	60	17	
12.	Brideville FC (Dublin)	22	6	3	13	32	51	15	
		264	114	36	114	571	571	264	

Top goal-scorers 1936-37

1)	Bob SLATER	(Waterford AFC/Shelbourne FC)	20
2)	Harry LITHERLAND	(Sligo Rovers FC)	19
3)	Hugh O'DONNELL	(Bray Unknowns FC)	16
	Timothy O'KEEFE	(Waterford AFC)	16

\# Dolphin FC (Dublin) resigned from the league at the end of the season.

Elected: Limerick AFC (Limerick)

FAI Cup Final   (Dalymount Park, Dublin – 18/04/1937 – 24,000)

WATERFORD AFC (WATERFORD)   2-1   St. James's Gate AFC (Dublin)
Noonan, O'Keeffe   *(H.T. 1-0)*   *Merry*

Waterford: Robinson, Foyle, McDonald, Walsh, Fullerton, Attigan, Phelan, Gill, Noonan, McGourty, O'Keeffe.
St James's Gate: Webster, Stewart, Daly, O'Reilly, Lennon, Cummins, Kennedy, Merry, Rigby, Comerford, Geoghegan.

Semi-Finals

St. James's Gate AFC (Dublin)	4-0	Fearon's Athletic FC (Dublin)
Waterford AFC (Waterford)	4-1	Longford Town FC (Longford)

Quarter-Finals

Cork FC (Cork)	0-1	Fearon's Athletic FC (Dublin)
Longford Town FC (Longford)	2-1	Drumcondra AFC (Dublin)
St. James's Gate AFC (Dublin)	6-2	Sligo Rovers FC (Sligo)
Waterford AFC (Waterford)	2-0	Shamrock Rovers FC (Dublin)

1937-38

Free State Football League Division "A" 1937-38	Bohemian FC	Bray Unknowns	Brideville FC	Cork FC	Drumcondra	Dundalk FC	Limerick FC	St. James's Gt.	Shamrock R.	Shelbourne FC	Sligo Rovers	Waterford AFC
Bohemian FC		4-3	2-3	2-0	6-1	2-2	3-2	1-3	2-3	2-4	5-1	2-3
Bray Unknowns FC	4-3		0-4	5-1	2-1	3-2	2-0	3-1	1-3	0-3	1-5	1-0
Brideville FC	4-2	3-0		4-1	0-0	0-0	3-1	3-1	2-2	3-0	3-2	3-1
Cork FC	2-7	4-1	1-2		1-0	0-3	3-2	3-8	2-3	5-4	5-5	1-8
Drumcondra AFC	1-4	3-2	3-2	0-1		0-2	2-2	2-0	4-5	1-1	3-0	1-4
Dundalk FC	1-1	0-0	2-1	3-1	5-2		4-0	3-4	4-0	3-1	4-0	4-1
Limerick FC	2-1	4-2	1-1	3-0	3-0	0-1		2-1	0-3	3-0	1-1	0-3
St. James's Gate AFC	5-1	5-0	4-1	5-2	1-4	5-0	3-1		4-1	1-1	7-1	0-4
Shamrock Rovers FC	6-1	2-4	2-2	3-0	8-1	1-5	1-0	2-1		3-1	3-1	6-1
Shelbourne FC	2-1	3-1	2-1	2-3	3-2	0-1	0-0	0-2	5-5		1-1	2-2
Sligo Rovers FC	6-1	2-2	1-3	4-1	7-1	4-2	5-3	1-2	4-7	1-0		1-1
Waterford AFC	2-2	3-0	7-3	4-1	8-0	3-2	4-4	4-2	2-2	6-1	5-2	

	Division "A"	Pd	Wn	Dw	Ls	GF	GA	Pts
1.	SHAMROCK ROVERS FC (DUBLIN)	22	14	4	4	71	47	32
2.	Waterford AFC (Waterford)	22	13	5	4	76	40	31
3.	Dundalk FC (Dundalk)	22	13	4	5	53	29	30
4.	Brideville FC (Dublin)	22	12	5	5	51	35	29
5.	St. James's Gate AFC (Dublin)	22	13	1	8	65	40	27
6.	Sligo Rovers FC (Sligo)	22	7	5	10	55	61	19
7.	Shelbourne FC (Dublin)	22	6	6	10	36	47	18
8.	Brat Unknowns FC (Bray)	22	8	2	12	37	56	18
9.	Bohemian FC (Dublin)	22	7	3	12	55	60	17
10.	Limerick AFC (Limerick)	22	6	5	11	34	43	17
11.	Cork FC (Cork)	22	6	1	15	38	78	13 *
12.	Drumcondra AFC (Dublin)	22	5	3	14	32	67	13
		264	110	44	110	603	603	264

Top goal-scorers 1937-38

1) William BYRNE (St. James's Gate AFC) 25
2) Frank FULLEN (Bohemian FC) 22
3) Timothy O'KEEFE (Waterford AFC) 21

* Cork FC (Cork) changed their club name to Cork City FC for next season.

FAI Cup Final   (Dalymount Park, Dublin – 10/04/1938 – 30,000)

ST. JAMES'S GATE AFC (DUBLIN) 2-1 Dundalk FC (Dundalk)
Comerford, Gaskins (H.T. 1-0) *Rigby*

St James's Gate: Webster, Stewart, Doyle, O'Reilly, Gaskins, Lennon, Kennedy, Balfe, Comerford, Reid, Geoghegan.
Dundalk: Tizard, O'Neill, Hoy, McAfee, Bowden, Lunn, Mardle, Patterson, Rigby, Donnelly, Griffiths.

Semi-Finals

Dundalk FC (Dundalk)	2-1	Shamrock Rovers FC (Dublin)
St. James's Gate AFC (Dublin)	2-2, 3-2	Distillery FC (Dublin)

Quarter-Finals

Drumcondra AFC (Dublin)	0-4	Distillery FC (Dublin)
Limerick AFC (Limerick)	1-1, 2-5	St. James's Gate AFC (Dublin)
Shamrock Rovers FC (Dublin)	1-1, 1-1, 2-1	Bray Unknowns FC (Bray)
Waterford AFC (Waterford)	2-3	Dundalk FC (Dundalk)

1938-39

Free State Football League Division "A" 1938-39	Bohemian FC	Bray Unknowns FC	Brideville FC	Cork City FC	Drumcondra AFC	Dundalk FC	Limerick AFC	St. James's Gate	Shamrock Rovers FC	Shelbourne FC	Sligo Rovers FC	Waterford AFC
Bohemian FC	■	3-2	2-2	2-1	2-3	0-2	4-2	2-0	1-3	3-0	2-2	2-3
Bray Unknowns FC	3-1	■	2-1	3-1	0-1	3-0	2-1	2-4	2-4	1-1	3-1	2-2
Brideville FC	3-2	2-2	■	2-1	2-5	2-0	2-2	3-1	3-3	5-2	1-1	2-2
Cork City FC	3-0	4-2	4-0	■	3-2	2-2	2-1	5-2	2-3	2-2	0-2	3-2
Drumcondra AFC	0-1	1-4	2-1	0-1	■	3-3	1-1	3-1	1-4	0-1	1-1	2-2
Dundalk FC	3-2	2-1	3-0	4-1	2-2	■	4-0	1-1	0-2	5-0	1-1	5-1
Limerick AFC	0-2	7-0	1-0	2-1	3-2	2-1	■	0-3	0-2	4-2	3-0	3-2
St. James's Gate AFC	1-1	3-1	3-5	5-1	3-3	2-3	4-1	■	4-2	7-3	3-0	4-1
Shamrock Rovers FC	2-2	5-3	3-0	3-1	3-1	3-2	0-0	4-2	■	0-1	3-3	5-1
Shelbourne FC	3-0	1-0	1-0	2-1	3-4	2-2	0-2	3-1	2-3	■	3-2	4-1
Sligo Rovers FC	4-0	2-1	6-1	4-2	1-0	1-1	3-0	5-1	0-1	3-2	■	7-1
Waterford AFC	4-7	2-2	1-0	1-1	3-1	0-2	1-1	2-1	1-2	2-2	1-1	■

	Division "A"	Pd	Wn	Dw	Ls	GF	GA	Pts
1.	SHAMROCK ROVERS FC (DUBLIN)	22	16	4	2	60	32	36
2.	Sligo Rovers FC (Sligo)	22	10	7	5	50	31	27
3.	Dundalk FC (Dundalk)	22	10	7	5	48	31	27
4.	St. James's Gate AFC (Dublin)	22	10	3	9	59	48	23
5.	Limerick AFC (Limerick)	22	9	4	9	36	38	22
6.	Shelbourne FC (Dublin)	22	9	4	9	40	48	22
7.	Bohemian FC (Dublin)	22	8	4	10	41	46	20
8.	Drumcondra AFC (Dublin)	22	6	6	10	38	45	18
9.	Bray Unknowns FC (Bray)	22	7	4	11	41	49	18
10.	Brideville FC (Dublin)	22	6	6	10	37	49	18
11.	Cork City FC (Cork)	22	7	3	12	39	49	17
12.	Waterford AFC (Waterford)	22	4	8	10	36	59	16
		264	102	60	102	525	525	264

Top goal-scorers 1938-39

1)	Patrick BRADSHAW	(St. James's Gate AFC)	22
2)	Tom DAVIS	(Cork City FC/Dundalk FC)	18
	Patrick LEENEY	(Bray Unknowns FC)	18

Note: Drumcondra AFC 0-1 Shelbourne FC was abandoned after the crowd invaded the field, but the result at the time of the abandonment was allowed to stand.

FAI Cup Final   (Dalymount Park, Dublin – 23/03/1939 – 30,000)

SHELBOURNE FC (DUBLIN)　　　　　　　1-1　　　　　　　　Sligo Rovers FC (Sligo)
Smyth　　　　　　　　　　　　　　　(H.T. 0-1)　　　　　　　　　　　　　　Dean

Shelbourne: Webster, Glen, Preston, Sharkey, Little, Lennon, Drain, Weir, Flynn, Balfe, Smyth.
Sligo Rovers: Cranstown, McDaid, Livesley, Hay, Peachey, Burns, Began, O'Connor, Dean, Johnstone, Monaghan.

Final Replay   (Dalymount Park, Dublin – 03/05/1939 – 25,000)

SHELBOURNE FC (DUBLIN)　　　　　　　1-0　　　　　　　　Sligo Rovers FC (Sligo)
Glen　　　　　　　　　　　　　　　(H.T. 1-0)

Shelbourne: Webster, Glen, Preston, Sharkey, Little, Lennon, Priestley, Weir, Flynn, Balfe, Smyth.
Sligo Rovers: Cranstown, McDaid, Livesley, Hay, Peachey, Graham, Began, O'Connor, Dean, Johnstone, Monaghan.

Semi-Finals

Shelbourne FC (Dublin)	1-0	Bohemian FC (Dublin)
Sligo Rovers FC (Sligo)	2-1	Dundalk FC (Dundalk)

Quarter-Finals

Bohemian FC (Dublin)	3-1	Cork Bohemians FC (Cork)
Bray Unknowns FC (Bray)	2-2, 2-2, 0-1	Shelbourne FC (Dublin)
Dundalk FC (Dundalk)	4-0	Waterford AFC (Waterford)
Sligo Rovers FC (Sligo)	2-1	Distillery FC (Dublin)

1939-40

Free State Football League Division "A" 1939-40	Bohemian FC	Bray Unknowns FC	Brideville FC	Cork City FC	Drumcondra AFC	Dundalk FC	Limerick AFC	St. James's Gate AFC	Shamrock Rovers FC	Shelbourne FC	Sligo Rovers FC	Waterford AFC
Bohemian FC	■	3-1	0-0	4-2	1-1	1-3	3-1	2-3	1-4	1-1	3-1	3-0
Bray Unknowns FC	6-2	■	1-3	7-2	3-1	1-1	6-0	0-5	2-3	4-2	3-1	4-0
Brideville FC	1-2	4-1	■	1-2	1-3	3-2	1-1	0-3	1-2	5-2	1-4	2-2
Cork City FC / Cork United FC	2-1	2-0	1-3	■	1-1	5-2	3-0	0-3	1-2	2-1	4-1	4-1
Drumcondra AFC	2-0	3-1	4-4	0-2	■	2-5	3-3	0-1	1-0	1-0	3-5	3-2
Dundalk FC	1-0	2-0	1-0	0-1	2-3	■	4-1	3-2	4-0	3-2	1-2	3-2
Limerick AFC	2-2	0-1	3-1	1-1	0-5	0-3	■	2-4	0-3	0-2	2-4	1-1
St. James's Gate AFC	6-1	3-2	4-0	1-0	1-1	3-0	5-3	■	1-2	2-2	3-2	2-1
Shamrock Rovers FC	2-0	4-2	2-3	3-2	2-4	2-1	4-1	2-5	■	1-1	2-2	5-2
Shelbourne FC	0-1	4-2	2-2	1-0	1-3	1-1	8-1	1-0	3-3	■	1-1	2-1
Sligo Rovers FC	3-2	2-1	4-2	0-0	6-2	3-1	9-1	1-3	1-1	3-2	■	3-1
Waterford AFC	4-3	5-1	3-1	1-3	4-3	2-2	2-0	2-3	1-2	2-2	5-2	■

	Division "A"	Pd	Wn	Dw	Ls	GF	GA	Pts	
1.	ST. JAMES'S GATE AFC (DUBLIN)	22	17	2	3	63	27	36	
2.	Shamrock Rovers FC (Dublin)	22	13	4	5	51	39	30	
3.	Sligo Rovers FC (Sligo)	22	12	4	6	60	44	28	#
4.	Dundalk FC (Dundalk)	22	11	3	8	45	36	25	
5.	Cork City FC / Cork United FC (Cork)	22	11	3	8	40	34	25	*
6.	Drumcondra AFC (Dublin)	22	10	5	7	49	45	25	
7.	Shelbourne FC (Dublin)	22	6	8	8	41	39	20	
8.	Bohemian FC (Dublin)	22	7	4	11	36	46	18	
9.	Bray Unknowns FC (Bray)	22	8	1	13	49	52	17	
10.	Brideville FC (Dublin)	22	6	5	11	39	49	17	
11.	Waterford AFC (Waterford)	22	6	4	12	44	54	16	
12.	Limerick AFC (Limerick)	22	1	5	16	23	75	7	
		264	108	48	108	540	540	264	

Top goal-scorers 1939-40

1)	Patrick BRADSHAW	(St. James's Gate AFC)	29
2)	Patrick LEENEY	(Bray Unknowns FC)	16
3)	Jimmy DUNNE	(Shamrock Rovers FC)	15
	Joe McALEER	(Sligo Rovers FC)	15
	Timothy O'KEEFE	(Waterford AFC)	15

St. James's Gate AFC 1-0 Cork United FC on 24/03/1940 was abandoned after 81 minutes due to a pitch invasion. The final 9 minutes were played on 20/04/1940 (no further goals were scored), prior to the St. James's Gate AFC v Brideville and Shelbourne FC v Cork United FC matches on that day.

* Cork City FC (Cork) was dissolved on 13 February 1940, however the club was re-formed immediately as Cork United FC (Cork) and took on the playing record and fixtures of the defunct club. In the above chart the results of Cork United FC are shown underlined.

\# Sligo Rovers FC (Sligo) resigned from the league which was reduced to 11 clubs for next season.

FAI Cup Final   (Dalymount Park, Dublin – 21/04/1940 – 38,509)

SHAMROCK ROVERS FC (DUBLIN)	3-0	Sligo Rovers FC (Sligo)
Ward, Fallon, Dunne	(H.T. 1-0)	

Shamrock Rovers: McCarthy, Clarke, Healey, Finnegan, Bryson, Creevey, Ward, Dunne, Clark, Cameron, Fallon.
Sligo Rovers: Twomey, Thompson, Powell, McCann, Peachey, Arrigan, Began, Gregg, McAleer, Connor, Prout.

Semi-Finals

Shamrock Rovers FC (Dublin)	2-0	Bray Unknowns FC (Bray)
Sligo Rovers FC (Sligo)	2-1	St. James's Gate AFC (Dublin)

Quarter-Finals

Brideville FC (Dublin)	0-2	Sligo Rovers FC (Sligo)
Drumcondra AFC (Dublin)	0-2	Shamrock Rovers FC (Dublin)
St. James's Gate AFC (Dublin)	2-0	Distillery FC (Dublin)
Waterford AFC (Waterford)	2-2, 0-2	Bray Unknowns FC (Bray)

1940-41

Free State Football League Division "A" 1940-41	Bohemian FC	Bray Unknowns FC	Brideville FC	Cork United FC	Drumcondra AFC	Dundalk FC	Limerick AFC	St. James's Gate AFC	Shamrock Rovers FC	Shelbourne FC	Waterford AFC
Bohemian FC	■	2-2	6-2	1-3	6-4	6-1	2-2	1-2	2-2	2-2	5-1
Bray Unknowns FC	1-3	■	2-2	1-3	3-4	3-1	3-1	3-1	0-2	0-0	2-4
Brideville FC	4-2	4-0	■	0-3	2-4	3-0	2-4	1-5	1-4	1-2	3-2
Cork United FC	1-2	2-1	4-1	■	1-1	1-0	7-1	5-0	4-2	2-1	1-2
Drumcondra AFC	2-1	5-1	3-2	1-4	■	1-0	0-0	3-5	6-1	2-2	3-2
Dundalk FC	4-0	6-1	7-2	1-3	5-3	■	2-0	3-2	4-1	2-0	0-3
Limerick AFC	2-3	2-1	0-2	1-3	3-0	2-1	■	0-1	1-3	1-0	2-2
St. James's Gate AFC	1-2	2-1	2-2	1-1	1-0	4-2	1-2	■	4-3	2-2	1-2
Shamrock Rovers FC	3-4	3-1	5-1	0-0	4-1	2-2	5-0	1-5	■	3-1	2-3
Shelbourne FC	2-2	3-1	0-1	2-2	1-1	0-2	0-0	3-2	0-2	■	1-2
Waterford AFC	3-0	5-2	2-3	4-0	6-0	5-0	6-3	4-2	3-0	1-1	■

Play-off (Mardyke, Cork – 11/05/1941)

Arrangements were made for a title play-off at the above venue and date but the players of Waterford AFC could not come to agree suitable terms with the club and thus refused to play. As a result the championship was awarded to Cork United FC.

	Division "A"	Pd	Wn	Dw	Ls	GF	GA	Pts	
1.	CORK UNITED FC (CORK)	20	13	4	3	50	23	30	
1.	Waterford AFC (Waterford)	20	14	2	4	62	31	30	#
3.	Bohemian FC (Dublin)	20	9	5	6	52	44	23	
4.	Shamrock Rovers FC (Dublin)	20	9	3	8	48	43	21	
5.	St. James's Gate AFC (Dublin)	20	9	3	8	44	41	21	
6.	Drumcondra AFC (Dublin)	20	8	4	8	44	50	20	
7.	Dundalk FC (Dundalk)	20	9	1	10	43	42	19	
8.	Brideville FC (Dublin)	20	7	2	11	39	57	16	
9.	Limerick AFC (Limerick)	20	6	4	10	27	44	16	
10.	Shelbourne FC (Dublin)	20	3	9	8	23	31	15	
11.	Bray Unknowns FC (Bray)	20	3	3	14	29	55	9	
		220	90	40	90	461	461	220	

Top goal-scorers 1940-41

1) Michael O'FLANAGAN   (Bohemian FC)   19
2) Johnny JOHNSTONE   (Waterford AFC)   17
   Timothy O'KEEFE   (Waterford AFC)   17

\# As a result of the above decision regarding the championship Waterford AFC resigned from the league which was reduced to 10 clubs for next season.

FAI Cup Final   (Dalymount Park, Dublin – 20/04/1941 – 30,132)

CORK UNITED FC (CORK)   2-2   Waterford AFC (Waterford)
O'Reilly 2   *(H.T. 1-1)*   *O'Driscoll, Johnstone*

Cork: Foley, McGowan, Duffy, Hooks, O'Riordan, McKenna, O'Reilly, McFarlane, McCarthy, O'Neill, Madden.
Waterford: Daly, J.Hartery, Myers, O'Mahoney, Phelan, Walsh, O'Driscoll, Coad, Johnstone, M.Hartery, O'Keeffe.

Final Replay   (Dalymount Park, Dublin – 23/04/1941 – 13,057)

CORK UNITED FC (CORK)   3-1   Waterford AFC (Waterford)
O'Reilly 2, McCarthy   (H.T. 1-1)   *Johnstone*

Cork United: Foley, McGowan, Duffy, Hooks, O'Riordan, McKenna, O'Reilly, McFarlane, McCarthy, O'Neill, Madden.
Waterford: Daly, J.Hartery, Myers, O'Mahoney, Phelan, Walsh, O'Driscoll, Coad, Johnstone, M.Hartery, O'Keeffe.

Semi-Finals

Cork United FC (Cork)	3-0	Dundalk FC (Dundalk)
Waterford AFC (Waterford)	2-2, 1-1, 3-2	Shamrock Rovers FC (Dublin)

Quarter-Finals

Cork United FC (Cork)	4-2	Drumcondra AFC (Dublin)
Limerick AFC (Limerick)	3-5	Waterford AFC (Waterford)
Shamrock Rovers FC (Dublin)	3-1	Brideville FC (Dublin)
Shelbourne FC (Dublin)	4-4, 3-3, 0-2	Dundalk FC (Dundalk)

1941-42

Free State Football League Division "A" 1941-42	Bohemian FC	Bray Unknowns FC	Brideville FC	Cork United FC	Drumcondra AFC	Dundalk FC	Limerick AFC	St. James's Gate AFC	Shamrock Rovers FC	Shelbourne FC
Bohemian FC	■	4-0	2-3	0-1	0-4	0-0	1-0	2-2	1-1	3-4
Bray Unknowns FC	2-2	■	1-2	0-2	2-2	1-4	2-4	1-7	0-1	1-2
Brideville FC	3-2	2-2	■	1-6	2-2	2-1	3-2	1-4	1-3	0-0
Cork United FC	2-1	4-0	3-0	■	4-0	3-1	3-2	5-0	2-3	3-0
Drumcondra AFC	2-4	2-1	2-2	4-4	■	0-2	2-2	2-1	0-6	2-1
Dundalk FC	3-3	4-1	4-1	2-2	6-2	■	2-0	2-3	2-1	3-1
Limerick AFC	3-1	6-0	1-1	1-4	3-0	4-1	■	-:+	2-0	0-5
St. James's Gate AFC	1-2	3-2	4-4	1-1	6-1	4-3	1-1	■	0-1	0-1
Shamrock Rovers FC	1-1	7-1	4-0	4-4	2-1	5-4	2-1	2-0	■	7-1
Shelbourne FC	4-0	3-0	1-1	0-1	1-1	3-1	5-0	4-4	2-2	■

	Division "A"	Pd	Wn	Dw	Ls	GF	GA	Pts	
1.	CORK UNITED FC (CORK)	18	13	4	1	54	20	30	
2.	Shamrock Rovers FC (Dublin)	18	12	4	2	52	23	28	
3.	Shelbourne FC (Dublin)	18	8	5	5	38	29	21	
4.	Dundalk FC (Dundalk)	18	8	3	7	45	36	19	
5.	St. James's Gate AFC (Dublin)	18	6	5	7	41	35	19	*
6.	Brideville FC (Dublin)	18	5	7	6	29	44	17	
7.	Limerick AFC (Limerick)	18	7	3	8	32	33	15	*
8.	Bohemian FC (Dublin)	18	4	6	8	29	36	14	
9.	Drumcondra AFC (Dublin)	18	4	6	8	29	49	14	
10.	Bray Unknowns FC (Bray)	18	-	3	15	17	61	3	
		180	67	46	67	366	366	180	

Top goal-scorers 1941-42

1) Thomas BYRNE   (Limerick AFC)   20
2) Arthur KELLY   (Dundalk FC)   15
3) Owen MADDEN   (Cork United FC)   14

After a protest the result of the Limerick AFC 3-1 St. James's Gate AFC match on 11/01/42 was deleted from the records and the points were awarded to St. James's Gate AFC (shown in results chart as -:+).

FAI Cup Final   (Dalymount Park, Dublin – 26/04/1942 – 34,298)

DUNDALK FC (DUNDALK)   3-1   Cork United FC (Cork)
Kelly 2, Lavery   *(H.T. 0-0)*   *O'Reilly*

Dundalk FC: Matier, O'Neill, Crawley, Donnelly, Leathem, Grice, Barlow, McArdle, Kelly, Lavery, McCartney.
Cork United: Foley, Hayes, Duffy, McGowan, O'Riordan, Noonan, O'Reilly, Burke McCarthy, O'Neill, Madden.

Semi-Finals

Cork United FC (Cork)	4-2	Drumcondra AFC (Dublin)
Dundalk FC (Dundalk)	1-1, 2-1	Shamrock Rovers FC (Dublin)

Quarter-Finals

Bray Unknowns FC (Bray)	3-3, 1-6	Shamrock Rovers FC (Dublin)
Cork United FC (Cork)	1-0	St. James's Gate AFC (Dublin)
Drumcondra AFC (Dublin)	2-2, 3-1	Bohemian FC (Dublin)
Shelbourne FC (Dublin)	1-2	Dundalk FC (Dundalk)

1942-43

Free State Football League Division "A" 1942-43	Bohemian FC	Bray Unknowns FC	Brideville FC	Cork United FC	Drumcondra AFC	Dundalk FC	Limerick AFC	St. James's Gate AFC	Shamrock Rovers FC	Shelbourne FC
Bohemian FC	■	3-0	3-1	1-0	4-2	1-1	4-1	1-2	1-1	0-5
Bray Unknowns FC	1-1	■	5-4	0-4	1-4	0-5	2-4	0-5	1-2	0-2
Brideville FC	1-1	4-0	■	0-2	0-3	0-0	2-2	0-1	1-0	1-0
Cork United FC	4-0	5-0	2-0	■	1-1	1-0	4-3	4-1	1-1	3-0
Drumcondra AFC	2-4	4-1	3-3	1-3	■	3-2	4-2	1-1	0-3	4-2
Dundalk FC	1-0	3-1	2-2	3-0	2-4	■	4-3	4-2	2-0	3-2
Limerick AFC	3-1	7-0	5-1	1-0	0-2	1-3	■	3-1	0-2	2-0
St. James's Gate AFC	4-1	6-1	2-1	0-3	2-2	1-1	0-2	■	1-1	0-0
Shamrock Rovers FC	1-0	7-1	3-2	1-4	2-6	0-2	5-1	3-0	■	3-4
Shelbourne FC	4-2	2-0	5-2	1-1	1-1	1-2	3-1	2-2	1-1	■

	Division "A"	Pd	Wn	Dw	Ls	GF	GA	Pts	
1.	CORK UNITED FC (CORK)	18	12	3	3	42	14	27	
2.	Dundalk FC (Dundalk)	18	11	4	3	40	22	26	
3.	Drumcondra AFC (Dublin)	18	9	5	4	47	34	23	
4.	Shamrock Rovers FC (Dublin)	18	8	4	6	36	28	20	
5.	Shelbourne FC (Dublin)	18	7	5	6	35	28	19	
6.	St. James's Gate AFC (Dublin)	18	6	6	6	31	30	18	
7.	Limerick AFC (Limerick)	18	8	1	9	41	38	17	
8.	Bohemian FC (Dublin)	18	6	4	8	28	34	16	
9.	Brideville FC (Dublin)	18	3	5	10	25	39	11	#
10.	Bray Unknowns FC (Bray)	18	1	1	16	14	72	3	#
		180	71	38	71	339	339	180	

Top goal-scorers 1942-43

1)	Sean McCARTHY	(Cork United FC)	16
2)	David WALSH	(Limerick AFC)	13
3)	Patrick COAD	(Shamrock Rovers FC)	12
	Donald McDONALD	(Dundalk FC)	12
	Tommy McNAMARA	(Drumcondra AFC)	12

\# Bray Unknowns FC (Bray) and Brideville FC (Dublin) were not re-elected to the league which was reduced to 8 clubs for next season.

FAI Cup Final   (Dalymount Park, Dublin – 18/04/1943 – 30,549)

DRUMCONDRA AFC (DUBLIN)   2-1   Cork United FC (Cork)
McGrane, McNamara   *(H.T. 1-0)*   *O'Reilly*

Drumcondra: Flynn, O'Rourke, Clarke, Mulville, McGlynn, O'Mara, Ward, Daly, McNamara, Dyer, McGrane.
Cork United: McAlinden, Hayes, Duffy, McGowan, Curtin, Forde, O'Reilly, Dunne, McCarthy, Madden, O'Driscoll.

Semi-Finals

Cork United FC (Cork)	2-2, 2-0	Brideville FC (Dublin)
Drumcondra AFC (Dublin)	0-0, 3-3, 4-2	Limerick AFC (Limerick)

Quarter-Finals

Dundalk FC (Dundalk)	2-2, 0-4	Drumcondra AFC (Dublin)
Shamrock Rovers FC (Dublin)	1-2	Brideville FC (Dublin)

Cork United FC (Cork) and Limerick AFC (Limerick) both received byes

1943-44

Free State Football League Division "A" 1943-44	Bohemian FC	Cork United FC	Drumcondra AFC	Dundalk FC	Limerick AFC	St. James's Gate AFC	Shamrock Rovers FC	Shelbourne FC
Bohemian FC	■	3-1	2-2	0-1	2-1	3-1	3-2	1-3
Cork United FC	2-1	■	6-3	0-0	2-0	5-1	1-3	3-2
Drumcondra AFC	3-2	3-2	■	3-0	0-2	2-0	0-4	1-2
Dundalk FC	5-2	3-2	2-0	■	2-4	3-0	1-1	0-3
Limerick AFC	2-0	3-0	2-2	3-0	■	4-0	3-2	3-3
St. James's Gate AFC	3-1	0-7	1-2	0-4	2-3	■	2-2	0-1
Shamrock Rovers FC	4-3	2-2	1-2	0-0	4-4	7-0	■	3-1
Shelbourne FC	2-2	4-3	2-1	1-0	0-0	3-2	5-3	■

Division "A"

		Pd	Wn	Dw	Ls	GF	GA	Pts	
1.	SHELBOURNE FC (DUBLIN)	14	9	3	2	32	22	21	
2.	Limerick AFC (Limerick)	14	8	4	2	34	19	20	
3.	Shamrock Rovers FC (Dublin)	14	5	5	4	38	27	15	
4.	Dundalk FC (Dundalk)	14	6	3	5	21	19	15	
5.	Cork United FC (Cork)	14	6	2	6	36	28	14	
6.	Drumcondra AFC (Dublin)	14	6	2	6	24	28	14	
7.	Bohemian FC (Dublin)	14	4	2	8	25	32	10	
8.	St. James's Gate AFC (Dublin)	14	1	1	12	12	47	3	#
		112	45	22	45	222	222	112	

Top goal-scorers 1943-44

1) Sean McCARTHY   (Cork United FC)   16
2) Patrick COAD   (Shamrock Rovers FC)   15
   Patrick O'LEARY   (Limerick FC)   15

\# St. James's Gate AFC (Dublin) were not re-elected for the next season.   Elected: Brideville FC (Dublin)

FAI Cup Final   (Dalymount Park, Dublin – 16/04/1944 – 34,000)

SHAMROCK ROVERS FC (DUBLIN)   3-2   Shelbourne FC (Dublin)
Rogers, Gannon o.g., Crowe   (H.T. 3-1)   *Fallon, McCluskey*

Shamrock Rovers: Palmer, Nolan, Clarke, Doherty, Byrne, Farrell, Delaney, Coad, Crowe, Rogers, Eglinton.
Shelbourne: Kiernan, Whelan, Olphert, Gannon, Kinsella, Mullally, Kennedy, Cassidy, McCluskey, Wall, Fallon.

Semi-Finals

| Shamrock Rovers FC (Dublin) | 2-0, 5-2 | Drumcondra AFC (Dublin) |
| Shelbourne FC (Dublin) | 1-1, 3-1 | Dundalk FC (Dundalk) |

Round 1

Bohemian FC (Dublin)	2-4, 1-1	Drumcondra AFC (Dublin)
Dundalk FC (Dundalk)	5-1, 0-1	Cork United FC (Cork)
St. James's Gate AFC (Dublin)	1-3, 1-3	Shelbourne FC (Dublin)
Shamrock Rovers FC (Dublin)	5-1, 2-2	Limerick AFC (Limerick)

1944-45

Free State Football League Division "A" 1944-45	Bohemian FC	Brideville FC	Cork United FC	Drumcondra AFC	Dundalk FC	Limerick AFC	Shamrock Rovers FC	Shelbourne FC
Bohemian FC	■	1-1	2-4	0-1	2-1	0-0	1-1	3-1
Brideville FC	2-1	■	0-9	4-7	2-1	2-2	0-0	0-3
Cork United FC	4-1	5-1	■	6-1	3-2	3-2	6-0	5-2
Drumcondra AFC	4-4	3-1	3-1	■	4-2	1-1	0-0	0-1
Dundalk FC	3-0	2-2	1-5	2-2	■	3-0	1-1	1-0
Limerick AFC	1-0	6-3	5-4	5-3	9-1	■	3-0	3-0
Shamrock Rovers FC	4-2	2-0	3-2	3-1	3-1	2-0	■	1-3
Shelbourne FC	3-0	2-2	1-2	2-2	0-1	3-1	0-0	■

Division "A"

		Pd	Wn	Dw	Ls	GF	GA	Pts	
1.	CORK UNITED FC (CORK)	14	11	-	3	59	24	22	
2.	Limerick AFC (Limerick)	14	7	3	4	38	25	17	
3.	Shamrock Rovers FC (Dublin)	14	6	5	3	20	20	17	
4.	Drumcondra AFC (Dublin)	14	5	5	4	32	32	15	
5.	Shelbourne FC (Dublin)	14	5	3	6	21	21	13	
6.	Dundalk FC (Dundalk)	14	4	3	7	22	33	11	
7.	Brideville FC (Dublin)	14	2	5	7	20	44	9	#
8.	Bohemian FC (Dublin)	14	2	4	8	17	30	8	
		112	42	28	42	229	229	112	

Top goal-scorers 1944-45

1) Sean McCARTHY (Cork United FC) 26
2) Joseph Noel DUNNE (Limerick AFC) 15
3) Seamus DARCY (Limerick AFC) 10
   Jack O'DRISCOLL (Cork United FC) 10

Brideville FC (Dublin) were not re-elected to the league for next season.   Elected: Waterford AFC (Waterford)

FAI Cup Final (Dalymount Park, Dublin – 22/04/1945 – 44,238)

SHAMROCK ROVERS FC (DUBLIN)   1-0   Bohemian FC (Dublin)
Gregg   *(H.T. 0-0)*

Shamrock Rovers: Palmer, Clarke, Coyle, Doherty, Byrne, Farrell, Delaney, Coad, Gregg, Rogers, Eglinton.
Bohemian: Collins, Glennon, Richardson, Nash, Molloy, Waters, K.O'Flanagan, Kelly, Burns, Morris, M.O'Flanagan.

Semi-Finals

Bohemian FC (Dublin)	2-1, 1-2, 2-0	Cork United FC (Cork)
Dundalk FC (Dundalk)	3-0, 0-5	Shamrock Rovers FC (Dublin)

Round 1

Drumcondra AFC (Dublin)	0-2, 0-5	Cork United FC (Cork)
Dundalk FC (Dundalk)	2-0, 1-2	Brideville FC (Dublin)
Shamrock Rovers FC (Dublin)	2-3, 3-1	Limerick AFC (Limerick)
Shelbourne FC (Dublin)	2-2, 0-4	Bohemian FC (Dublin)

1945-46

Free State Football League Division "A" 1945-46	Bohemian FC	Cork United FC	Drumcondra AFC	Dundalk FC	Limerick AFC	Shamrock Rovers FC	Shelbourne FC	Waterford AFC
Bohemian FC		1-1	0-2	1-4	2-1	1-5	3-1	0-1
Cork United FC	3-1		9-1	6-2	2-1	2-1	6-0	0-1
Drumcondra AFC	2-3	1-1		5-3	3-1	2-2	4-3	3-1
Dundalk FC	3-1	2-2	1-2		2-2	5-3	2-2	3-3
Limerick AFC	0-1	4-6	1-2	2-1		2-0	4-1	2-0
Shamrock Rovers FC	7-2	2-4	2-5	3-3	2-0		6-0	4-1
Shelbourne FC	4-1	0-3	3-3	2-4	5-0	1-2		3-1
Waterford AFC	2-2	3-1	4-2	3-1	1-5	3-1	5-1	

	Division "A"	Pd	Wn	Dw	Ls	GF	GA	Pts
1.	CORK UNITED FC (CORK)	14	9	3	2	46	20	21
2.	Drumcondra AFC (Dublin)	14	8	3	3	37	34	19
3.	Waterford AFC (Waterford)	14	7	2	5	29	28	16
4.	Shamrock Rovers FC (Dublin)	14	6	2	6	40	31	14
5.	Dundalk FC (Dundalk)	14	4	5	5	36	37	13
6.	Limerick AFC (Limerick)	14	5	1	8	25	28	11
7.	Bohemian FC (Dublin)	14	4	2	8	19	36	10
8.	Shelbourne FC (Dublin)	14	3	2	9	26	44	8
		112	46	20	46	258	258	112

Top goal-scorers 1945-46

1) Patrick O'LEARY   (Cork United FC)   15
2) Tommy EGLINTON   (Shamrock Rovers FC)   11
   Tommy McCORMACK   (Drumcondra AFC)   11
   Michael O'FLANAGAN   (Bohemian FC)   11

FAI Cup Final   (Dalymount Park, Dublin – 21/04/1946 – 34,248)

DRUMCONDRA AFC (DUBLIN)	2-1	Shamrock Rovers FC (Dublin)
McCormack, Henderson	*(H.T. 1-1)*	*Coad*

Drumcondra: Keogh, Martin, Barnwell, R.Lawlor, Clarke, O'Mara, Henderson, Delaney, McCormack, J.Lawlor, Ward.
Shamrock Rovers: Collins, Clarke, Glennon, Kelly, Byrne, Farrell, Cochrane, Coad, Delaney, McAlinden, Eglinton.

Semi-Finals

Cork United FC (Cork)	2-0, 2-4, 1-4	Shamrock Rovers FC (Dublin)
Shelbourne FC (Dublin)	2-1, 0-1, 1-4	Drumcondra AFC (Dublin)

Round 1

Bohemian FC (Dublin)	0-1, 0-0	Cork United FC (Cork)
Dundalk FC (Dundalk)	2-2, 0-1	Shamrock Rovers FC (Dundalk)
Shelbourne FC (Dublin)	3-3, 3-0	Limerick AFC (Dublin)
Waterford AFC (Waterford)	3-2, 0-6	Drumcondra AFC (Dublin)

1946-47

Free State Football League Division "A" 1946-47	Bohemian	Cork United	Drumcondra	Dundalk FC	Limerick	Shamrock R.	Shelbourne	Waterford
Bohemian FC	■	4-1	1-5	3-1	6-0	1-3	4-3	1-2
Cork United FC	6-1	■	4-1	5-1	2-0	1-1	1-1	4-1
Drumcondra AFC	3-2	3-2	■	4-4	0-2	3-2	2-0	1-0
Dundalk FC	1-3	2-5	1-0	■	3-0	2-1	1-2	3-0
Limerick AFC	2-2	0-3	4-1	2-2	■	2-2	1-2	1-1
Shamrock Rovers FC	3-3	4-2	1-2	5-1	3-1	■	1-2	3-0
Shelbourne FC	1-1	4-2	1-1	6-2	3-0	1-4	■	4-2
Waterford AFC	2-1	4-2	1-3	1-1	1-1	0-1	2-4	■

	Division "A"	Pd	Wn	Dw	Ls	GF	GA	Pts
1.	SHELBOURNE FC (DUBLIN)	14	8	3	3	34	24	19
2.	Drumcondra AFC (Dublin)	14	8	2	4	29	25	18
3.	Shamrock Rovers FC (Dublin)	14	7	3	4	34	21	17
4.	Cork United FC (Cork)	14	7	2	5	40	27	16
5.	Bohemian FC (Dublin)	14	5	3	6	33	33	13
6.	Dundalk FC (Dundalk)	14	4	3	7	25	37	11
7.	Waterford AFC (Waterford)	14	3	3	8	17	30	9
8.	Limerick AFC (Limerick)	14	2	5	7	16	31	9
		112	44	24	44	228	228	112

Top goal-scorers 1946-47

1)	Patrick COAD	(Shamrock Rovers FC)	11
	Alf HANSON	(Shelbourne FC)	11
3)	Sean MCCARTHY	(Cork United FC)	10
	Michael O'FLANAGAN	(Bohemian FC)	10

FAI Cup Final   (Dalymount Park, Dublin – 20/04/1947 – 20,198)

CORK UNITED FC (CORK)	2-2	Bohemian FC (Dublin)
Denning o.g., McCarthy	*(H.T. 2-1)*	*M.O'Flanagan, Halpin pen.*

Cork: Foley, McGowan, D.Noonan, O'Reilly, Burke, P.Noonan, O'Driscoll, McCarthy, O'Leary, Moroney, Madden.
Bohemian: Denning, Cleary, Eccles, Cameron, Nolan, Halpin, Smith, Morris, M.O'Flanagan, O'Kelly, Kirby.

Final Replay   (Dalymount Park, Dublin – 23/04/1947 – 5,519)

CORK UNITED FC (CORK)	2-0	Bohemian FC (Dublin)
McCarthy, Moroney	*(H.T. 2-0)*	

Cork: Foley, McGowan, D.Noonan, O'Reilly, Burke, P.Noonan, O'Driscoll, McCarthy, O'Leary, Moroney, Madden.
Bohemian: Denning, Richardson, Eccles, Cameron, Nolan, Halpin, Smith, Morris, M.O'Flanagan, O'Kelly, Kirby.

Semi-Finals

Bohemian FC (Dublin)	3-2, 3-3	Shelbourne FC (Dublin)
Cork United FC (Cork)	1-0, 3-3	Limerick AFC (Limerick)

Round 1

Bohemian FC (Dublin)	3-0, 1-2	Drumcondra AFC (Dublin)
Cork United FC (Cork)	9-1, 1-1	Waterford AFC (Waterford)
Dundalk FC (Dundalk)	1-0, 1-3	Limerick AFC (Limerick)
Shelbourne FC (Dublin)	0-1, 1-0, 5-2	Shamrock Rovers FC (Dublin)

1947-48

Free State Football League Division "A" 1947-48	Bohemian FC	Cork United FC	Drumcondra AFC	Dundalk FC	Limerick AFC	Shamrock Rovers FC	Shelbourne FC	Waterford AFC
Bohemian FC	■	1-2	1-5	0-2	5-2	0-1	3-6	1-0
Cork United FC	1-1	■	3-4	0-0	6-2	4-3	1-2	1-2
Drumcondra AFC	0-2	2-2	■	2-0	1-1	3-1	1-4	3-2
Dundalk FC	3-0	2-2	2-0	■	2-0	1-1	2-2	4-0
Limerick AFC	4-2	3-1	1-1	2-0	■	1-1	2-1	0-2
Shamrock Rovers FC	0-0	2-2	3-3	4-0	2-1	■	2-2	3-2
Shelbourne FC	1-2	5-3	0-3	1-1	2-0	2-1	■	2-1
Waterford AFC	2-1	1-1	0-1	0-2	1-3	3-2	2-0	■

	Division "A"	Pd	Wn	Dw	Ls	GF	GA	Pts
1.	DRUMCONDRA AFC (DUBLIN)	14	7	4	3	29	22	18
2.	Dundalk FC (Dundalk)	14	6	5	3	21	14	17
3.	Shelbourne FC (Dublin)	14	7	3	4	30	24	17
4.	Shamrock Rovers FC (Dublin)	14	4	6	4	26	24	14
5.	Limerick AFC (Limerick)	14	5	3	6	22	27	13
6.	Cork United FC (Cork)	14	3	6	5	29	30	12
7.	Waterford AFC (Waterford)	14	5	1	8	18	24	11
8.	Bohemian FC (Dublin)	14	4	2	8	19	29	10
		112	41	30	41	194	194	112

Top goal-scorers 1947-48

1)	Sean McCARTHY	(Cork United FC)	13
2)	John LAWLOR	(Drumcondra AFC)	10
3)	Brendan CARROLL	(Shelbourne FC)	9
	Patrick COAD	(Shamrock Rovers FC)	9

Elected: Sligo Rovers FC (Sligo), Transport FC (Bray)

The League was extended to 10 clubs for next season

FAI Cup Final   (Dalymount Park, Dublin – 11/04/1948 – 33,812)

SHAMROCK ROVERS FC (DUBLIN)   2-1   Drumcondra AFC (Dublin)
Coad, Kirby   *(H.T. 1-1)*   *Henderson*

Shamrock Rovers: Collins, Clarke, Coyle, Nash, Rogers, Dunne, Glennon, Coad, Gregg, Treacy, Kirby.
Drumcondra: Keogh, Robinson, Barnwell, Kinsella, Clarke, Mulville, Giles, Lawlor, Delaney, Daly, Henderson.

Semi-Finals

Cork United FC (Cork)	1-1, 0-2	Drumcondra AFC (Dublin)
Shamrock Rovers FC (Dublin)	8-2	St. Patrick's Athletic FC (Dublin)

Quarter-Finals

Drumcondra AFC (Dublin)	1-0	Shelbourne FC (Dublin)
Shamrock Rovers FC (Dublin)	2-1	Waterford AFC (Waterford)

Cork United FC (Cork) and St. Patrick's Athletic FC (Dublin) both received byes

1948-49

Free State Football League Division "A" 1948-49	Bohemian	Cork Athletic	Drumcondra	Dundalk FC	Limerick	Shamrock R.	Shelbourne	Sligo Rovers	Transport	Waterford
Bohemian FC		2-2	1-3	1-4	2-3	2-1	0-6	1-2	2-2	3-2
Cork Athletic FC	3-1		2-4	0-2	2-0	3-4	2-5	3-2	3-0	0-2
Drumcondra AFC	3-2	1-0		1-0	1-1	1-1	2-2	2-1	2-1	1-4
Dundalk FC	2-2	2-1	0-0		2-1	2-1	1-1	1-1	1-2	4-0
Limerick AFC	2-1	5-2	0-1	3-2		1-1	0-2	3-2	1-1	1-5
Shamrock Rovers FC	2-2	3-1	2-3	3-0	0-0		2-0	2-2	2-2	4-1
Shelbourne FC	0-0	0-1	3-4	0-1	3-1	1-0		2-1	3-1	2-2
Sligo Rovers FC	3-1	5-2	0-1	3-4	1-1	1-1	1-4		1-1	0-3
Transport FC	4-3	2-6	1-1	3-3	6-2	1-1	2-2	4-3		2-0
Waterford AFC	5-2	1-0	2-3	1-2	1-2	2-3	2-3	1-2	5-0	

	Division "A"	Pd	Wn	Dw	Ls	GF	GA	Pts	
1.	DRUMCONDRA AFC (DUBLIN)	18	12	5	1	34	23	29	
2.	Shelbourne FC (Dublin)	18	9	5	4	39	23	23	
3.	Dundalk FC (Dundalk)	18	9	5	4	33	24	23	
4.	Shamrock Rovers FC (Dublin)	18	6	8	4	33	25	20	
5.	Transport FC (Bray)	18	5	8	5	35	41	18	
6.	Limerick AFC (Limerick)	18	6	5	7	27	35	17	
7.	Waterford AFC (Waterford)	18	7	1	10	39	34	15	
8.	Sligo Rovers FC (Sligo)	18	4	5	9	31	37	13	
9.	Cork Athletic FC (Cork)	18	6	1	11	33	41	13	#
10.	Bohemian FC (Dublin)	18	2	5	11	28	49	9	
		180	66	48	66	332	332	180	

Top goal-scorers 1948-49

1) Bernard LESTER (Transport FC) 12
   Eugene NOONAN (Waterford AFC) 12
   Patrick O'LEARY (Cork Athletic FC) 12

\# Cork United FC (Cork) resigned from the league on 10th October 1948 after competing in the Dublin City Cup and 2 games in the League of Ireland Shield. The club then disbanded but a new club Cork Athletic FC (Cork) was founded with virtually the same personnel etc. The new club was elected to the league in place of Cork United FC.

FAI Cup Final (Dalymount Park, Dublin – 10/04/1949 – 28,539)

DUNDALK FC (DUNDALK)	3-0	Shelbourne FC (Dublin)
J.Walsh 2, Henderson	(H.T. 2-0)	

Dundalk: Anderson, Fearon, Maguire, Murphy, Skivington, Matthews, P.Walsh, McElhinney, Henderson, Hamilton, J.Walsh.

Shelbourne: Tapkin, Murphy, Haughey, Rooney, Nolan, Keely, Colfer, Fitzsimmons, Carroll, Desmond, Malone.

Semi-Finals

Drumcondra AFC (Dublin)	2-2, 1-2	Dundalk FC (Dundalk)
Shelbourne FC (Dublin)	3-1	Waterford AFC (Waterford)

Quarter-Finals

Drumcondra AFC (Dublin)	4-0	Transport FC (Bray)
St. Patrick's Athletic FC (Dublin)	0-1	Shelbourne FC (Dublin)

Dundalk FC (Dundalk) and Waterford AFC (Waterford) both received byes

1949-50

League of Ireland Division "A" 1949-50	Bohemian FC	Cork Athletic FC	Drumcondra AFC	Dundalk FC	Limerick AFC	Shamrock Rovers FC	Shelbourne FC	Sligo Rovers FC	Transport FC	Waterford AFC
Bohemian FC	■	1-1	0-3	3-5	2-0	2-2	0-1	1-2	0-0	0-4
Cork Athletic FC	2-1	■	1-2	1-0	8-3	3-0	3-1	2-2	3-2	2-0
Drumcondra AFC	3-1	1-2	■	0-0	3-2	0-4	2-2	0-0	3-0	3-0
Dundalk FC	0-1	3-2	1-1	■	2-1	1-1	3-2	0-0	5-0	2-1
Limerick AFC	0-0	2-2	1-1	3-3	■	4-3	1-1	2-1	1-1	1-1
Shamrock Rovers FC	7-2	2-5	0-1	3-1	4-0	■	3-1	5-1	1-2	1-0
Shelbourne FC	4-0	1-1	0-0	4-3	3-1	3-0	■	2-2	3-1	3-3
Sligo Rovers FC	3-1	2-1	2-4	2-1	2-0	1-0	4-0	■	0-1	1-1
Transport FC	5-0	1-2	1-2	1-3	1-1	1-1	1-2	3-0	■	0-0
Waterford AFC	4-1	2-2	4-3	5-2	4-3	2-2	1-1	6-3	2-2	■

	Division "A"	Pd	Wn	Dw	Ls	GF	GA	Pts
1.	CORK ATHLETIC FC (CORK)	18	10	5	3	43	26	25
2.	Drumcondra AFC (Dublin)	18	9	6	3	32	21	24
3.	Shelbourne FC (Dublin)	18	7	7	4	34	29	21
4.	Waterford AFC (Waterford)	18	6	8	4	40	32	20
5.	Dundalk FC (Dundalk)	18	7	5	6	35	31	19
6.	Sligo Rovers FC (Sligo)	18	7	5	6	28	30	19
7.	Shamrock Rovers FC (Dublin)	18	7	4	7	39	30	18
8.	Transport FC (Bray)	18	4	6	8	23	29	14
9.	Limerick AFC (Limerick)	18	2	8	8	26	42	12
10.	Bohemian FC (Dublin)	18	2	4	12	16	46	8
		180	61	58	61	316	316	180

Top goal-scorers 1949-50

1) David McCULLOCH   (Waterford AFC)   19
2) Patrick O'LEARY   (Cork Athletic FC)   13
3) Johnny VAUGHAN   (Cork Athletic FC)   12

FAI Cup Final   (Dalymount Park, Dublin – 23/04/1950 – 27,807)

TRANSPORT FC (BRAY)   2-2   Cork Athletic FC (Cork)
Lester, Duggan   (H.T. 0-2)   *O'Leary, Cronin*

Transport: Carroll, Meighan, Loughran, Gibney, Woods, Kennedy, P.Doyle, Kearns, Duggan, Lester, Smith.
Cork Athletic: Healy, O'Reilly, D.Noonan, Warner, Burke, Cantwell, Vaughan, Broderick, O'Leary, Cronin, Lennox.

Final Replay   (Dalymount Park, Dublin – 26/04/1950 – 21,123)

TRANSPORT FC (BRAY)   2-2 (aet)   Cork Athletic FC (Cork)
Smith, Loughran   (H.T. 0-1)   *O'Reilly pen., Lennox*

Cork Athletic: Healy, O'Reilly, O'Connell, Warner, Burke, Cantwell, Vaughan, Broderick, O'Leary, Cronin, Lennox.
Transport: Carroll, Meighan, Loughran, Gibney, M.Doyle, Kennedy, N.Doyle, Kearns, Duggan, Lester, Smith.

Final 2nd Replay (Dalymount Park, Dublin – 05/05/1950)

TRANSPORT FC (BRAY)	3-1	Cork Athletic FC (Cork)
Lester 2, Duggan	*(H.T. 1-1)*	*Vaughan*

Transport: Carroll, Meighan, Loughran, Gibney, Collins, Kennedy, P.Doyle, Kearns, Duggan, Lester, Smith.
Cork Athletic: Healy, O'Reilly, D.Noonan, Warner, Burke, Cantwell, Vaughan, Broderick, O'Leary, Cronin, Lennox.

Semi-Finals

Cork Athletic FC (Cork)	1-1, 2-2, 4-2	St. Patrick's Athletic FC (Dublin)
Transport FC (Bray)	2-1	Sligo Rovers FC (Sligo)

Quarter-Finals

A.O.H. (Cork)	0-1	St. Patrick's Athletic FC (Dublin)
Bohemian FC (Dublin)	1-2	Transport FC (Bray)
Shamrock Rovers FC (Dublin)	1-1, 1-2	Cork Athletic FC (Cork)
Sligo Rovers FC (Sligo)	2-0	Albert Rovers FC (Cork)

1950-51

League of Ireland Division "A" 1950-51	Bohemian FC	Cork Athletic FC	Drumcondra AFC	Dundalk FC	Limerick AFC	Shamrock Rovers FC	Shelbourne FC	Sligo Rovers FC	Transport FC	Waterford AFC
Bohemian FC	■	1-2	1-2	1-1	3-1	2-0	1-1	1-0	2-2	0-0
Cork Athletic FC	5-0	■	3-3	5-1	4-1	1-0	2-1	4-2	3-0	3-1
Drumcondra AFC	2-2	2-1	■	1-1	3-0	2-2	0-3	1-2	2-1	4-0
Dundalk FC	3-3	4-1	0-3	■	0-0	1-4	2-1	2-3	2-3	5-2
Limerick AFC	4-2	1-2	4-4	2-1	■	3-2	1-4	3-1	1-1	2-4
Shamrock Rovers FC	4-1	1-0	1-1	2-3	2-0	■	1-1	0-2	3-2	1-2
Shelbourne FC	2-3	2-2	0-2	3-2	5-2	3-2	■	2-2	0-1	3-0
Sligo Rovers FC	1-2	1-0	1-1	4-3	2-0	4-2	3-1	■	2-0	5-0
Transport FC	2-1	1-5	0-1	2-1	4-2	2-3	0-3	0-0	■	1-1
Waterford AFC	0-2	0-3	4-3	4-3	4-0	0-3	1-2	3-4	2-3	■

	Division "A"	Pd	Wn	Dw	Ls	GF	GA	Pts	
1.	CORK ATHLETIC FC (CORK)	18	12	2	4	46	22	26	
2.	Sligo Rovers FC (Sligo)	18	11	3	4	39	25	25	
3.	Drumcondra AFC (Dublin)	18	8	7	3	37	26	23	
4.	Shelbourne FC (Dublin)	18	8	4	6	37	27	20	
5.	Bohemian FC (Dublin)	18	7	6	5	30	32	20	
6.	Shamrock Rovers FC (Dublin)	18	7	3	8	33	30	17	
7.	Transport FC (Bray)	18	5	4	9	25	36	14	*
8.	Dundalk FC (Dundalk)	18	4	4	10	35	44	12	
9.	Waterford AFC (Waterford)	18	5	2	11	28	47	12	
10.	Limerick AFC (Limerick)	18	4	3	11	27	48	11	
		180	71	38	71	337	337	180	

Top goal-scorers 1950-51

1)	Desmond GLYNN	(Drumcondra AFC)	20
2)	Johnny VAUGHAN	(Cork Athletic FC)	14
3)	Martin COLFER	(Shelbourne FC)	10
	Patrick GALLACHER	(Dundalk FC)	10
	George GRAY	(Sligo Rovers FC)	10

Elected: Evergreen United FC (Cork), St. Patrick's Athletic FC (Dublin)

The League was extended to 12 clubs for next season

*   Transport FC (Bray) moved their home base from Bray to the city of Dublin as Transport FC (Dublin).

FAI Cup Final   (Dalymount Park, Dublin – 22/04/1951 – 38,912)

CORK ATHLETIC FC (CORK)	1-1	Shelbourne FC (Dublin)
O'Leary	*(H.T. 1-0)*	*Carberry*

Cork Athletic: Courtney, P.Noonan, D.Noonan, O'Mahoney, Burke, Cotter, Vaughan, Cronin, O'Leary, McAlea, Lennox.

Shelbourne: Brien, Haughey, Mulligan, Fitzpatrick, Curtis, Keely, Cunningham, Lynam, Colfer, Malone, Carberry.

Final Replay   (Dalymount Park, Dublin – 29/04/1951 – 22,010)

CORK ATHLETIC FC (CORK)	1-0	Shelbourne FC (Dublin)
Vaughan	*(H.T. 1-0)*	

Cork Athletic: Courtney, P.Noonan, O'Connell, O'Mahoney, Burke, Cotter, Vaughan, Cronin, O'Leary, McAlea, Lennox.

Shelbourne: Brien, Haughey, Mulligan, Fitzpatrick, Curtis, Keely, Cunningham, Lynam, Colfer, Malone, Carberry.

Semi-Finals

Cork Athletic FC (Cork)	2-0	Sligo Rovers FC (Sligo)
Shelbourne FC (Dublin)	1-0	Drumcondra AFC (Dublin)

Quarter-Finals

Drumcondra AFC (Dublin)	2-0	Bohemian FC (Dublin)
Limerick AFC (Limerick)	0-1, 1-1, 0-6	Cork Athletic FC (Cork)

(1st match was abandoned after 77 minutes due to a pitch invasion. 2nd match was played at Dalymount Park)

Shamrock Rovers FC (Dublin)	1-2	Shelbourne FC (Dublin)
Sligo Rovers FC (Sligo)	2-0	Dundalk FC (Dundalk)

1951-52

League of Ireland Division "A" 1951-52	Bohemian FC	Cork Athletic FC	Drumcondra AFC	Dundalk FC	Evergreen United	Limerick AFC	St. Patrick's Ath.	Shamrock Rovers	Shelbourne FC	Sligo Rovers FC	Transport FC	Waterford AFC
Bohemian FC	■	4-1	3-2	3-1	3-1	2-0	1-5	1-4	3-2	1-2	3-0	1-4
Cork Athletic FC	2-2	■	1-0	2-2	1-3	5-0	0-1	2-1	3-4	1-4	2-2	3-1
Drumcondra AFC	0-0	0-2	■	3-2	4-1	4-0	1-3	1-0	6-1	3-1	5-0	2-3
Dundalk FC	1-1	2-5	2-1	■	2-1	6-0	1-1	0-2	0-3	1-1	3-3	4-0
Evergreen United FC	1-0	2-0	3-2	3-1	■	1-1	1-1	0-3	1-2	5-0	4-2	4-3
Limerick AFC	0-3	3-0	0-0	3-3	2-5	■	2-3	0-3	1-1	1-2	1-1	3-1
St. Patrick's Athletic FC	3-2	1-0	1-2	5-2	5-1	4-2	■	1-0	6-1	3-1	4-3	3-2
Shamrock Rovers FC	1-0	3-1	1-1	1-1	3-1	2-0	3-1	■	3-2	6-0	0-1	1-2
Shelbourne FC	2-1	3-2	4-4	3-1	3-1	4-0	3-1	1-1	■	6-2	5-2	1-1
Sligo Rovers FC	3-0	1-0	2-1	4-2	3-1	6-0	2-1	1-1	4-4	■	2-1	3-2
Transport FC	2-1	2-1	1-3	3-0	0-1	5-1	1-2	0-3	1-2	2-3	■	5-2
Waterford AFC	4-2	3-2	2-2	2-0	1-3	4-0	3-4	1-1	0-2	4-2	2-6	■

	Division "A"	Pd	Wn	Dw	Ls	GF	GA	Pts
1.	ST. PATRICK'S ATHLETIC FC (DUBLIN)	22	16	2	4	59	34	34
2.	Shelbourne FC (Dublin)	22	13	5	4	59	44	31
3.	Shamrock Rovers FC (Dublin)	22	12	5	5	43	18	29
4.	Sligo Rovers FC (Sligo)	22	13	3	6	49	46	29
5.	Evergreen United FC (Cork)	22	11	2	9	44	42	24
6.	Drumcondra AFC (Dublin)	22	9	5	8	47	33	23
7.	Bohemian FC (Dublin)	22	8	3	11	37	41	19
8.	Waterford AFC (Waterford)	22	8	3	11	47	54	19
9.	Transport FC (Dublin)	22	7	3	12	43	50	17
10.	Cork Athletic FC (Cork)	22	6	3	13	36	44	15
11.	Dundalk FC (Dundalk)	22	4	7	11	37	50	15
12.	Limerick AFC (Limerick)	22	2	5	15	20	65	9
		264	109	46	109	521	521	264

Top goal-scorers 1951-52

1) Shay GIBBONS (St. Patrick's Athletic FC) 26
2) Rory DWYER (Shelbourne FC) 22
3) Desmond GLYNN (Drumcondra AFC) 20

FAI Cup Final (Dalymount Park, Dublin – 20/04/1952 – 26,479)

DUNDALK FC (DUNDALK)	1-1	Cork Athletic FC (Cork)
Martin	(H.T. 0-0)	O'Leary

Dundalk: Durkan, Ralph, Traynor, Gavin, Clarke, McCourt, McDonagh, Fearon, Martin, Mullen, Maloney.
Cork: Courtney, P.Noonan, D.Noonan, Moloney, Burke, Cotter, Vaughan, Broderick, O'Leary, Cronin, Lennox.

Final Replay (Dalymount Park, Dublin – 23/04/1952 – 20,753)

DUNDALK FC (DUNDALK)	3-0	Cork Athletic FC (Cork)
Fearon, Maloney, Mullen	(H.T. 1-0)	

Dundalk: Durkan, Ralph, Traynor, Gavin, Clarke, McCourt, McDonagh, Fearon, Martin, Mullen, Maloney.
Cork: Waters, P.Noonan, D.Noonan, Moloney, Burke, Cotter, Vaughan, O'Mahoney, O'Leary, Cronin, Lennox.

Semi-Finals

Cork Athletic FC (Cork)	4-3	Sligo Rovers FC (Sligo)
Dundalk FC (Dundalk)	2-2, 6-4	Waterford AFC (Waterford)

Quarter-Finals

A.O.H. (Cork)	0-4	Dundalk FC (Dundalk)
Shamrock Rovers FC (Dublin)	1-2	Cork Athletic FC (Cork)
Shelbourne FC (Dublin)	3-3, 0-1	Waterford AFC (Waterford)
Sligo Rovers FC (Sligo)	3-1	Drumcondra AFC (Dublin)

1952-53

League of Ireland Division "A" 1952-53	Bohemian FC	Cork Athletic FC	Drumcondra AFC	Dundalk FC	Evergreen United	Limerick AFC	St. Patrick's Ath.	Shamrock Rovers	Shelbourne FC	Sligo Rovers FC	Transport FC	Waterford AFC
Bohemian FC	■	1-2	1-3	0-4	1-1	2-0	3-7	2-1	0-3	2-0	4-2	0-0
Cork Athletic FC	6-1	■	3-3	2-0	2-1	2-2	2-1	0-1	2-0	1-4	1-2	4-2
Drumcondra AFC	6-1	1-1	■	2-1	0-1	3-0	0-0	1-0	1-1	3-1	1-1	4-4
Dundalk FC	5-1	1-0	2-2	■	3-2	2-1	1-1	0-0	2-2	0-4	5-2	4-0
Evergreen United FC	2-1	1-0	3-1	5-0	■	2-2	1-3	0-3	1-2	1-1	1-2	4-2
Limerick AFC	4-3	1-4	1-1	6-3	2-0	■	2-2	4-1	2-4	2-0	1-1	2-1
St. Patrick's Athletic FC	2-0	6-2	1-2	4-2	2-3	3-0	■	3-1	1-1	3-3	1-2	4-1
Shamrock Rovers FC	1-0	6-2	4-3	2-2	2-1	1-2	2-0	■	2-0	2-0	3-0	1-2
Shelbourne FC	2-1	6-1	2-3	2-0	3-1	3-0	1-0	1-2	■	4-1	1-1	4-0
Sligo Rovers FC	4-1	1-2	2-2	2-2	1-1	2-1	1-1	0-2	2-2	■	3-1	4-3
Transport FC	1-1	2-0	2-4	2-1	1-0	2-3	3-3	1-1	1-2	0-4	■	5-1
Waterford AFC	2-1	4-2	1-3	3-5	1-4	2-1	1-1	3-2	0-0	1-2	1-1	■

	Division "A"	Pd	Wn	Dw	Ls	GF	GA	Pts
1.	SHELBOURNE FC (DUBLIN)	22	12	6	4	46	24	30
2.	Drumcondra AFC (Dublin)	22	10	9	3	49	33	29
3.	Shamrock Rovers FC (Dublin)	22	12	3	7	40	27	27
4.	St. Patrick's Athletic FC (Dublin)	22	8	8	6	49	34	24
5.	Sligo Rovers FC (Sligo)	22	8	7	7	42	37	23
6.	Dundalk FC (Dundalk)	22	8	6	8	45	45	22
7.	Limerick AFC (Limerick)	22	8	5	9	39	44	21
8.	Cork Athletic FC (Cork)	22	9	3	10	41	47	21
9.	Transport FC (Dublin)	22	7	7	8	35	42	21
10.	Evergreen United FC (Cork)	22	8	4	10	36	35	20
11.	Waterford AFC (Waterford)	22	5	5	12	35	58	15
12.	Bohemian FC (Dublin)	22	4	3	15	27	58	11
		264	99	66	99	484	484	264

Top goal-scorers 1952-53

1)	Shay GIBBONS	(St. Patrick's Athletic FC)	22
2)	James ROWE	(Drumcondra AFC)	16
3)	Liam COLL	(Sligo Rovers FC)	13
	Rory DWYER	(Shelbourne FC)	13
	Desmond GLYNN	(Drumcondra AFC)	13
	Michael LIPPER	(Transport FC)	13

FAI Cup Final (Dalymount Park, Dublin – 26/04/1953 – 17,396)

CORK ATHLETIC FC (CORK) 2-2 Evergreen United FC (Cork)
Carter, D.Noonan *(H.T. 1-0)* *Venner, O'Neill*

Cork Athletic: Courtney, McCarthy, D.Noonan, Moloney, O'Callaghan, McGrath, Vaughan, Broderick, O'Leary, Carter, Cotter.

Evergreen United: Barrett, Doolin, Taylor, Madden, Burke, Lynch, Moloney, Doran, McCarthy, O'Neill, Venner.

Final Replay (Dalymount Park, Dublin – 29/04/1953 – 6,000)

CORK ATHLETIC FC (CORK) 2-1 Evergreen United FC (Cork)
Lennox, Carter *(H.T. 1-0)* *O'Neill*

Cork Athletic: Courtney, McCarthy, D.Noonan, Moloney, Coughlan, McGrath, Vaughan, Broderick, O'Leary, Carter, Lennox.

Evergreen United: Barrett, Doolin, Hayes, Madden, Burke, Lynch, Moloney, Doran, McCarthy, O'Neill, Venner.

Semi-Finals

Cork Athletic FC (Cork)	2-1	Limerick AFC (Limerick)
Evergreen United FC (Cork)	1-0	St. Patrick's Athletic FC (Dublin)

Quarter-Finals

Evergreen United FC (Cork)	1-1, 1-0	Jacobs AFC (Dublin)
Limerick AFC (Limerick)	1-1, 1-1, 0-0, 2-1	Longford Town FC (Longford)
St. Patrick's Athletic FC (Dublin)	0-0, 1-0	Sligo Rovers FC (Sligo)
Waterford AFC (Waterford)	2-3	Cork Athletic FC (Cork)

1953-54

League of Ireland Division "A" 1953-54	Bohemian FC	Cork Athletic FC	Drumcondra AFC	Dundalk FC	Evergreen United	Limerick AFC	St. Patrick's Ath.	Shamrock Rovers	Shelbourne FC	Sligo Rovers FC	Transport FC	Waterford AFC
Bohemian FC	■	3-1	0-2	4-1	2-2	4-1	1-2	0-2	2-2	4-1	1-1	1-2
Cork Athletic FC	2-1	■	2-0	2-1	2-1	4-1	2-2	3-1	1-0	2-2	3-2	0-2
Drumcondra AFC	1-2	1-1	■	4-0	3-0	0-0	7-2	1-1	1-0	2-1	0-2	1-0
Dundalk FC	3-2	1-2	1-3	■	2-2	3-1	1-1	1-3	1-2	2-1	3-0	2-2
Evergreen United FC	2-0	3-0	2-1	4-1	■	4-4	3-1	1-0	3-1	2-1	3-1	
Limerick AFC	0-1	3-2	2-2	5-2	0-3	■	2-0	1-1	2-1	2-0	4-4	2-2
St. Patrick's Athletic FC	1-4	0-2	1-1	6-1	0-2	2-2	■	0-1	2-1	0-0	2-0	2-5
Shamrock Rovers FC	1-0	10-2	2-3	1-0	1-0	1-1	0-0	■	4-1	2-1	2-0	7-1
Shelbourne FC	1-0	2-1	3-0	1-0	1-1	2-3	2-1	1-1	■	2-0	3-2	3-1
Sligo Rovers FC	2-2	2-0	2-2	3-2	2-1	3-2	2-1	1-0	2-3	■	3-0	3-0
Transport FC	5-3	3-4	1-2	3-2	3-2	1-2	0-0	1-1	5-2	3-1	■	5-3
Waterford AFC	1-4	5-2	0-0	2-2	2-2	1-2	4-1	1-1	4-2	2-0	4-0	■

	Division "A"	Pd	Wn	Dw	Ls	GF	GA	Pts
1.	SHAMROCK ROVERS FC (DUBLIN)	22	11	8	3	44	20	30
2.	Evergreen United FC (Cork)	22	11	6	5	44	29	28
3.	Drumcondra AFC (Dublin)	22	10	7	5	37	25	27
4.	Cork Athletic FC (Cork)	22	11	3	8	40	46	25
5.	Limerick AFC (Limerick)	22	8	8	6	42	43	24
6.	Shelbourne FC (Dublin)	22	10	3	9	35	35	23
7.	Waterford AFC (Waterford)	22	8	6	8	45	45	22
8.	Bohemian FC (Dublin)	22	8	4	10	41	36	20
9.	Sligo Rovers FC (Sligo)	22	8	4	10	33	37	20
10.	Transport FC (Dublin)	22	7	4	11	42	49	18
11.	St. Patrick's Athletic FC (Dublin)	22	4	7	11	27	43	15
12.	Dundalk FC (Dundalk)	22	4	4	14	32	54	12
		264	100	64	100	462	462	264

Top goal-scorers 1953-54

1) Daniel JORDAN   (Bohemian FC)   14
2) Patrick AMBROSE   (Shamrock Rovers FC)   13
3) Christy BERGIN   (Waterford AFC)   12
   Eddie DORAN   (Evergreen United FC)   12

FAI Cup Final   (Dalymount Park, Dublin – 25/04/1954 – 20,000)

DRUMCONDRA AFC (DUBLIN)	1-0	St. Patrick's Athletic FC (Dublin)
Byrne o.g.	*(H.T. 0-0)*	

Drumcondra: Neville, Noonan, Lynch, Kinsella, Robinson, Coffey, Rowe, Daly, Duffy, Glynn, Henderson.

St. Patrick's Athletic: Collins, Deacy, Crawford, Boland, Byrne, Nelson, O'Brien, White, Fitzgerald, O'Rourke, Haverty.

Semi-Finals

Drumcondra AFC (Dublin)	2-1	Shamrock Rovers FC (Dublin)
St. Patrick's Athletic FC (Dublin)	0-0, 1-0	Cork Athletic FC (Cork)

Quarter-Finals

Cork Athletic FC (Cork)	2-0	Bohemian FC (Dublin)
Evergreen United FC (Cork)	0-0, 0-1	St. Patrick's Athletic FC (Dublin)
Shelbourne FC (Dublin)	0-2	Drumcondra AFC (Dublin)
Transport FC (Dublin)	1-2	Shamrock Rovers FC (Dublin)

1954-55

League of Ireland Division "A" 1954-55	Bohemian FC	Cork Athletic FC	Drumcondra AFC	Dundalk FC	Evergreen United	Limerick AFC	St. Patrick's Ath.	Shamrock Rovers	Shelbourne FC	Sligo Rovers FC	Transport FC	Waterford AFC
Bohemian FC	■	3-1	0-2	2-1	3-1	6-1	1-2	5-1	1-4	2-1	2-1	1-4
Cork Athletic FC	4-4	■	2-0	2-6	4-1	4-1	1-1	3-3	4-2	4-1	3-1	4-3
Drumcondra AFC	6-2	1-2	■	1-0	2-1	0-0	0-3	1-2	2-3	0-0	1-1	0-5
Dundalk FC	0-2	2-2	0-6	■	3-3	3-1	0-3	1-2	1-3	4-0	3-4	1-2
Evergreen United FC	2-0	1-1	1-2	4-0	■	2-3	0-1	2-3	1-4	4-1	0-0	2-5
Limerick AFC	3-1	0-1	0-5	1-2	2-1	■	0-2	1-2	2-1	1-2	5-2	4-2
St. Patrick's Athletic FC	2-1	5-2	1-0	10-3	1-0	3-2	■	0-5	4-6	5-2	3-0	4-1
Shamrock Rovers FC	7-0	7-1	1-3	7-3	1-4	3-0	2-2	■	2-0	3-3	6-0	2-3
Shelbourne FC	3-0	3-2	2-2	2-1	5-0	3-1	1-4	1-1	■	1-3	0-1	1-6
Sligo Rovers FC	3-1	2-1	1-2	3-4	2-2	0-1	1-2	1-0	2-4	■	3-0	1-2
Transport FC	1-2	2-1	1-0	0-0	1-1	0-1	1-4	1-2	0-7	2-1	■	1-3
Waterford AFC	5-2	2-4	2-2	6-1	2-1	5-2	2-0	2-1	1-6	4-1	3-2	■

	Division "A"	Pd	Wn	Dw	Ls	GF	GA	Pts
1.	ST. PATRICK'S ATHLETIC FC (DUBLIN)	22	17	2	3	62	31	36
2.	Waterford AFC (Waterford)	22	16	1	5	70	43	33
3.	Shamrock Rovers FC (Dublin)	22	12	4	6	63	37	28
4.	Shelbourne FC (Dublin)	22	13	2	7	62	41	28
5.	Cork Athletic FC (Cork)	22	10	5	7	53	51	25
6.	Drumcondra AFC (Dublin)	22	9	5	8	38	30	23
7.	Bohemian FC (Dublin)	22	9	1	12	41	55	19
8.	Limerick AFC (Limerick)	22	8	1	13	32	50	17
9.	Sligo Rovers FC (Sligo)	22	6	3	13	34	49	15
10.	Transport FC (Dublin)	22	5	4	13	22	51	14
11.	Evergreen United FC (Cork)	22	4	5	13	34	46	13
12.	Dundalk FC (Dundalk)	22	5	3	14	39	66	13
		264	114	36	114	550	550	264

Top goal-scorers 1954-55

1) Jimmy GAULD (Waterford AFC) 30
2) Shay GIBBONS (St. Patrick's Athletic FC) 28
3) Rory DWYER (Shelbourne FC) 19

FAI Cup Final   (Dalymount Park, Dublin – 24/04/1955 – 33,041)

SHAMROCK ROVERS FC (DUBLIN)   1-0   Drumcondra AFC (Dublin)
Tuohy   *(H.T. 0-0)*

Shamrock Rovers: O'Callaghan, Burke, Mackey, Nolan, Keogh, Hennessy, McCann Peyton, Ambrose, Gannon, Tuohy.

Drumcondra: Neville, Noonan, Lynch, Kinsella, Robinson, Glynn, Henderson, Rowe, Duffy, O'Hara, Pownall.

Semi-Finals

| Drumcondra AFC (Dublin) | 2-2, 2-1 | Waterford AFC (Waterford) |
| Shamrock Rovers FC (Dublin) | 3-0 | Longford Town FC (Longford) |

Quarter-Finals

Evergreen United FC (Cork)	0-2	Drumcondra AFC (Dublin)
Shamrock Rovers FC (Dublin)	3-0	Shelbourne FC (Dublin)
Transport FC (Dublin)	2-3	Longford Town FC (Longford)
Waterford AFC (Waterford)	5-1	St. Patrick's Athletic FC (Dublin)

1955-56

League of Ireland Division "A" 1955-56	Bohemian FC	Cork Athletic FC	Drumcondra AFC	Dundalk FC	Evergreen United	Limerick AFC	St. Patrick's Ath.	Shamrock Rovers	Shelbourne FC	Sligo Rovers FC	Transport FC	Waterford AFC
Bohemian FC	■	2-1	3-0	2-2	0-2	1-1	2-0	3-2	1-2	4-0	1-1	3-1
Cork Athletic FC	1-0	■	4-3	5-0	1-0	4-1	1-2	0-2	3-3	1-2	3-1	1-0
Drumcondra AFC	1-1	2-0	■	2-5	2-3	2-0	2-0	3-4	2-2	3-1	4-2	1-4
Dundalk FC	0-1	2-0	3-2	■	0-1	3-3	3-3	1-2	3-2	1-1	2-1	3-2
Evergreen United FC	2-0	1-1	1-2	2-2	■	3-1	1-3	1-2	2-1	1-0	1-2	4-2
Limerick AFC	0-0	2-2	3-1	2-0	0-2	■	3-4	2-1	2-2	4-1	3-2	1-3
St. Patrick's Athletic FC	3-1	3-2	4-2	4-0	2-1	3-0	■	2-4	3-2	4-0	3-2	2-0
Shamrock Rovers FC	4-0	3-1	1-2	2-1	1-1	3-2	2-1	■	2-1	4-0	6-0	1-2
Shelbourne FC	3-1	2-0	2-1	3-0	3-1	7-1	1-3	1-2	■	1-3	3-1	1-4
Sligo Rovers FC	6-2	4-3	4-0	4-2	0-3	3-2	1-3	0-4	4-2	■	4-0	5-3
Transport FC	2-1	3-1	1-3	5-3	0-0	0-1	1-6	3-1	1-1	1-2	■	1-2
Waterford AFC	2-0	5-3	3-1	5-1	3-1	7-1	3-3	3-1	2-0	2-2	8-3	■

	Division "A"	Pd	Wn	Dw	Ls	GF	GA	Pts
1.	ST. PATRICK'S ATHLETIC FC (DUBLIN)	22	16	2	4	61	34	34
2.	Shamrock Rovers FC (Dublin)	22	15	1	6	54	30	31
3.	Waterford AFC (Waterford)	22	14	2	6	66	39	30
4.	Evergreen United FC (Cork)	22	10	4	8	34	28	24
5.	Sligo Rovers FC (Sligo)	22	11	2	9	47	50	24
6.	Shelbourne FC (Dublin)	22	8	4	10	45	42	20
7.	Bohemian FC (Dublin)	22	7	5	10	29	36	19
8.	Drumcondra AFC (Dublin)	22	8	2	12	41	51	18
9.	Cork Athletic FC (Cork)	22	7	3	12	38	43	17
10.	Dundalk FC (Dundalk)	22	6	5	11	37	54	17
11.	Limerick AFC (Limerick)	22	6	5	11	35	54	17
12.	Transport FC (Dublin)	22	5	3	14	33	59	13
		264	113	38	113	520	520	264

Top goal-scorers 1955-56

1)	Shay GIBBONS	(St. Patrick's Athletic FC)	21
2)	Patrick AMBROSE	(Shamrock Rovers FC)	20
3)	Patrick O'ROURKE	(St. Patrick's Athletic FC)	17

FAI Cup Final   (Dalymount Park, Dublin – 29/04/1956 – 35,017)

SHAMROCK ROVERS FC (DUBLIN)	3-2	Cork Athletic FC (Cork)
Hamilton, Hennessy, Nolan	*(H.T. 0-2)*	*Delaney, Murphy*

Shamrock R.: O'Callaghan, Burke, Nolan, Coad, Mackey, Hennessy, McCann, Peyton, Ambrose, Hamilton, Tuohy.
Cork Ath.: O'Toole, P.Noonan, D.Noonan, Moloney, Coughlan, Daly, Horgan, Collins, Delaney, Murphy, Wallace.

Semi-Finals

Cork Athletic FC (Cork)	0-0, 5-1	Waterford AFC (Waterford)
Shamrock Rovers FC (Dublin)	2-1	Dublin Workman's Club FC (Dublin)

Quarter-Finals

Cork Athletic FC (Cork)	0-0, 2-1	Evergreen United FC (Cork)
Dublin Workman's Club FC (Dublin)	0-0, 1-0	Bray Wanderers AFC (Bray)
Shamrock Rovers FC (Cork)	3-0	Drumcondra AFC (Dublin)
Transport FC (Dublin)	1-1, 0-1	Waterford AFC (Waterford)

1956-57

League of Ireland Division "A" 1956-57	Bohemian FC	Cork Athletic FC	Drumcondra AFC	Dundalk FC	Evergreen United	Limerick AFC	St. Patrick's Ath.	Shamrock Rovers	Shelbourne FC	Sligo Rovers FC	Transport FC	Waterford AFC
Bohemian FC	■	3-0	0-3	0-0	1-0	0-2	0-3	1-4	0-1	1-4	2-2	1-3
Cork Athletic FC	2-1	■	3-3	1-0	2-4	2-0	0-2	4-3	1-3	3-3	1-3	1-1
Drumcondra AFC	1-0	4-2	■	5-1	1-1	4-1	3-0	1-1	2-2	0-0	4-1	3-1
Dundalk FC	4-2	1-1	2-2	■	4-1	0-1	1-2	1-2	2-2	0-1	2-2	2-0
Evergreen United FC	4-1	2-0	2-2	2-1	■	1-1	4-0	1-2	2-1	1-0	2-3	2-2
Limerick AFC	2-2	0-2	0-1	2-3	0-2	■	2-3	1-1	1-6	0-2	2-3	1-2
St. Patrick's Athletic FC	3-3	1-1	1-2	1-1	2-5	3-2	■	1-6	1-2	2-2	0-2	3-1
Shamrock Rovers FC	6-0	5-1	5-0	3-1	4-1	3-0	4-0	■	2-2	3-1	1-0	1-1
Shelbourne FC	3-0	2-2	2-2	2-1	0-5	1-0	6-1	2-5	■	3-0	1-1	1-0
Sligo Rovers FC	5-0	2-0	0-4	3-3	1-1	2-0	4-2	2-2	3-0	■	2-2	2-1
Transport FC	1-1	2-2	1-1	2-2	2-1	6-1	0-0	0-0	5-4	0-1	■	3-2
Waterford AFC	3-1	1-1	2-1	3-1	1-4	10-2	4-2	3-5	3-1	1-2	4-1	■

	Division "A"	Pd	Wn	Dw	Ls	GF	GA	Pts	
1.	SHAMROCK ROVERS FC (DUBLIN)	22	15	6	1	68	24	36	
2.	Drumcondra AFC (Dublin)	22	11	9	2	49	28	31	
3.	Sligo Rovers FC (Sligo)	22	11	7	4	42	29	29	
4.	Evergreen United FC (Cork)	22	11	5	6	48	31	27	
5.	Transport FC (Dublin)	22	8	10	4	42	36	26	
6.	Shelbourne FC (Dublin)	22	10	6	6	47	39	24	*
7.	Waterford AFC (Waterford)	22	9	4	9	49	41	22	
8.	Cork Athletic FC (Cork)	22	5	8	9	32	46	18	#
9.	St. Patrick's Athletic FC (Dublin)	22	6	5	11	33	55	17	
10.	Dundalk FC (Dundalk)	22	4	8	10	33	40	16	
11.	Bohemian FC (Dublin)	22	2	5	15	20	56	9	
12.	Limerick AFC (Limerick)	22	2	3	17	21	59	7	
		264	94	76	94	484	484	262	

Top goal-scorers 1956-57

1)	Thomas HAMILTON	(Shamrock Rovers FC)	15
	Donal LEAHY	(Evergreen United FC)	15
3)	Austin NOONAN	(Evergreen United FC)	13

* Shelbourne FC (Dublin) had 2 points deducted by a League of Ireland committee.

\# Cork Athletic FC (Cork) resigned from the league and disbanded.   Elected: Cork Hibernians FC (Cork)

FAI Cup Final (Dalymount Park, Dublin – 28/04/1957 – 30,000)

DRUMCONDRA AFC (DUBLIN)　　　　2-0　　　　Shamrock Rovers FC (Dublin)
Fullam pen., Coleman　　　　*(H.T. 1-0)*

Drumcondra: Kelly, Fullam, McConnell, Healy, O'Neill, Rowe, Pownall, Gorman, Lawlor, McCourt, Coleman.
Shamrock Rovers: Darcy, Burke, Keogh, Nolan, Mackey, Hennessy, McCann, Peyton, Ambrose, Coad, Tuohy.

Semi-Finals

Drumcondra AFC (Dublin)	5-2	Evergreen United FC (Cork)
Shamrock Rovers FC (Dublin)	1-1, 3-1	Limerick AFC (Limerick)

Quarter-Finals

Cork Athletic FC (Cork)	1-1, 1-4	Limerick AFC (Limerick)
Dublin Workman's Club FC (Dublin)	0-1	Drumcondra AFC (Dublin)
Shamrock Rovers FC (Dublin)	2-1	Sligo Rovers FC (Sligo)
Waterford AFC (Waterford)	3-3, 0-3	Evergreen United FC (Cork)

1957-58

League of Ireland Division "A" 1957-58	Bohemian FC	Cork Hibernians FC	Drumcondra AFC	Dundalk FC	Evergreen United	Limerick AFC	St. Patrick's Athletic	Shamrock Rovers	Shelbourne FC	Sligo Rovers FC	Transport FC	Waterford AFC
Bohemian FC	■	3-1	3-7	2-2	2-1	2-0	0-2	2-4	0-3	6-1	2-2	1-1
Cork Hibernians FC	3-3	■	3-2	4-2	2-7	2-0	3-5	2-1	2-4	3-1	0-1	1-3
Drumcondra AFC	3-2	5-0	■	3-0	1-1	4-0	2-1	1-2	2-1	5-0	0-1	1-0
Dundalk FC	3-2	8-2	0-1	■	0-1	1-3	3-3	1-0	0-2	3-1	1-0	1-2
Evergreen United FC	4-2	2-1	1-2	4-2	■	1-0	4-1	1-2	3-0	5-1	4-1	3-0
Limerick AFC	2-0	5-2	1-1	3-2	2-2	■	0-0	2-4	3-3	2-0	1-0	1-2
St. Patrick's Athletic FC	1-0	1-2	2-2	0-2	0-3	3-0	■	3-0	4-0	2-2	5-0	4-1
Shamrock Rovers FC	6-0	1-1	3-0	0-1	6-2	2-0	1-2	■	1-0	5-1	8-2	3-2
Shelbourne FC	0-1	3-0	0-1	5-2	2-0	4-1	0-1	2-1	■	1-1	2-0	2-3
Sligo Rovers FC	3-0	3-0	2-3	4-2	2-1	0-2	2-2	0-2	1-1	■	0-6	1-5
Transport FC	2-1	2-0	0-3	1-1	0-2	2-2	2-2	0-1	2-5	3-4	■	3-2
Waterford AFC	1-2	4-3	0-2	3-1	1-1	3-1	3-1	1-2	0-1	2-2	4-0	■

Division "A"	Pd	Wn	Dw	Ls	GF	GA	Pts
1. DRUMCONDRA AFC (DUBLIN)	22	15	3	4	51	23	33
2. Shamrock Rovers FC (Dublin)	22	15	1	6	55	26	31
3. Evergreen United FC (Cork)	22	13	3	6	53	30	29
4. St. Patrick's Athletic FC (Dublin)	22	10	6	6	45	32	26
5. Shelbourne FC (Dublin)	22	11	3	8	41	29	25
6. Waterford AFC (Waterford)	22	10	3	9	43	37	23
7. Limerick AFC (Limerick)	22	7	5	10	31	40	19
8. Dundalk FC (Dundalk)	22	7	3	12	38	46	17
9. Bohemian FC (Dublin)	22	6	4	12	36	52	16
10. Transport FC (Dublin)	22	6	4	12	30	50	16
11. Sligo Rovers FC (Sligo)	22	5	5	12	32	61	15
12. Cork Hibernians FC (Cork)	22	6	2	14	37	66	14
	264	111	42	111	492	492	264

Top goal-scorers 1957-58

1) Donal LEAHY   (Evergreen United FC)   16
2) Johnny McGEEHAN   (Transport FC)   15
   Austin NOONAN   (Evergreen United FC)   15

Note: Drumcondra AFC 1-2 Shamrock Rovers FC on 26/01/58 was abandoned after 65 minutes due to crowd encroachment onto the field of play. However, the result was allowed to stand.

FAI Cup Final   (Dalymount Park, Dublin – 20/04/1958 – 27,000)

DUNDALK FC (DUNDALK)   1-0   Shamrock Rovers FC (Dublin)
Gannon   (H.T. 0-0)

Dundalk: McNeill, Ralph, Finn, McDonagh, Robinson, Noonan, McGahon, Gannon, Gilmore, Toner, Kerr.
Shamrock R.: O'Callaghan, Burke, Mackey, Nolan, Farrell, Hennessy, McCann, Carroll, Ambrose, Coad, Tuohy.

Semi-Finals

Dundalk FC (Dundalk)   1-0   Shelbourne FC (Dublin)
Shamrock Rovers FC (Dublin)   1-0   St. Patrick's Athletic FC (Dublin)

Quarter-Finals

Limerick AFC (Limerick)   0-0, 0-3   Dundalk FC (Dundalk)
St. Patrick's Athletic FC (Dublin) 3-1   Evergreen United FC (Cork)
Shelbourne FC (Dublin)   0-0, 2-2, 1-0   Waterford AFC (Waterford)
Sligo Rovers FC (Sligo)   1-1, 2-3   Shamrock Rovers FC (Dublin)

1958-59

League of Ireland Division "A" 1958-59	Bohemian FC	Cork Hibernians	Drumcondra AFC	Dundalk FC	Evergreen United	Limerick AFC	St. Patrick's Ath.	Shamrock Rovers	Shelbourne FC	Sligo Rovers FC	Transport FC	Waterford AFC
Bohemian FC	■	2-1	0-1	1-1	1-3	2-2	2-3	0-0	1-0	2-1	3-1	1-3
Cork Hibernians FC	6-1	■	0-1	1-0	1-0	1-3	0-2	3-3	2-2	2-1	1-1	0-4
Drumcondra AFC	2-0	1-0	■	3-0	2-1	3-2	0-2	2-4	0-2	1-1	0-1	0-1
Dundalk FC	1-0	2-3	2-3	■	1-1	3-1	3-1	1-3	3-3	4-1	3-0	0-2
Evergreen United FC	8-2	1-0	3-2	4-1	■	2-1	3-0	0-1	2-1	0-1	3-3	3-1
Limerick AFC	3-0	0-0	2-4	3-0	1-0	■	6-1	1-1	1-2	4-0	1-4	3-2
St. Patrick's Athletic FC	2-1	3-2	1-2	6-1	1-3	2-4	■	3-4	2-5	3-5	2-1	2-0
Shamrock Rovers FC	4-1	4-1	3-0	4-1	0-2	1-1	3-1	■	0-2	4-1	1-0	3-2
Shelbourne FC	0-1	2-2	0-0	5-0	2-2	0-0	5-1	1-4	■	0-2	0-5	2-1
Sligo Rovers FC	2-3	3-1	1-1	2-3	3-2	1-3	3-0	0-3	0-0	■	3-5	1-3
Transport FC	3-0	2-1	0-2	2-1	0-2	0-3	0-6	0-3	0-0	2-0	■	0-1
Waterford AFC	3-1	5-1	0-0	3-2	2-4	2-3	6-1	6-5	4-1	5-2	1-0	■

	Division "A"	Pd	Wn	Dw	Ls	GF	GA	Pts	
1.	SHAMROCK ROVERS FC (DUBLIN)	22	15	4	3	58	29	34	
2.	Evergreen United FC (Cork)	22	13	3	6	49	27	29	*
3.	Waterford AFC (Waterford)	22	14	1	7	58	36	29	
4.	Limerick AFC (Limerick)	22	11	5	6	48	31	27	
5.	Drumcondra AFC (Dublin)	22	11	4	7	30	26	26	
6.	Shelbourne FC (Dublin)	22	7	8	7	35	33	22	
7.	Transport FC (Dublin)	22	8	3	11	30	37	19	
8.	St. Patrick's Athletic FC (Dublin)	22	9	-	13	45	59	18	
9.	Cork Hibernians FC (Cork)	22	5	5	12	29	43	15	
10.	Sligo Rovers FC (Sligo)	22	6	3	13	34	51	15	
11.	Dundalk FC (Dundalk)	22	6	3	13	34	53	15	
12.	Bohemian FC (Dublin)	22	6	3	13	25	50	15	
		264	111	42	111	475	475	264	

Top goal-scorers 1958-59

1) Donal LEAHY   (Evergreen United FC)   22
2) Alfred HALE   (Waterford AFC)   18
3) Peter FITZGERALD   (Waterford AFC)   16

Note: Cork Hibernians FC 1-1 Transport FC match on 21/12/58 was abandoned at half-time. The result was allowed to stand as at the time of abandonment.

* Evergreen United FC (Cork) changed name to Cork Celtic FC (Cork) prior to next season.

FAI Cup Final   (Dalymount Park, Dublin – 19/04/1959 – 22,000)

ST. PATRICK'S ATHLETIC FC (DUBLIN)   2-2   Waterford AFC (Waterford)
Hunt o.g., McGeehan   *(H.T. 1-1)*   *J.Fitzgerald, O'Brien o.g.*

St. Patrick's Athletic: Lowry, White, O'Brien, T.Dunne, Boucher, O'Reilly, Curtin, Whelan, McGeehan, J.Dunne, Peyton.

Waterford: Dunphy, Hunt, Slattery, D.Hale. Martin, Griffin, D.Fitzgerald, J.Fitzgerald, P.Fitzgerald, Halpin, Coady.

Final Replay   (Dalymount Park, Dublin – 22/04/1959 – 22,800)

ST. PATRICK'S ATHLETIC FC (DUBLIN)   2-2, 2-1   Waterford AFC (Waterford)
McGeehan, Peyton   *(H.T. 1-0)*   *P.Fitzgerald*

St. Patrick's Athletic: Lowry, White, O'Brien, T.Dunne, Boucher, O'Reilly, Curtin, O'Rourke, McGeehan, J.Dunne, Peyton.

Waterford: Dunphy, Hunt, Slattery, D.Hale. Martin, Griffin, D.Fitzgerald, J.Fitzgerald, P.Fitzgerald, Brett, Coady.

Semi-Finals

| St. Patrick's Athletic FC (Dublin) | 1-0 | Cork Hibernians FC (Cork) |
| Waterford AFC (Waterford) | 1-0 | Limerick AFC (Limerick) |

Quarter-Finals

Bohemian FC (Dublin)	1-1, 0-3	Cork Hibernians FC (Cork)
Chapelizod AFC (Dublin)	1-4	St. Patrick's Athletic FC (Dublin)
Drumcondra AFC (Dublin)	2-2, 1-1, 1-1, 0-2	Limerick AFC (Limerick)
Dundalk FC (Dundalk)	1-2	Waterford AFC (Waterford)

1959-60

League of Ireland Division "A" 1959-60	Bohemian FC	Cork Celtic FC	Cork Hibernians FC	Drumcondra AFC	Dundalk FC	Limerick AFC	St. Patrick's Athletic FC	Shamrock Rovers FC	Shelbourne FC	Sligo Rovers FC	Transport FC	Waterford AFC
Bohemian FC		1-1	0-1	0-3	1-6	1-6	1-6	1-4	0-2	-2	1-1	0-1
Cork Celtic FC	7-1		2-1	2-2	2-5	4-0	5-2	3-3	4-3	4-3	3-1	4-0
Cork Hibernians FC	3-0	3-3		3-1	1-3	2-1	3-4	3-1	1-1	3-1	10-1	4-4
Drumcondra AFC	4-0	3-5	4-1		0-1	2-1	0-2	1-1	3-2	6-0	6-1	0-3
Dundalk FC	2-1	4-0	0-2	3-1		0-1	3-2	4-2	0-2	4-2	3-0	2-2
Limerick AFC	4-0	2-1	2-1	1-0	2-1		2-0	1-0	3-1	3-2	2-1	5-0
St. Patrick's Athletic FC	3-0	2-1	4-1	2-4	0-2	3-2		1-3	3-3	2-1	1-0	1-0
Shamrock Rovers FC	5-0	2-1	1-2	1-2	2-0	2-1	1-4		2-2	8-0	1-0	6-1
Shelbourne FC	4-1	2-0	2-0	2-1	0-0	3-2	2-1	0-2		3-3	3-0	0-2
Sligo Rovers FC	1-1	3-4	1-3	1-0	6-5	1-4	7-2	0-2	3-6		4-1	1-2
Transport FC	2-0	0-5	0-7	0-1	1-1	0-1	3-0	3-2	0-3	1-2		1-6
Waterford AFC	3-3	1-5	1-2	3-1	2-1	1-0	0-1	1-3	2-2	1-0	4-1	

	Division "A"	Pd	Wn	Dw	Ls	GF	GA	Pts
1.	LIMERICK AFC (LIMERICK)	22	15	-	7	46	26	30
2.	Cork Celtic FC (Celtic)	22	12	4	6	66	44	28
3.	Shelbourne FC (Dublin)	22	11	6	5	48	33	28
4.	Shamrock Rovers FC (Dublin)	22	12	3	7	54	31	27
5.	Dundalk FC (Dundalk)	22	12	3	7	50	32	27
6.	Cork Hibernians FC (Cork)	22	12	3	7	57	37	27
7.	St. Patrick's Athletic FC (Dublin)	22	12	1	9	46	44	25
8.	Waterford AFC (Waterford)	22	10	4	8	40	43	24
9.	Drumcondra AFC (Dublin)	22	10	2	10	45	35	22
10.	Sligo Rovers FC (Sligo)	22	5	3	14	44	67	13
11.	Transport FC (Dublin)	22	3	2	17	18	66	8
12.	Bohemian FC (Dublin)	22	-	5	17	15	71	5
		264	114	36	114	529	529	264

Top goal-scorers 1959-60

1) Austin NOONAN (Cork Celtic FC) 27
2) Tommy COLLINS (Cork Hibernians FC) 21
3) Donal LEAHY (Cork Celtic FC) 20

FAI Cup Final (Dalymount Park, Dublin – 24/04/1960 – 32,308)

SHELBOURNE FC (DUBLIN)　　　　2-0　　　　Cork Hibernians FC (Cork)
Barber, Wilson　　　　　　　　*(H.T. 1-0)*

Shelbourne: Flood, Tony Dunne, O'Brien, Theo Dunne, Strahan, Kelly, Wilson, Doyle, Barber, Hennessey, Conroy.
Cork Hibernians: S.O'Brien, Lane, O'Flynn, T.O'Brien, Dougan, Morley, Vaughan, Maguire, Collins, Tully, Aherne.

Semi-Finals

Cork Hibernians FC (Cork)	1-0		Waterford AFC (Waterford)
Shelbourne FC (Dublin)	4-1		Dundalk FC (Dundalk)

Quarter-Finals

Cork Hibernians FC (Cork)	0-0, 3-2	Sligo Rovers FC (Sligo)
Dundalk FC (Dundalk)	4-1	Transport FC (Dublin)
Limerick AFC (Limerick)	1-3	Waterford AFC (Waterford)
Shamrock Rovers FC (Dublin)	1-1, 0-3	Shelbourne FC (Dublin)

1960-61

League of Ireland Division "A" 1960-61	Bohemian FC	Cork Celtic FC	Cork Hibernians	Drumcondra AFC	Dundalk FC	Limerick AFC	St. Patrick's Ath.	Shamrock Rovers	Shelbourne FC	Sligo Rovers FC	Transport FC	Waterford AFC
Bohemian FC	■	1-2	2-2	1-0	2-5	0-1	0-4	0-2	3-3	5-0	1-0	1-1
Cork Celtic FC	3-1	■	3-0	4-3	1-2	2-3	5-0	0-1	0-2	3-1	4-2	0-0
Cork Hibernians FC	2-1	1-2	■	1-2	0-0	3-1	1-1	1-0	1-1	2-2	2-0	2-2
Drumcondra AFC	6-1	0-2	2-0	■	3-0	2-0	6-0	1-1	2-1	8-0	4-0	3-0
Dundalk FC	1-0	2-2	2-0	3-1	■	1-0	1-2	3-1	4-3	5-2	1-0	1-3
Limerick AFC	2-1	2-1	4-0	1-2	0-2	■	0-1	2-2	3-2	4-0	3-1	1-3
St. Patrick's Athletic FC	3-0	3-2	3-1	0-2	2-1	1-0	■	3-2	0-2	7-1	1-1	4-0
Shamrock Rovers FC	1-1	2-2	3-3	2-0	2-4	0-0	2-2	■	0-1	8-1	3-0	2-1
Shelbourne FC	2-0	0-3	3-4	1-2	4-2	1-1	0-1	1-3	■	5-5	0-1	2-2
Sligo Rovers FC	2-3	2-9	3-3	3-5	3-1	2-2	0-3	0-1	1-6	■	2-4	2-4
Transport FC	6-1	1-1	2-1	0-1	2-1	0-3	1-2	0-1	0-2	4-0	■	2-3
Waterford AFC	4-0	2-1	3-0	0-4	4-1	0-2	0-0	3-1	3-1	5-3	2-0	■

	Division "A"	Pd	Wn	Dw	Ls	GF	GA	Pts
1.	DRUMCONDRA AFC (DUBLIN)	22	16	1	2	59	21	33
2.	St. Patrick's Athletic FC (Dublin)	22	14	4	4	43	28	32
3.	Waterford AFC (Waterford)	22	12	5	5	45	33	29
4.	Cork Celtic FC (Cork)	22	11	4	7	52	31	26
5.	Dundalk FC (Dundalk)	22	12	2	8	43	37	26
6.	Shamrock Rovers FC (Dublin)	22	9	7	6	40	29	25
7.	Limerick AFC (Limerick)	22	10	4	8	35	27	24
8.	Shelbourne FC (Dublin)	22	7	5	10	43	41	19
9.	Cork Hibernians FC (Cork)	22	5	8	9	30	42	18
10.	Transport FC (Dublin)	22	6	2	14	27	39	14
11.	Bohemian FC (Dublin)	22	4	4	14	25	52	12
12.	Sligo Rovers FC (Sligo)	22	1	4	17	35	97	6
		264	107	50	107	477	477	264

Top goal-scorers 1960-61

1) Dan McCAFFREY (Drumcondra AFC) 29
2) Donal LEAHY (Cork Celtic FC) 21
3) Jimmy HASTY (Dundalk FC) 17

FAI Cup Final (Dalymount Park, Dublin – 23/04/1961 – 22,000)

ST. PATRICK'S ATHLETIC FC (DUBLIN)   2-1   Drumcondra AFC (Dublin)
White, Peyton   (H.T. 1-1)   *McCaffrey*

St. Patrick's: Lowry, White, Dunne, Clarke, McCarthy, O'Reilly, Curtin, O'Rourke, Redmond, Whelan, Peyton.
Drumcondra: M.Smyth, Fullam, Girvan, S.Smith, Prole, Rowe, Keogh, Halpin, McCaffrey, Morissey, Pownall.

Semi-Finals

Cork Hibernians FC (Cork)	1-2	St. Patrick's Athletic FC (Dublin)
Drumcondra AFC (Dublin)	4-1	Waterford AFC (Waterford)

Quarter-Finals

Jacobs AFC (Dublin)	0-0, 1-2	Cork Hibernians FC (Cork)
St. Patrick's Athletic FC (Dublin)	2-1	Shelbourne FC (Dublin)
Shamrock Rovers FC (Dublin)	0-1	Waterford AFC (Waterford)
Tycor Athletic FC (Waterford)	0-2	Drumcondra AFC (Dublin)

1961-62

League of Ireland Division "A" 1961-62	Bohemian FC	Cork Celtic FC	Cork Hibernians FC	Drumcondra AFC	Dundalk FC	Limerick AFC	St. Patrick's Athletic FC	Shamrock Rovers FC	Shelbourne FC	Sligo Rovers FC	Transport FC	Waterford AFC
Bohemian FC		2-2	3-3	1-5	2-1	1-2	1-4	2-3	1-0	5-0	2-0	2-1
Cork Celtic FC	3-1		5-1	1-0	4-1	1-1	0-2	4-0	1-1	8-1	5-1	4-1
Cork Hibernians FC	2-1	2-3		2-0	2-2	1-1	0-1	1-1	1-2	4-1	4-0	1-1
Drumcondra AFC	2-1	2-1	1-1		4-1	2-4	2-3	0-2	1-1	5-1	4-2	2-1
Dundalk FC	2-0	1-2	4-1	1-1		1-2	0-1	0-2	2-2	3-0	5-0	4-1
Limerick AFC	2-0	4-1	1-2	2-3	1-1		2-1	1-1	1-2	6-3	3-3	1-0
St. Patrick's Athletic FC	2-2	2-8	2-2	3-1	2-3	1-2		0-5	0-2	4-1	5-3	3-2
Shamrock Rovers FC	3-2	1-3	3-0	4-3	3-1	2-0	3-1		1-2	0-0	4-2	2-0
Shelbourne FC	0-0	3-0	1-2	3-2	1-0	3-1	3-3	6-2		7-0	2-1	2-1
Sligo Rovers FC	4-4	0-2	2-3	1-1	2-5	1-4	0-1	1-3	2-7		6-4	1-5
Transport FC	1-5	0-6	1-1	1-1	1-2	0-4	1-6	3-1	1-2	2-1		1-3
Waterford AFC	4-2	0-4	1-2	3-3	2-2	2-0	3-1	0-5	0-3	4-3	4-1	

Play-off (Dalymount Park, Dublin – 02/05/1962)

SHELBOURNE FC (DUBLIN)	1-0	Cork Celtic FC (Cork)

	Division "A"	Pd	Wn	Dw	Ls	GF	GA	Pts	
1.	Shelbourne FC (Dublin)	22	15	5	2	55	23	35	PO
1.	Cork Celtic FC (Cork)	22	16	3	3	71	24	35	PO
3.	Shamrock Rovers FC (Dublin)	22	14	3	5	51	32	31	
4.	St. Patrick's Athletic FC (Dublin)	22	11	3	8	48	46	25	
5.	Cork Hibernians FC (Cork)	22	8	8	6	37	36	25	*
6.	Limerick AFC (Limerick)	22	10	5	7	41	34	24	*
7.	Drumcondra AFC (Dublin)	22	8	6	8	45	40	22	
8.	Dundalk FC (Dundalk)	22	8	5	9	42	36	21	
9.	Bohemian FC (Dublin)	22	6	5	11	40	46	17	
10.	Waterford AFC (Waterford)	22	7	3	12	30	40	17	
11.	Transport FC (Dublin)	22	2	3	17	29	76	7	#
12.	Sligo Rovers FC (Sligo)	22	1	3	18	31	87	5	#
		264	106	52	106	529	529	264	

Top goal-scorers 1961-62

1) Eddie BAILHAM   (Shamrock Rovers FC)   21
2) Donal LEAHY   (Cork Celtic FC)   18
3) Eric BARBER   (Shelbourne FC)   15
   Austin NOONAN   (Cork Celtic FC)   15

* After a protest the result of the Cork Hibernians FC 1-1 Limerick AFC match was annulled. Both points were awarded to Cork Hibernians FC and no goals were recorded in the final table.

\# Sligo Rovers FC (Sligo) and Transport FC (Dublin) were not re-elected to the league which was reduced to 10 clubs for next season.

FAI Cup Final (Dalymount Park, Dublin – 29/04/1962 – 32,000)

SHAMROCK ROVERS FC (DUBLIN)   4-1   Shelbourne FC (Dublin)
Ambrose 2, Hamilton 2   *(H.T. 2-1)*   *Barber*

Shamrock Rovers: Henderson, Keogh, Courtney, Nolan, T.Farrell, E.Farrell, O'Neill, Hamilton, Bailham, Ambrose, O'Connell.

Shelbourne: Heavey, Carroll, O'Brien, Bonham, Strahan, Roberts, Wilson, Hannigan, Barber, Hennessy, Conroy.

Semi-Finals

Shamrock Rovers FC (Dublin)	1-1, 5-2	Waterford AFC (Waterford)
Shelbourne FC (Dublin)	3-0	St. Patrick's Athletic FC (Dublin)

Quarter-Finals

Bohemian FC (Dublin)	0-1	Shamrock Rovers FC (Dublin)
Pike Rovers FC (Limerick)	1-2	Shelbourne FC (Dublin)
St. Patrick's Athletic FC (Dublin)	1-0	Cork Celtic FC (Cork)
Waterford AFC (Waterford)	1-0	Drumcondra AFC (Dublin)

1962-63

League of Ireland Division "A" 1962-63	Bohemian FC	Cork Celtic FC	Cork Hibernians FC	Drumcondra AFC	Dundalk FC	Limerick AFC	St. Patrick's Athletic FC	Shamrock Rovers FC	Shelbourne FC	Waterford AFC
Bohemian FC	■	1-1	0-1	0-1	2-2	2-0	1-2	0-0	2-2	1-3
Cork Celtic FC	2-1	■	1-1	5-0	2-2	3-2	1-1	2-2	3-3	4-2
Cork Hibernians FC	2-1	0-1	■	0-1	1-0	0-1	0-1	3-2	1-0	3-3
Drumcondra AFC	2-1	2-1	1-2	■	0-0	2-1	3-0	2-1	4-0	2-0
Dundalk FC	5-1	2-1	2-0	5-2	■	3-0	4-1	1-3	2-1	2-2
Limerick AFC	3-0	0-0	3-3	3-3	0-2	■	3-0	1-0	1-4	2-3
St. Patrick's Athletic FC	1-1	1-5	1-1	1-5	2-2	2-0	■	1-4	2-3	3-6
Shamrock Rovers FC	3-1	0-0	5-2	2-0	1-1	0-1	1-1	■	5-0	2-4
Shelbourne FC	2-1	0-0	1-0	2-2	2-1	1-0	1-2	2-4	■	2-3
Waterford AFC	3-3	2-1	1-2	3-1	2-3	2-1	6-1	3-1	2-3	■

Division "A"	Pd	Wn	Dw	Ls	GF	GA	Pts
1. DUNDALK FC (DUNDALK)	18	9	6	3	39	23	24
2. Waterford AFC (Waterford)	18	10	3	5	50	37	23
3. Drumcondra AFC (Dublin)	18	10	3	5	33	27	23
4. Cork Celtic FC (Cork)	18	6	9	3	33	22	21
5. Shamrock Rovers FC (Dublin)	18	7	5	6	36	25	19
6. Cork Hibernians FC (Cork)	18	7	4	7	22	25	18
7. Shelbourne FC (Dublin)	18	7	4	7	29	35	19
8. Limerick AFC (Limerick)	18	5	3	10	22	30	13
9. St. Patrick's Athletic FC (Dublin)	18	4	5	9	23	47	13
10. Bohemian FC (Dublin)	18	1	6	11	19	35	8
	180	66	48	66	306	306	180

Top goal-scorers 1962-63

1) Michael LYNCH   (Waterford AFC)   12
2) Jackie MOONEY   (Shamrock Rovers FC)   11
3) Jimmy HASTY   (Dundalk FC)   9

Elected: Drogheda FC (Drogheda), Sligo Rovers FC (Sligo)

The league was extended to 12 clubs for next season

FAI Cup Final (Dalymount Park, Dublin – 21/04/1963 – 15,000)

SHELBOURNE FC (DUBLIN)   2-0   Cork Hibernians FC (Cork)
Roberts, Bonham pen.   *(H.T. 1-0)*

Shelbourne: Heavey, Carroll, Bonham, Roberts, Strahan, Corrigan, Wilson, Hannigan, Barber, Hennessy, Conroy.
Cork: Brohan, Lane, Morley, Allen, O'Mahoney, O'Callaghan, Aherne, Hamilton, Kingston, Wallace, Eglinton.

Semi-Finals

Cork Hibernians FC (Cork)	4-1	Limerick AFC (Limerick)
Shelbourne FC (Dublin)	2-0	Shamrock Rovers FC (Dublin)

Quarter-Finals

Drumcondra AFC (Dublin)	3-3, 0-2	Shelbourne FC (Dublin)
Dundalk FC (Dundalk)	1-2	Cork Hibernians FC (Cork)
Limerick AFC (Limerick)	2-2, 2-1	Transport FC (Dublin)
Shamrock Rovers FC (Dublin)	7-3	Bohemian FC (Dublin)

1963-64

League of Ireland Division "A" 1963-64	Bohemian FC	Cork Celtic FC	Cork Hibernians FC	Drogheda FC	Drumcondra AFC	Dundalk FC	Limerick AFC	St. Patrick's Athletic FC	Shamrock Rovers FC	Shelbourne FC	Sligo Rovers FC	Waterford AFC
Bohemian FC		1-3	2-3	3-2	0-1	2-2	1-3	1-1	1-2	0-2	1-4	0-0
Cork Celtic FC	4-1		0-0	2-1	1-2	0-3	1-1	0-0	0-1	3-2	4-0	5-3
Cork Hibernians FC	2-0	1-3		3-2	2-0	1-1	4-1	1-1	0-0	0-0	3-2	2-1
Drogheda FC	1-0	1-1	2-2		1-2	1-6	0-2	0-2	0-1	3-1	0-1	3-1
Drumcondra AFC	2-1	3-4	1-0	1-1		0-4	1-2	3-3	1-1	2-0	3-0	0-1
Dundalk FC	0-0	2-1	4-2	6-2	1-0		4-2	3-2	2-1	1-1	0-0	3-0
Limerick AFC	4-1	1-1	2-2	2-1	3-1	2-2		1-1	0-2	3-0	3-0	4-0
St. Patrick's Athletic FC	1-0	3-2	2-0	1-2	1-3	1-0	2-2		0-0	5-2	6-1	4-1
Shamrock Rovers FC	7-1	2-2	1-0	5-5	4-1	3-1	6-2	1-1		4-2	7-2	4-1
Shelbourne FC	3-0	3-3	2-3	0-0	4-1	3-1	1-2	3-2	0-4		6-0	4-2
Sligo Rovers FC	3-3	2-2	2-1	1-1	0-3	1-0	1-2	1-1	4-4	3-3		1-0
Waterford AFC	2-0	3-7	2-6	1-2	4-0	2-3	0-2	2-1	1-8	0-4	0-1	

	Division "A"	Pd	Wn	Dw	Ls	GF	GA	Pts
1.	SHAMROCK ROVERS FC (DUBLIN)	22	14	7	1	68	27	35
2.	Dundalk FC (Dundalk)	22	12	6	4	49	27	30
3.	Limerick AFC (Limerick)	22	12	6	4	46	32	30
4.	Cork Celtic FC (Cork)	22	9	8	5	49	36	26
5.	St. Patrick's Athletic FC (Dublin)	22	8	9	5	41	29	25
6.	Cork Hibernians FC (Cork)	22	9	7	6	38	31	25
7.	Shelbourne FC (Dublin)	22	8	5	9	46	42	21
8.	Drumcondra AFC (Dublin)	22	9	3	10	31	38	21
9.	Sligo Rovers FC (Sligo)	22	6	7	9	30	53	17 *
10.	Drogheda FC (Drogheda)	22	5	6	11	31	44	16
11.	Waterford AFC (Waterford)	22	4	1	17	27	64	9
12.	Bohemian FC (Dublin)	22	1	5	16	19	52	7
		264	97	70	97	475	475	262

Top goal-scorers 1963-64

1) Eddie BAILHAM (Shamrock Rovers FC) 18
   Jimmy HASTY (Dundalk FC) 18
   Johnny KINGSTON (Cork Hibernians FC) 18

Note: The Cork Hibernians FC 0-0 Shelbourne FC and Sligo Rovers FC 0-3 Drumcondra AFC matches were both abandoned but the score at the time of abandonment was allowed to stand.

* Sligo Rovers FC (Sligo) had 2 points deducted by the League of Ireland for an infringement of the league rules.

FAI Cup Final   (Dalymount Park, Dublin – 26/04/1964 – 35,500)

SHAMROCK ROVERS FC (DUBLIN)   1-1   Cork Celtic FC (Cork)
Mooney   (H.T. 0-0)   *Leahy*

Shamrock Rovers: Dunne, Keogh, Courtney, Nolan, Farrell, Fullam, O'Neill, Mooney, Bailham, Ambrose, Tuohy.
Cork: Blount, O'Flynn, O'Mahoney, Cowhie, Coughlan, Millington, O'Donovan, Noonan, Leahy, Casey, McCarthy.

Final Replay   (Dalymount Park, Dublin – 29/04/1964 – 23,600)

SHAMROCK ROVERS FC (DUBLIN)   2-1   Cork Celtic FC (Cork)
Bailham 2   *(H.T. 0-0)*   *Casey*

Shamrock Rovers: Dunne, Keogh, Courtney, Nolan, Farrell, Fullam, Byrne, Mooney, Bailham, Ambrose, Tuohy.
Cork: Blount, O'Flynn, O'Mahoney, Cowhie, Lynam, Millington, O'Donovan, Noonan, Leahy, Casey, McCarthy.

Semi-Finals

Cork Celtic FC (Cork)	2-0	Bohemian FC (Dublin)
Shamrock Rovers FC (Dublin)	1-0	Drumcondra AFC (Dublin)

Quarter-Finals

Drumcondra AFC (Dublin)	1-0	Drogheda FC (Drogheda)
Jacobs AFC (Dublin)	2-3	Bohemian FC (Dublin)
Limerick AFC (Limerick)	0-1	Shamrock Rovers FC (Dublin)
Shelbourne FC (Dublin)	1-3	Cork Celtic FC (Cork)

1964-65

League of Ireland Division "A" 1964-65	Bohemian FC	Cork Celtic FC	Cork Hibernians FC	Drogheda FC	Drumcondra AFC	Dundalk FC	Limerick AFC	St. Patrick's Athletic FC	Shamrock Rovers FC	Shelbourne FC	Sligo Rovers FC	Waterford AFC
Bohemian FC	■	2-0	1-0	2-0	0-0	2-0	3-1	1-0	1-2	5-1	1-0	1-1
Cork Celtic FC	2-2	■	1-0	6-2	3-0	1-4	1-2	2-1	1-2	2-0	3-0	1-0
Cork Hibernians FC	1-0	1-0	■	4-0	1-2	3-3	3-1	2-0	2-0	3-0	2-2	5-3
Drogheda FC	1-1	1-0	1-1	■	1-2	0-1	2-1	1-0	0-0	2-0	0-1	0-1
Drumcondra AFC	2-2	3-0	2-0	3-1	■	3-1	2-1	1-0	2-0	2-1	2-0	2-1
Dundalk FC	3-3	1-0	1-2	1-3	1-2	■	2-1	0-1	1-1	1-2	1-0	2-0
Limerick AFC	2-2	2-2	3-3	1-0	2-3	1-4	■	1-2	2-1	0-2	1-5	1-3
St. Patrick's Athletic FC	4-1	3-6	2-1	1-0	3-0	1-1	2-2	■	0-1	2-3	4-0	5-1
Shamrock Rovers FC	2-0	1-0	1-1	4-1	2-1	5-1	2-1	4-1	■	3-1	3-0	3-2
Shelbourne FC	2-0	3-0	2-3	1-1	2-1	1-1	2-1	6-2	3-1	■	0-2	3-2
Sligo Rovers FC	0-6	2-2	2-0	2-1	0-0	2-1	1-1	1-1	1-0	3-1	■	3-1
Waterford AFC	0-2	2-0	2-3	1-1	0-0	3-0	1-1	1-2	0-2	0-2	0-3	■

	Division "A"	Pd	Wn	Dw	Ls	GF	GA	Pts
1.	DRUMCONDRA AFC (DUBLIN)	22	14	4	4	35	22	32
2.	Shamrock Rovers FC (Dublin)	22	14	3	5	40	22	31
3.	Bohemian FC (Dublin)	22	10	7	5	38	24	27
4.	Cork Hibernians FC (Cork)	22	11	5	6	41	29	27
5.	Sligo Rovers FC (Sligo)	22	10	5	7	30	31	25
6.	Shelbourne FC (Dublin)	22	11	2	9	38	37	24
7.	St. Patrick's Athletic FC (Dublin)	22	9	3	10	37	36	21
8.	Cork Celtic FC (Cork)	22	8	3	11	33	34	19
9.	Dundalk FC (Dundalk	22	7	5	10	31	37	19
10.	Drogheda FC (Drogheda)	22	5	5	12	19	34	15
11.	Limerick AFC (Limerick)	22	3	6	13	29	48	12
12.	Waterford AFC (Waterford)	22	4	4	14	25	42	12
		264	106	52	106	396	396	264

Top goal-scorers 1964-65

1) Jackie MOONEY   (Shamrock Rovers FC)   16
2) Eric BARBER   (Shelbourne FC)   14
   Noel BATES   (St. Patrick's Athletic FC) 14

FAI Cup Final   (Dalymount Park, Dublin – 25/04/1965 – 22,000)

SHAMROCK ROVERS FC (DUBLIN)   1-1   Limerick AFC (Limerick)
Dunne   (H.T. 0-0)   *Mulvey*

Shamrock Rovers: Smyth, Keogh, Courtney, Nolan, Farrell, Mulligan, O'Neill, Mooney, Dunne, Fullam, Tuohy.
Limerick: Fitzpatrick, Quinn, Casey, Finucane, Fenton, McNamara, O'Connor, Mulvey, Mitchell, O'Rourke, Doyle (Linnane).

Final Replay   (Dalymount Park, Dublin – 28/04/1965 – 19,436)

SHAMROCK ROVERS FC (DUBLIN)   1-0   Limerick AFC (Limerick)
Fullam   (H.T. 0-0)

Shamrock Rovers: Smyth, Keogh, Courtney, Nolan, Farrell, Mulligan, O'Neill, Mooney, Dunne, Fullam, O'Connell.
Limerick: Fitzpatrick, Quinn, Casey, Finucane, Fenton, McNamara, O'Connor, Mulvey, Mitchell, O'Rourke, Linnane.

Semi-Finals

Cork Celtic FC (Cork)	0-3	Shamrock Rovers FC (Dublin)
Limerick AFC (Limerick)	1-0	Drumcondra AFC (Dublin)

Quarter-Finals

Cork Celtic FC (Cork)	1-1, 1-0	Belgrove FC (Dublin)
St. Patrick's Athletic FC (Dublin)	1-1, 1-2	Limerick AFC (Limerick)
Shamrock Rovers FC (Dublin)	3-1	Dundalk FC (Dundalk)
Shelbourne FC (Dublin)	1-2	Drumcondra AFC (Dublin)

1965-66

League of Ireland Division "A" 1965-66	Bohemian FC	Cork Celtic FC	Cork Hibernians FC	Drogheda FC	Drumcondra AFC	Dundalk FC	Limerick AFC	St. Patrick's Athletic	Shamrock Rovers	Shelbourne FC	Sligo Rovers FC	Waterford AFC
Bohemian FC	■	2-0	6-0	4-1	2-1	3-1	3-1	0-2	2-4	2-0	2-0	0-1
Cork Celtic FC	2-3	■	4-3	4-3	1-1	1-1	2-3	2-4	1-1	1-3	3-3	0-1
Cork Hibernians FC	3-2	1-1	■	3-2	0-0	3-0	0-2	0-3	0-2	0-3	2-1	0-0
Drogheda FC	0-2	0-1	2-1	■	1-2	0-2	0-3	0-1	0-2	1-1	1-2	1-3
Drumcondra AFC	3-1	1-3	2-1	0-0	■	1-2	2-1	2-0	0-3	1-0	0-1	2-3
Dundalk FC	1-0	4-1	3-6	4-0	0-2	■	0-2	2-1	0-2	2-0	2-0	0-1
Limerick AFC	2-0	3-2	2-4	1-1	2-2	0-1	■	2-2	1-1	0-2	3-3	1-2
St. Patrick's Athletic FC	3-4	1-0	2-1	2-0	1-3	4-4	1-3	■	1-2	1-3	1-3	2-6
Shamrock Rovers FC	2-3	3-1	6-1	4-0	5-1	2-1	5-2	1-2	■	7-1	2-1	0-1
Shelbourne FC	2-0	5-0	2-0	2-1	4-2	1-1	1-1	0-1	1-1	■	0-1	3-5
Sligo Rovers FC	1-1	1-1	1-0	1-0	1-1	2-1	0-0	2-0	0-0	1-2	■	0-1
Waterford AFC	0-4	4-1	5-1	3-1	3-3	3-0	1-1	3-0	3-4	1-1	3-1	■

	Division "A"	Pd	Wn	Dw	Ls	GF	GA	Pts
1.	WATERFORD AFC (WATERFORD)	22	16	4	2	53	26	36
2.	Shamrock Rovers FC (Dublin)	22	15	4	3	59	23	34
3.	Bohemian FC (Dublin)	22	13	1	8	46	30	27
4.	Shelbourne FC (Dublin)	22	10	5	7	37	30	25
5.	Sligo Rovers FC (Sligo)	22	8	7	7	26	26	23
6.	Limerick AFC (Limerick)	22	7	8	7	36	35	22
7.	Drumcondra AFC (Dublin)	22	8	6	8	32	35	22
8.	Dundalk FC (Dundalk)	22	9	3	10	32	35	21
9.	St. Patrick's Athletic FC (Dublin)	22	9	2	11	35	43	20
10.	Cork Hibernians FC (Cork)	22	6	3	13	30	51	15
11.	Cork Celtic FC (Cork)	22	4	6	12	32	51	14
12.	Drogheda FC (Drogheda)	22	1	3	18	15	48	5
		264	106	52	106	433	433	264

Top goal-scorers 1965-66

1) Michael LYNCH   (Waterford AFC)   17
2) Seamus COAD   (Waterford AFC)   14
   Bobby GILBERT   (Shamrock Rovers FC)   14
   Liam TUOHY   (Shamrock Rovers FC)   14

FAI Cup Final   (Dalymount Park, Dublin – 24/04/1966 – 26,898)

SHAMROCK ROVERS FC (DUBLIN)   2-0   Limerick AFC (Limerick)
O'Connell, O'Neill   (H.T. 0-0)

Shamrock Rovers: Smyth, Keogh, Courtney, Mulligan, Nolan, Fullam, O'Neill, Tyrell, Gilbert, O'Connell, Hayes.
Limerick: Fitzpatrick, Quinn, Casey, Finucane, Fenton, McNamara, O'Connor, Hamilton, Mulvey, O'Brien, Curtin.

Semi-Finals

Limerick AFC (Limerick)	0-0, 3-0	Sligo Rovers FC (Sligo)
Shamrock Rovers FC (Dublin)	2-2, 4-2	Waterford AFC (Waterford)

Quarter-Finals

Cork Celtic FC (Cork)	1-1, 0-3	Sligo Rovers FC (Sligo)
Dalkey United FC (Dalkey)	0-2	Waterford AFC (Waterford)
Limerick AFC (Limerick)	3-0	Dundalk FC (Dundalk)
Shamrock Rovers FC (Dublin)	1-1, 1-0	Shelbourne FC (Dublin)

1966-67

League of Ireland Division "A" 1966-67	Bohemian FC	Cork Celtic FC	Cork Hibernians	Drogheda FC	Drumcondra AFC	Dundalk FC	Limerick AFC	St. Patrick's Ath.	Shamrock Rovers	Shelbourne FC	Sligo Rovers FC	Waterford AFC
Bohemian FC	■	6-0	2-1	6-1	2-1	3-0	0-0	0-1	0-2	3-0	1-0	2-2
Cork Celtic FC	2-4	■	0-0	2-0	4-2	1-4	2-4	1-2	0-0	0-3	0-0	3-0
Cork Hibernians FC	0-1	2-3	■	0-1	1-2	0-0	1-0	4-3	4-2	2-1	0-3	1-4
Drogheda FC	2-1	5-1	1-2	■	0-3	1-3	1-1	2-2	1-0	2-1	2-2	4-3
Drumcondra AFC	2-2	3-0	2-2	1-1	■	1-2	1-1	2-2	0-3	1-1	3-1	3-4
Dundalk FC	3-0	5-0	0-0	3-0	2-0	■	3-0	2-2	2-0	6-0	1-2	3-0
Limerick AFC	1-0	4-0	3-2	2-2	0-2	2-3	■	2-0	0-2	1-0	0-0	1-2
St. Patrick's Athletic FC	3-2	3-4	4-3	1-3	1-2	1-3	2-2	■	1-1	6-3	5-1	5-4
Shamrock Rovers FC	1-2	1-2	1-1	2-1	4-1	2-1	0-1	1-3	■	2-2	1-2	2-1
Shelbourne FC	1-3	1-2	1-2	2-0	2-2	1-3	1-3	3-0	1-3	■	2-1	1-4
Sligo Rovers FC	0-3	3-1	3-0	3-1	0-0	1-1	4-1	3-0	2-1	3-1	■	3-2
Waterford AFC	4-2	0-2	2-3	1-0	3-1	2-4	1-2	3-2	3-0	5-4	3-0	■

	Division "A"	Pd	Wn	Dw	Ls	GF	GA	Pts
1.	DUNDALK FC (DUNDALK)	22	15	4	3	54	19	34
2.	Bohemian FC (Dublin)	22	12	3	7	45	27	27
3.	Sligo Rovers FC (Sligo)	22	11	5	6	37	29	27
4.	Limerick AFC (Limerick)	22	9	6	7	31	29	24
5.	Waterford AFC (Waterford)	22	11	1	10	53	48	23
6.	St. Patrick's Athletic FC (Dublin)	22	8	5	9	49	51	21
7.	Shamrock Rovers FC (Dublin)	22	8	4	10	31	31	20
8.	Drumcondra AFC (Dublin)	22	6	8	8	35	38	20
9.	Cork Hibernians FC (Cork)	22	7	5	10	31	39	19
10.	Drogheda FC (Drogheda)	22	7	5	10	31	42	19
11.	Cork Celtic FC (Cork)	22	8	3	11	30	52	19
12.	Shelbourne FC (Dublin)	22	4	3	15	32	54	11
		264	106	52	106	459	459	264

Top goal-scorers 1966-67

1)	Johnny BROOKS	(Sligo Rovers FC)	15
	Daniel HALE	(Dundalk FC)	15
3)	Ben HANNIGAN	(Dundalk FC)	14

FAI Cup Final   (Dalymount Park, Dublin – 23/04/1967 – 12,000)

SHAMROCK ROVERS FC (DUBLIN)   3-2   St. Patrick's Athletic FC (Dublin)
O'Neill pen., Leech, Dixon   (H.T. 1-2)   *Dunne, Bates*

Shamrock Rovers: Smyth, Keogh, Courtney, Fullam, Mulligan, Kearin, O'Neill, Dixon, Gilbert, Leech, Kinsella.
St. Patrick's: Lowry, Dowling, O'Reilly, Roche, Boucher, Hennessy, Monaghan, Dunne, Bates, Campbell, Peyton.

Semi-Finals

St. Patrick's Athletic FC (Dublin)   1-0   Drogheda FC (Drogheda)
Shamrock Rovers FC (Dublin)   1-1, 3-0   Dundalk FC (Dundalk)

Quarter-Finals

Bohemian FC (Dublin)	0-2	Drogheda FC (Drogheda)
Dundalk FC (Dundalk)	1-1, 1-0	Cork Hibernians FC (Cork)
Limerick AFC (Limerick)	0-1	St. Patrick's Athletic FC (Dublin)
Shamrock Rovers FC (Dublin)	2-1	Home Farm FC (Dublin)

1967-68

League of Ireland Division "A" 1967-68	Bohemian FC	Cork Celtic FC	Cork Hibernians FC	Drogheda FC	Drumcondra AFC	Dundalk FC	Limerick AFC	St. Patrick's Athletic FC	Shamrock Rovers FC	Shelbourne FC	Sligo Rovers FC	Waterford AFC
Bohemian FC	■	0-0	0-1	1-0	0-2	1-5	1-2	4-1	1-2	2-3	0-0	1-3
Cork Celtic FC	1-0	■	1-0	2-0	1-1	3-2	3-1	2-0	1-4	3-2	3-0	2-0
Cork Hibernians FC	5-2	1-2	■	0-0	1-1	2-1	1-2	1-0	0-2	2-1	1-2	0-5
Drogheda FC	2-1	1-1	2-1	■	2-2	1-0	2-5	2-1	1-1	3-0	3-1	0-2
Drumcondra AFC	2-0	2-0	0-1	2-2	■	0-1	2-0	1-2	3-3	0-1	3-2	1-4
Dundalk FC	4-1	1-3	1-0	3-2	1-0	■	5-1	0-0	2-1	3-1	3-0	0-2
Limerick AFC	2-1	3-2	1-1	1-2	1-2	2-3	■	4-0	3-2	1-1	3-0	0-1
St. Patrick's Athletic FC	2-2	2-2	1-0	1-4	2-1	0-4	8-0	■	0-0	2-1	1-0	0-1
Shamrock Rovers FC	4-1	2-1	1-1	0-1	4-0	1-1	2-1	2-1	■	1-2	7-0	3-2
Shelbourne FC	4-1	1-1	1-0	0-1	2-2	1-2	1-2	2-3	2-0	■	4-0	0-4
Sligo Rovers FC	0-0	1-3	2-0	2-2	1-1	2-1	1-0	7-1	1-2	0-1	■	2-0
Waterford AFC	3-0	3-3	0-0	2-0	4-3	0-1	4-0	6-1	1-0	3-1	9-0	■

	Division "A"	Pd	Wn	Dw	Ls	GF	GA	Pts
1.	WATERFORD AFC (WATERFORD)	22	16	2	4	59	18	34
2.	Dundalk FC (Dundalk)	22	14	2	6	44	24	30
3.	Cork Celtic FC (Cork)	22	12	6	4	40	27	30
4.	Shamrock Rovers FC (Dublin)	22	11	5	6	44	26	27
5.	Drogheda FC (Drogheda)	22	10	6	6	33	29	26
6.	Limerick AFC (Limerick)	22	9	2	11	35	45	20
7.	Shelbourne FC (Dublin)	22	8	3	11	32	36	19
8.	Drumcondra AFC (Dublin)	22	6	7	9	31	35	19
9.	St. Patrick's Athletic FC (Dublin)	22	7	4	11	29	46	18
10.	Cork Hibernians FC (Cork)	22	6	5	11	19	28	17
11.	Sligo Rovers FC (Sligo)	22	6	4	12	24	48	16
12.	Bohemian FC (Dublin)	22	2	4	16	20	48	8
		264	107	50	107	410	410	264

Top goal-scorers 1967-68

1)	Carl DAVENPORT	(Cork Celtic FC)	15
	Ben HANNIGAN	(Dundalk FC)	15
3)	Alfred HALE	(Waterford AFC)	14

FAI Cup Final (Dalymount Park, Dublin – 21/04/1968 – 39,128)

SHAMROCK ROVERS FC (DUBLIN)   3-0   Waterford AFC (Waterford)

Leech 2, Lawlor

Shamrock Rovers: Smyth, Gregg, Courtney, Kearin, Brady, Fullam, O'Neill, Lawlor, Gilbert, Leech, Richardson.
Waterford: Thomas, Bryan, Morissey, Maguire, Morley, McGeough, O'Neill, Hale, Lynch, Coad, Matthews.

Semi-Finals

Shamrock Rovers FC (Dublin)	3-0	Dundalk FC (Dundalk)
Waterford AFC (Waterford)	2-1	Drumcondra AFC (Dublin)

Quarter-Finals

Dundalk FC (Dundalk)	1-0	Limerick AFC (Limerick)
Home Farm FC (Dublin)	1-2	Drumcondra AFC (Dublin)
Shamrock Rovers FC (Dublin)	1-0	Shelbourne FC (Dublin)
Waterford AFC (Waterford)	6-0	St. Patrick's Athletic FC (Dublin)

1968-69

League of Ireland Division "A" 1968-69	Bohemian FC	Cork Celtic FC	Cork Hibernians FC	Drogheda FC	Drumcondra AFC	Dundalk FC	Limerick AFC	St. Patrick's Ath.	Shamrock Rovers FC	Shelbourne FC	Sligo Rovers FC	Waterford AFC
Bohemian FC	■	4-2	1-2	0-4	1-0	1-1	1-2	0-1	0-3	5-1	1-2	2-2
Cork Celtic FC	1-0	■	1-2	1-0	2-4	3-3	2-0	1-3	0-2	1-1	3-1	1-1
Cork Hibernians FC	2-0	2-0	■	3-2	2-0	1-2	0-2	6-1	2-0	3-1	1-0	1-0
Drogheda FC	1-1	3-3	1-2	■	2-1	1-2	3-1	1-1	2-1	4-1	1-0	0-2
Drumcondra AFC	5-1	5-1	2-2	0-1	■	0-5	0-1	1-1	2-2	4-2	2-1	1-2
Dundalk FC	6-0	3-0	0-2	0-1	3-1	■	2-0	2-1	1-5	4-0	3-2	2-3
Limerick AFC	2-0	2-1	0-2	2-1	2-2	0-3	■	2-1	3-1	3-3	0-2	1-1
St. Patrick's Athletic FC	2-0	4-2	4-0	1-0	1-1	0-3	2-1	■	1-6	6-2	2-0	1-1
Shamrock Rovers FC	2-2	4-2	3-1	2-2	2-0	2-1	2-0	3-0	■	4-0	2-1	1-2
Shelbourne FC	1-0	2-1	1-1	2-2	3-4	2-2	1-1	1-4	1-7	■	1-1	2-5
Sligo Rovers FC	2-0	1-1	2-1	1-1	1-0	1-5	1-3	4-1	0-1	2-2	■	0-2
Waterford AFC	6-1	3-2	4-1	3-2	7-3	3-1	5-2	5-3	5-1	5-0	1-2	■

	Division "A"	Pd	Wn	Dw	Ls	GF	GA	Pts
1.	WATERFORD AFC (WATERFORD)	22	16	4	2	68	30	36
2.	Shamrock Rovers FC (Dublin)	22	14	3	5	56	28	31
3.	Cork Hibernians FC (Cork)	22	14	2	6	39	27	30
4.	Dundalk FC (Dundalk)	22	13	3	6	54	29	29
5.	St. Patrick's Athletic FC (Dublin)	22	10	4	8	41	42	24
6.	Drogheda FC (Drogheda)	22	8	6	8	35	30	22
7.	Limerick AFC (Limerick)	22	9	4	9	30	36	22
8.	Sligo Rovers FC (Sligo)	22	8	4	10	29	32	20
9.	Drumcondra AFC (Dublin)	22	6	5	11	38	44	17
10.	Shelbourne FC (Dublin)	22	2	8	12	30	69	12
11.	Cork Celtic FC (Cork)	22	3	5	14	28	52	11
12.	Bohemian FC (Dublin)	22	3	4	15	21	50	10
		264	106	52	106	469	469	264

Top goal-scorers 1968-69

1) Michael LEECH   (Shamrock Rovers FC)   19
2) Turlough O'CONNOR   (Dundalk FC)   17
3) Alfred HALE   (Waterford AFC)   16
   John O'NEILL   (Waterford AFC)   16

Elected: Athlone Town AFC (Athlone), Finn Harps FC (Ballybofey)

The league was extended to 14 clubs for next season

FAI Cup Final   (Dalymount Park, Dublin – 20/04/1969 – 28,000)

SHAMROCK ROVERS FC (DUBLIN)   1-1   Cork Celtic FC (Cork)
Keogh o.g.   *(H.T. 0-1)*   *Carroll*

Shamrock Rovers: Smyth, Canavan, Courtney, Mulligam, Pugh, Kearin, O'Neill, Hannigan, Leech (Brophy), Lawlor, Kinsella.
Cork Celtic: Taylor, Keogh, O'Mahoney, Ronayne, Hefferman, McCullough, Shortt, Carroll, Leahy, Wilson, McCarthy.

Final Replay   (Dalymount Park, Dublin – 23/04/1969 – 18,000)

SHAMROCK ROVERS FC (DUBLIN)   4-1   Cork Celtic FC (Cork)
Leech 2, Kearin, Richardson   *(H.T. 2-0)*   *McCarthy*

Shamrock Rovers: Smyth, Canavan, Courtney, Mulligam, Pugh, Kearin, O'Neill, Richardson, Leech (Brophy), Lawlor, Brophy.
Cork Celtic: Taylor, Keogh, O'Mahoney, Ronayne, Hefferman, McCullough, Shortt, Carroll, Leahy, Wilson, McCarthy.

Semi-Finals

Cork Celtic FC (Cork)   1-1, 1-1, 0-0, 1-0   Limerick AFC (Limerick)
Shamrock Rovers FC (Dublin)   1-1, 1-0   Shelbourne FC (Dublin)

Quarter-Finals

Cork Celtic FC (Cork)   2-1   St. Patrick's Athletic FC (Dublin)
Limerick AFC (Limerick)   1-0   Waterford AFC (Waterford)
Longford Town FC (Longford)   0-2   Shelbourne FC (Dublin)
Shamrock Rovers FC (Dublin)   4-0   Ringmahon Rangers FC (Cork)

1969-70

League of Ireland Division "A" 1969-70	Athlone Town	Bohemian FC	Cork Celtic FC	Cork Hibernians	Drogheda FC	Drumcondra AFC	Dundalk FC	Finn Harps FC	Limerick AFC	St. Patrick's Ath.	Shamrock Rovers	Shelbourne FC	Sligo Rovers FC	Waterford AFC
Athlone Town AFC	■	3-2	2-2	2-1	2-1	4-0	1-2	1-3	1-2	1-3	2-2	1-2	1-0	1-1
Bohemian FC	3-2	■	0-1	0-2	1-1	4-4	3-0	4-1	1-4	2-0	1-2	1-0	1-0	1-2
Cork Celtic FC	1-1	4-1	■	0-1	3-1	1-0	0-1	2-3	1-1	2-1	0-2	0-1	3-0	1-1
Cork Hibernians FC	3-1	2-2	1-0	■	1-0	0-0	1-1	1-1	3-1	1-1	3-0	1-0	0-0	
Drogheda FC	1-3	1-1	3-0	0-1	■	2-0	0-1	1-0	0-1	2-0	2-2	0-0	2-2	1-1
Drumcondra AFC	3-1	0-3	2-2	0-1	1-1	■	1-3	4-4	2-1	4-2	0-5	3-2	6-4	0-2
Dundalk FC	1-2	3-1	1-2	1-4	0-3	2-1	■	2-0	0-0	2-1	1-1	2-2	2-0	6-1
Finn Harps FC	1-0	2-0	2-1	3-1	1-1	3-2	6-2	■	1-0	2-2	2-2	1-1	2-2	2-4
Limerick AFC	6-1	0-1	2-1	1-0	0-0	3-0	1-1	3-1	■	1-0	1-0	2-1	0-1	1-0
St. Patrick's Athletic FC	3-4	1-0	3-2	2-1	2-1	2-0	1-5	3-1	2-1	■	2-3	1-2	0-1	1-4
Shamrock Rovers FC	2-0	2-1	1-3	2-2	2-0	0-0	3-1	4-0	2-0	3-1	■	1-1	4-1	4-1
Shelbourne FC	2-0	3-2	1-1	1-2	6-1	2-0	1-2	2-1	1-1	3-1	1-0	■	0-0	2-3
Sligo Rovers FC	1-3	2-1	2-0	0-1	2-1	4-1	2-1	3-2	2-1	3-0	3-1	1-1	■	1-5
Waterford AFC	1-0	3-2	4-1	1-1	4-0	6-1	0-0	3-2	3-1	1-0	2-4	1-0	1-0	■

	Division "A"	Pd	Wn	Dw	Ls	GF	GA	Pts
1.	WATERFORD AFC (WATERFORD)	26	16	6	4	55	33	38
2.	Shamrock Rovers FC (Dublin)	26	14	8	4	55	29	36
3.	Cork Hibernians FC (Cork)	26	13	9	4	35	20	35
4.	Limerick AFC (Limerick)	26	12	6	8	35	24	30
5.	Dundalk FC (Dundalk)	26	12	6	8	42	37	30
6.	Shelbourne FC (Dublin)	26	10	7	9	38	32	27
7.	Finn Harps FC (Ballybofey)	26	10	6	10	48	51	26
8.	Sligo Rovers FC (Sligo)	26	11	4	11	37	41	26
9.	Cork Celtic FC (Celtic)	26	8	6	12	34	38	22
10.	Athlone Town AFC (Athlone)	26	9	4	13	40	49	22
11.	Bohemian FC (Dublin)	26	8	4	14	39	45	20
12.	Drogheda FC (Drogheda)	26	5	9	12	26	37	19
13.	St. Patrick's Athletic FC (Dublin)	26	8	1	17	35	54	17
14.	Drumcondra AFC (Dublin)	26	5	6	15	35	64	16
		364	141	82	141	554	554	364

Top goal-scorers 1969-70

1) Brendan BRADLEY (Finn Harps FC) 18
2) Dave WIGGINTON (Cork Hibernians FC) 17
3) Eric BARBER (Shamrock Rovers FC) 15
   John MATTHEWS (Waterford AFC) 15

FAI Cup Final (Dalymount Park, Dublin – 19/04/1970 – 16,000)

BOHEMIAN FC (DUBLIN)   0-0   Sligo Rovers FC (Sligo)

Bohemian: Lowry, Doran, Fullam, Nolan, Parkes, Conway, T.Kelly, Swan, O'Connell, Hamill, M.Kelly.
Sligo Rovers: Lally, Turner, Fallon, Pugh, Stenson, Burns, McCluskey, Fagan, Cooke, Mitchell, Brooks.

Final Replay   (Dalymount Park, Dublin – 22/04/1970 – 11,000)

BOHEMIAN FC (DUBLIN)　　　　　　　　　0-0　　　　　　　　　　　Sligo Rovers FC (Sligo)

Bohemian: Lowry, Doran, Fullam, Nolan, Parkes, Conway, T.Kelly, Swan, O'Connell, Hamill, M.Kelly.
Sligo Rovers: Lally, Turner, Fallon, Pugh, Stenson, Burns, McCluskey, Fagan, Cooke, Mitchell, Brooks.

Final 2nd Replay   (Dalymount Park, Dublin – 03/05/1970 – 22,000)

BOHEMIAN FC (DUBLIN)　　　　　　　　　2-1　　　　　　　　　　　Sligo Rovers FC (Sligo)
Fullam, O'Connell　　　　　　　　　　*(H.T. 0-1)*　　　　　　　　　　　　　　*Cooke*

Bohemian: Lowry, Doran, Fullam, Nolan, Parkes, Conway (O'Sullivan), T.Kelly, Swan, O'Connell, Hamill, M. Kelly (Clarke).
Sligo: Lally, Turner, Fallon, Pugh, Stenson (McKiernan), Burns, McCluskey, Fagan, Cooke, Mitchell, Brooks.

Semi-Finals

Bohemian FC (Dublin)	1-0	Dundalk FC (Dundalk)
Sligo Rovers FC (Sligo)	0-0, 2-1	Cork Hibernians FC (Cork)

Quarter-Finals

Athlone Town AFC (Athlone)	0-0, 0-2	Dundalk FC (Dundalk)
Bohemian FC (Dublin)	1-0	Shelbourne FC (Dublin)
Sligo Rovers FC (Sligo)	4-0	Rialto FC (Dublin)
Waterford AFC (Waterford)	1-2	Cork Hibernians FC (Cork)

1970-71

League of Ireland Division "A" 1970-71	Athlone Town AFC	Bohemian FC	Cork Celtic FC	Cork Hibernians	Drogheda FC	Drumcondra AFC	Dundalk FC	Finn Harps FC	Limerick AFC	St. Patrick's Ath.	Shamrock Rovers	Shelbourne FC	Sligo Rovers FC	Waterford AFC
Athlone Town AFC	■	1-1	1-0	1-1	1-4	4-0	0-0	3-5	1-3	3-4	2-4	0-0	1-0	0-3
Bohemian FC	3-2	■	1-0	0-0	6-2	1-0	1-0	1-3	1-0	2-0	1-0	3-2	0-0	1-1
Cork Celtic FC	1-0	1-1	■	1-2	2-0	5-2	2-0	3-1	3-2	2-1	1-3	0-0	2-2	1-1
Cork Hibernians FC	0-0	1-0	2-1	■	3-1	3-0	2-1	3-0	0-0	5-0	0-1	1-1	0-0	0-1
Drogheda FC	0-1	0-0	1-0	1-2	■	0-0	2-4	1-1	0-1	3-1	1-3	0-1	0-1	1-0
Drumcondra AFC	1-2	0-2	0-2	1-2	1-4	■	0-3	1-3	0-1	5-3	2-2	0-1	3-1	1-4
Dundalk FC	2-0	0-0	0-2	0-3	1-1	1-1	■	3-0	0-0	3-0	1-2	2-0	4-1	2-2
Finn Harps FC	1-2	0-1	1-1	2-1	5-1	3-1	1-0	■	4-3	2-1	2-3	4-0	4-1	4-0
Limerick AFC	2-1	3-2	1-1	0-0	1-0	2-3	1-1	1-2	■	4-2	0-0	0-0	5-0	0-1
St. Patrick's Athletic FC	2-1	1-1	1-1	2-2	0-1	0-0	2-2	1-1	1-1	■	1-2	2-0	1-0	1-0
Shamrock Rovers FC	1-4	2-2	1-1	0-0	2-0	2-1	3-3	3-1	3-1	4-2	■	1-0	1-2	2-0
Shelbourne FC	2-1	2-1	1-4	0-0	2-1	2-1	0-0	2-1	1-2	4-1	5-0	■	3-0	0-1
Sligo Rovers FC	0-1	0-4	1-6	1-3	3-1	0-0	5-2	2-2	3-0	4-3	4-3	2-2	■	2-2
Waterford AFC	3-2	4-2	1-1	2-2	4-1	3-2	2-2	3-1	1-2	2-1	1-1	2-1	5-1	■

Play-off   (Dalymount Park, Dublin – 25/04/1971)

CORK HIBERNIANS FC (CORK)　　　　　　3-1　　　　　　　　　Shamrock Rovers FC (Dublin)

	Division "A"	Pd	Wn	Dw	Ls	GF	GA	Pts
1.	Cork Hibernians FC (Cork)	26	12	11	3	38	17	25
1.	Shamrock Rovers FC (Dublin)	26	14	7	5	49	38	35
3.	Waterford AFC (Waterford)	26	13	8	5	49	34	34
4.	Bohemian FC (Dublin)	26	12	9	5	38	25	33
5.	Cork Celtic FC (Cork)	26	11	9	6	44	27	31
6.	Finn Harps FC (Ballybofey)	26	13	4	9	54	42	30
7.	Limerick AFC (Limerick)	26	10	8	8	36	31	28
8.	Shelbourne FC (Dublin)	26	10	7	9	32	30	27
9.	Dundalk FC (Dundalk)	26	7	11	8	37	33	25
10.	Athlone Town AFC (Athlone)	26	8	5	13	35	43	21
11.	Sligo Rovers FC (Sligo)	26	7	7	12	36	58	21
12.	St. Patrick's Athletic FC (Dublin)	26	5	7	14	34	55	17
13.	Drogheda FC (Drogheda)	26	6	4	16	27	46	16
14.	Drumcondra AFC (Dublin)	26	3	5	18	26	56	11
		364	131	102	131	535	535	364

Top goal-scorers 1970-71

1) Brendan BRADLEY   (Finn Harps FC)   20
2) John MATTHEWS   (Waterford AFC)   17
3) Turlough O'CONNOR   (Dundalk FC)   16

FAI Cup Final   (Dalymount Park, Dublin – 18/04/1971 – 16,000)

LIMERICK AFC (LIMERICK)   0-0   Drogheda FC (Drogheda)

Limerick: Fitzpatrick, Bourke, Hall, Finucane, Byrnes, O'Mahoney, Coad (Hamilton), McEvoy, Shortt, Barrett, Meaney.

Drogheda: Baxter, Dowling, Meagan, Shawcross, Jacenuik, McSwiney, Cooke, McEwan, Whelan, Cullen, Fairclough (Conroy).

Final Replay   (Dalymount Park, Dublin – 21/04/1971 – 15,000)

LIMERICK AFC (LIMERICK)   3-0   Drogheda FC (Drogheda)
Barrett, Hamilton 2   (H.T. 0-0)

Limerick: Fitzpatrick, Bourke (Hamilton), Hall, Finucane, Byrnes, O'Mahoney, Coad, McEvoy, Shortt, Barrett, Meaney.

Drogheda: Baxter, Dowling, Meagan, Shawcross, Jacenuik, McSwiney, Cooke, McEwan, Whelan (Fairclough), Cullen, Conroy.

Semi-Finals

| Drogheda FC (Drogheda) | 0-0, 2-1 | Cork Hibernians FC (Cork) |
| Limerick AFC (Limerick) | 1-0 | St. Patrick's Athletic FC (Dublin) |

Quarter-Finals

Cork Hibernians FC (Cork)	2-2, 1-1, 5-0	Finn Harps FC (Ballybofey)
Limerick AFC (Limerick)	0-0, 3-1	Bohemian FC (Dublin)
Shamrock Rovers FC (Dublin)	2-5	Drogheda FC (Drogheda)
Sligo Rovers FC (Sligo)	1-2	St. Patrick's Athletic FC (Dublin)

1971-72

League of Ireland Division "A" 1971-72	Athlone Town AFC	Bohemian FC	Cork Celtic FC	Cork Hibernians FC	Drogheda FC	Drumcondra AFC	Dundalk FC	Finn Harps FC	Limerick AFC	St. Patrick's Athletic FC	Shamrock Rovers FC	Shelbourne FC	Sligo Rovers FC	Waterford AFC
Athlone Town AFC		1-2	4-4	1-5	2-1	1-1	4-4	2-5	1-0	2-1	3-2	1-0	2-2	1-2
Bohemian FC	1-1		1-0	1-0	4-0	2-1	2-1	4-1	3-0	2-0	2-2	4-1	1-1	1-1
Cork Celtic FC	2-0	2-1		0-3	0-0	1-2	4-2	0-1	1-0	3-3	3-2	0-3	1-0	0-1
Cork Hibernians FC	1-0	2-0	4-1		8-1	3-1	4-1	3-0	6-0	2-0	3-1	4-0	3-1	2-3
Drogheda FC	3-1	1-2	1-3	0-0		5-1	0-1	3-0	1-0	1-3	3-3	0-0	5-0	0-1
Drumcondra AFC	0-2	1-2	1-0	0-4	1-1		2-0	1-3	2-1	0-0	2-2	1-1	0-1	0-3
Dundalk FC	1-0	0-1	4-1	0-4	0-3	1-0		3-2	5-2	0-0	1-0	1-1	2-1	3-0
Finn Harps FC	7-0	3-1	5-2	0-1	2-0	4-1	4-1		2-1	0-1	5-3	2-1	3-0	2-0
Limerick AFC	1-1	0-0	2-2	1-0	2-1	4-1	2-1	1-3		2-2	2-4	0-1	0-1	0-3
St. Patrick's Athletic FC	1-2	0-2	1-1	3-1	1-0	2-2	2-0	1-3	2-1		0-1	1-0	3-2	1-3
Shamrock Rovers FC	3-0	1-0	1-2	0-0	3-0	4-1	3-1	1-3	3-0	1-0		2-1	6-2	1-2
Shelbourne FC	3-5	0-2	0-0	1-0	0-0	1-2	0-1	1-0	1-1	1-1	0-1		5-3	2-2
Sligo Rovers FC	1-1	0-3	2-2	0-4	2-0	1-0	1-3	1-2	3-4	1-2	2-1	0-4		4-7
Waterford AFC	3-2	4-1	2-1	1-3	2-0	3-0	3-2	1-0	3-2	3-2	3-1	3-2	7-2	

	Division "A"	Pd	Wn	Dw	Ls	GF	GA	Pts	
1.	WATERFORD AFC (WATERFORD)	26	21	2	3	66	35	44	
2.	Cork Hibernians FC (Cork)	26	19	2	5	70	17	40	
3.	Bohemian FC (Dublin)	26	16	5	5	45	24	37	
4.	Finn Harps FC (Ballybofey)	26	18	-	8	62	34	36	
5.	Shamrock Rovers FC (Dublin)	26	12	4	10	52	41	28	
6.	St. Patrick's Athletic FC (Dublin)	26	9	7	10	33	36	25	
7.	Dundalk FC (Dundalk)	26	11	3	12	39	46	25	
8.	Cork Celtic FC (Cork)	26	8	7	11	36	46	23	
9.	Shelbourne FC (Dublin)	26	6	8	12	30	37	22	*
10.	Athlone Town AFC (Athlone)	26	8	7	11	40	56	21	*
11.	Drogheda FC (Drogheda)	26	6	6	14	30	42	18	
12.	Drumcondra AFC (Dublin)	26	5	6	15	24	52	16	**
13.	Limerick AFC (Limerick)	26	5	5	16	29	53	15	
14.	Sligo Rovers FC (Sligo)	26	5	4	17	34	71	14	
		364	149	66	149	590	590	364	

Top goal-scorers 1971-72

1) Alfred HALE (Waterford AFC) 22
   Anthony MARSDEN (Cork Hibernians FC) 22
3) Brendan BRADLEY (Finn Harps FC) 18

* After the match Athlone Town AFC 1-0 Shelbourne FC played on 17/10/1971, both points were awarded to Shelbourne FC

** Drumcondra AFC (Dublin) were taken over by, and merged into Home Farm FC (Dublin) and their club name changed to Home Farm-Drumcondra FC (Dublin) for next season.

FAI Cup Final (Dalymount Park, Dublin – 23/04/1972 – 22,500)

CORK HIBERNIANS FC (CORK)   3-0   Waterford AFC (Waterford)
Dennehy 3   *(H.T. 0-0)*

Cork Hibernians: Grady, Bacuzzi, O'Mahoney, Sheehan, Herrick, Lawson, Sweeney, Finnegan, Marsden, Wigginton, Dennehy.

Waterford: Thomas, Bryan, Cottle, Morley, Maguire, O'Neill, McGeough, Matthews, Hale, Kirby (House), Humphries.

Semi-Finals

Cork Hibernians FC (Cork)	1-0	St. Patrick's Athletic FC (Dublin)
Waterford AFC (Waterford)	4-2	Dundalk FC (Dundalk)

Quarter-Finals

Cork Hibernians FC (Cork)	6-0	Drumcondra AFC (Dublin)
Drogheda FC (Drogheda)	2-4	Waterford AFC (Waterford)
Limerick AFC (Limerick)	0-0, 1-1, 1-2	Dundalk FC (Dundalk)
St. Patrick's Athletic FC (Dublin)	1-0	Shamrock Rovers FC (Dublin)

1972-73

League of Ireland Division "A" 1972-73	Athlone Town AFC	Bohemian FC	Cork Celtic FC	Cork Hibernians FC	Drogheda FC	Dundalk FC	Finn Harps FC	Home Farm-Drumcondra	Limerick AFC	St. Patrick's Athletic FC	Shamrock Rovers FC	Shelbourne FC	Sligo Rovers FC	Waterford AFC
Athlone Town AFC	■	1-2	2-0	2-1	4-1	1-0	1-3	2-4	4-1	1-0	1-2	3-3	1-0	0-1
Bohemian FC	2-0	■	1-0	1-1	3-1	2-1	2-3	5-3	1-0	3-0	3-2	1-0	0-1	0-3
Cork Celtic FC	1-2	0-2	■	2-2	1-1	3-0	0-2	4-1	3-1	0-1	0-1	1-5	1-2	1-5
Cork Hibernians FC	2-0	2-1	4-0	■	1-1	2-0	2-0	6-0	0-0	1-2	2-1	1-1	2-3	3-1
Drogheda FC	0-1	1-6	4-2	0-1	■	2-2	0-0	1-1	0-2	1-2	1-3	1-1	2-3	1-4
Dundalk FC	1-2	0-1	2-0	0-4	1-1	■	1-2	0-1	2-1	1-1	1-0	0-1	0-1	0-4
Finn Harps FC	1-2	3-2	0-0	2-1	2-1	1-1	■	4-2	2-1	4-2	5-0	3-0	2-1	3-2
Home Farm-Drumcondra	1-1	0-1	0-0	0-4	1-1	0-3	3-1	■	0-2	2-3	1-0	0-6	2-0	1-0
Limerick AFC	1-1	1-1	1-2	1-3	4-1	2-0	1-2	2-0	■	1-1	0-2	3-1	2-1	0-0
St. Patrick's Athletic FC	1-1	0-0	0-1	3-3	2-0	1-1	1-3	2-2	3-2	■	1-1	2-2	0-1	2-3
Shamrock Rovers FC	1-0	0-0	2-0	2-2	3-0	6-0	1-3	4-0	0-0	3-3	■	1-0	3-0	1-3
Shelbourne FC	0-1	1-4	2-4	1-1	3-0	3-0	1-2	1-3	3-0	2-2	3-0	■	6-1	0-1
Sligo Rovers FC	0-3	1-2	0-2	1-2	1-0	1-1	1-4	1-1	0-3	0-2	3-2	1-4	■	1-3
Waterford AFC	2-1	0-0	7-1	2-0	2-0	5-1	3-2	5-0	2-0	4-0	0-3	4-0	1-0	■

Division "A"	Pd	Wn	Dw	Ls	GF	GA	Pts	
1. WATERFORD AFC (WATERFORD)	26	20	2	4	67	21	42	
2. Finn Harps FC (Ballybofey)	26	19	3	4	59	32	41	
3. Bohemian FC (Dublin)	26	16	5	5	46	25	37	
4. Cork Hibernians FC (Cork)	26	13	8	5	53	27	34	
5. Shamrock Rovers FC (Dublin)	26	12	6	8	45	32	30	
6. Athlone Town AFC (Athlone)	26	13	4	9	38	31	30	
7. St. Patrick's Athletic FC (Dublin)	26	7	11	8	37	43	25	
8. Shelbourne FC (Dublin)	26	9	6	11	50	40	24	
9. Limerick AFC (Limerick)	26	8	6	12	32	35	20	*
10. Sligo Rovers FC (Sligo)	26	8	2	16	25	51	20	*
11. Home Farm-Drumcondra AFC (Dublin)	26	6	7	13	29	60	19	**
12. Cork Celtic FC (Cork)	26	7	4	15	29	50	18	
13. Dundalk FC (Dundalk)	26	4	6	16	19	48	14	
14. Drogheda FC (Drogheda)	26	1	8	17	22	56	10	
	364	143	78	143	551	551	364	

Top goal-scorers 1972-73

1) Alfred HALE   (Waterford AFC)   20
   Terry HARKIN   (Finn Harps FC)   20
3) John MATTHEWS   (Waterford AFC)   14

*   After the Limerick AFC 2-1 Sligo Rovers FC match played on 08/10/1972 both points were awarded to Sligo Rovers FC.

** Home Farm-Drumcondra AFC (Dublin) changed to Home Fram FC (Dublin) for next season, the club's original name prior to their take over of Drumcondra AFC (Dublin) in 1971.

FAI Cup Final   (Dalymount Park, Dublin – 22/04/1973 – 12,500)

Shelbourne FC (Dublin)	0-0	CORK HIBERNIANS FC (CORK)

Shelbourne: P. Roche, Gannon, B.Roche, McDonnell (Mulhall), O'Brien, Newman, Rogers, Hannigan, McKenna, McNaughton, Barber.

Cork Hibernians: D.O'Mahoney, Bacuzzi, N.O'Mahoney, Sheehan, Brohan Sweeney, Lawson, Allen, Wiggington, Humphries, Coyne.

Final Replay   (Flower Lodge – 29/04/1973 – 11,000)

Shelbourne FC (Dublin)	0-1	CORK HIBERNIANS FC (CORK)
	(H.T. 0-0)	*Humphries*

Shelbourne: P. Roche, Gannon, B.Roche, McDonnell (Mulhall), O'Brien, Newman (Doyle), Rogers (Dunning), Hannigan, McKenna, McNaughton, Barber.

Cork Hibernians: D.O'Mahoney, Bacuzzi, N.O'Mahoney (Connolly), Sheehan, Brohan Sweeney, Lawson, Allen, Wiggington, Humphries, Coyne.

Semi-Finals

Cork Hibernians FC (Cork)	2-0	Limerick AFC (Limerick)
Shelbourne FC (Dublin)	0-0, 2-2, 1-0	Cork Celtic FC (Cork)

Quarter-Finals

Cork Celtic FC (Cork)	3-0	Bohemian FC (Dublin)
Cork Hibernians FC (Cork)	0-0, 2-0	Waterford AFC (Waterford)
Limerick AFC (Limerick)	1-0	Shamrock Rovers FC (Dublin)
Shelbourne FC (Dublin)	0-0, 1-0	Dalkey United FC (Dalkey)

1973-74

League of Ireland Division "A" 1973-74	Athlone Town AFC	Bohemian FC	Cork Celtic FC	Cork Hibernians	Drogheda FC	Dundalk FC	Finn Harps FC	Home Farm FC	Limerick AFC	St. Patrick's Ath.	Shamrock Rovers	Shelbourne FC	Sligo Rovers FC	Waterford AFC
Athlone Town AFC	■	1-2	0-1	0-1	1-3	0-2	1-3	2-0	4-1	1-0	1-2	2-0	3-0	0-2
Bohemian FC	2-3	■	7-0	0-2	3-1	1-0	1-0	4-0	3-0	7-0	0-1	2-0	2-1	1-0
Cork Celtic FC	1-0	0-0	■	1-3	6-0	1-0	1-1	2-0	2-1	3-0	4-0	2-1	1-1	1-0
Cork Hibernians FC	2-0	3-4	1-2	■	2-2	2-1	0-0	3-0	2-1	2-0	3-1	3-0	3-2	1-1
Drogheda FC	3-1	0-5	2-3	0-4	■	3-1	2-3	1-1	0-1	2-3	2-1	1-1	2-3	2-2
Dundalk FC	1-1	1-0	1-1	2-3	3-0	■	1-1	0-1	2-1	2-1	1-3	3-1	3-0	3-2
Finn Harps FC	3-1	2-1	1-2	0-0	3-0	0-1	■	7-1	0-1	4-0	1-1	3-2	3-2	2-4
Home Farm FC	1-0	1-0	0-1	0-0	2-0	1-2	1-3	■	1-0	0-2	0-0	0-2	2-0	2-2
Limerick AFC	0-0	0-2	0-0	2-1	2-3	4-1	0-3	1-1	■	4-2	1-0	1-1	2-3	0-4
St. Patrick's Athletic FC	1-0	0-1	1-2	0-2	1-3	3-1	2-1	1-1	2-3	■	1-0	3-2	0-1	0-1
Shamrock Rovers FC	0-0	0-1	1-1	2-0	2-1	2-1	0-2	2-1	2-1	0-0	■	3-1	1-0	3-5
Shelbourne FC	1-2	0-2	1-3	1-1	1-3	0-3	1-2	2-2	3-3	1-3	4-1	■	2-1	1-4
Sligo Rovers FC	0-1	0-3	1-3	1-2	2-1	3-4	0-1	3-0	1-1	1-2	1-0	0-2	■	1-3
Waterford AFC	6-0	2-2	2-6	0-1	2-2	1-1	1-2	0-0	2-1	0-1	0-3	5-0	4-0	■

	Division "A"	Pd	Wn	Dw	Ls	GF	GA	Pts
1.	CORK CELTIC FC (CORK)	26	18	6	2	50	25	42
2.	Bohemian FC (Dublin)	26	18	2	6	56	18	38
3.	Cork Hibernians FC (Cork)	26	16	6	4	47	23	38
4.	Fin Harps FC (Ballybofey)	26	15	5	6	51	27	35
5.	Waterford AFC (Waterford)	26	11	7	8	55	36	29
6.	Dundalk FC (Dundalk)	26	12	4	10	41	36	28
7.	Shamrock Rovers FC (Dublin)	26	11	5	10	31	33	27
8.	St. Patrick's Athletic FC (Dublin)	26	10	2	14	29	45	22
9.	Limerick AFC (Limerick)	26	7	6	13	32	45	20
10.	Home Farm FC (Dublin)	26	6	8	12	19	40	20
11.	Drogheda FC (Drogheda)	26	7	5	14	39	59	19
12.	Athlone Town AFC (Athlone)	26	8	3	15	25	38	19
13.	Sligo Rovers FC (Sligo)	26	6	2	18	28	51	14
14.	Shelbourne FC (Dublin)	26	4	5	17	31	58	13
		364	149	66	149	534	534	364

Top goal-scorers 1973-74

1)	Terry FLANAGAN	(Bohemian FC)	18
	Turlough O'CONNOR	(Bohemian FC)	18
3)	Brendan BRADLEY	(Finn Harps FC)	12
	Donal MURPHY	(Shamrock Rovers FC)	12
	Frank O'NEILL	(Cork Celtic FC)	12

FAI Cup Final   (Dalymount Park, Dublin – 21/04/1974 – 14,000)

FINN HARPS FC (BALLYBOFEY)   3-1   St. Patrick's Athletic FC (Dublin)

Ferry, Bradley 2   *(H.T. 1-1)*   *Byrne*

Finn Harps: Murray, McGranaghan, Sheridan, T.O'Doherty, Hutton, McGrory, McDowell, Smith (D.O'Doherty), McGee, Bradley, Ferry.

St. Patrick's Athletic: Lally, Burkett, Reynolds, Doyle, Myles, Byrne, Flanagan, Munroe, O'Sullivan, Smith (Dempsey), Shields.

Semi-Finals

Finn Harps FC (Ballybofey)	5-0	Athlone Town AFC (Athlone)
St. Patrick's Athletic FC (Dublin)	1-0	Drogheda FC (Drogheda)

Quarter-Finals

Athlone Town AFC (Athlone)	2-1	Transport FC (Dublin)
Bohemian FC (Dublin)	1-1, 0-2	Finn Harps FC (Ballybofey)
Cork Hibernians FC (Cork)	1-2	St. Patrick's Athletic FC (Dublin)
Drogheda FC (Drogheda)	0-0, 4-3	Waterford AFC (Waterford)

1974-75

League of Ireland Division "A" 1974-75	Athlone Town AFC	Bohemian FC	Cork Celtic FC	Cork Hibernians FC	Drogheda FC	Dundalk FC	Finn Harps FC	Home Farm FC	Limerick AFC	St. Patrick's Athletic	Shamrock Rovers	Shelbourne FC	Sligo Rovers FC	Waterford AFC
Athlone Town AFC		1-1	2-3	1-0	0-0	2-0	4-4	2-2	4-0	2-0	2-1	2-1	4-2	3-1
Bohemian FC	1-0		1-0	1-0	2-0	3-1	3-0	0-1	2-1	1-0	2-0	1-0	0-0	1-0
Cork Celtic FC	1-0	1-1		2-2	1-1	3-1	2-3	0-0	2-2	3-1	2-2	2-1	2-1	2-3
Cork Hibernians FC	3-0	2-1	3-0		3-1	4-1	4-1	2-2	7-0	1-1	1-0	0-2	0-1	2-2
Drogheda FC	3-3	0-0	0-0	0-1		0-0	4-3	2-1	0-1	1-1	0-2	0-0	2-4	4-2
Dundalk FC	0-0	0-1	3-2	1-0	1-1		1-2	4-1	2-3	3-0	1-0	3-2	1-0	2-2
Finn Harps FC	1-1	1-1	3-3	1-1	4-4	2-2		1-0	3-1	4-0	2-3	2-2	4-1	5-1
Home Farm FC	2-1	0-2	1-1	0-2	4-2	0-2	2-3		2-0	0-1	0-2	0-0	0-1	3-5
Limerick AFC	0-2	0-1	0-4	0-0	0-1	0-1	2-2	3-1		0-1	3-1	3-1	1-0	2-3
St. Patrick's Athletic FC	4-1	1-2	3-3	0-0	0-2	3-1	1-1	2-2	3-1		3-1	1-0	2-1	0-1
Shamrock Rovers FC	2-3	1-2	1-2	2-2	0-1	1-1	1-0	3-2	1-1	2-1		2-3	4-1	2-1
Shelbourne FC	0-1	0-2	4-0	2-2	1-1	1-2	1-2	0-1	0-0	2-1	2-2		2-1	0-2
Sligo Rovers FC	0-2	0-2	2-1	1-0	1-1	2-2	1-3	1-2	1-0	1-2	0-2	1-5		2-1
Waterford AFC	0-2	2-2	3-1	3-0	2-1	1-1	4-2	2-2	2-3	0-0	0-2	4-1	1-1	

	Division "A"	Pd	Wn	Dw	Ls	GF	GA	Pts	
1.	BOHEMIAN FC (DUBLIN)	26	18	6	2	36	12	42	
2.	Athlone Town AFC (Athlone)	26	13	7	6	45	32	33	
3.	Finn Harps FC (Ballybofey)	26	10	10	6	59	50	30	
4.	Cork Hibernians FC (Cork)	26	10	9	7	42	26	29	
5.	Dundalk FC (Dundalk)	26	10	8	8	37	36	28	
6.	Waterford AFC (Waterford)	26	10	7	9	48	46	27	
7.	Cork Celtic FC (Cork)	26	8	10	8	43	44	26	
8.	Shamrock Rovers FC (Dublin)	26	10	5	11	40	38	25	
9.	Drogheda FC (Drogheda)	26	6	12	8	32	37	24	*
10.	St. Patrick's Athletic FC (Dublin)	26	8	7	11	30	37	23	
11.	Home Farm FC (Dublin)	26	7	6	13	31	43	20	
12.	Limerick FC (Limerick)	26	7	6	13	28	46	20	
13.	Shelbourne FC (Dublin)	26	6	7	13	33	38	19	
14.	Sligo Rovers FC (Sligo)	26	7	4	15	27	46	18	
		364	130	104	130	531	531	364	

Top goal-scorers 1974-75

1) Brendan BRADLEY   (Finn Harps FC)   21
2) Michael LEECH   (Waterford AFC)   11
3) Frank DEVLIN   (Home Farm FC)   10
   Anthony MARSDEN   (Cork Hibernians FC)   10
   John MATTHEWS   (Waterford AFC)   10

* Drogheda FC (Drogheda) changed their club name to Drogheda United FC (Drogheda) for next season.

FAI Cup Final   (Dalymount Park, Dublin – 27/04/1975 – 10,000)

HOME FARM FC (DUBLIN)   1-0   Shelbourne FC (Dublin)
Devlin   *(H.T. 1-0)*

Home Farm: Grace, Smith, Daly, D.Keely, Brophy, Dempsey, Hughes, J.Keely, Higgins, Devlin, Murray.
Shelbourne: W.Byrne, Gannon, McKenna, McDonnell, Dunning, Cervi, T.Byrne (Devine), Hannon, McNaughton, Lawlor, Barber.

Semi-Finals

Cork Hibernians FC (Cork)   1-1, 0-1   Shelbourne FC (Dublin)
Home Farm FC (Dublin)   3-2   St. Patrick's Athletic FC (Dublin)

Quarter-Finals

Bohemian FC (Dublin)   1-1, 0-1   Cork Hibernians FC (Cork)
Home Farm FC (Dublin)   3-2   Cork Celtic FC (Cork)
St. Patrick's Athletic FC (Dublin)   1-0   C.Y.M. (Dublin)
Shelbourne FC (Dublin)   1-0   Shamrock Rovers FC (Dublin)

1975-76

League of Ireland Division "A" 1975-76	Athlone Town AFC	Bohemian FC	Cork Celtic FC	Cork Hibernians FC	Drogheda United FC	Dundalk FC	Finn Harps FC	Home Farm FC	Limerick AFC	St. Patrick's Athletic FC	Shamrock Rovers FC	Shelbourne FC	Sligo Rovers FC	Waterford AFC
Athlone Town AFC		1-1	2-1	2-1	3-2	0-1	3-2	4-2	5-5	2-0	3-1	2-1	0-2	0-1
Bohemian FC	2-0		2-2	0-0	2-2	1-1	1-2	3-2	6-2	6-0	1-0	3-0	3-1	2-0
Cork Celtic FC	1-2	1-0		1-1	0-2	2-1	0-2	3-1	2-0	3-1	3-1	0-0	3-0	3-4
Cork Hibernians FC	5-0	1-2	1-1		2-1	1-1	0-2	2-0	2-1	2-0	1-1	2-2	3-0	1-1
Drogheda United FC	1-0	2-2	2-1	1-1		1-2	2-3	1-1	2-1	0-1	2-1	1-0	1-0	2-2
Dundalk FC	3-0	2-2	3-2	1-0	4-1		1-1	2-2	1-0	2-2	5-2	4-1	3-2	1-1
Finn Harps FC	1-2	2-1	0-3	3-1	7-0	0-2		2-1	4-2	1-0	2-2	2-1	6-1	1-1
Home Farm FC	5-0	1-1	0-1	1-1	0-3	0-0	1-1		1-1	1-2	1-1	1-5	4-2	2-4
Limerick AFC	3-0	1-1	2-1	0-1	3-4	1-4	1-3	0-1		1-2	1-2	2-0	1-2	2-1
St. Patrick's Athletic FC	1-1	0-1	1-2	1-2	3-1	2-2	3-3	1-3	0-5		1-0	1-3	1-4	0-2
Shamrock Rovers FC	1-2	1-0	2-2	1-0	2-3	0-3	1-1	0-0	1-0	0-1		0-4	0-2	3-3
Shelbourne FC	2-3	0-0	2-1	0-3	2-2	1-2	0-1	5-1	3-1	2-4	2-0		0-0	2-2
Sligo Rovers FC	1-1	1-1	0-1	1-2	0-3	1-1	2-4	2-1	0-0	1-1	3-2	2-2		1-1
Waterford AFC	3-2	0-0	2-1	0-1	2-0	0-2	3-1	7-2	0-1	3-2	3-2	4-2	4-1	

Division "A"

		Pd	Wn	Dw	Ls	GF	GA	Pts	
1.	DUNDALK FC (DUNDALK)	26	15	10	1	54	26	40	
2.	Finn Harps FC (Ballybofey)	26	15	6	5	57	35	36	
3.	Waterford AFC (Waterford)	26	13	8	5	54	37	34	
4.	Bohemian FC (Dublin)	26	10	12	4	44	25	32	
5.	Cork Hibernians FC (Cork)	26	11	9	6	37	24	31	#
6.	Drogheda United FC (Drogheda)	26	11	6	9	42	45	28	
7.	Athlone Town AFC (Athlone)	26	12	4	10	40	49	28	
8.	Cork Celtic FC (Cork)	26	11	5	10	41	34	27	
9.	Shelbourne FC (Dublin)	26	7	7	12	42	44	21	
10.	Sligo Rovers FC (Sligo)	26	6	8	12	32	49	20	
11.	St. Patrick's Athletic FC (Dublin)	26	7	5	14	31	53	19	
12.	Home Farm FC (Dublin)	26	4	9	13	35	54	17	
13.	Limerick AFC (Limerick)	26	6	4	16	37	49	16	
14.	Shamrock Rovers FC (Dublin)	26	4	7	15	27	49	15	
		364	132	100	132	573	573	364	

Top goal-scorers 1975-76

1) Brendan BRADLEY (Finn Harps FC) 29
2) Turlough O'CONNOR (Bohemian FC) 16
3) Michael LEECH (Waterford AFC) 15
   Bobby TAMBLING (Cork Celtic FC) 15

\# Cork Hibernians FC (Cork) resigned from the league at the end of the season and disbanded.

Elected: Albert Rovers FC (Cork)

From the next season goal-difference replaced goal-average in deciding places for teams level on points.

FAI Cup Final   (Dalymount Park, Dublin – 18/04/1976 – 10,400)

BOHEMIAN FC (DUBLIN)   1-0   Drogheda United FC (Drogheda)
Shelly   *(H.T. 0-0)*

Bohemian: Smyth, Gregg, O'Brien, Kelly, Burke, Fullam, Byrne, P.O'Connor, T.O'Connor, Shelly, Ryan (Grimes).
Drogheda United: L.Byrne, Campbell (Clarke), McGuigan, Donnelly, Roche, Brunton, O'Halloran, Stephens, D.Byrne, Muckian.

Semi-Finals

Bohemian FC (Dublin)	1-1, 5-0	Sligo Rovers FC (Sligo)
Drogheda United FC (Drogheda)	1-0	Finn Harps FC (Ballybofey)

Quarter-Finals

Cork Celtic FC (Cork)	0-1	Bohemian FC (Dublin)
Drogheda United FC (Drogheda)	1-0	St. Patrick's Athletic FC (Dublin)
Shelbourne FC (Dublin)	0-2	Finn Harps FC (Ballybofey)
Sligo Rovers FC (Sligo)	4-2	Athlone Town AFC (Athlone)

1976-77

League of Ireland Division "A" 1976-77	Albert Rovers FC	Athlone Town AFC	Bohemian FC	Cork Celtic FC	Drogheda United	Dundalk FC	Finn Harps FC	Home Farm FC	Limerick AFC	St. Patrick's Athletic	Shamrock Rovers	Shelbourne FC	Sligo Rovers FC	Waterford AFC
Albert Rovers FC	■	0-4	0-1	1-5	1-2	0-0	2-2	1-2	4-2	0-0	1-2	2-1	0-1	1-3
Athlone Town AFC	3-1	■	3-1	1-1	2-2	1-3	1-2	4-0	1-0	0-0	4-2	2-3	0-5	3-1
Bohemian FC	1-0	4-1	■	3-1	3-1	1-3	6-0	2-0	1-1	0-2	1-0	2-1	0-3	0-1
Cork Celtic FC	1-0	2-2	2-3	■	4-1	0-1	1-2	3-0	5-2	0-0	1-1	4-2	2-1	5-2
Drogheda United FC	4-0	4-2	2-2	6-3	■	2-2	2-2	5-0	1-1	2-1	1-0	3-0	0-0	2-2
Dundalk FC	0-2	4-3	1-3	3-1	0-1	■	2-0	6-3	2-1	3-0	2-3	1-1	3-1	2-1
Finn Harps FC	2-0	1-1	1-2	2-2	1-7	2-1	■	0-0	5-1	2-0	3-1	1-2	0-1	3-1
Home Farm FC	1-1	1-2	0-1	2-0	0-2	3-1	2-2	■	2-0	1-2	1-2	1-3	0-2	0-3
Limerick AFC	0-1	2-1	1-2	0-2	2-1	2-2	1-2	3-2	■	0-2	1-1	1-3	1-3	0-1
St. Patrick's Athletic FC	3-1	0-0	1-5	5-0	0-0	1-1	1-1	2-1	1-1	■	2-0	1-1	0-1	2-1
Shamrock Rovers FC	0-1	1-0	1-2	0-2	1-2	1-3	3-1	0-0	0-4	1-0	■	2-3	0-2	0-2
Shelbourne FC	1-1	3-0	1-1	1-0	1-1	3-2	2-2	1-0	0-1	2-0	1-3	■	1-1	1-6
Sligo Rovers FC	1-0	2-1	1-2	2-1	3-1	4-2	2-1	5-1	1-0	1-2	3-1	1-0	■	0-0
Waterford AFC	0-0	1-1	1-1	1-0	1-1	2-1	1-0	2-0	1-1	2-2	3-0	1-1	2-1	■

	Division "A"	Pd	Wn	Dw	Ls	GF	GA	Pts
1.	SLIGI ROVERS FC (SLIGO)	26	18	3	5	48	20	39
2.	Bohemian FC (Dublin)	26	17	4	5	50	29	38
3.	Drogheda United FC (Drogheda)	26	12	10	4	56	34	34
4.	Waterford AFC (Waterford)	26	12	9	5	42	28	33
5.	Dundalk FC (Dundalk)	26	12	5	9	51	42	29
6.	St. Patrick's Athletic FC (Dublin)	26	9	10	7	30	27	28
7.	Shelbourne FC (Dublin)	26	10	8	8	39	40	28
8.	Finn Harps FC (Ballybofey)	26	9	8	9	40	45	26
9.	Cork Celtic FC (Cork)	26	10	5	11	48	44	25
10.	Athlone Town AFC (Athlone)	26	8	7	11	43	46	23
11.	Shamrock Rovers FC (Dublin)	26	7	3	16	26	46	17
12.	Limerick AFC (Limerick)	26	5	6	15	29	47	16
13.	Albert Rovers FC (Cork)	26	5	6	15	21	42	16 *
14.	Home Farm FC (Dublin)	26	4	4	18	22	55	12
		364	138	88	138	545	545	364

Top goal-scorers 1976-77

1) Sydney WALLACE (Waterford AFC) 16
2) Turlough O'CONNOR (Bohemian FC) 15
3) Gary HULMES (Sligo Rovers FC) 13
   Paul McGEE (Sligo Rovers FC) 13

Note: The matches Albert Rovers 0-0 St. Patrick's Athletic on 27/02/1977 and Sligo Rovers FC 0-0 Waterford AFC on 09/01/1977 were abandoned but the result of both at the time of abandonment was allowed to stand.

* Albert Rovers FC (Cork) changed their club name to Cork Albert FC (Cork) for next season.

Elected: Galway Rovers FC (Galway), Thurles Town FC (Thurles)

The league was extended to 16 clubs for next season

FAI Cup Final (Dalymount Park, Dublin – 01/05/1977 – 17,000)

DUNDALK FC (DUNDALK)   2-0   Limerick AFC (Limerick)

Flanagan 2   (H.T. 1-0)

Dundalk: Blackmore, B.McConville, McManus, T.McConville, McLaughlin, Braddish, McDowell, Dainty, Mick Lawlor, Flanagan, Cananagh.

Limerick: Fitzpatrick, Nolan, Fitzgerald, O'Mahoney, Herick, Deacy, Meaney, Walsh (Lymer), Kennedy, Duggan, Kirby.

Semi-Finals

Dundalk FC (Dundalk)	1-1, 1-0	St. Patrick's Athletic FC (Dublin)
Limerick AFC (Limerick)	0-0, 1-1, 2-1	Drogheda United FC (Drogheda)

Quarter-Finals

Bohemian FC (Dublin)	1-1, 0-1	St. Patrick's Athletic FC (Dublin)
Cork Celtic FC (Cork)	0-1	Dundalk FC (Dundalk)
Drogheda United FC (Drogheda)	1-1, 3-2	Shelbourne FC (Dublin)
Limerick AFC (Limerick)	0-0, 1-0	Waterford AFC (Waterford)

1977-78

League of Ireland Division "A" 1977-78	Athlone Town	Bohemian FC	Cork Alberts FC	Cork Celtic FC	Drogheda Utd.	Dundalk FC	Finn Harps FC	Galway Rovers	Home Farm FC	Limerick AFC	St. Patrick's Ath.	Shamrock Rov.	Shelbourne FC	Sligo Rovers FC	Thurles Town	Waterford AFC
Athlone Town AFC	■	2-2	2-1	2-2	2-0	1-0	1-2	0-0	4-2	1-1	2-2	2-2	3-3	1-2	2-1	1-3
Bohemian FC	0-0	■	6-0	3-1	2-0	7-2	3-0	3-0	4-0	0-0	3-2	3-0	0-0	2-0	0-0	7-3
Cork Alberts FC	3-1	1-1	■	1-1	1-2	3-0	1-0	0-0	3-0	0-0	1-0	0-0	2-2	0-1	1-0	1-2
Cork Celtic FC	1-3	0-3	0-0	■	1-4	0-0	1-3	2-0	1-0	2-0	1-3	2-6	1-1	1-3	2-0	2-2
Drogheda United FC	2-1	1-1	3-1	3-0	■	0-0	3-0	4-0	4-1	0-0	2-1	0-0	2-1	1-1	1-1	2-0
Dundalk FC	0-2	2-2	1-3	2-3	1-1	■	0-4	2-0	0-0	2-0	1-0	0-1	6-2	0-1	3-0	4-0
Finn Harps FC	2-0	3-0	0-1	7-4	3-3	4-2	■	3-1	1-3	1-0	2-0	0-0	1-0	2-1	0-0	1-2
Galway Rovers FC	3-2	0-0	0-4	1-1	0-1	1-1	2-3	■	1-2	1-1	0-0	1-4	1-1	1-1	2-1	0-3
Home Farm FC	1-1	0-8	2-0	0-0	0-2	1-1	0-1	2-0	■	0-1	1-0	0-0	2-1	2-3	3-1	0-1
Limerick AFC	1-0	3-4	1-0	3-2	1-0	2-2	4-2	0-0	1-3	■	2-0	1-1	3-0	0-0	3-0	2-2
St. Patrick's Athletic	2-0	2-0	2-0	2-1	1-1	1-2	0-3	4-0	1-1	1-0	■	1-0	1-2	0-0	2-1	2-1
Shamrock Rovers FC	1-1	0-0	2-1	4-0	2-2	2-0	0-1	2-0	4-1	1-0	2-1	■	4-1	2-1	2-1	1-1
Shelbourne FC	0-3	1-2	1-0	0-0	0-4	1-1	3-4	1-0	3-0	0-0	1-1	0-0	■	0-0	2-0	0-2
Sligo Rovers FC	0-1	1-5	2-2	1-1	1-0	0-1	1-2	4-0	4-1	3-0	1-0	0-0	3-0	■	6-2	0-1
Thurles Town FC	0-0	1-0	3-4	0-1	1-3	2-6	1-4	0-1	1-1	1-6	1-1	0-2	1-5	1-5	■	1-1
Waterford AFC	1-2	0-3	0-1	1-0	3-2	2-1	1-1	1-0	4-1	0-0	3-1	1-0	3-0	2-1	0-0	■

	Division "A"	Pd	Wn	Dw	Ls	GF	GA	Pts	
1.	BOHEMIAN FC (DUBLIN)	30	17	10	3	74	35	44	
2.	Finn Harps FC (Ballybofey)	30	19	4	7	60	38	42	
3.	Drogheda United FC (Drogheda)	30	15	10	5	53	27	40	
4.	Shamrock Rovers FC (Dublin)	30	14	12	4	45	22	40	
5.	Waterford AFC (Waterford)	30	16	7	7	46	37	39	
6.	Sligo Rovers FC (Sligo)	30	13	8	9	47	31	34	
7.	Limerick AFC (Limerick)	30	10	12	8	36	29	32	
8.	Athlone Town AFC (Athlone)	30	10	11	9	43	40	31	
9.	Cork Alberts FC (Cork)	30	11	8	11	36	35	30	*
10.	St. Patrick's Athletic FC (Dublin)	30	10	7	13	34	35	27	
11.	Dundalk FC (Dundalk)	30	9	9	12	43	46	27	
12.	Shelbourne FC (Dublin)	30	6	11	13	32	50	23	
13.	Home Farm FC (Dublin)	30	8	7	15	30	56	23	
14.	Cork Celtic FC (Cork)	30	6	10	14	34	58	22	
15.	Galway Rovers FC (Galway)	30	3	10	17	16	53	16	
16.	Thurles Town FC (Thurles)	30	1	8	21	22	69	10	
		480	168	144	168	651	651	480	

Top goal-scorers 1977-78

1) Turlough O'CONNOR   (Bohemian FC)   24
2) Cathal MUCKIAN   (Drogheda United FC) 21
3) Sydney WALLACE   (Waterford AFC)   18

* Albert Rovers FC (Cork) had changed their name pre-season to Cork Albert FC (Cork) but in October 1977 changed again. This time their name was changed to Cork Alberts FC (Cork) (i.e. an added 's' was added to Albert).

FAI Cup Final   (Dalymount Park, Dublin – 30/04/1978 – 12,500)

SHAMROCK ROVERS FC (DUBLIN)   1-0   Sligo Rovers FC (Sligo)
Treacy pen.   *(H.T. 0-0)*

Shamrock Rovers: O'Neill, Gannon (O'Sullivan) O'Leary, Synnott, Fullam, Dunphy, Giles, Meagan, Murray, Treacy, Lynex.

Sligo Rovers: Patterson, Fielding, Rutherford, Stenson, Fox, Gilligan, Fagan, Tobin, Cavanagh, Hulmes, Delamere (McLoughlin).

Semi-Finals

Shamrock Rovers FC (Dublin)	2-1	Waterford AFC (Waterford)
Sligo Rovers FC (Sligo)	1-0	Drogheda United FC (Drogheda)

Quarter-Finals

Cork Alberts FC (Cork)	1-2	Sligo Rovers FC (Sligo)
Drogheda United FC (Drogheda)	1-0	Limerick AFC (Limerick)
Dundalk FC (Dundalk)	0-0, 0-1	Shamrock Rovers FC (Dublin)
Home Farm FC (Dublin)	0-2	Waterford AFC (Waterford)

1978-79

League of Ireland Division "A" 1978-79	Athlone Town	Bohemian FC	Cork Alberts FC	Cork Celtic FC	Drogheda United	Dundalk FC	Finn Harps FC	Galway Rovers FC	Home Farm FC	Limerick AFC	St. Patrick's Ath.	Shamrock Rovers	Shelbourne FC	Sligo Rovers FC	Thurles Town FC	Waterford AFC
Athlone Town AFC	■	1-0	2-1	2-0	1-2	2-2	2-0	2-2	2-2	0-1	3-0	2-0	4-1	1-3	6-2	3-1
Bohemian FC	1-0	■	2-0	6-0	3-3	0-0	2-0	3-1	1-1	1-0	3-0	0-1	2-1	2-1	2-2	1-0
Cork Alberts FC	0-0	1-2	■	6-1	1-3	1-1	1-3	3-2	1-1	0-1	0-0	0-3	2-5	0-0	1-0	2-2
Cork Celtic FC	1-2	1-0	1-0	■	0-2	0-3	0-2	2-2	0-2	0-0	0-2	0-2	2-2	1-2	0-1	0-1
Drogheda United FC	1-1	2-4	5-1	0-0	■	1-0	0-1	6-2	2-1	2-1	4-3	2-0	3-0	1-1	3-1	2-2
Dundalk FC	3-0	1-0	3-0	2-0	1-0	■	1-1	2-1	2-0	2-0	5-1	3-2	3-1	1-1	4-1	0-3
Finn Harps FC	2-3	1-3	2-0	4-0	0-2	2-1	■	4-1	4-1	2-5	1-1	2-1	2-2	1-0	3-3	3-1
Galway Rovers FC	0-4	2-6	2-1	2-1	0-1	2-2	2-3	■	1-6	1-4	1-0	0-2	4-2	1-2	2-2	1-1
Home Farm FC	4-1	2-1	0-1	2-2	4-1	0-1	1-0	2-1	■	2-0	3-0	0-0	2-1	2-1	1-2	0-1
Limerick AFC	1-1	0-0	2-2	5-1	1-1	0-2	0-0	3-1	1-0	■	1-1	0-0	1-0	0-1	2-1	1-1
St. Patrick's Athletic	4-1	0-3	0-3	4-1	1-3	2-2	0-3	3-2	1-1	0-1	■	1-2	1-4	1-0	3-1	3-0
Shamrock Rovers FC	2-1	0-1	2-3	4-0	2-1	1-2	4-0	3-0	2-1	2-1	2-0	■	1-0	4-0	1-2	0-1
Shelbourne FC	2-2	0-0	1-1	3-1	1-2	0-3	1-3	2-1	0-2	0-4	3-1	0-0	■	1-1	1-1	2-2
Sligo Rovers FC	0-1	0-2	1-1	3-0	2-4	1-2	2-1	2-1	0-0	0-1	2-0	0-1	1-2	■	2-0	3-4
Thurles Town FC	0-5	0-2	0-1	0-1	2-1	1-3	0-5	2-1	3-2	0-2	2-2	0-1	4-2	2-1	■	0-1
Waterford AFC	3-1	0-0	2-1	1-0	3-0	1-0	1-1	3-2	0-2	1-0	5-1	2-0	2-1	2-2	1-0	■

	Division "A"	Pd	Wn	Dw	Ls	GF	GA	Pts	
1.	DUNDALK FC (DUNDALK)	30	19	7	4	57	25	45	
2.	Bohemian FC (Dublin)	30	18	7	5	53	21	43	
3.	Drogheda United FC (Drogheda)	30	17	6	7	60	40	42	+2
4.	Waterford AFC (Waterford)	30	17	8	5	48	32	42	
5.	Shamrock Rovers FC (Dublin)	30	17	3	10	45	25	37	
6.	Limerick AFC (Limerick)	30	13	9	8	39	25	36	+1
7.	Athlone Town AFC (Athlone)	30	14	7	9	56	41	35	
8.	Finn Harps FC (Ballybofey)	30	15	6	9	56	41	34	-2
9.	Home Farm FC (Dublin)	30	13	7	10	47	33	33	
10.	Sligo Rovers FC (Sligo)	30	9	7	14	35	40	25	
11.	Cork Alberts FC (Cork)	30	7	9	14	35	49	23	*
12.	Thurles Town FC (Thurles)	30	8	5	17	35	62	23	+2
13.	Shelbourne FC (Dublin)	30	6	9	15	41	58	21	
14.	St. Patrick's Athletic FC (Dublin)	30	7	6	17	36	62	20	
15.	Galway Rovers FC (Galway)	30	4	5	21	41	79	13	
16.	Cork Celtic FC (Cork)	30	3	5	22	16	67	8	-3#
		480	187	106	187	700	700	480	

Top goal-scorers 1978-79

1) John DELAMERE   (Shelbourne FC/Sligo Rovers FC)   17
2) Hilary CARLYLE   (Dundalk FC)   16
3) Turlough O'CONNOR (Bohemian FC)   15

Note: After the matches Cork Celtic 0-0 Limerick, Drogheda United 0-1 Finn Harps and Thurles Town 0-1 Cork Celtic the League of Ireland awarded 1 point to Limerick from Cork Celtic and 2 points to Drogheda United and Thurles Town from Finn Harps and Cork Celtic respectively.

\# Cork Celtic FC (Cork) resigned from the league at the end of the season and disbanded.

* Cork Alberts FC (Cork) changed their club name to Cork United FC (Cork) for next season.

Limerick AFC (Limerick) changed their club name to Limerick United FC (Limerick) for next season.

Elected: University College Dublin AFC (Dublin)

FAI Cup Final   (Dalymount Park, Dublin – 22/04/1979 – 14,000)

DUNDALK FC (DUNDALK)   2-0   Waterford AFC (Waterford)

Byrne, Carlyle   *(H.T. 1-0)*

Dundalk: Blackmore, T.McConville, Keely, Dunning, Martin, Lawlor, Flanagan, Mick Lawlor, Byrne, Dainty, Carlyle, Muckian,

Waterford: Thomas, O'Mahoney, Dunphy, Finucane, Gardiner, Madigan, Jackson, McCarthy, Smith, Wallace, Matthews.

Semi-Finals

Dundalk FC (Dundalk)	2-1	Cork Alberts FC (Cork)
Waterford AFC (Waterford)	2-1	Shamrock Rovers FC (Dublin)

Quarter-Finals

Drogheda United FC (Drogheda)	1-1, 0-2	Cork Alberts FC (Cork)
Dundalk FC (Dundalk)	2-0	Finn Harps FC (Ballybofey)
Galway Rovers FC (Galway)	0-1	Waterford AFC (Waterford)
Shamrock Rovers FC (Dublin)	2-0	Limerick AFC (Limerick)

1979-80

League of Ireland Division "A" 1979-80	Athlone Town AFC	Bohemian FC	Cork United FC	Drogheda United FC	Dundalk FC	Finn Harps FC	Galway Rovers FC	Home Farm FC	Limerick AFC	St. Patrick's Athletic	Shamrock Rovers	Shelbourne FC	Sligo Rovers FC	Thurles Town FC	University College	Waterford AFC
Athlone Town AFC	■	2-1	2-1	4-0	0-1	0-1	6-0	2-0	1-1	1-0	4-1	3-0	0-2	3-0	6-0	0-0
Bohemian FC	3-3	■	1-0	1-1	1-0	4-0	0-0	1-2	1-0	0-0	0-2	4-1	0-0	1-0	3-0	0-2
Cork United FC	2-1	0-3	■	1-2	0-4	1-3	2-0	0-1	1-1	2-1	1-1	4-3	0-1	1-3	1-2	0-0
Drogheda United FC	1-2	3-1	2-0	■	0-2	2-3	0-0	1-2	1-4	0-3	1-1	2-2	1-1	1-1	1-2	1-1
Dundalk FC	1-0	1-0	3-0	1-1	■	0-1	7-2	0-0	1-0	3-0	1-0	9-0	3-2	2-0	6-0	0-0
Finn Harps FC	1-2	0-2	2-0	0-1	0-0	■	2-0	4-3	2-3	1-1	0-0	6-0	2-1	2-0	2-1	3-1
Galway Rovers FC	1-0	1-1	1-0	1-1	0-2	1-3	■	0-1	0-2	2-0	1-2	3-5	2-0	0-1	1-0	2-2
Home Farm FC	0-3	1-1	0-1	2-2	1-1	0-0	1-2	■	0-1	2-0	2-0	1-0	0-1	1-0	0-1	1-5
Limerick United FC	0-0	1-0	4-1	1-1	2-0	1-0	1-0	4-0	■	0-0	2-1	4-0	3-1	5-0	2-0	1-1
St. Patrick's Athletic	1-1	1-4	1-0	0-2	0-1	1-4	0-1	3-1	2-1	■	3-3	2-0	4-5	4-1	1-1	1-1
Shamrock Rovers FC	0-1	1-1	6-0	1-1	1-1	2-0	2-0	3-0	1-2	3-1	■	5-0	4-0	1-1	7-1	2-1
Shelbourne FC	1-4	0-1	1-0	1-4	0-3	1-2	2-4	0-2	1-4	1-2	0-0	■	1-1	1-1	4-1	1-1
Sligo Rovers FC	3-3	2-1	3-1	1-1	0-1	1-0	2-2	1-0	2-3	1-2	1-6	1-0	■	2-2	0-0	1-0
Thurles Town FC	0-0	3-1	3-0	0-0	0-2	1-1	1-2	3-1	3-3	2-3	1-2	3-2	2-2	■	3-1	4-2
University College Dublin	0-5	1-4	1-2	1-1	0-3	2-3	1-2	0-2	0-7	1-1	1-2	5-1	1-0	0-2	■	0-1
Waterford AFC	2-1	2-1	0-0	1-1	2-0	1-1	0-1	2-0	3-4	1-1	1-1	1-1	0-2	2-2	2-0	■

	Division "A"	Pd	Wn	Dw	Ls	GF	GA	Pts
1.	LIMERICK UNITED FC (LIMERICK)	30	20	7	3	67	24	47
2.	Dundalk FC (Dundalk)	30	20	6	4	59	13	46
3.	Athlone Town AFC (Athlone)	30	16	7	7	60	24	39
4.	Shamrock Rovers FC (Dublin)	30	14	10	6	61	29	38
5.	Finn Harps FC (Ballybofey)	30	16	6	8	49	33	38
6.	Bohemian FC (Dublin)	30	12	8	10	42	30	32
7.	Waterford AFC (Waterford)	30	8	15	7	38	33	31
8.	Sligo Rovers FC (Sligo)	30	11	9	10	40	45	31
9.	Thurles Town FC (Thurles)	30	9	10	11	43	48	28
10.	Drogheda United FC (Drogheda)	30	6	16	8	36	41	28
11.	Galway Rovers FC (Galway)	30	11	6	13	32	47	28
12.	St. Patrick's Athletic FC (Dublin)	30	9	9	12	39	46	27
13.	Home Farm FC (Dublin)	30	10	5	15	27	42	25
14.	Cork United FC (Cork)	30	6	4	20	22	56	16
15.	University College Dublin AFC (Dublin)	30	5	4	21	24	75	14
16.	Shelbourne FC (Dublin)	30	3	6	21	30	83	12
		480	176	128	176	669	669	480

Top goal-scorers 1979-80

1)	Alan CAMPBELL	(Shamrock Rovers FC)	22
2)	Anthony MORRIS	(Limerick United FC)	19
3)	Neville STEEDMAN	(Thurles Town FC)	17

FAI Cup Final   (Dalymount Park, Dublin – 20/04/1980 – 18,000)

WATERFORD AFC (WATERFORD)   1-0   St. Patrick's Athletic FC (Dublin)
Gardiner   *(H.T. 1-0)*

Waterford: Thomas, O'Mahoney, Dunphy, Finucane, Gardiner, Meagan, Madigan, McCarthy (Jackson), Murray, Wallace (Coady), Kirk.

St. Patrick's Athletic: Grace, Higgins, Roche, Murphy, Munnelly (Daly), O'Donnell, Malone, Hynes, Carthy (Wright), Jameson, Kirwan.

Semi-Finals

St. Patrick's Athletic FC (Dublin)	1-0	Bohemian FC (Dublin)
Waterford AFC (Waterford)	1-1, 3-2	Limerick United FC (Limerick)

Quarter-Finals

Bohemian FC (Dublin)	2-1	Galway Rovers FC (Galway)
Dundalk FC (Dundalk)	0-1	Limerick United FC (Limerick)
St. Patrick's Athletic FC (Dublin)	1-1, 2-1	Home Farm FC (Dublin)
Waterford AFC (Waterford)	1-0	Athlone Town AFC (Athlone)

1980-81

League of Ireland Division "A" 1980-81	Athlone Town AFC	Bohemian FC	Cork United FC	Drogheda United FC	Dundalk FC	Finn Harps FC	Galway Rovers FC	Home Farm FC	Limerick AFC	St. Patrick's Athletic FC	Shamrock Rovers FC	Shelbourne FC	Sligo Rovers FC	Thurles Town FC	University College Dublin	Waterford AFC
Athlone Town AFC	■	1-1	5-1	5-1	2-1	3-2	2-0	2-1	0-0	2-0	1-1	2-0	3-1	3-2	4-1	2-0
Bohemian FC	1-1	■	1-1	1-1	1-1	2-2	1-0	0-0	1-1	0-0	0-0	0-2	5-0	2-0	1-1	0-1
Cork United FC	1-1	2-1	■	2-1	1-1	0-1	1-0	0-2	0-2	1-1	0-0	3-0	1-2	0-1	1-0	0-1
Drogheda United FC	2-3	2-2	4-1	■	1-1	3-1	2-3	1-1	1-0	2-5	2-0	1-1	3-1	1-3	1-3	1-3
Dundalk FC	0-3	1-2	3-0	5-2	■	2-0	3-1	3-2	0-1	3-1	2-1	2-1	1-0	6-1	3-0	3-0
Finn Harps FC	0-1	0-1	1-0	0-0	1-2	■	3-2	6-2	0-2	2-1	2-0	1-0	2-1	1-0	2-0	1-2
Galway Rovers FC	0-2	0-0	0-1	0-1	1-1	1-1	■	0-1	1-2	1-0	0-1	2-0	2-2	1-1	0-1	0-0
Home Farm FC	2-1	1-0	1-3	0-1	0-4	0-2	2-3	■	1-2	0-1	0-1	1-1	1-3	2-2	1-0	2-4
Limerick United FC	0-2	0-0	1-3	3-0	0-0	0-0	0-0	2-1	■	2-0	1-2	3-1	2-1	2-1	4-1	0-0
St. Patrick's Athletic	0-1	3-3	2-6	0-3	3-1	4-3	2-3	2-1	0-2	■	1-0	6-0	2-2	2-0	1-1	2-0
Shamrock Rovers FC	0-3	2-2	2-0	1-2	1-2	2-1	1-2	2-0	2-1	1-1	■	1-0	4-2	2-1	0-0	1-0
Shelbourne FC	1-4	1-2	2-3	2-5	0-2	4-1	0-0	1-1	2-0	1-0	0-2	■	3-0	3-0	2-2	1-1
Sligo Rovers FC	1-0	0-1	2-1	2-0	0-3	0-3	3-1	3-4	0-2	1-3	0-3	1-0	■	3-1	4-1	2-1
Thurles Town FC	0-3	0-3	0-2	1-0	1-4	3-1	2-1	1-3	3-5	5-0	2-3	1-0	2-5	■	1-1	0-1
University College Dublin	1-2	1-2	3-1	2-2	0-1	1-1	2-0	3-0	0-4	2-1	0-0	4-2	1-3	3-3	■	0-1
Waterford AFC	1-3	0-2	1-1	3-1	1-2	1-1	1-1	1-1	2-3	0-2	1-1	1-0	1-0	2-0	1-2	■

	Division "A"	Pd	Wn	Dw	Ls	GF	GA	Pts
1.	ATHLONE TOWN AFC (ATHLONE)	30	23	5	2	67	22	51
2.	Dundalk FC (Dundalk)	30	20	5	5	63	28	45
3.	Limerick United FC (Limerick)	30	17	7	6	47	25	41
4.	Bohemian FC (Dublin)	30	10	16	4	38	25	36
5.	Shamrock Rovers FC (Dublin)	30	14	8	8	37	29	36
6.	Finn Harps FC (Ballybofey)	30	12	6	12	41	39	30
7.	Waterford AFC (Waterford)	30	11	8	11	32	35	30
8.	St. Patrick's Athletic FC (Dublin)	30	11	6	13	45	48	28
9.	Cork United FC (Cork)	30	11	6	13	37	42	28
10.	Drogheda United FC (Drogheda)	30	10	7	13	47	55	27
11.	Sligo Rovers FC (Sligo)	30	12	2	16	45	57	26
12.	University College Dublin AFC (Dublin)	30	8	9	13	37	49	25
13.	Galway Rovers FC (Galway)	30	6	9	15	26	39	21 *
14.	Home Farm FC (Dublin)	30	7	6	17	34	55	20
15.	Shelbourne FC (Dublin)	30	6	6	18	31	52	18
16.	Thurles Town FC (Thurles)	30	7	4	19	38	65	18
		480	185	110	185	665	665	480

Top goal-scorers 1980-81

1) Eugene DAVIS   (Athlone Town AFC)   23
2) Brendan BRADLEY   (Sligo Rovers FC)   18
3) Michael FAIRCLOUGH (Dundalk FC)   16
   Michael O'CONNOR   (Athlone Town AFC)   16

* Galway Rovers FC (Galway) changed their club name to Galway United FC (Galway) for next season.

The points system was changed for next season to:

Away win = 4 points • Home win = 3 points • Away draw = 2 points • Home draw = 1 point • Defeat = 0 points

FAI Cup Final   (Dalymount Park, Dublin – 26/04/1981 – 12,000)

DUNDALK FC (DUNDALK)	2-0	Sligo Rovers FC (Sligo)
Archibold, Fairclough	*(H.T. 0-0)*	

Dundalk: Blackmore, T.McConville, Keely, Dunning, Martin Lawlor (O'Doherty), Byrne, Flanagan, McKenna, Archibold, Fairclough, Crawley (Duff).

Sligo Rovers: McIntyre, Ferry, Sheridan, O'Doherty (McDonnell), McGeever, McGroarty, Fagan, Doherty, McLoughlin, Bradley, Patton (Coyle).

Semi-Finals

Dundalk FC (Dundalk)	1-0	Finn Harps FC (Ballybofey)
Sligo Rovers FC (Sligo)	2-2, 1-0	Waterford AFC (Waterford)

Quarter-Finals

Cobh Ramblers FC (Cobh)	1-4	Finn Harps FC (Ballybofey)
Drogheda United FC (Drogheda)	0-0, 0-1	Dundalk FC (Dundalk)
Limerick United FC (Limerick)	1-1, 1-3	Waterford AFC (Waterford)
Sligo Rovers FC (Sligo)	3-0	Home Farm FC (Dublin)

1981-82

League of Ireland Division "A" 1981-82	Athlone Town AFC	Bohemian FC	Cork United FC	Drogheda United FC	Dundalk FC	Finn Harps FC	Galway United FC	Home Farm FC	Limerick AFC	St. Patrick's Athletic FC	Shamrock Rovers FC	Shelbourne FC	Sligo Rovers FC	Thurles Town FC	University College Dublin	Waterford AFC
Athlone Town AFC	■	1-2	3-1	1-0	1-2	2-0	4-0	1-1	1-2	2-1	2-0	3-0	1-3	8-0	2-2	4-0
Bohemian FC	1-0	■	0-1	3-0	0-0	3-1	4-1	0-0	0-0	3-0	3-1	2-1	1-1	4-0	1-1	2-0
Cork United FC	2-3	2-1	■	5-1	0-2	0-1	1-0	5-2	1-0	2-2	1-0	1-1	1-3	2-0	1-0	1-3
Drogheda United FC	1-4	0-0	3-2	■	1-1	4-0	2-2	3-1	2-2	0-1	0-1	1-1	6-1	6-1	2-0	1-2
Dundalk FC	7-1	1-4	3-0	5-1	■	3-0	4-0	2-1	1-0	2-0	0-1	0-3	1-0	3-0	2-0	3-1
Finn Harps FC	2-4	1-3	3-0	1-2	0-2	■	1-2	2-3	0-1	3-2	0-2	0-2	1-2	5-1	3-1	0-0
Galway United FC	1-4	0-0	1-0	1-1	1-2	3-0	■	0-1	0-3	1-2	1-3	1-1	0-0	3-7	0-2	3-0
Home Farm FC	0-4	0-1	1-1	3-0	2-3	4-1	3-3	■	0-0	0-4	0-2	0-1	1-2	0-2	1-0	1-2
Limerick United FC	2-2	0-1	1-0	3-1	2-4	2-2	2-0	0-0	■	2-0	2-1	4-3	7-1	6-0	2-2	1-3
St. Patrick's Athletic	3-2	0-0	1-3	1-1	0-1	2-1	1-1	2-0	1-0	■	3-0	2-1	2-3	4-1	1-0	3-1
Shamrock Rovers FC	0-3	2-1	4-1	1-0	1-1	3-1	4-0	1-0	1-1	2-0	■	1-0	1-0	7-0	1-0	2-1
Shelbourne FC	3-1	0-2	2-0	2-2	0-3	1-1	5-2	3-3	0-3	0-2	1-2	■	1-4	2-2	3-0	2-0
Sligo Rovers FC	3-0	0-2	3-3	1-1	2-1	5-1	1-0	2-3	1-1	2-1	0-1	1-0	■	2-0	4-1	1-0
Thurles Town FC	2-3	1-4	1-1	2-3	0-0	0-7	1-1	0-2	0-3	1-4	0-3	1-2	4-3	■	0-2	0-2
University College Dublin	1-2	1-1	2-0	0-0	1-1	1-1	0-1	1-0	3-2	2-2	1-1	1-0	1-3	2-2	■	0-1
Waterford AFC	0-1	2-1	3-3	2-0	1-1	1-3	3-1	0-1	3-2	2-2	0-1	1-3	2-1	2-0	1-2	■

	Division "A"	Pd	AW	HW	AD	HD	Ls	GF	GA	Pts	
1.	DUNDALK FC (DUNDALK)	30	8	12	6	-	4	61	24	80	
2.	Shamrock Rovers FC (Dublin)	30	9	12	1	2	6	50	23	76	
3.	Bohemian FC (Dublin)	30	8	9	4	5	4	50	18	72	
4.	Athlone Town AFC (Athlone)	30	9	9	1	2	9	70	42	67	
5.	Sligo Rovers FC (Sligo)	30	7	9	2	3	9	55	45	62	
6.	Limerick United FC (Limerick)	30	5	8	5	4	8	56	34	58	
7.	St. Patrick's Athletic FC (Dublin)	30	5	9	3	3	10	49	39	56	
8.	Waterford AFC (Waterford)	30	6	6	1	3	14	39	46	47	*
9.	Shelbourne FC (Dublin)	30	5	5	3	4	13	44	46	45	
10.	Cork United FC (Cork)	30	2	8	4	2	14	41	50	42	#
11.	Drogheda United FC (Drogheda)	30	2	6	5	5	12	45	50	41	
12.	Home Farm FC (Dublin)	30	5	3	4	3	15	34	48	40	
13.	University College Dublin AFC (Dublin)	30	3	4	3	7	13	30	41	37	
14.	Finn Harps FC (Ballybofey)	30	3	4	3	1	19	42	61	31	
15.	Galway United FC (Galway)	30	2	3	4	4	17	30	62	29	
16.	Thurles Town FC (Thurles)	30	2	1	2	3	22	29	96	18	#
		480	81	108	51	51	189	725	725	801	

Top goal-scorers 1981-82

1) Michael O'CONNOR   (Athlone Town AFC)   22
2) Liam BUCKLEY   (Shamrock Rovers FC)   21
3) Gus GILLIGAN   (Sligo Rovers FC)   16
   Jim MAHON   (St. Patrick's Athletic FC) 16

* Waterford AFC (Waterford) changed their club name to Waterford United FC (Waterford) for next season.

\# Cork United FC (Cork) were expelled from the league, the club was then dissolved. Thurles Town FC (Thurles) resigned from the league.

The league was reduced to 14 clubs for next season.

FAI Cup Final   (Dalymount Park, Dublin – 02/05/1982 – 12,000)

LIMERICK UNITED FC (LIMERICK)	1-0	Bohemian FC (Dublin)

Storan

Limerick United: Fitzpatrick, Nolan, Storan, O'Mahoney, Finucane, Hand (Douglas), Nodwell, Walsh, Ward, Gaynor, Hulmes (Kennedy)

Bohemian: O'Neill, Connell, McDonagh, McCormack, Lawless, Doolin, Kelly (Reynor), Kinsella), King, O'Brien, Jameson, Shelly.

Semi-Finals

Bohemian FC (Dublin)	3-3, 0-0, 1-1, 2-1	Dundalk FC (Dundalk)
Limerick United FC (Limerick)	1-1, 1-0	Athlone Town AFC (Athlone)

Quarter-Finals

Athlone Town AFC (Athlone)	1-0	Shamrock Rovers FC (Dublin)
Dundalk FC (Dundalk)	2-0	Galway United FC (Galway)
Limerick United FC (Limerick)	4-0	Aer Lingus FC (Dublin)
University College Dublin AFC (Dublin)	1-2	Bohemian FC (Dublin)

1982-83

League of Ireland Division "A" 1982-83	Athlone Town AFC	Bohemian FC	Drogheda United FC	Dundalk FC	Finn Harps FC	Galway United FC	Home Farm FC	Limerick AFC	St. Patrick's Athletic	Shamrock Rovers FC	Shelbourne FC	Sligo Rovers FC	University College	Waterford AFC
Athlone Town AFC		3-1	2-1	2-0	3-0	4-1	3-1	2-0	3-1	2-1	2-1	4-1	5-2	4-0
Bohemian FC	0-1		0-2	0-0	1-0	2-1	1-0	1-1	1-2	3-2	4-2	2-2	2-0	2-1
Drogheda United FC	0-1	1-1		3-1	0-0	2-1	5-0	1-2	5-1	0-0	1-0	0-1	2-0	3-1
Dundalk FC	0-1	0-0	1-0		1-2	2-2	2-0	1-0	1-0	0-0	2-0	1-0	3-0	2-1
Finn Harps FC	3-3	0-0	2-3	0-1		2-4	2-0	1-1	1-1	0-1	1-0	1-1	5-1	0-1
Galway United FC	1-1	3-2	0-1	0-5	2-3		1-1	1-3	0-1	1-0	2-3	0-0	1-2	1-3
Home Farm FC	1-4	0-2	0-4	0-1	1-3	1-3		2-1	0-2	1-3	3-4	1-2	4-3	1-2
Limerick United FC	0-2	0-2	0-0	0-1	4-3	1-1	5-0		1-2	2-0	5-1	4-0	3-1	1-2
St. Patrick's Athletic FC	1-2	0-3	1-3	1-2	2-1	3-0	1-1	1-1		1-0	1-2	3-1	1-0	1-1
Shamrock Rovers FC	1-1	3-0	0-1	2-1	0-1	0-2	2-1	4-0	1-1		6-1	3-1	1-0	4-0
Shelbourne FC	4-1	1-1	0-2	2-0	1-1	0-0	3-1	4-3	1-0	2-2		4-3	1-0	5-2
Sligo Rovers FC	2-2	0-2	1-1	1-1	0-2	1-4	3-1	1-0	3-3	0-0	0-0		1-2	2-4
University College Dublin	0-2	1-4	1-1	0-3	1-1	1-1	5-2	0-3	2-5	2-2	2-5	2-0		1-3
Waterford United FC	1-1	0-5	1-1	0-0	0-1	0-0	1-1	1-2	2-2	1-1	0-3	1-0	2-0	

	Division "A"	Pd	Wn	Dw	Ls	GF	GA	Pts	
1.	ATHLONE TOWN AFC (ATHLONE)	26	20	5	1	61	24	65	
2.	Drogheda United FC (Drogheda)	26	14	7	5	43	18	49	
3.	Dundalk FC (Dundalk)	26	14	6	6	32	17	48	
4.	Bohemian FC (Dublin)	26	13	7	6	42	26	46	
5.	Shelbourne FC (Dublin)	26	13	5	8	50	45	44	
6.	Shamrock Rovers FC (Dublin)	26	10	8	8	39	25	38	
7.	St. Patrick's Athletic FC (Dublin)	26	10	7	8	38	38	37	
8.	Limerick United FC (Limerick)	26	10	5	11	43	35	35	#
9.	Finn Harps FC (Ballybofey)	26	9	8	9	36	33	35	
10.	Waterford United FC (Waterford)	26	8	8	10	31	44	32	
11.	Galway United FC (Galway)	26	6	8	12	33	44	26	
12.	Sligo Rovers FC (Sligo)	26	4	9	13	27	48	21	
13.	University College Dublin AFC (Dublin)	26	4	4	18	29	63	16	
14.	Home Farm FC (Dublin)	26	2	3	21	24	68	9	
		364	137	90	137	528	528	501	

Top goal-scorers 1982-83

1) Noel LARKIN   (Athlone Town AFC)   18
2) Brendan BRADLEY   (Finn Harps FC)   17
   Kieran McCABE   (Shelbourne FC)   17

Win = 3 points • Draw = 1 point • Defeat = 0 points

* Some members of Limerick United FC (Limerick) broke away from the club and formed a new club under the name of Limerick City FC (Limerick). After much wrangling between the 2 clubs which eventually ended in the High Court, Limerick City FC were elected to the league in place of Limerick United FC which resulted in the older club being wound up and dissolved.

FAI Cup Final (Dalymount Park, Dublin – 24/04/1983 – 8,500)

SLIGO ROVERS FC (SLIGO)　　　　　　2-1　　　　　　　　Bohemian FC (Dublin)
Stenson, McLoughlin　　　　　　　　(H.T. 0-1)

Sligo: Oakley, Ferry, Rutherford (Fielding), Stenson, Fox, Savage, Fagan, McDonnell, McLoughlin, Gilligan, Elliot.
Bohemian: O'Neill, Connell, Murphy, Kinsella, Lawless, Doolin, Walker, Reynor (Shelly), O'Brien, Jameson, Eviston (Murphy).

Semi-Finals

Bohemian FC (Dublin)	0-0, 0-0, 3-0	Drogheda United FC (Drogheda)
Cobh Ramblers FC (Cobh)	1-1, 2-2, 0-0, 2-0, 3-3	Sligo Rovers FC (Sligo)

Quarter-Finals

Athlone Town AFC (Athlone)	0-2	Bohemian FC (Dublin)
Cobh Ramblers FC (Cobh)	1-0	Finn Harps FC (Ballybofey)
Limerick United FC (Limerick)	0-1	Drogheda United FC (Drogheda)
Sligo Rovers FC (Sligo)	2-1	Shamrock Rovers FC (Dublin)

1983-84

League of Ireland Division "A" 1983-84	Athlone Town	Bohemian FC	Drogheda United	Dundalk FC	Finn Harps FC	Galway United FC	Home Farm FC	Limerick AFC	St. Patrick's Athletic	Shamrock Rovers	Shelbourne FC	Sligo Rovers FC	University College	Waterford AFC
Athlone Town AFC	■	1-1	2-1	2-0	3-0	2-1	3-0	3-0	3-1	1-1	2-1	3-1	0-1	2-1
Bohemian FC	1-0	■	5-1	0-0	1-2	0-0	1-0	1-1	0-0	2-1	3-1	3-0	0-0	1-2
Drogheda United FC	1-4	0-1	■	0-3	2-1	2-1	3-0	0-1	3-1	0-7	2-2	1-3	1-0	3-1
Dundalk FC	0-2	1-1	3-0	■	1-2	1-0	3-1	2-2	1-2	0-1	5-3	4-0	0-2	3-2
Finn Harps FC	1-1	0-1	2-3	1-1	■	3-2	3-0	0-2	2-2	2-1	1-1	3-2	1-2	3-2
Galway United FC	0-0	0-1	2-2	2-1	3-3	■	1-2	3-0	1-3	0-3	0-2	1-0	0-0	2-0
Home Farm FC	2-3	0-3	0-4	1-1	0-0	1-1	■	1-2	0-4	0-5	0-5	2-1	0-2	1-3
Limerick City FC	1-2	2-0	2-1	2-2	0-2	1-0	2-0	■	3-2	0-1	1-1	4-1	2-0	1-0
St. Patrick's Athletic FC	3-2	1-1	3-0	0-1	2-0	1-2	0-0	1-0	■	0-4	3-3	2-0	1-1	0-2
Shamrock Rovers FC	4-0	1-1	2-0	1-1	5-1	4-1	1-0	1-1	1-0	■	3-1	5-0	2-1	2-0
Shelbourne FC	2-0	1-1	1-3	0-0	5-0	1-1	1-0	0-2	1-0	3-2	■	2-1	0-0	2-1
Sligo Rovers FC	1-2	3-4	2-3	0-2	2-2	0-2	0-2	0-4	2-1	0-2	0-0	■	0-0	0-2
University College Dublin	2-1	1-3	2-1	1-1	0-0	0-0	1-2	0-0	3-2	0-2	1-0	2-1	■	0-1
Waterford United FC	1-0	1-3	2-0	3-1	2-1	0-0	1-0	2-2	1-1	0-2	2-2	0-0	2-2	■

Division "A"	Pd	Wn	Dw	Ls	GF	GA	Pts
1. SHAMROCK ROVERS FC (DUBLIN)	26	19	4	3	64	15	42
2. Bohemian FC (Dublin)	26	13	10	3	39	20	36
3. Athlone Town AFC (Athlone)	26	15	4	7	44	28	34
4. Limerick City FC (Limerick)	26	13	7	6	38	26	33
5. Shelbourne FC (Dublin)	26	9	10	7	41	34	28
6. University College Dublin AFC (Dublin)	26	9	10	7	24	23	28
7. Dundalk FC (Dundalk)	26	9	9	8	38	31	27
8. Waterford United FC (Waterford)	26	10	6	10	34	34	26
9. Finn Harps FC (Ballybofey)	26	8	8	10	36	46	24
10. St. Patrick's Athletic FC (Dublin)	26	8	7	11	36	37	23
11. Drogheda United FC (Drogheda)	26	10	2	14	37	54	22
12. Galway United FC (Galway)	26	6	9	11	26	33	21
13. Home Farm FC (Dublin)	26	4	4	18	16	54	12
14. Sligo Rovers FC (Sligo)	26	2	4	20	20	58	8
	364	135	94	135	493	493	364

Top goal-scorers 1983-84

1) Alan CAMPBELL   (Shamrock Rovers FC)   24
2) Brendan BRADLEY   (Finn Harps FC)   16
3) Liam BUCKLEY   (Shamrock Rovers FC)   14

Elected: Cork City FC (Cork), Longford Town FC (Longford)

The league was extended to 16 clubs for next season

FAI Cup Final   (Dalymount Park, Dublin – 29/04/1984 – 8,000)

UNIVERSITY COLLEGE DUBLIN AFC   0-0   Shamrock Rovers FC (Dublin)

U.C.D.: O'Neill, Lawlor, O'Doherty, Dunning, Moran, Gaffney, Dignam, Cullen, Reynolds (Murphy), Devlin, Hanrahan.

Shamrock Rovers: J.Byrne, Whelan (Eviston), McDonagh, Keely, Coady, Steedman, King, P.Byrne, Neville, Campbell, Buckley.

Final Replay   (Tolka Park, Dublin – 04/05/1984 – 6,500)

UNIVERSITY COLLEGE DUBLIN AFC   2-1   Shamrock Rovers FC (Dublin)
Hanrahan, O'Doherty   (H.T. 1-0)   *McDonagh pen.*

U.C.D.: O'Neill, Lawlor, O'Doherty, Dunning, Moran, Gaffney, Dignam, Cullen, Murphy, Devlin, Hanrahan.

Shamrock Rovers: J.Byrne, Whelan (Eviston), McDonagh, Keely, Coady, Steedman, King, P.Byrne, Neville, Campbell, Buckley.

Semi-Finals

Shamrock Rovers FC (Dublin)	1-1, 1-0	Shelbourne FC (Dublin)
University College Dublin AFC (Dublin)	1-0	Waterford United FC (Waterford)

Quarter-Finals

Home Farm FC (Dublin)	1-2	University College Dublin AFC (Dublin)
Limerick City FC (Limerick)	0-1	Shamrock Rovers FC (Dublin)
Shelbourne FC (Dublin)	1-0	Galway United FC (Galway)
Waterford United FC (Waterford)	2-1	Finn Harps FC (Ballybofey)

1984-85

League of Ireland Division "A" 1984-85	Athlone Town AFC	Bohemian FC	Cork City FC	Drogheda United FC	Dundalk FC	Finn Harps FC	Galway United FC	Home Farm FC	Limerick AFC	Longford Town FC	St. Patrick's Athletic FC	Shamrock Rovers FC	Shelbourne FC	Sligo Rovers FC	University College Dublin	Waterford AFC
Athlone Town AFC	■	1-2	3-0	1-1	1-1	3-1	0-0	3-4	4-1	1-3	2-0	0-0	3-0	0-0	0-1	1-0
Bohemian FC	2-1	■	0-1	2-0	2-1	1-2	2-1	4-0	1-2	4-1	6-1	2-0	1-0	2-0	3-2	2-1
Cork City FC	1-4	1-1	■	1-2	1-0	3-0	2-1	2-1	0-0	1-0	1-1	0-3	3-1	0-4	0-0	3-1
Drogheda United FC	0-1	1-2	2-1	■	0-0	0-1	1-1	1-3	4-3	6-2	1-3	0-2	1-2	3-3	1-1	4-2
Dundalk FC	0-2	1-1	1-0	4-1	■	1-3	3-1	2-1	2-1	1-0	0-0	1-1	0-1	2-2	0-0	1-3
Finn Harps FC	0-5	0-1	1-1	4-5	1-4	■	1-5	1-0	1-2	0-0	3-1	1-2	1-2	1-1	2-2	1-4
Galway United FC	3-5	1-0	1-2	2-2	2-0	2-2	■	3-1	2-0	2-1	2-0	0-1	2-3	5-0	0-0	2-2
Home Farm FC	0-2	1-3	0-1	1-1	1-1	4-2	3-1	■	3-2	1-1	1-2	0-2	2-1	3-1	1-1	2-0
Limerick City FC	0-1	2-1	3-1	6-0	0-0	5-0	4-1	3-0	■	3-0	3-2	1-4	2-2	2-2	3-0	1-0
Longford Town FC	2-3	1-3	1-1	2-4	1-2	1-1	1-3	1-4	1-0	■	0-6	1-2	3-0	1-3	0-1	
St. Patrick's Athletic	0-2	1-1	1-0	1-0	3-2	5-1	1-1	1-0	1-3	1-2	■	0-2	0-0	0-0	0-2	1-1
Shamrock Rovers FC	2-0	1-0	3-1	3-0	2-0	3-2	1-0	0-2	1-1	6-1	4-0	■	3-2	4-0	1-0	4-1
Shelbourne FC	3-1	2-3	0-0	0-0	1-2	1-2	2-2	0-2	1-2	3-1	1-0	0-0	■	2-0	3-3	0-3
Sligo Rovers FC	0-1	0-3	2-1	1-1	1-1	2-2	2-2	2-1	2-0	1-0	1-2	2-3	2-1	■	0-1	1-1
University College Dublin	1-1	1-1	0-0	1-1	3-0	3-0	1-1	1-1	1-3	2-1	2-0	1-0	3-1	1-1	■	3-0
Waterford United FC	0-2	1-1	2-1	4-0	3-1	2-1	0-0	2-0	2-3	2-0	1-2	2-2	1-1	2-0	0-1	■

	Division "A"	Pd	Wn	Dw	Ls	GF	GA	Pts	
1.	SHAMROCK ROVERS FC (DUBLIN)	30	22	5	3	63	21	49	
2.	Bohemian FC (Dublin)	30	19	5	6	57	29	43	
3.	Athlone Town AFC (Athlone)	30	17	6	7	54	28	40	
4.	University College Dublin AFC (Dublin)	30	12	14	4	41	26	38	
5.	Limerick City FC (Limerick)	30	16	5	9	61	40	37	
6.	Galway United FC (Galway)	30	9	11	10	49	43	29	
7.	Waterford United FC (Waterford)	30	11	7	12	44	41	29	
8.	Dundalk FC (Dundalk)	30	9	10	11	34	39	28	
9.	Cork City FC (Cork)	30	10	8	12	30	39	28	
10.	Home Farm FC (Dublin)	30	11	5	14	43	47	27	
11.	St. Patrick's Athletic FC (Dublin)	30	10	7	13	36	45	27	
12.	Shelbourne FC (Dublin)	30	9	8	13	39	46	26	
13.	Sligo Rovers FC (Sligo)	30	7	12	11	34	47	26	R
14.	Drogheda United FC (Drogheda)	30	7	10	13	43	60	24	R
15.	Finn Harps FC (Ballybofey)	30	6	7	17	38	71	19	R
16.	Longford Town FC (Longford)	30	3	4	23	27	71	10	R
		480	178	124	178	693	693	480	

Top goal-scorers 1984-85

1) Tommy GAYNOR   (Limerick City FC)   17
   Michael O'CONNOR   (Athlone Town AFC)   17
3) Jackie JAMESON   (Bohemian FC)   15

The league was extended to 2 divisions (Premier Division and Division One) of 12 and 10 clubs respectively for next season. Division One consisted of the bottom 4 clubs of Division "A" and 6 newly elected clubs.

Elected: Bray Wanderers AFC (Bray), Cobh Ramblers FC (Cobh), Derry City FC (Derry), E.M.F.A. (Kilkenny), Monaghan United FC (Monaghan), Newcastle United FC (Newcastlewest)

FAI Cup Final   (Dalymount Park, Dublin – 28/04/1985 –7,000)

SHAMROCK ROVERS FC (DUBLIN)   1-0   Galway United FC (Galway)
Larkin   (H.T. 0-0)

Shamrock Rovers: J.Byrne, Neville, Keely, McDonagh, Brady, O'Brien, P.Byrne, King, Coady, Larkin, M.Byrne.
Galway United: Lally, Daly, Gardiner, Bonner, Nolan, Beacy, Mannion, McDonnell, Murphy, Cassidy, Glynn (Mernagh).

Semi-Finals

Galway United FC (Galway)	2-2, 1-0	Limerick City FC (Limerick)
Shamrock Rovers FC (Dublin)	2-1	Athlone Town AFC (Athlone)

Quarter-Finals

Drogheda United FC (Drogheda)	2-3	Shamrock Rovers FC (Dublin)
Limerick City FC (Limerick)	3-1	Waterford United FC (Waterford)
Shelbourne FC (Dublin)	0-0, 1-4	Galway United FC (Galway)
University College Dublin AFC (Dublin)	1-3	Athlone Town AFC (Athlone)

1985-86

League of Ireland Premier Division 1985-86	Athlone Town AFC	Bohemian FC	Cork City FC	Dundalk FC	Galway United FC	Home Farm FC	Limerick AFC	St. Patrick's Athletic	Shamrock Rovers FC	Shelbourne FC	University College	Waterford AFC
Athlone Town AFC	■	1-2	1-1	0-0	0-0	0-2	4-0	0-0	2-3	1-0	1-1	2-0
Bohemian FC	1-0	■	0-2	0-0	2-2	1-0	3-1	1-1	1-1	2-2	2-0	1-1
Cork City FC	0-2	1-2	■	1-4	0-2	1-1	1-4	2-2	0-3	0-1	1-2	1-1
Dundalk FC	3-2	0-0	2-2	■	2-1	0-1	2-1	0-1	1-0	1-0	3-0	0-0
Galway United FC	2-0	0-2	3-1	1-1	■	3-0	3-0	2-1	1-3	6-1	3-0	2-0
Home Farm FC	2-2	0-1	0-1	0-3	0-1	■	1-3	0-0	2-3	1-0	1-0	0-0
Limerick City FC	0-1	0-0	5-2	1-2	1-1	4-1	■	1-1	3-1	5-0	3-0	1-1
St. Patrick's Athletic FC	0-1	2-1	2-1	1-0	0-0	2-0	1-3	■	0-2	1-1	2-0	2-2
Shamrock Rovers FC	5-1	3-0	4-0	1-0	2-2	4-0	1-0	0-1	■	1-0	1-0	1-0
Shelbourne FC	0-0	1-1	0-2	0-3	0-3	0-0	0-4	0-0	1-1	■	5-3	0-2
University College Dublin AFC	2-0	3-3	2-2	1-2	1-2	0-3	0-4	1-3	1-4	0-2	■	1-1
Waterford United FC	3-2	1-1	1-1	2-5	2-2	1-0	2-1	1-0	1-0	3-1	2-1	■

	Premier Division	Pd	Wn	Dw	Ls	GF	GA	Pts	
1.	SHAMROCK ROVERS FC (DUBLIN)	22	15	3	4	44	17	33	
2.	Galway United FC (Galway)	22	12	7	3	42	19	31	
3.	Dundalk FC (Dundalk)	22	12	6	4	35	16	30	
4.	Bohemian FC (Dublin)	22	8	11	3	27	22	27	
5.	Waterford United FC (Waterford)	22	8	10	4	27	25	26	
6.	St. Patrick's Athletic FC (Dublin)	22	8	9	5	23	19	25	
7.	Limerick City FC (Limerick)	22	10	4	8	45	28	24	
8.	Athlone Town AFC (Athlone)	22	6	7	9	23	27	19	
9.	Home Farm FC (Dublin)	22	5	5	12	15	30	15	
10.	Cork City FC (Cork)	22	3	7	12	23	44	13	
11.	Shelbourne FC (Dublin)	22	3	7	12	15	40	13	R
12.	University College Dublin AFC (Dublin)	22	2	4	16	19	51	8	R
		264	92	80	92	338	338	264	

Top goal-scorers 1985-86

1) Tommy GAYNOR (Limerick City FC) 15
2) Paul McGEE (Galway United FC) 13
3) Colm McGONIGLE (Galway United FC) 12

League of Ireland Division One 1985-86	Bray Wanderers	Cobh Ramblers	Derry City FC	Drogheda United	E.M.F.A. Kilkenny	Finn Harps FC	Longford Town	Monaghan United	Newcastle United	Sligo Rovers FC
Bray Wanderers AFC	■	3-0	1-1	2-0	3-1	0-0	0-1	1-0	2-1	1-1
Cobh Ramblers FC	0-3	■	0-3	1-0	2-1	2-1	1-1	2-1	2-0	0-0
Derry City FC	1-1	3-0	■	0-0	0-1	1-0	1-2	4-1	3-0	0-2
Drogheda United FC	1-2	1-0	1-1	■	3-0	1-1	2-2	0-0	2-0	3-2
E.M.F.A. Kilkenny	1-2	0-0	1-1	2-2	■	1-2	2-2	2-2	2-2	1-2
Finn Harps FC	0-0	0-0	2-7	2-2	3-1	■	1-2	4-0	2-3	0-2
Longford Town FC	0-3	1-0	5-1	1-0	3-2	1-1	■	3-1	3-0	0-0
Monaghan United FC	1-2	2-2	0-2	0-2	3-1	2-0	3-0	■	0-3	0-1
Newcastle United FC	0-3	2-1	1-1	2-0	4-2	2-2	0-1	0-2	■	0-2
Sligo Rovers FC	1-1	3-1	0-1	0-0	1-0	4-2	5-1	3-1	3-1	■

	Division One	Pd	Wn	Dw	Ls	GF	GA	Pts	
1.	Bray Wanderers AFC (Bray)	18	11	6	1	30	10	28	P
2.	Sligo Rovers FC (Sligo)	18	11	5	2	32	13	27	P
3.	Longford Town FC (Longford)	18	10	5	3	29	23	25	
4.	Derry City FC (Derry)	18	8	6	4	31	18	22	
5.	Drogheda United FC (Drogheda)	18	5	8	5	20	18	18	
6.	Cobh Ramblers FC (Cobh)	18	5	5	8	14	25	15	
7.	Finn Harps FC (Ballybofey)	18	3	7	8	23	31	13	
8.	Newcastle United FC (Newcastlewest)	18	5	3	10	21	33	13	*
9.	Monaghan United FC (Monaghan)	18	4	3	11	19	32	11	
10.	E.M.F.A. (Kilkenny)	18	1	6	11	21	37	8	
		180	63	54	63	240	240	180	

* Newcastle United FC (Newcastlewest) changed their name to Newcastlewest FC (Newcastlewest) for next season.

FAI Cup Final (Dalymount Park, Dublin – 27/04/86 – 11,500)

SHAMROCK ROVERS FC (DUBLIN)   2-0   Waterford United FC (Waterford)
Brady, Synnott o.g.   (H.T. 2-0)

Shamrock Rovers: J.Byrne, Kenny, Neville, Eccles, Brady, Doolin, P.Byrne, O'Brien, Coady, Larkin, M.Byrne.
Waterford United: Flavin, Grace (Bollard), Power, Synnott, Burns, Donnelly, Macken, McCabe (McCarthy(, Kearns, Bennett, Reid.

Semi-Finals

Shamrock Rovers FC (Dublin)	4-1, 4-2	Cork City FC (Cork)
Waterford United FC (Waterford)	1-1, 3-1	St. Patrick's Athletic FC (Dublin)

Quarter-Finals

Bohemian FC (Dublin)	1-2	Shamrock Rovers FC (Dublin)
Cobh Ramblers FC (Cobh)	1-3	St. Patrick's Athletic FC (Dublin)
Cork City FC (Cork)	1-0	Derry City FC (Derry)
Waterford United FC (Waterford)	2-1	Dundalk FC (Dundalk)

1986-87

League of Ireland Premier Division 1986-87	Athlone Town	Bohemian FC	Bray Wanderers	Cork City FC	Dundalk FC	Galway United FC	Home Farm FC	Limerick AFC	St. Patrick's Ath.	Shamrock Rovers	Sligo Rovers FC	Waterford AFC
Athlone Town AFC		0-1	2-1	3-1	1-1	0-0	1-2	1-2	2-3	0-2	0-1	0-0
Bohemian FC	2-1		2-0	2-1	2-2	5-3	3-1	1-0	0-1	1-1	2-1	1-3
Bray Wanderers AFC	2-2	1-3		1-0	0-1	1-1	2-3	3-2	0-0	1-3	2-1	3-0
Cork City FC	3-1	1-1	0-1		1-2	0-1	3-2	1-2	2-1	1-2	3-2	1-2
Dundalk FC	1-0	0-0	1-0	3-0		2-3	4-0	2-1	0-0	2-0	2-0	1-2
Galway United FC	2-0	0-0	2-1	1-1	1-2		2-1	0-0	2-1	0-1	1-2	0-0
Home Farm FC	0-1	1-2	2-1	1-4	2-1	1-3		0-1	1-1	1-3	1-3	1-5
Limerick City FC	3-1	0-1	1-3	1-3	2-2	1-0	1-0		2-1	0-3	0-1	2-4
St. Patrick's Athletic FC	1-0	1-1	0-0	2-2	0-0	1-0	0-1	1-1		1-3	1-0	2-1
Shamrock Rovers FC	1-0	3-2	4-1	2-0	5-0	3-1	3-0	2-1	1-1		4-1	2-1
Sligo Rovers FC	1-1	0-0	1-1	0-0	1-8	2-1	1-2	2-1	0-2	1-3		2-2
Waterford United FC	5-1	2-0	2-0	1-2	0-3	0-1	3-1	6-0	2-1	0-0	1-0	

	Premier Division	Pd	Wn	Dw	Ls	GF	GA	Pts	
1.	SHAMROCK ROVERS FC (DUBLIN)	22	18	3	1	51	16	39	
2.	Dundalk FC (Dundalk)	22	12	6	4	40	21	30	
3.	Bohemian FC (Dublin)	22	11	7	4	32	23	29	
4.	Waterford United FC (Waterford)	22	12	4	6	42	24	28	
5.	St. Patrick's Athletic FC (Dublin)	22	7	9	6	22	21	23	
6.	Galway United FC (Galway)	22	8	6	8	25	25	22	
7.	Cork City FC (Cork)	22	7	4	11	30	34	18	
8.	Bray Wanderers AFC (Bray)	22	6	5	11	25	33	17	
9.	Limerick City FC (Limerick)	22	7	3	12	24	38	17	
10.	Sligo Rovers FC (Sligo)	22	6	5	11	23	38	17	
11.	Home Farm FC (Dublin)	22	6	1	15	24	48	13	R
12.	Athlone Town AFC (Athlone)	22	3	5	14	18	35	11	R
		264	103	58	103	356	356	264	

Top goal-scorers 1986-87

1) Michael BYRNE   (Shamrock Rovers FC)   12
2) Dave BARRY   (Cork City FC)   10
   Desmond GORMAN   (Dundalk FC)   10
   Noel LARKIN   (Shamrock Rovers FC)   10
   Martin REID   (Waterford United FC) 10

League of Ireland Division One 1986-87	Cobh Ramblers FC	Derry City FC	Drogheda United	E.M.F.A. Kilkenny	Finn Harps FC	Longford Town FC	Monaghan United	Newcastlewest FC	Shelbourne FC	University College
Cobh Ramblers FC	■	0-1	3-1	0-0	1-2	3-1	2-2	1-2	2-3	4-2
Derry City FC	2-1	■	3-1	3-2	1-1	4-2	3-1	5-1	3-0	1-2
Drogheda United FC	2-2	0-1	■	2-1	5-1	4-0	5-1	3-0	1-1	3-0
E.M.F.A. Kilkenny	2-2	0-2	0-2	■	1-2	4-0	1-1	2-1	1-3	0-1
Finn Harps FC	2-1	1-4	3-0	4-0	■	5-0	1-0	0-1	2-2	1-0
Longford Town FC	1-5	1-5	0-0	0-0	3-1	■	0-0	1-2	0-1	2-3
Monaghan United FC	3-0	0-2	0-3	3-1	0-2	2-3	■	1-1	0-3	3-4
Newcastlewest FC	2-2	0-2	1-3	1-2	0-1	4-2	1-1	■	0-2	0-0
Shelbourne FC	4-1	1-2	3-4	2-0	3-2	5-0	2-1	2-0	■	1-1
University College Dublin	0-1	0-1	2-2	2-0	2-1	1-0	0-1	2-0	0-1	■

	Division One	**Pd**	**Wn**	**Dw**	**Ls**	**GF**	**GA**	**Pts**	
1.	Derry City FC (Derry)	18	16	1	1	45	14	33	P
2.	Shelbourne FC (Dublin)	18	12	3	3	39	20	27	P
3.	Drogheda United FC (Drogheda)	18	10	4	4	41	22	24	
4.	Finn Harps FC (Ballybofey)	18	10	2	6	32	24	22	
5.	University College Dublin AFC (Dublin)	18	8	3	7	22	22	19	
6.	Cobh Ramblers FC (Cobh)	18	5	5	8	31	32	15	
7.	Newcastlewest FC (Newcastlewest)	18	4	4	10	17	32	12	
8.	Monaghan United FC (Monaghan)	18	3	5	10	20	34	11	
9.	E.M.F.A. (Kilkenny)	18	3	4	11	17	31	10	
10.	Longford Town FC (Longford)	18	2	3	13	16	49	7	
		180	73	34	73	280	280	180	

FAI Cup Final   (Dalymount Park, Dublin – 26/04/1987 – 8,569)

SHAMROCK ROVERS FC (DUBLIN)   3-0   Dundalk FC (Dundalk)
Kenny pen., M.Byrne, Larkin   (H.T. 1-0)

Shamrock: J.Byrne, Kenny, Eccles, Neville, Brady, Doolin, P.Byrne, Dignam, Murphy, Larkin, M.Byrne.
Dundalk: O'Neill, Lawless, McCue, Lawlor, Murray, Wyse, Kehoe, McNulty, Gorman, Eviston, Malone.

Semi-Finals

Dundalk FC (Dundalk)	1-2, 1-0, 3-0	Bohemian FC (Dublin)
Sligo Rovers FC (Sligo)	0-0, 1-1, 0-1	Shamrock Rovers FC (Dublin)

Quarter-Finals

Bohemian FC (Dublin)	2-1	Derry City FC (Derry)
Galway United FC (Galway)	0-1	Sligo Rovers FC (Sligo)
Rockmount AFC (Whitchurch)	0-2	Dundalk FC (Dundalk)
St. Patrick's Athletic FC (Dublin)	0-0, 0-1	Shamrock Rovers FC (Dublin)

1987-88

League of Ireland Premier Division 1987-88

	Bohemian FC	Bray Wanderers AFC	Cork City FC	Derry City FC	Dundalk FC	Galway United FC	Limerick AFC	St. Patrick's Athletic FC	Shamrock Rovers FC	Shelbourne FC	Sligo Rovers FC	Waterford AFC
Bohemian FC (Dublin)		1-0			0-1	2-0		1-1		3-2		
		1-1	5-1	3-1	3-2	0-0	3-0	2-0	1-4	1-0	4-2	0-0
Bray Wanderers AFC (Bray)			1-1	0-1		1-2			1-3	1-2	3-0	
	0-4		1-3	0-6	2-3	1-3	0-0	1-3	1-3	0-1	3-3	0-0
Cork City FC (Cork)	0-1				1-1		0-0	0-1			3-0	
	2-2	2-1		1-0	0-2	1-3	1-1	0-0	0-0	2-1	3-1	1-2
Derry City FC (Derry)	0-1		0-1			3-2			0-3			
	3-2	0-0	7-2		3-0	3-0	5-0	0-3	0-1	0-0	4-0	1-2
Dundalk FC (Dundalk)	0-2	5-1		3-2			4-0	1-1				1-1
	0-0	2-0	3-1	2-0		2-1	2-1	0-2	1-1	3-1	1-0	1-0
Galway United FC (Galway)		3-1	1-1	2-0				2-2		1-0	3-1	
	1-1	2-0	1-1	3-1	1-0		0-2	1-0	3-2	0-2	5-1	2-2
Limerick City FC (Limerick)		3-0			1-5			0-4	5-0	2-0		
	0-2	0-0	1-1	2-2	0-3	3-0		0-3	1-4	2-0	1-0	2-1
St. Patrick's Athletic FC (Dublin)	1-0	1-1	1-0		3-0		2-0					0-2
	2-2	0-1	3-0	3-0	2-2	0-0	4-1		1-1	2-1	4-2	1-1
Shamrock Rovers FC (Dublin)		2-0	1-3	0-1	0-0			2-0		2-0		
	1-1	7-1	2-2	2-1	0-1	1-0	2-0	0-2		0-1	2-1	1-1
Shelbourne FC (Dublin)	2-2		1-1		0-1		2-0					1-1
	1-3	1-1	1-2	0-1	0-2	1-1	4-1	1-0	1-2	***	1-1	0-2
Sligo Rovers FC (Sligo)		0-3	2-7	0-0			0-1		1-1			0-2
	3-2	1-2	0-2	0-3	2-2	1-0	1-2	1-3	2-0	1-0		1-7
Waterford United FC (Waterford)	1-1	0-1		0-0		1-0	0-0		0-2			
	0-1	1-1	1-2	3-1	2-3	1-1	1-1	0-1	0-0	2-1	3-0	

Premier Division

		Pd	Wn	Dw	Ls	GF	GA	Pts	
1.	DUNDALK FC (DUNDALK)	33	19	8	6	54	32	46	
2.	St. Patrick's Athletic FC (Dublin)	33	18	9	6	52	25	45	
3.	Bohemian FC (Dublin)	33	17	11	5	57	32	45	
4.	Shamrock Rovers FC (Dublin)	33	16	9	8	53	30	41	
5.	Galway United FC (Galway)	33	15	10	8	48	34	40	
6.	Waterford United FC (Waterford)	33	10	14	9	40	31	34	
7.	Cork City FC (Cork)	33	12	10	11	41	47	34	
8.	Derry City FC (Derry)	33	13	5	15	59	44	31	
9.	Limerick City FC (Limerick)	33	9	7	17	33	60	25	
10.	Shelbourne FC (Dublin)	33	8	8	17	31	44	24	
11.	Bray Wanderers FC (Bray)	33	4	10	19	27	65	18	R
12.	Sligo Rovers FC (Sligo)	33	4	5	24	30	81	13	R
		396	145	106	145	525	525	396	

Top goal-scorers 1987-88

1) Jonathan SPEAK   (Derry City FC)   24
2) Paul McGEE   (Galway United FC)   20
3) Desmond GORMAN   (Dundalk FC)   14
4) Mick BENNETT   (Waterford United FC)   13
   Patrick DILLON   (St. Patrick's Athletic FC) 13

League of Ireland Division One 1987-88

	Athlone Town AFC	Cobh Ramblers FC	Drogheda United FC	E.M.F.A.	Finn Harps FC	Home Farm FC	Longford Town FC	Monaghan United FC	Newcastlewest FC	University College Dublin
Athlone Town AFC (Athlone)	■	2-1			1-2	1-0	0-1			2-0
		0-1	2-1	3-1	1-0	2-0	2-0	2-1	2-1	3-1
Cobh Ramblers FC (Cobh)		■	1-0	3-1	1-0		2-0	2-0		
	0-2		2-0	3-0	1-1	4-5	2-1	1-0	3-0	0-0
Drogheda United FC (Drogheda)	0-4		■	1-0		3-1	2-0	2-1		
	1-3	2-1		3-0	1-4	2-1	3-1	4-1	0-1	0-2
E.M.F.A. (Kilkenny)	0-1			■	2-4		1-1			
	2-1	1-2	3-1		2-2	2-2	2-1	3-2	3-2	3-1
Finn Harps FC (Ballybofey)		5-4			■	2-1		3-0	1-0	0-4
	2-0	0-1	3-0	0-0		4-1	0-0	1-4	2-3	1-0
Home Farm FC (Dublin)		1-0	2-0	6-0		■			1-2	1-2
	0-0	0-2	0-2	2-1	0-2		2-0	2-0	5-5	3-1
Longford Town FC (Longford)				1-1	0-1		■	1-1	0-0	
	1-0	0-0	3-0	2-0	1-0	2-6		0-3	2-1	2-1
Monaghan United FC (Monaghan)	1-3		2-1		2-2			■	0-1	1-1
	1-2	0-1	3-2	2-1	0-0	2-2	0-1		4-3	0-0
Newcastlewest FC (Newcastlewest)	0-1	1-2	4-1						■	0-0
	3-0	1-2	0-1	1-3	2-3	1-2	0-0	1-1		2-0
University College Dublin AFC (Dublin)		3-0	2-3	2-0			2-1			■
	1-3	3-3	3-0	1-1	2-2	1-2	2-0	1-3	1-0	

	Division One	Pd	Wn	Dw	Ls	GF	GA	Pts	
1.	Athlone Town AFC (Athlone)	27	19	1	7	42	22	39	P
2.	Cobh Ramblers FC (Cobh)	27	17	4	6	41	24	38	P
3.	Finn Harps FC (Ballybofey)	27	13	7	7	45	33	33	
4.	Home Farm FC (Dublin)	27	12	5	10	50	42	29	
5.	University College Dublin AFC (Dublin)	27	9	7	11	37	36	25	
6.	Drogheda United FC (Drogheda)	27	12	-	15	38	48	24	
7.	Longford Town FC (Longford)	27	8	7	12	23	35	23	
8.	Monaghan United FC (Monaghan)	27	7	7	13	34	43	21	
9.	Newcastlewest FC (Newcastlewest)	27	7	5	15	36	42	19	
10.	E.M.F.A. (Kilkenny)	27	7	5	15	34	55	19	
		270	111	48	111	380	380	270	

FAI Cup Final   (Dalymount Park, Dublin – 01/05/1988 – 21,000)

DUNDALK FC (DUNDALK)   1-0   Derry City FC (Derry)

Cleary 20' pen.

Dundalk: O'Neill, Lawless, Cleary, McCue, Malone, Lawlor, Wyse (O'Connor 71'), Murray, Kehoe, Eviston, Gorman.

Derry City: Roberts, Vaudequin, Curran, Gauld, McGuinness, Carlyle, Bayly, Healy (Cunningham), Plummer, Da Gama, Speak.

Semi-Finals

Dundalk FC (Dundalk)	1-0, 3-0	St. Patrick's Athletic FC (Dublin)
Longford Town FC (Longford)	0-2, 2-4	Derry City FC (Derry)

Quarter-Finals

Dundalk FC (Dundalk)	0-0, 1-0	Cork City FC (Cork)
Home Farm FC (Dublin)	0-3	Derry City FC (Derry)
Longford Town FC (Longford)	1-0	Newcastlewest FC (Newcastlewest)
St. Patrick Athletic FC (Dublin)	2-2, 2-1	Limerick City FC (Limerick)

1988-89

League of Ireland Premier Division 1988-89	Athlone Town	Bohemian FC	Cobh Ramblers	Cork City FC	Derry City FC	Dundalk FC	Galway United	Limerick AFC	St. Patrick's Ath.	Shamrock Rovers	Shelbourne FC	Waterford AFC
Athlone Town AFC (Athlone)	■	4-1		0-1	1-2		0-3	0-1			1-2	
	■	0-2	0-0	1-0	1-0	1-2	0-0	0-0	1-1	3-1	0-1	0-1
Bohemian FC (Dublin)		■	1-1	1-2	0-1			0-1		1-0	4-0	
	0-1	■	2-0	3-0	0-2	1-1	1-1	4-2	1-3	2-2	1-0	3-0
Cobh Ramblers FC (Cobh)	2-1	0-2	■			1-2	1-2		1-1			
	0-0	0-2	■	0-1	2-5	1-0	0-0	0-1	1-2	1-1	2-2	4-0
Cork City FC (Cork)	2-1		1-1	■	0-2		4-0		0-1	0-0		
	1-2	0-0	3-0	■	0-1	1-2	0-0	0-2	0-1	0-0	2-1	3-0
Derry City FC (Derry)		2-0			■	2-0	2-1		1-0	0-1		2-0
	3-0	3-0	5-0	4-2	■	1-1	5-1	1-1	1-0	1-1	2-3	2-0
Dundalk FC (Dundalk)			3-1	1-0		■	1-1		2-1	1-0		
	0-0	1-1	3-1	2-0	1-1	■	5-2	2-0	2-1	2-1	2-2	3-0
Galway United FC (Galway)	1-2	4-0					■	0-3		2-0		2-1
	2-4	2-1	0-1	2-1	0-3	1-2	■	1-5	1-1	1-1	0-2	0-0
Limerick City FC (Limerick)		1-0		1-1	1-3	2-5		■	3-1			2-1
	1-0	3-1	3-3	2-0	1-1	1-2	2-1	■	0-0	4-1	1-0	2-2
St. Patrick's Athletic FC (Dublin)			0-0	0-0		0-1	1-1		■	2-1		
	0-0	2-0	3-0	2-1	1-0	0-1	3-0	0-0	■	0-0	1-1	2-0
Shamrock Rovers FC (Dublin)	2-1	3-0					0-0	0-1		■		4-0
	0-1	3-1	1-2	2-2	0-2	1-1	0-2	3-2	0-4	■	1-1	1-0
Shelbourne FC (Dublin)	0-2		0-2		1-3		1-0	0-1		1-1	■	
	1-0	0-2	3-2	0-1	0-5	0-0	2-0	2-3	0-0	0-0	■	1-0
Waterford United FC (Waterford)		1-0	1-2		1-1			1-2		2-0		■
	0-2	0-3	2-0	0-0	1-2	1-1	0-3	1-2	1-4	2-0	0-0	■

	Premier Division	Pd	Wn	Dw	Ls	GF	GA	Pts	
1.	DERRY CITY FC (DERRY)	33	24	5	4	70	21	53	
2.	Dundalk FC (Dundalk)	33	20	11	2	55	27	51	
3.	Limerick City FC (Limerick)	33	18	9	6	57	37	45	
4.	St. Patrick's Athletic FC (Dublin)	33	16	11	6	40	19	43	
5.	Bohemian FC (Dublin)	33	12	6	15	41	43	30	
6.	Athlone Town AFC (Athlone)	33	11	7	15	30	33	29	
7.	Shamrock Rovers FC (Dublin)	33	8	13	12	34	42	29	
8.	Cork City FC (Cork)	33	8	10	15	29	36	26	
9.	Shelbourne FC (Dublin)	33	8	10	15	26	40	26	
10.	Galway United FC (Galway)	33	8	9	16	34	56	25	
11.	Cobh Ramblers FC (Cobh)	33	6	9	18	29	54	21	R
12.	Waterford United FC (Waterford)	33	6	6	21	21	58	18	R
		396	145	106	145	466	466	396	

Top goal-scorers 1988-89

1)	William HAMILTON	(Limerick City FC)	21
2)	Derek SWAN	(Bohemian FC)	16
3)	Liam COYLE	(Derry City FC)	14
4)	Mark ENNIS	(St. Patrick's Athletic FC)	12
	Jonathan SPEAK	(Derry City FC)	12

League of Ireland Division One 1988-89	Bray Wanderers AFC	Drogheda United FC	E.M.F.A.	Finn Harps FC	Home Farm FC	Longford Town FC	Monaghan United FC	Newcastlewest FC	Sligo Rovers FC	University College Dublin
Bray Wanderers AFC (Bray)		1-2		3-1			2-1	2-1	1-1	
		0-0	0-0	2-2	1-2	0-1	4-1	2-1	2-1	0-0
Drogheda United FC (Drogheda)	2-1		0-0	1-0	1-1				1-0	
	2-1		3-0	0-1	2-1	3-0	3-2	2-2	1-0	1-1
E.M.F.A. (Kilkenny)				1-1		0-1	2-3	0-3	0-0	
	1-2	0-1		1-4	1-3	0-2	2-2	0-2	0-0	1-4
Finn Harps FC (Ballybofey)	0-1		0-0		2-0		2-0			
	0-3	0-1	1-0		1-2	2-1	4-0	0-0	1-2	0-0
Home Farm FC (Dublin)				0-1		0-1	1-2		3-1	
	1-0	3-3	0-1	1-2		7-1	5-0	1-1	1-1	0-0
Longford Town FC (Longford)	0-2	0-2	3-2						1-1	
	0-0	1-0	1-0	1-1	1-2		1-1	0-0	2-0	0-3
Monaghan United FC (Monaghan)	1-1	0-3		1-3		2-1				
	0-3	3-0	1-1	1-1	0-0	1-2		1-1	2-2	1-1
Newcastlewest FC (Newcastlewest)		3-1		2-1	0-0	2-1	0-3			
	2-2	1-1	0-1	0-0	0-0	3-2	2-1		0-0	1-1
Sligo Rovers FC (Sligo)		0-1				0-1	0-0	1-0		
	3-5	0-1	1-2	0-1	0-1	3-1	0-1	3-3		0-1
University College Dublin AFC (Dublin)			0-0	3-1		0-0	5-1	1-0		
	0-1	1-2	2-0	0-1	0-0	4-0	1-0	4-2	2-1	

	Division One	Pd	Wn	Dw	Ls	GF	GA	Pts	
1.	Drogheda United FC (Drogheda)	27	16	7	4	38	22	39	P
2.	University College Dublin AFC (Dublin)	27	11	12	4	36	16	34	P
3.	Bray Wanderers AFC (Bray)	27	13	8	6	41	25	34	
4.	Finn Harps FC (Ballybofey)	27	12	8	7	30	19	32	
5.	Home Farm FC (Dublin)	27	9	10	8	38	28	28	
6.	Newcastlewest FC (Newcastlewest)	27	7	13	7	33	37	27	
7.	Monaghan United FC (Monaghan)	27	6	11	10	28	42	23	
8.	Longford Town FC (Longford)	27	9	5	13	25	43	23	
9.	E.M.F.A. (Kilkenny)	27	4	8	15	18	41	16	*
10.	Sligo Rovers FC (Sligo)	27	4	6	17	23	37	14	
		270	91	88	91	310	310	270	

* E.M.F.A. (Kilkenny) changed their club name to Kilkenny City FC (Kilkenny) for next season.

FAI Cup Final   (Dalymount Park, Dublin – 30/04/1989 – 20,100)

DERRY CITY FC (DERRY)   0-0   Cork City FC (Cork)

Derry City: Dalton, Gauld, Keay, Neville, Brady, Carlyle, Doolin, Healey, Coady (Larkin 58'), Coyle, Speak.
Cork City: Harrington, Murphy, Healy, Carey, Long, Bowdren, Conroy, Barry, Freyne, Caulfield, Nugent.

Final Replay   (Dalymount Park, Dublin – 07/05/1989 – 13,000)

DERRY CITY FC (DERRY)   1-0   Cork City FC (Cork)
Healy 12'

Cork City: Harrington, Murphy, Long, Healy, Carey, Freyne, Barry, Conroy, Nugent, Nagle (Duggan 53'), Caulfield.
Derry City: Dalton, Vaudequin, Brady, Keay (Coady 87'), Neville, Doolin, Carlyle, Larkin, Coyle (Speak 81'), Gauld, Healy.

Semi-Finals

Cork City FC (Cork)	0-1, 1-0, 4-0	Bray Wanderers AFC (Bray)
Derry City FC (Derry)	3-0, 1-1	Shamrock Rovers FC (Dublin)

Quarter-Finals

Bray Wanderers AFC (Bray)	0-0, 1-0	Drogheda United FC (Drogheda)
Derry City FC (Derry)	3-0	Longford Town FC (Longford)
Dundalk FC (Dundalk)	2-2, 0-1	Cork City FC (Cork)
Home Farm FC (Dublin)	1-1, 0-1	Shamrock Rovers FC (Dublin)

1989-90

League of Ireland Premier Division 1989-90	Athlone Town AFC	Bohemian FC	Cork City FC	Derry City FC	Drogheda United FC	Dundalk FC	Galway United FC	Limerick AFC	St. Patrick's Athletic	Shamrock Rovers FC	Shelbourne FC	University College
Athlone Town AFC (Athlone)	■	0-4	0-1			0-0			0-1		2-1
		1-1	0-0	0-3	1-1	0-1	3-3	3-2	1-0	0-3	1-1	1-1
Bohemian FC (Dublin)	1-0	■	0-0		1-0		0-0				1-2
	2-1		0-0	1-3	4-0	0-2	1-0	2-1	1-2	1-2	1-0	3-0
Cork City FC (Cork)		1-0	■	2-0	2-0			0-1		4-0	
	2-0	0-2		0-0	1-1	0-1	0-0	2-1	0-3	1-1	0-1	2-0
Derry City FC (Derry)				■	2-2		3-0	7-0		1-1	1-1	3-0
	6-1	1-0	2-0		2-0	0-0	9-1	2-0	0-1	5-0	1-0	2-0
Drogheda United FC (Drogheda)	0-1	1-2			■			0-2	1-0	2-2
	0-0	0-1	0-1	2-0		0-1	0-2	1-0	2-1	1-1	1-0
Dundalk FC (Dundalk)	3-2		0-0	1-3	3-1	■		0-1	1-2		
	2-0	1-1	1-2	0-2	1-0		3-0	4-0	2-1	1-0	4-3	5-0
Galway United FC (Galway)	3-1	1-2	1-1		2-1	1-1	■	1-1			
	2-1	2-3	2-1	0-6	2-0	1-0		3-0	2-2	1-2	1-4	2-0
Limerick City FC (Limerick)		1-3		1-1		1-1	0-3	■	2-0		
	2-2	0-1	2-1	1-2	0-0	0-1	4-0		0-1	0-1	0-0	3-1
St. Patrick's Athletic FC (Dublin)	1-1	0-0		1-1		0-0			■	3-1		4-0
	2-1	1-0	1-0	2-0	2-1	2-1	3-2	2-1		0-3	1-0	1-0
Shamrock Rovers FC (Dublin)		2-1	0-0			1-1	2-1			■	2-3	1-0
	2-0	3-1	0-1	1-1	2-1	0-0	1-1	0-1	1-1		1-4	2-1
Shelbourne FC (Dublin)	1-1	2-0			0-4	4-0		0-3			■
	1-1	0-0	0-1	0-0	2-0	0-0	1-0	2-0	1-1	1-3		1-1
University College Dublin AFC (Dublin)		1-2		1-0	0-3	1-0	1-1			1-1		■
	0-2	3-1	2-1	0-3	1-0	3-3	0-1	1-2	1-2	1-3	1-2	

	Premier Division	**Pd**	**Wn**	**Dw**	**Ls**	**GF**	**GA**	**Pts**	
1.	ST. PATRICK'S ATHLETIC FC (DUBLIN)	33	22	8	3	51	22	52	
2.	Derry City FC (Derry)	33	20	9	4	72	18	49	
3.	Dundalk FC (Dundalk)	33	17	8	8	50	26	42	
4.	Shamrock Rovers FC (Dublin)	33	16	8	9	45	37	40	
5.	Cork City FC (Cork)	33	14	9	10	35	24	37	
6.	Bohemian FC (Dublin)	33	14	7	12	35	32	35	
7.	Shelbourne FC (Dublin)	33	10	13	10	39	39	33	
8.	Galway United FC (Galway)	33	10	9	14	39	61	29	
9.	Limerick City FC (Limerick)	33	7	8	18	28	50	22	
10.	Athlone Town AFC (Athlone)	33	5	12	16	28	53	22	
11.	Drogheda United FC (Drogheda)	33	5	8	20	20	44	18	R
12.	University College Dublin AFC (Dublin)	33	6	5	22	25	61	17	R
		396	146	104	146	467	467	396	

Top goal-scorers 1989-90

1) Mark ENNIS   (St. Patrick's Athletic FC)   19
2) Paul McGEE   (Galway United FC)   15
3) Robbie COUSINS   (Dundalk FC)   14

League of Ireland Division One 1989-90

Team	Bray	Cobh	Finn Harps	Home Farm	Kilkenny	Longford	Monaghan	Newcastlewest	Sligo	Waterford
Bray Wanderers AFC (Bray)	■	3-0	1-0	1-3	2-1					
	■	2-1	1-0	1-2	0-0	4-0	0-2	3-2	0-0	4-1
Cobh Ramblers FC (Cobh)	2-1	■			1-0		3-0	0-0		1-3
	1-1	■	3-0	0-1	2-3	3-0	2-1	1-2	0-1	1-3
Finn Harps FC (Ballybofey)		1-0	■			2-1	4-1	0-1		
	1-2	3-1	■	0-0	0-1	1-1	0-0	3-2	2-0	3-0
Home Farm FC (Dublin)		0-1	0-1	■		0-2	5-0	3-0		
	0-0	2-0	1-0	■	2-0	2-0	2-0	2-0	0-1	0-2
Kilkenny City FC (Kilkenny)		0-2	2-1		■	1-0	2-0			
	2-1	0-0	6-2	1-0	■	0-1	4-0	1-3	0-1	1-0
Longford Town FC (Longford)			0-2	0-0	0-0	■	0-2			1-6
	0-0	2-2	0-2	0-1	0-3	■	2-0	1-0	0-1	0-3
Monaghan United FC (Monaghan)	0-3	0-2					■	0-3	0-4	
	1-3	0-2	2-1	1-1	3-3	1-3	■	3-1	1-3	0-6
Newcastlewest FC (Newcastlewest)	0-2				1-1	2-2		■		2-1
	0-1	3-1	0-2	1-0	1-1	0-0	0-1	■	0-1	1-2
Sligo Rovers FC (Sligo)	1-2		1-0	1-1	1-1		5-0		■	
	1-0	0-0	0-0	1-1	0-1	0-0	3-1	2-0	■	0-0
Waterford United FC (Waterford)	2-1		1-0	2-0	2-1			1-1		■
	0-2	2-1	1-1	0-2	1-1	8-1	3-1	3-1	1-1	■

Division One (Play-off)

Sligo Rovers FC (Sligo)   1-0, 0-2   Waterford United FC (Waterford)

	Division One	Pd	Wn	Dw	Ls	GF	GA	Pts	
1.	Waterford United FC (Waterford)	27	16	5	6	58	28	37	P
1.	Sligo Rovers FC (Sligo)	27	13	11	3	30	12	37	P
3.	Bray Wanderers AFC (Bray)	27	15	5	7	41	23	35	
4.	Kilkenny City FC (Kilkenny)	27	14	7	6	40	24	35	
5.	Home Farm FC (Dublin)	27	12	5	10	27	16	29	
6.	Finn Harps FC (Ballybofey)	27	11	5	11	32	30	27	
7.	Cobh Ramblers FC (Cobh)	27	10	5	12	33	31	25	
8.	Longford Town FC (Longford)	27	4	9	14	15	46	17	
9.	Newcastlewest FC (Newcastlewest)	27	5	4	18	23	51	14	#
10	Monaghan United FC (Monaghan)	27	5	4	18	23	61	14	
		270	105	60	105	322	322	270	

\# Newcastlewest FC (Newcastlewest) resigned from the league in order to make improvements to their stadium. They were replaced by St. James's Gate AFC (Dublin).

FAI Cup Final (Lansdowne Road, Dublin – 13/05/1990 – 29,000)

BRAY WANDERERS AFC (BRAY)	3-0	St. Francis FC (Dublin)

Ryan 20' pen., 60', 81' pen.

Bray Wanderers: Moran, McKeever, Doohan, Phillips, Cosgrave, Nugent, Judge, Reynolds, Finnegen (Kealy 87'), Ryan, McDermott (Corcoran 87').

St. Francis: Matthews, O'Reilly, Gibbons, Kerr, T.Coleman, G.Coleman, Hilliard, Connolly, Murphy, Toner, Byrne (McGivern 86').

Semi-Finals

Bray Wanderers AFC (Bray)	2-1	Derry City FC (Derry)
St. Francis FC (Dublin)	1-0	Bohemian FC (Dublin)

Quarter-Finals

Bohemian FC (Dublin)	2-0	Cork City FC (Cork)
Bray Wanderers AFC (Bray)	1-0	Galway United FC (Galway)
Derry City FC (Derry)	1-1, 1-1 (aet) (4-3 on penalties)	St. Patrick's Athletic FC (Dublin)
Newcastlewest FC (Newcastlewest)	0-3	St. Francis FC (Dublin)

1990-91

League of Ireland Premier Division 1990-91	Athlone Town	Bohemian FC	Cork City FC	Derry City FC	Dundalk FC	Galway United	Limerick AFC	St. Patrick's Ath.	Shamrock Rvs.	Shelbourne FC	Sligo Rovers FC	Waterford AFC
Athlone Town AFC (Athlone)	■	1-0			1-3	2-2		2-1		0-1	1-2	
	■	3-0	1-1	1-4	0-1	0-1	0-1	1-1	0-2	0-5	0-2	1-1
Bohemian FC (Dublin)		■	1-1		0-0		2-1	1-2	0-1	1-1		
	0-1	■	0-1	0-0	0-2	3-0	2-0	0-1	2-3	1-0	0-2	1-1
Cork City FC (Cork)	2-1		■		0-1	1-0	2-2		0-0			2-0
	2-0	1-0	■	1-1	0-0	1-0	1-0	0-0	1-1	0-0	1-0	1-0
Derry City FC (Derry)	0-1	2-1	1-3	■	0-1		1-0					--
	5-0	1-1	0-0	■	0-1	6-1	1-0	0-1	0-0	2-0	1-1	6-1
Dundalk FC (Dundalk)		3-0		--	■	2-0		0-0		2-0		1-0
	3-0	4-1	1-1	1-0	■	2-0	3-0	3-0	0-0	1-5	0-2	0-0
Galway United FC (Galway)				2-1		■	4-1		0-1	3-5		1-1
	0-2	1-0	1-3	3-1	2-3	■	1-2	0-4	2-4	2-1	0-2	2-1
Limerick City FC (Limerick)	1-0	2-3		0-2	0-3		■			0-3		0-2
	0-0	0-2	1-6	0-4	0-4	0-3	■	2-1	2-1	0-4	1-1	1-2
St. Patrick's Athletic FC (Dublin)			0-3			0-0	1-1	■		1-0	1-0	
	3-0	2-0	1-1	1-0	0-0	4-0	3-0	■	2-1	1-1	2-0	2-0
Shamrock Rovers FC (Dublin)	3-1			2-5	1-2		2-4		■		0-0	
	0-0	0-2	4-0	1-1	0-0	2-0	4-1	0-0	■	2-3	2-1	3-1
Shelbourne FC (Dublin)			0-2	1-0			3-1		1-0	■	1-1	3-0
	0-0	1-1	0-2	1-0	1-2	3-1	5-0	1-2	3-0	■	2-1	4-0
Sligo Rovers FC (Sligo)			1-2	0-0	0-0	0-1					■	3-0
	1-0	1-0	0-1	0-0	2-0	3-1	1-1	0-0	2-1	2-2	■	1-0
Waterford United FC (Waterford)	2-1	2-1		1-4			0-1	0-3				■
	3-1	1-1	0-2	0-2	1-3	0-1	1-0	0-5	0-3	0-1	0-1	■

Premier Division	Pd	Wn	Dw	Ls	GF	GA	Pts	
1. DUNDALK FC (DUNDALK)	33	22	8	3	52	17	52	
2. Cork City FC (Cork)	33	19	12	2	45	18	50	
3. St. Patrick's Athletic FC (Dublin)	33	17	10	6	46	21	44	
4. Shelbourne FC (Dublin)	33	18	6	9	59	30	42	
5. Sligo Rovers FC (Sligo)	33	13	12	8	34	22	38	
6. Shamrock Rovers FC (Dublin) ·	33	14	9	10	51	37	37	
7. Derry City FC (Derry)	33	13	9	11	51	28	35	
8. Galway United FC (Galway)	33	9	5	19	34	61	23	
9. Bohemian FC (Dublin)	33	7	8	18	27	42	22	
10. Athlone Town AFC (Athlone)	33	6	7	20	22	53	19	
11. Waterford United FC (Waterford)	33	6	5	22	22	62	17	R
12. Limerick City FC (Limerick)	33	6	5	22	21	73	17	R
	396	150	96	150	464	464	396	

Top goal-scorers 1990-91

1) Peter HANRAHAN   (Dundalk FC)   18
2) Patrick MORLEY   (Cork City FC)   15
3) Vinny ARKINS   (Shamrock Rovers FC)   14
   Paul NEWE   (Shelbourne FC)   14
5) Mark ENNIS   (St. Patrick's Athletic FC) 12
   Pat FENLON   (St. Patrick's Athletic FC) 12

League of Ireland Division One 1990-91	Bray Wanderers AFC	Cobh Ramblers FC	Drogheda United FC	Finn Harps FC	Home Farm FC	Kilkenny City FC	Longford Town FC	Monaghan United FC	St. James's Gate AFC	University College Dublin
Bray Wanderers AFC (Bray)		0-2	0-0					3-1	3-0	2-0
		1-2	0-0	1-1	2-0	1-1	3-0	2-0	0-2	1-0
Cobh Ramblers FC (Cobh)			1-0	5-0	0-1		3-0			
	0-0		0-2	2-1	1-0	0-0	1-1	3-0	0-1	1-0
Drogheda United FC (Drogheda)		3-1					2-0	1-1	2-2	
	2-0	2-0		2-0	2-1	1-1	3-1	3-2	2-1	2-0
Finn Harps FC (Ballybofey)	0-1		1-0		2-0	3-0	0-1		0-2	
	2-2	1-0	0-0		2-2	3-1	5-0	2-1	0-3	2-1
Home Farm FC (Dublin)	0-3		0-1			0-0				1-2
	0-2	2-2	0-1	4-2		1-1	3-0	3-3	0-3	1-2
Kilkenny City FC (Kilkenny)	0-1		1-4	1-1			2-0			3-0
	0-2	0-0	1-1	1-2	1-3		0-0	2-0	3-0	1-1
Longford Town FC (Longford)	2-1	3-1						0-2	0-1	
	0-1	1-1	0-0	1-3	0-0	3-3		1-3	0-1	0-2
Monaghan United FC (Monaghan)			0-1	1-2	2-1	0-2			2-2	
	0-3	1-2	0-1	2-3	0-1	1-1	2-1		1-2	0-4
St. James's Gate AFC (Dublin)		0-1			2-0	1-0				3-2
	1-3	0-2	0-0	1-3	2-1	1-2	1-2	2-4		1-5
University College Dublin AFC (Dublin)		0-0	0-0	0-1			1-0			
	1-2	0-0	1-1	1-0	3-0	0-1	3-1	2-0	0-1	

	Division One	Pd	Wn	Dw	Ls	GF	GA	Pts	
1.	Drogheda United FC (Drogheda)	27	15	11	1	38	14	41	P
2.	Bray Wanderers AFC (Bray)	27	16	6	5	40	17	38	P
3.	Cobh Ramblers FC (Cobh)	27	12	8	7	31	20	32	
4.	Finn Harps FC (Ballybofey)	27	14	4	9	40	30	32	
5.	St. James's Gate AFC (Dublin)	27	13	3	11	37	38	29	
6.	University College Dublin AFC (Dublin)	27	11	5	11	32	25	27	
7.	Kilkenny City FC (Kilkenny)	27	7	11	9	29	32	25	
8.	Home Farm FC (Dublin)	27	5	7	15	26	46	17	
9.	Longford Town FC (Longford)	27	5	7	15	20	44	17	
10	Monaghan United FC (Monaghan)	27	4	4	19	27	54	12	
		270	102	66	102	320	320	270	

FAI Cup Final   (Lansdowne Road, Dublin – 12/05/1991 – 15,257)

GALWAY UNITED FC (GALWAY)   1-0   Shamrock Rovers FC (Dublin)

Glynn 85'

Galway United: McIntyre, Rodgers, Cleary, Nolan, Morris-Burke (Lally 65'), P.Campbell, Wyse (Cassidy 86'), Carpenter, Mernagh, Kane, Glynn.

Shamrock Rovers: Kavanagh, Connell, Murphy, Eccles, Cooney, Devine (Power 86'), D.Campbell, Poutch (O'Connor 86'), Treacy, Larkins, Swan.

Semi-Finals

Kilkenny City FC (Kilkenny)	0-1	Shamrock Rovers FC (Dublin)
St. James's Gate AFC (Dublin)	1-3	Galway United FC (Galway)

Quarter-Finals

Athlone Town AFC (Athlone)	0-0, 0-1	Shamrock Rovers FC (Dublin)
Kilkenny City FC (Kilkenny)	1-0	Ashtown Villa FC (Ashtown)
Limerick City FC (Limerick)	1-2	Galway United FC (Galway)
Waterford United AFC (Waterford)	0-1	St. James's Gate AFC (Dublin)

1991-92

League of Ireland Premier Division 1991-92

	Athlone Town AFC	Bohemian FC	Bray Wanderers AFC	Cork City FC	Derry City FC	Drogheda United FC	Dundalk FC	Galway United FC	St. Patrick's Athletic FC	Shamrock Rovers FC	Shelbourne FC	Sligo Rovers FC
Athlone Town AFC (Athlone)	■		3-2			2-1	0-1				1-2	1-1
	■	0-0	0-0	0-0	0-1	1-1	1-2	2-1	2-3	2-2	0-2	0-0
Bohemian FC (Dublin)	1-0	■		1-2	1-1	2-3			0-0			
	2-0	■	2-0	2-1	0-1	2-0	1-2	2-1	2-1	1-1	0-0	1-1
Bray Wanderers AFC (Bray)	0-1	1-0	■	2-1			0-2	0-0		0-2		
	1-1	1-0	■	0-0	0-3	1-1	0-2	2-0	0-1	0-0	0-1	1-2
Cork City FC (Cork)		1-0		■	0-0		2-1	2-1	1-0			
	1-1	1-1	2-0	■	0-0	0-0	4-0	2-0	3-1	0-0	2-2	1-0
Derry City FC (Derry)	2-2		0-0	0-1	■	0-2			3-1		3-1	
	2-0	0-1	2-0	2-0	■	7-1	0-0	1-0	1-1	0-0	3-2	0-0
Drogheda United FC (Drogheda)	1-2		0-1		1-0	■		1-0		0-0		0-3
	2-1	0-3	0-1	1-3	0-2	■	2-2	0-0	0-0	0-0	0-3	1-1
Dundalk FC (Dundalk)		0-0	1-1		0-0		■			1-3		0-1
	4-1	0-1	4-0	3-0	1-1	1-1	■	2-1	1-0	0-0	0-2	1-0
Galway United FC (Galway)		3-2			1-1		2-2	■	1-0	2-2	0-5	
	1-0	4-4	1-1	1-2	0-2	1-2	0-2	■	4-0	0-2	1-3	5-1
St. Patrick's Athletic FC (Dublin)	6-3	1-3			2-1	2-1	0-2		■		1-2	
	1-1	3-2	2-1	2-4	0-1	3-1	1-0	1-1	■	1-1	1-1	1-1
Shamrock Rovers FC (Dublin)	2-1		1-1			1-1		2-1		■		1-2
	2-0	1-3	2-0	1-3	0-1	0-1	1-1	3-0	1-1	■	1-2	2-0
Shelbourne FC (Dublin)		2-1		0-1	0-5	2-1			2-1		■	0-0
	2-0	1-2	3-0	3-3	1-0	1-0	1-1	1-1	1-0	0-1	■	1-0
Sligo Rovers FC (Sligo)		1-2	0-1	0-2			3-0	0-0				■
	1-2	0-0	1-2	2-1	2-2	2-3	1-2	5-1	0-0	0-1	1-4	■

	Premier Division	**Pd**	**Wn**	**Dw**	**Ls**	**GF**	**GA**	**Pts**	
1.	SHELBOURNE FC (DUBLIN)	33	21	7	5	57	29	49	
2.	Derry City FC (Derry)	33	17	10	6	49	21	44	
3.	Cork City FC (Cork)	33	16	11	6	47	30	43	
4.	Dundalk FC (Dundalk)	33	14	12	7	44	31	40	
5.	Bohemian FC (Dublin)	33	14	9	10	45	34	37	
6.	Shamrock Rovers FC (Dublin)	33	9	15	9	33	30	33	
7.	St. Patrick's Athletic FC (Dublin)	33	9	11	13	38	46	29	
8.	Bray Wanderers AFC (Bray)	33	8	10	15	17	37	26	
9.	Sligo Rovers FC (Sligo)	33	7	11	15	33	42	25	
10.	Drogheda United FC (Drogheda)	33	6	13	14	23	46	24	*
11.	Athlone Town AFC (Athlone)	33	6	11	16	31	50	23	R
12.	Galway United FC (Galway)	33	7	8	18	37	58	22	R
		396	134	128	134	454	454	395	

* Drogheda United FC (Drogheda) had 1 point deducted for a registration irregularity.

Top goal-scorers 1991-92

1) John CAULFIELD   (Cork City FC)   16
2) Mark ENNIS   (St. Patrick's Athletic FC) 15
3) Gary HAYLOCK   (Shelbourne FC)   13
   Jonathan SPEAK   (Derry City FC)   13
5) Pat MORLEY   (Cork City FC)   11
   Michael O'CONNOR   (Athlone Town AFC)   11

League of Ireland Division One 1991-92	Cobh Ramblers FC	Finn Harps FC	Home Farm FC	Kilkenny City FC	Limerick AFC	Longford Town FC	Monaghan United FC	St. James's Gate AFC	University College Dublin AFC	Waterford AFC
Cobh Ramblers FC (Cobh)	■		0-0		0-0		2-2	1-0	1-3	
	■	1-2	5-1	0-0	1-2	1-1	1-1	1-0	1-1	2-0
Finn Harps FC (Ballybofey)	0-1	■					0-1	0-1	1-3	
	1-1	■	2-2	2-5	0-3	1-1	2-2	0-0	4-0	0-3
Home Farm FC (Dublin)	0-1	1-2	■		0-0	0-1				
	0-0	1-2	■	4-0	0-1	0-3	2-2	0-2	0-0	1-0
Kilkenny City FC (Kilkenny)		1-1	1-1	■			1-2		0-2	
	0-1	3-2	2-1	■	0-2	3-1	1-2	4-0	1-1	0-0
Limerick City FC (Limerick)	1-1	2-0		1-1	■	4-2				
	1-2	5-2	1-1	4-1	■	1-1	3-3	1-0	1-2	2-0
Longford Town FC (Longford)		0-4		1-0		■	1-0		0-1	
	0-2	1-2	1-4	4-2	1-1	■	2-0	0-0	1-0	1-1
Monaghan United FC (Monaghan)	0-0	1-0	2-1	1-1	1-2		■			
	1-2	1-1	0-0	2-4	0-2	1-0	■	1-3	1-1	1-1
St. James's Gate AFC (Dublin)			0-1		0-2	1-0	3-3	■		0-1
	1-0	1-1	0-2	2-1	0-0	2-1	0-1	■	0-3	2-2
University College Dublin AFC (Dublin)			2-0	4-0	4-0		1-2	0-1	■	
	3-0	1-2	1-1	2-1	1-2	5-1	1-1	1-0	■	0-0
Waterford United FC (Waterford)			1-1		2-2	2-1	3-2		3-0	■
	1-1	0-2	1-1	1-2	1-1	3-0	1-0	3-0	1-1	■

	Division One	Pd	Wn	Dw	Ls	GF	GA	Pts	
1.	Limerick City FC (Limerick)	27	14	10	3	47	27	38	P*
2.	Waterford United FC (Waterford)	27	11	11	5	39	25	33	P
3.	Cobh Ramblers FC (Cobh)	27	10	12	5	29	22	32	
4.	University College Dublin AFC (Dublin)	27	11	8	8	37	25	30	
5.	St. James's Gate AFC (Dublin)	27	9	7	11	23	32	25	
6.	Finn Harps FC (Ballybofey)	27	8	8	11	36	42	24	
7.	Monaghan United FC (Monaghan)	27	6	12	9	32	39	24	
8.	Kilkenny City FC (Kilkenny)	27	7	8	12	35	44	22	
9.	Home Farm FC (Dublin)	27	5	11	11	26	33	21	
10	Longford Town FC (Longford)	27	7	7	13	26	41	21	
		270	88	94	88	330	330	270	

*   Limerick City FC (Limerick) changed their club name to Limerick FC (Limerick) for next season.

FAI Cup Final   (Lansdowne Road, Dublin – 10/05/1992 – 17,000)

BOHEMIAN FC (DUBLIN)   1-0   Cork City FC (Cork)

Tilson 78'

Bohemian: Connolly, Broughan, Best, Whelan, P.Byrne. King, A.Byrne, Fenlon, T.Byrne. Lawless, Tilson.
Cork City: Harrington, Murphy, Daly, Bannon, Napier (Long 85'), Cotter (Glynn 80'), Hyde, Barry, McCabe, Morley, Caulfield.

Semi-Finals

Bohemian FC (Dublin)	0-0, 3-1	St. James's Gate AFC (Dublin)
Cork City FC (Cork)	1-0	St. Patrick's Athletic FC (Dublin)

Quarter-Finals

Bohemian FC (Dublin)	1-1, 1-0	Shelbourne FC (Dublin)
Cork City FC (Cork)	2-0	Limerick City FC (Limerick)
St. James's Gate AFC (Dublin)	2-1	Monaghan United FC (Monaghan)
St. Patrick's Athletic FC (Dublin)	1-0	Bray Wanderers AFC (Bray)

1992-93

League of Ireland Premier Division 1992-93	Bohemian FC	Bray Wanderers	Cork City FC	Derry City FC	Drogheda United	Dundalk FC	Limerick AFC	St. Patrick's Ath.	Shamrock Rovers	Shelbourne FC	Sligo Rovers FC	Waterford AFC
Bohemian FC (Dublin)	■	2-0	1-1		0-1	1-0			1-1			
	■	2-0	0-2	0-0	2-0	1-1	1-1	0-0	2-1	1-1	4-0	6-0
Bray Wanderers AFC (Bray)		■		1-0			0-0	1-2		2-0		0-1
	0-4	■	1-1	1-2	1-1	1-1	0-2	1-1	0-5	0-1	2-0	1-1
Cork City FC (Cork)	1-1		■	2-1	2-0	3-0			1-2			
	1-4	2-0	■	1-1	2-0	4-1	0-1	2-1	2-0	2-1	1-1	1-0
Derry City FC (Derry)	2-1		1-1	■		1-0	1-1			0-2		
	0-2	0-0	0-1	■	3-1	1-0	1-1	1-0	1-0	0-0	0-0	1-0
Drogheda United FC (Drogheda)		0-1			■		2-0	0-0			1-0	1-2
	0-0	1-0	0-0	0-1	■	0-2	2-2	1-1	1-4	0-2	1-1	1-0
Dundalk FC (Dundalk)	1-0		0-0	1-1		■	0-0	--	1-0			
	1-1	1-1	3-1	0-0	1-1	■	1-0	0-0	2-1	2-1	1-1	4-0
Limerick City FC (Limerick)	0-2		0-1	1-1	0-1		■			0-2		
	0-0	0-0	1-1	0-0	2-3	0-1	■	2-0	0-0	1-1	1-0	2-2
St. Patrick's Athletic FC (Dublin)		0-0			0-1			■	2-1		0-1	4-0
	1-1	1-1	2-1	1-1	2-2	0-0	0-0	■	1-0	0-0	2-0	2-1
Shamrock Rovers FC (Dublin)			1-1		0-3		1-0		■	0-0	0-0	
	0-1	6-1	2-3	1-2	0-0	0-1	1-4	1-1	■	2-2	0-0	4-0
Shelbourne FC (Dublin)	0-0		2-0	1-1			0-1	1-1		■	4-0	6-0
	1-4	1-0	6-2	1-2	3-2	4-1	3-1	1-1	1-1	■	4-0	6-0
Sligo Rovers FC (Sligo)		0-0			1-1		3-1	0-0			■	1-1
	1-1	1-0	0-3	0-0	0-0	1-1	1-0	1-0	0-1	0-1	■	1-2
Waterford United FC (Waterford)		1-0			4-0		1-1	1-1		1-0		■
	1-0	1-2	0-3	2-0	3-3	5-4	0-3	0-2	2-3	2-1	0-1	■

League of Ireland Premier Division 1992-93 2nd Play-off	Cork City FC	Bohemian FC	Shelbourne FC
Cork City FC (Cork)		1-0	3-2
Bohemian FC (Dublin)	---		2-1
Shelbourne FC (Dublin)	---	---	

League of Ireland Premier Division 1992-93 Play-off	Shelbourne FC	Bohemian FC	Cork City FC
Shelbourne FC (Dublin)		0-0	1-0
Bohemian FC (Dublin)	2-1		0-0
Cork City FC (Cork)	1-1	1-0	

2nd Play-off

		Pd	Wn	Dw	Ls	GF	GA	Pts
1.	CORK CITY FC (CORK)	2	2	-	-	4	2	4
2.	Bohemian FC (Dublin)	2	1	-	1	2	2	2
3.	Shelbourne FC (Dublin)	2	-	-	2	3	5	-
		6	3	-	3	9	9	6

All matches in the 2nd play-off were played on neutral venues

Play-off

		Pd	Wn	Dw	Ls	GF	GA	Pts
1.	Shelbourne FC (Dublin)	4	1	2	1	3	3	4
1.	Bohemian FC (Dublin)	4	1	2	1	2	2	4
1.	Cork City FC (Cork)	4	1	2	1	2	2	4
		12	3	6	3	7	7	12

Final (1-6)

		Pd	Wn	Dw	Ls	GF	GA	Pts	
1.	Bohemian FC (Dublin)	32	13	14	5	46	19	40	
1.	Shelbourne FC (Dublin)	32	15	10	7	53	29	40	
1.	Cork City FC (Cork)	32	16	8	8	47	34	40	
4.	Dundalk FC (Dundalk)	32	13	13	6	35	28	39	
5.	Derry City FC (Derry)	32	11	15	6	26	23	37	
6.	Limerick FC (Limerick)	32	6	15	11	27	31	27	

Final (7-12)

		Pd	Wn	Dw	Ls	GF	GA	Pts	
7.	St. Patrick's Athletic FC (Dublin)	32	7	16	9	27	27	30	
8.	Shamrock Rovers FC (Dublin)	32	8	12	12	39	35	28	
9.	Drogheda United FC (Drogheda)	32	7	13	12	29	41	27	
10.	Waterford United FC (Waterford)	32	10	7	15	34	59	27	PO
11.	Sligo Rovers FC (Sligo)	32	6	14	12	16	32	26	R
12.	Bray Wanderers AFC (Bray)	32	5	13	14	19	40	23	R
		384	117	150	117	398	398	384	

	Premier Division (1st Phase)	Pd	Wn	Dw	Ls	GF	GA	Pts
1.	Bohemian FC (Dublin)	22	10	10	2	37	12	30
2.	Cork City FC (Cork)	22	12	5	5	36	25	29
3.	Derry City FC (Derry)	22	9	10	3	17	12	28
4.	Shelbourne FC (Dublin)	22	10	7	5	42	24	27
5.	Dundalk FC (Dundalk)	22	8	10	4	29	24	26
6.	Limerick FC (Limerick)	22	6	11	5	24	18	23
7.	St. Patrick's Athletic FC (Dublin)	22	5	13	4	19	17	23
8.	Shamrock Rovers FC (Dublin)	22	6	6	10	33	27	18
9.	Drogheda United FC (Drogheda)	22	3	11	8	20	32	17
10.	Sligo Rovers FC (Sligo)	22	4	9	9	10	25	25
11.	Bray Wanderers AFC (Bray)	22	2	9	11	13	35	13
12.	Waterford United FC (Waterford)	22	5	3	14	22	51	13
		264	80	104	80	302	302	264

Top goal-scorers 1992-93

1)	Pat MORLEY	(Cork City FC)	17
2)	Paschal KEANE	(Waterford United FC)	16
3)	Padraig DUFFY	(Shelbourne FC)	15
4)	Pat FENLON	(Bohemian FC)	14
5)	Gary HAYLOCK	(Shelbourne FC)	13

Promotion/Relegation Play-offs (18/04/1993 + 25/04/1993)

Waterford United FC (Waterford)   2-2, 0-3   Monaghan United FC (Monaghan)

League of Ireland Division One 1992-93	Athlone Town	Cobh Ramblers	Finn Harps FC	Galway United	Home Farm FC	Kilkenny City	Longford Town	Monaghan United	St. James's Gate	University College
Athlone Town AFC (Athlone)	■			0-1	2-2			0-2	0-1	2-0
		0-0	1-2	3-2	1-1	0-1	2-1	2-0	0-0	1-2
Cobh Ramblers FC (Cobh)	2-0	■	0-0		1-0			1-1		
	1-1		2-1	0-0	1-1	0-1	0-0	2-2	3-1	1-1
Finn Harps FC (Ballybofey)	1-1		■		1-1	1-1	1-6	1-2		
	2-3	2-1		1-2	3-2	1-2	0-0	2-0	5-1	3-2
Galway United FC (Galway)		1-3	2-1	■		2-2			4-0	
	4-0	1-3	4-1		1-1	2-1	1-0	1-1	4-0	1-1
Home Farm FC (Dublin)			0-0		■	0-0		1-1	4-0	0-1
	1-0	2-1	0-1	3-4		3-0	1-1	0-1	3-1	0-1
Kilkenny City FC (Kilkenny)	2-4	0-0	.			■	3-3	1-2		0-1
	1-1	0-1	0-1	1-4	0-0		1-3	1-3	0-0	0-0
Longford Town FC (Longford)	1-1	3-1		1-0	2-0		■			
	0-5	2-2	3-1	1-3	1-0	2-2		2-2	2-0	2-0
Monaghan United FC (Monaghan)				0-2		1-0		■	2-0	1-1
	3-1	1-1	0-0	2-7	1-0	2-3	5-0		2-0	0-0
St. James's Gate AFC (Dublin)		0-3	0-0			1-1	1-2		■	1-1
	0-1	2-1	1-1	1-0	0-2	1-3	1-0	0-0		2-5
University College Dublin AFC (Dublin)		0-1	3-1	0-1			2-2			■
	1-1	0-1	0-0	0-2	3-0	5-0	3-1	2-1	1-1	

	Division One	Pd	Wn	Dw	Ls	GF	GA	Pts	
1.	Galway United FC (Galway)	27	16	6	5	56	27	39	P
2.	Cobh Ramblers FC (Cobh)	27	10	12	5	33	23	32	P
3.	Monaghan United FC (Monaghan)	27	11	10	6	38	31	32	PO
4.	University College Dublin AFC (Dublin)	27	10	10	7	36	26	30	
5.	Longford Town FC (Longford)	27	10	9	8	41	39	29	
6.	Athlone Town AFC (Athlone)	27	8	9	10	33	34	25	
7.	Finn Harps FC (Ballybofey)	27	8	9	10	34	40	25	
8.	Home Farm FC (Dublin)	27	6	10	11	28	29	22	
9.	Kilkenny City FC (Kilkenny)	27	5	11	11	27	43	21	
10.	St. James's Gate AFC (Dublin)	27	4	8	15	16	50	16	
		270	88	94	88	342	342	270	

FAI Cup Final   (Lansdowne Road, Dublin – 16/05/1993 – 11,000)

SHELBOURNE FC (DUBLIN) 1-0 Dundalk FC (Dundalk)

Costello 59'

Shelbourne: Byrne, Coyle, Neville, Whelan, Brady, Haylock, Doolin, Costello, Rutherford, Dully, O'Doherty (Browne 71').

Dundalk: O'Neill, Purdy, Coll, Murphy, Lawlor, Hanrahan, McNulty, Lawless, Cooney, Eviston (Doherty 79'), Irwin.

Semi-Finals

Dundalk FC (Dundalk)	1-0	St. Patrick's Athletic FC (Dublin)
Shelbourne FC (Dublin)	0-0, 3-2	Derry City FC (Derry)

Quarter-Finals

Derry City FC (Derry)	2-1	Shamrock Rovers FC (Dublin)
Dundalk FC (Dundalk)	2-0	Limerick FC (Limerick)
Glenmore Celtic FC (Dublin)	0-6	Shelbourne FC (Dublin)
Sligo Rovers FC (Sligo)	1-2	St. Patrick's Athletic FC (Dublin)

1993-94

League of Ireland Premier Division 1993-94	Bohemian FC	Cobh Ramblers	Cork City FC	Derry City FC	Drogheda United	Dundalk FC	Galway United FC	Limerick AFC	Monaghan United	St. Patrick's Ath.	Shamrock Rovers	Shelbourne FC
Bohemian FC (Dublin)	■	1-1	1-3				0-1				1-2	2-0
	■	2-0	3-4	2-0	0-1	1-0	3-0	1-0	0-0	0-0	2-0	1-0
Cobh Ramblers FC (Cobh)		■		1-0	1-1		1-0	1-2	0-1			
	0-0	■	2-1	1-3	1-2	0-2	0-2	0-0	2-0	0-1	1-3	1-1
Cork City FC (Cork)	3-1		■	4-2			2-0				2-1	1-1
	2-0	2-0	■	1-0	1-1	0-1	1-2	3-0	1-0	1-1	2-2	3-1
Derry City FC (Derry)	4-0	3-2		■	1-1					1-0	0-0	
	3-0	2-0	0-1	■	1-1	1-4	0-0	0-0	1-0	2-0	0-0	1-4
Drogheda United FC (Drogheda)		2-1			■	0-2		0-0	1-1	2-0		
	0-4	1-3	0-5	0-1	■	0-3	1-4	0-2	1-4	1-1	2-1	2-2
Dundalk FC (Dundalk)		0-0		4-0		■	2-0	1-1	0-2			
	1-1	0-2	2-2	2-2	0-1	■	0-0	0-0	1-3	0-2	1-2	5-1
Galway United FC (Galway)	3-1		0-1	2-1			■				2-3	2-5
	1-1	4-0	0-0	2-1	2-0	0-0	■	1-2	1-0	1-2	0-5	1-1
Limerick City FC (Limerick)		0-0			1-0	2-1		■	2-1	2-2		
	0-0	1-5	1-7	0-1	1-1	0-1	0-3	■	2-3	2-1	0-2	0-0
Monaghan United FC (Monaghan)		1-1			3-2	1-1		2-1	■	0-0		
	1-0	2-1	2-1	1-1	1-0	1-0	3-1	0-0	■	1-2	0-1	4-5
St. Patrick's Athletic FC (Dublin)		0-5			1-3	0-0		1-0	1-2	■		
	0-0	1-1	3-4	0-0	4-1	0-0	2-3	1-1	1-0	■	0-2	2-2
Shamrock Rovers FC (Dublin)	1-2		2-0	3-0			2-5				■	2-1
	2-1	3-0	3-0	0-1	2-0	0-0	3-1	7-3	2-1	1-0	■	2-0
Shelbourne FC (Dublin)	0-2		1-1	1-1			0-1			0-3		■
	2-1	1-0	0-1	2-0	1-0	1-2	1-1	3-0	3-0	1-0	1-0	■

Final (1-6) | Pd | Wn | Dw | Ls | GF | GA | Pts

1. SHAMROCK ROVERS FC (DUBLIN) — 32, 21, 3, 8, 62, 30, 66
2. Cork City FC (Cork) — 32, 17, 8, 7, 60, 36, 59
3. Galway United FC (Galway) — 32, 14, 8, 10, 47, 42, 50
4. Derry City FC (Derry) — 32, 12, 10, 10, 37, 35, 46
5. Shelbourne FC (Dublin) — 32, 11, 10, 11, 42, 42, 43
6. Bohemian FC (Dublin) — 32, 11, 8, 13, 34, 35, 41

Final (7-12) | Pd | Wn | Dw | Ls | GF | GA | Pts

7. Monaghan United FC (Monaghan) — 32, 13, 8, 11, 41, 38, 47
8. Dundalk FC (Dundalk) — 32, 10, 13, 9, 37, 27, 43
9. St. Patrick's Athletic FC (Dublin) — 32, 9, 12, 11, 32, 38, 39
10. Cobh Ramblers FC (Cobh) — 32, 8, 8, 16, 31, 41, 32 PO

11. Limerick FC (Limerick) — 32, 6, 11, 15, 23, 50, 29 R
12. Drogheda United FC (Drogheda) — 32, 7, 7, 18, 26, 58, 28 R

Totals: 384, 139, 106, 139, 472, 472, 523

	Premier Division (1st Phase)	Pd	Wn	Dw	Ls	GF	GA	Pts
1.	Shamrock Rovers FC (Dublin)	22	15	3	4	43	16	48
2.	Cork City FC (Cork)	22	11	6	5	41	24	39
3.	Shelbourne FC (Dublin)	22	10	7	3	33	25	37
4.	Galway United FC (Galway)	22	9	7	6	30	26	34
5.	Bohemian FC (Dublin)	22	8	7	7	23	17	31
6.	Derry City FC (Derry)	22	8	7	7	21	21	31
7.	Monaghan United FC (Monaghan)	22	9	3	10	27	27	30
8.	Dundalk FC (Dundalk)	22	7	8	7	25	20	29
9.	St. Patrick's Athletic FC (Dublin)	22	6	9	7	24	24	27
10.	Cobh Ramblers FC (Cobh)	22	5	4	13	20	34	19
11.	Limerick FC (Limerick)	22	3	8	11	15	40	17
12.	Drogheda United FC (Drogheda)	22	4	5	13	16	44	17
		264	95	74	95	318	318	359

Top goal-scorers 1993-94

1) Stephen GEOGHEGAN (Shamrock Rovers FC) 23
2) Pat MORLEY (Cork City FC) 16
3) John BRENNAN (Galway United FC) 14
4) Donnie FARRAGHER (Galway United FC) 13

Promotion/Relegation Play-offs (09/04/1994 + 16/04/1994)

Finn Harps FC (Ballybofey)   1-0, 0-3   Cobh Ramblers FC (Cobh)

League of Ireland Division One 1993-94	Athlone Town	Bray Wanderers	Finn Harps FC	Home Farm FC	Kilkenny City FC	Longford Town	St. James's Gate	Sligo Rovers FC	University College	Waterford AFC
Athlone Town AFC (Athlone)	■	0-0		1-1	2-3			0-2		
			1-1	1-0	2-2	0-0	2-1	3-1	2-1	2-0	2-2
Bray Wanderers AFC (Bray)		■		0-0		0-0		1-0	0-0	
	0-0		0-4	1-0	1-1	2-1	0-0	0-3	0-2	1-1
Finn Harps FC (Ballybofey)	1-0	1-0	■			3-1		2-0		1-1
	2-2	2-1		2-0	1-1	1-1	1-0	0-1	0-0	2-0
Home Farm FC (Dublin)			1-1	■		3-2	3-1	0-1		1-3
	1-1	3-2	3-1		1-1	-0	2-2	0-1	0-0	3-0
Kilkenny City FC (Kilkenny)		1-1	1-1	0-0	■			1-1	0-1	
	1-3	1-1	1-1	1-1		3-1	2-0	1-4	3-2	2-2
Longford Town FC (Longford)	0-2	1-1		3-1		■	5-3		1-2	
	0-0	1-0	2-0	3-2	2-1		1-4	0-0	1-2	2-1
St. James's Gate AFC (Dublin)	0-1		1-2		1-1		■			1-1
	0-2	1-1	1-1	2-3	2-2	0-1		0-0	0-2	0-0
Sligo Rovers FC (Sligo)		1-0		3-0	1-0	3-1		■		
	2-2	1-1	4-1	4-0	0-1	1-1	1-1		1-1	4-1
University College Dublin AFC (Dublin)	0-0		2-3	0-0		0-0	1-0		■	
	0-1	1-2	4-1	3-1	7-1	1-2	0-0	1-1		1-0
Waterford United FC (Waterford)	0-1				0-0		0-1	0-3		■
	1-1	0-0	6-0	4-2	0-0	2-2	3-1	2-1	1-1	

	Division One	Pd	Wn	Dw	Ls	GF	GA	Pts	
1.	Sligo Rovers FC (Sligo)	27	14	8	5	42	19	50	P
2.	Athlone Town AFC (Athlone)	27	11	13	3	34	22	46	P
3.	Finn Harps FC (Ballybofey)	27	11	9	7	35	35	42	PO
4.	University College Dublin AFC (Dublin)	27	10	10	7	37	23	40	
5.	Longford Town FC (Longford)	27	9	7	11	35	39	34	
6.	Home Farm FC (Dublin)	27	7	11	9	34	39	32	
7.	Waterford United FC (Waterford)	27	6	13	8	32	33	31	
8.	Kilkenny City FC (Kilkenny)	27	5	15	7	31	42	30	
9.	Bray Wanderers AFC (Bray)	27	4	15	8	17	27	27	
10	St. James's Gate AFC (Dublin)	27	1	13	13	23	41	16	
		270	78	114	78	320	320	348	

FAI Cup Final   (Lansdowne Road, Dublin – 15/05/1994 – 13,800)

SLIGO ROVERS FC (SLIGO)   1-0   Derry City FC (Derry)

Carr 72'

Sligo Rovers: McLean, McStay, Boyle, Dykes, McDonnell, Moran, Hastie, Carr, Kenny, Gabbiadini, Annand.
Derry City: O'Neill, Vaudequin, Curran, Gauld, McLaughlin, Hutton, McKever, O'Brien, Kinnaird, Lawless, Coyle (Heaney 85').

Semi-Finals

Bohemian FC (Dublin)	0-1	Derry City FC (Derry)
Sligo Rovers FC (Sligo)	1-0	Limerick FC (Limerick)

Quarter-Finals

Derry City FC (Derry)	1-0	St. Patrick's Athletic FC (Dublin)
Home Farm FC (Dublin)	1-1, 1-4	Bohemian FC (Dublin)
Limerick FC (Limerick)	2-1	Monaghan United FC (Monaghan)
Sligo Rovers FC (Sligo)	1-0	Cobh Ramblers FC (Cobh)

1994-95

League of Ireland Premier Division 1994-95	Athlone Town AFC	Bohemian FC	Cobh Ramblers FC	Cork City FC	Derry City FC	Dundalk FC	Galway United FC	Monaghan United FC	St. Patrick's Athletic FC	Shamrock Rovers FC	Shelbourne FC	Sligo Rovers FC
Athlone Town AFC (Athlone)	■	1-1	1-4	1-1			1-0		1-0			1-0
		0-0	0-2	2-3	0-1	0-2	1-1	1-1	2-2	4-2	0-0	0-0
Bohemian FC (Dublin)	2-2	■	3-0		0-0	2-0				1-2		
	3-1		4-1	1-2	0-0	2-0	3-0	3-0	1-1	2-4	3-3	0-1
Cobh Ramblers FC (Cobh)			■	1-0	1-1		5-0	0-1	0-2			
	0-0	0-1		0-0	0-0	2-2	1-2	0-2	1-0	0-3	0-0	1-1
Cork City FC (Cork)		1-2		■	0-2	0-1		1-3		0-1		2-0
	4-2	2-1	3-0		2-4	2-0	0-0	4-0	3-1	1-1	0-1	3-2
Derry City FC (Derry)		1-1			■	2-0		2-0	1-0	2-0		
	2-1	1-0	3-1	0-0		2-0	1-1	2-0	0-3	0-1	1-2	4-3
Dundalk FC (Dundalk)	1-0		1-0		2-0	■	2-0	6-0		1-1		
	2-1	2-0	2-1	1-3	1-1		1-0	0-0	2-0	2-1	1-0	1-1
Galway United FC (Galway)	0-1		1-0	0-1			■		2-4			4-2
	1-2	2-2	0-5	2-1	1-4	0-0		5-2	0-0	1-1	0-1	2-1
Monaghan United FC (Monaghan)		1-2		0-5		1-2		■	0-1	1-2		
	1-0	0-1	3-1	0-5	0-1	0-4	2-3		0-0	0-1	1-1	0-6
St. Patrick's Athletic FC (Dublin)	1-1	1-1		2-1		1-1			■			3-1
	1-1	0-0	5-0	3-4	1-1	1-0	4-2	2-0		3-3	1-0	5-0
Shamrock Rovers FC (Dublin)		0-2			2-1	1-1		1-1		■	0-3	0-2
	1-0	1-1	1-1	2-1	4-0	3-0	1-2	3-0	1-1		0-0	1-0
Shelbourne FC (Dublin)	3-1		3-0	1-0		2-1	3-1	1-1			■	
	2-2	0-2	1-1	2-0	3-0	1-0	2-3	0-2	0-2	3-1		1-3
Sligo Rovers FC (Sligo)		0-2	2-2		1-0	0-1		2-0		0-1		■
	0-0	1-0	3-1	3-2	0-0	0-1	0-0	2-1	4-1	1-0	1-2	

	Premier Division	**Pd**	**Wn**	**Dw**	**Ls**	**GF**	**GA**	**Pts**	
1.	DUNDALK FC (DUNDALK)	33	17	8	8	41	25	59	
2.	Derry City FC (Derry)	33	16	10	7	45	30	58	
3.	Shelbourne FC (Dublin)	33	16	9	8	45	32	57	
4.	Bohemian FC (Dublin)	33	14	11	8	48	30	53	
5.	St. Patrick's Athletic FC (Dublin)	33	13	14	6	53	36	53	
6.	Shamrock Rovers FC (Dublin)	33	14	9	10	45	36	51	
7.	Cork City FC (Cork)	33	15	4	14	55	42	49	
8.	Sligo Rovers FC (Sligo)	33	12	7	14	43	42	43	
9.	Galway United FC (Galway)	33	10	9	14	39	53	39	
10.	Athlone Town AFC (Athlone)	33	6	14	13	31	44	32	PO
11.	Cobh Ramblers FC (Cobh)	33	5	11	17	29	51	26	R
12.	Monaghan United FC (Monaghan)	33	5	4	24	22	75	19	R
		396	143	110	143	496	496	539	

Top goal-scorers 1994-95

1) John CAULFIELD   (Cork City FC)   15
2) Eddie ANNAND   (Sligo Rovers FC)   14
3) Vinny ARKINS   (Shelbourne FC)   13
   Ricky O'FLAHERTY   (Galway United FC)   13
5) Jason BYRNE   (St. Patrick's Athletic FC) 12

Promotion/Relegation Play-off

Finn Harps FC (Ballybofey)   0-0, 0-0 (aet) (3-5 on penalties)   Athlone Town AFC (Athlone)

League of Ireland Division One 1994-95	Bray Unknowns AFC	Drogheda United FC	Finn Harps FC	Home Farm FC	Kilkenny City FC	Limerick AFC	Longford Town FC	St. James's Gate AFC	University College Dublin AFC	Waterford AFC
Bray Unknowns AFC (Bray)	■	1-1	0-1		1-1	0-1	1-1			
	■	2-0	2-3	4-3	4-1	1-1	0-1	0-0	0-0	0-1
Drogheda United FC (Drogheda)		■	1-0	1-0		1-0			0-0	2-1
	3-1	■	0-4	1-2	6-0	2-2	3-0	1-1	1-0	0-0
Finn Harps FC (Ballybofey)			■	2-0	3-0			2-1	0-1	
	2-2	0-2	■	3-2	5-2	1-1	3-3	0-1	1-2	1-1
Home Farm FC (Dublin)	2-1			■	5-0	0-1			0-3	
	2-1	1-2	0-1	■	7-2	0-2	1-1	2-1	1-4	0-0
Kilkenny City FC (Kilkenny)		0-0			■	0-3	0-1	0-6		
	0-3	1-3	1-8	2-3	■	0-1	0-1	0-3	0-4	0-1
Limerick AFC (Limerick)			0-0			■	3-0	2-1	1-1	3-1
	0-1	0-2	0-0	0-2	1-0	■	2-0	2-2	0-3	0-0
Longford Town FC (Longford)		1-1	0-1	1-1			■			1-2
	1-0	1-3	0-2	2-2	3-2	1-1	■	2-0	0-2	0-1
St. James's Gate AFC (Dublin)	0-3	1-5		1-1		2-2		■	0-3	
	1-2	2-4	1-1	2-2	1-0	2-3	1-1	■	2-3	2-2
University College Dublin AFC (Dublin)	1-0			3-0		5-0			■	1-0
	2-0	2-2	3-0	3-0	3-0	1-0	0-1	4-0	■	0-2
Waterford United FC (Waterford)	1-1		2-0	5-2	2-1		1-1			■
	1-2	0-1	2-0	1-2	2-1	0-0	0-1	1-0	1-2	■

	Division One	**Pd**	**Wn**	**Dw**	**Ls**	**GF**	**GA**	**Pts**	
1.	University College Dublin AFC (Dublin)	27	20	4	3	56	12	64	P
2.	Drogheda United FC (Drogheda)	27	16	8	3	48	23	56	P
3.	Finn Harps FC (Ballybofey)	27	12	7	8	44	30	43	PO
4.	Limerick FC (Limerick)	27	11	10	6	30	22	43	
5.	Waterford United FC (Waterford)	27	11	8	8	31	24	41	
6.	Home Farm FC (Dublin)	27	9	6	12	43	47	33	
7.	Longford Town FC (Longford)	27	8	9	10	26	39	33	
8.	Bray Wanderers AFC (Bray)	27	8	8	11	33	31	32	
9.	St. James's Gate AFC (Dublin)	27	4	10	13	35	49	22	
10	Kilkenny City FC (Kilkenny)	27	-	2	25	14	83	2	
		270	99	72	99	360	360	369	

FAI Cup Final (Lansdowne Road, Dublin – 07/05/1995 – 14,000)

DERRY CITY FC (DERRY)   2-1   Shelbourne FC (Dublin)

Shelbourne: Gough, Costello, Dunne, Neville, Duffy, Byrne, Mooney, Flood, Arkins (Vaughan 89'), Geoghegan, Rutherford.

Semi-Finals

Bohemian FC (Dublin)	0-0, 0-0 (aet), 2-3 (aet)	Derry City FC (Derry)
Sligo Rovers FC (Sligo)	1-3	Shelbourne FC (Dublin)

Quarter-Finals

Avondale United FC (Cork)	0-4	Shelbourne FC (Dublin)
Bluebell United FC (Dublin)	0-4	Bohemian FC (Dublin)
Dundalk FC (Dundalk)	0-1	Derry City FC (Derry)
Shamrock Rovers FC (Dublin)	0-0, 0-2	Sligo Rovers FC (Sligo)

1995-96

League of Ireland Premier Division 1995-96	Athlone Town AFC	Bohemian FC	Cork City FC	Derry City FC	Drogheda United	Dundalk FC	Galway United FC	St. Patrick's Athletic	Shamrock Rovers	Shelbourne FC	Sligo Rovers FC	University College
Athlone Town AFC (Athlone)	■	0-3				0-0	1-0	2-2		4-3		
		2-5	2-4	1-1	0-2	0-0	0-2	0-1	2-0	1-2	1-2	1-0
Bohemian FC (Dublin)		■	1-0	1-1				0-0	1-0		1-2	3-1
	3-1		1-1	1-0	6-0	3-2	3-0	0-1	1-1	1-0	2-0	0-0
Cork City FC (Cork)	0-2		■	2-1		3-0	0-0		2-1			
	2-0	1-0		0-1	1-2	0-2	1-1	1-0	2-0	1-1	2-1	2-1
Derry City FC (Derry)	1-1		2-1	■	1-1	0-1				4-0		1-1
	5-3	1-1	2-0		1-0	1-1	2-0	5-1	1-1	1-2	1-2	3-1
Drogheda United FC (Drogheda)	0-1	0-1			■	2-1	6-1		1-3	0-1		
	0-1	2-5	2-2	2-2		3-2	3-0	1-3	1-2	1-1	0-0	0-1
Dundalk FC (Dundalk)		2-4	0-1			■		1-2	0-0		0-1	
	2-1	1-2	0-0	2-1	2-2		2-0	3-2	1-0	1-1	0-1	2-0
Galway United FC (Galway)		0-2		0-3		2-1	■		0-2	1-3		0-2
	2-2	1-5	3-1	1-1	0-3	0-1		0-1	1-1	1-1	2-3	1-1
St. Patrick's Athletic FC (Dublin)			1-1	3-2		3-0		■	2-2	3-0		2-0
	3-2	3-3	2-1	3-3	1-0	2-1	1-2		1-0	2-1	1-0	2-1
Shamrock Rovers FC (Dublin)	2-1		2-0	2-1	1-0				■			2-0
	1-1	1-0	1-1	2-0	1-1	1-0	2-1	0-1		0-1	0-2	0-2
Shelbourne FC (Dublin)		1-0		1-0	1-1	0-1			1-2	■	2-1	
	1-0	1-0	1-1	1-2	0-0	3-1	2-0	1-1	3-0		0-0	1-1
Sligo Rovers FC (Sligo)	2-1	4-1				0-2	1-1	3-1			■	
	4-2	0-0	3-1	1-1	1-0	3-3	3-2	0-0	0-1	0-1		2-0
University College Dublin AFC (Dublin)	1-2		2-1		4-1	0-0			3-2	3-1		■
	3-0	3-1	0-1	2-0	0-0	1-2	2-0	0-2	0-1	0-3	2-1	

	Premier Division	Pd	Wn	Dw	Ls	GF	GA	Pts	
1.	ST. PATRICK'S ATHLETIC FC (DUBLIN)	33	19	10	4	53	34	67	
2.	Bohemian FC (Dublin)	33	18	8	7	60	29	62	
3.	Sligo Rovers FC (Sligo)	33	16	7	10	45	38	55	
4.	Shelbourne FC (Dublin)	33	15	9	9	45	33	54	
5.	Shamrock Rovers FC (Dublin)	33	14	8	11	32	32	50	
6.	Derry City FC (Derry)	33	11	13	9	50	38	46	
7.	Dundalk FC (Dundalk)	33	11	9	13	38	39	42	
8.	University College Dublin AFC (Dublin)	33	12	6	15	38	40	42	
9.	Cork City FC (Cork)	33	12	8	13	37	41	41	*
10.	Athlone Town AFC (Athlone)	33	8	7	18	38	59	31	PO
11.	Drogheda United FC (Drogheda)	33	7	9	17	39	51	30	R
12.	Galway United FC (Galway)	33	5	6	22	26	67	21	R
		396	148	100	148	501	501	541	

* Cork City FC (Cork) had 3 points deducted for fielding an ineligible player. The club went into liquidation in January 1996 but were saved from extinction and moved from Bishopstown to Turner's Cross.

Top goal-scorers 1995-96

1)	Stephen GEOGHEGAN	(Shelbourne FC)	20
2)	Mick O'BYRNE	(University College Dublin AFC)	16
3)	Padraig MORAN	(Sligo Rovers FC)	14
	Ricky O'FLAHERTY	(St. Patrick's Athletic FC)	14
5)	Tommy GAYNOR	(Athlone Town AFC)	12
	Ian GILZEAN	(Sligo Rovers FC)	12

	Division One	Pd	Wn	Dw	Ls	GF	GA	Pts	
1.	Bray Wanderers AFC (Bray)	27	16	7	4	53	21	55	P
2.	Finn Harps FC (Ballybofey)	27	14	7	6	50	25	49	P
3.	Home Farm-Everton FC (Dublin)	27	14	4	9	44	33	46	PO
4.	Cobh Ramblers FC (Cobh)	27	10	13	4	30	18	43	
5.	St. James's Gate AFC (Dublin)	27	9	11	7	35	30	38	
6.	Limerick FC (Limerick)	27	10	6	11	38	34	36	
7.	Kilkenny City FC (Kilkenny)	27	9	8	10	32	35	35	
8.	Waterford United FC (Waterford)	27	9	7	11	37	39	34	
9.	Longford Town FC (Longford)	27	5	6	16	25	49	21	
10	Monaghan United FC (Monaghan)	27	2	5	20	11	71	11	
		270	98	74	98	355	355	368	

Home Farm FC (Dublin) changed to Home Farm-Everton FC (Dublin) under a player-exchange deal with English club Everton FC (Liverpool).

FAI Cup Final (Lansdowne Road, Dublin – 06/05/1996)

SHELBOURNE FC (DUBLIN)   1-1   St. Patrick's Athletic FC (Dublin)

Sheridan 86'   *Campbell 76'*

Shelbourne: Gough, Costello, Neville, Duffy (Rutherford 82'), D.Geoghegan, Sheridan, Kelly (McKop 66'), Flood, O'Rourke, Tilson, S.Geoghegan.

St, Patrick's Athletic: Byrne, Burke, McDonnell, D.Campbell, Carpenter, P.Campbell, Menagh, Gormley, Osam, O'Flaherty (Glynn 79'), Buckley (Reilly 69').

Final Replay (Lansdowne Road, Dublin – 13/05/1996)

SHELBOURNE FC (DUBLIN)   2-1   St. Patrick's Athletic FC (Dublin)

Sheridan 71', Geoghegan 82'   *Campbell 63'*

St. Patrick's Athletic: Byrne, Burke, McDonnell (P.Campbell 30'), D.Campbell, Carpenter, Osam (Reilly 45'), Menagh (Glynn 82'), Gormley, Buckley, Morris-Roe, O'Flaherty.

Shelbourne: Gough, Costello, Neville, Duffy, D.Geoghegan, Sheridan, Kelly (Rutherford 64'), Flood, O'Rourke, Tilson, S.Geoghegan.

Semi-Finals

Bohemian FC (Dublin)	0-0, 0-0 (aet), 1-2	St. Patrick's Athletic FC (Dublin)
Sligo Rovers FC (Sligo)	0-1	Shelbourne FC (Dublin)

Quarter-Finals

Cork City FC (Cork)	1-2	Sligo Rovers FC (Sligo)
Derry City FC (Derry)	0-3	Shelbourne FC (Dublin)
Finn Harps FC (Ballybofey)	0-0, 0-2	Bohemian FC (Dublin)
Wayside Celtic FC (Dublin)	0-3	St. Patrick's Athletic FC (Dublin)

1996-97

League of Ireland Premier Division 1996-97	Bohemian FC	Bray Wanderers AFC	Cork City FC	Derry City FC	Dundalk FC	Finn Harps FC	Home Farm-Everton	St. Patrick's Athletic	Shamrock Rovers FC	Shelbourne FC	Sligo Rovers FC	University College
Bohemian FC (Dublin)	■	1-0	0-2	0-0		0-1			0-0			
	■	1-0	1-0	1-1	3-0	3-1	1-1	2-1	1-1	1-1	0-2	1-0
Bray Wanderers AFC (Bray)	0-1	■		2-5	0-1	0-0			1-1		2-0	
	1-5	■	0-0	2-3	1-0	0-1	1-0	0-1	3-4	0-4	2-2	0-2
Cork City FC (Cork)		3-1	■		1-0	0-0		1-1	0-1	1-0		
	0-0	3-1	■	0-1	0-0	0-1	2-1	1-1	0-1	3-1	1-2	1-0
Derry City FC (Derry)		0-2	■			1-1	2-0	1-1		0-2		
	1-0	5-1	0-1	■	5-2	3-0	3-1	1-1	1-0	2-2	0-0	5-0
Dundalk FC (Dundalk)		0-4	0-1		■			2-2	1-3		1-1	
	0-2	2-1	0-1	2-4	■	1-1	2-1	1-0	4-1	0-1	2-1	2-2
Finn Harps FC (Ballybofey)	1-2		0-1	0-0		■	3-0		1-2		3-4	
	2-2	0-0	0-1	0-1	5-0	■	3-2	0-1	0-0	3-2	1-1	5-1
Home Farm-Everton FC (Dublin)	2-2	0-1			0-1		■		3-0			2-3
	0-3	1-1	0-2	0-2	0-0	2-3	■	0-2	0-0	0-3	0-0	0-1
St. Patrick's Athletic FC (Dublin)		2-1	0-0		2-1	3-1		■	2-2		4-2	
	5-0	2-2	1-1	1-1	2-2	2-0	1-2	■	0-0	1-1	2-2	1-1
Shamrock Rovers FC (Dublin)	3-1	2-2				2-3			■	6-4		0-0
	3-2	2-0	0-1	1-1	0-2	2-2	2-1	0-1	■	0-2	2-1	1-1
Shelbourne FC (Dublin)	0-1		1-1	0-1	2-0		1-1			■		1-0
	0-1	1-0	3-3	2-2	2-1	1-2	2-0	0-1	2-0	■	3-0	1-0
Sligo Rovers FC (Sligo)		0-1				3-2		1-1	0-3		■	2-0
	2-1	3-2	1-4	0-1	2-1	0-2	0-0	2-0	3-0	1-1	■	2-1
University College Dublin AFC (Dublin)	1-2		3-0	0-1	3-1	0-0		2-0				■
	0-2	2-1	2-1	1-0	1-0	4-0	0-0	0-1	1-0	1-3	1-1	■

	Premier Division	Pd	Wn	Dw	Ls	GF	GA	Pts	
1.	DERRY CITY FC (DERRY)	33	19	10	4	58	27	67	
2.	Bohemian FC (Dublin)	33	16	9	8	43	32	57	
3.	Shelbourne FC (Dublin)	33	15	9	9	52	36	54	
4.	Cork City FC (Cork)	33	15	9	9	38	24	54	
5.	St. Patrick's Athletic FC (Dublin)	33	13	14	6	45	33	53	
6.	Sligo Rovers FC (Sligo)	33	12	11	10	43	43	47	
7.	Shamrock Rovers FC (Dublin)	33	10	13	10	43	46	43	
8.	University College Dublin AFC (Dublin)	33	12	7	14	34	39	43	
9.	Finn Harps FC (Ballybofey)	33	10	9	14	41	43	39	
10.	Dundalk FC (Dundalk)	33	9	9	15	32	50	36	PO
11.	Bray Wanderers AFC (Bray)	33	5	8	29	30	59	23	R
12.	Home Farm-Everton FC (Dublin)	33	3	10	20	26	53	19	R
		396	139	118	139	485	485	535	

Top goal-scorers 1996-97

1) Stephen GEOGHEGAN (Shelbourne FC) 16
2) Tony COUSINS (Shamrock Rovers FC) 15
   Peter HUTTON (Derry City FC) 15
   Pat MORLEY (Shelbourne FC) 15
   Martin REILLY (St. Patrick's Athletic FC) 15

Promotion/Relegation Play-off

Dundalk FC (Dundalk)   3-0, 0-1   Waterford United FC (Waterford)

	Division One	Pd	Wn	Dw	Ls	GF	GA	Pts	
1.	Kilkenny City FC (Kilkenny)	27	15	10	2	47	20	55	P
2.	Drogheda United FC (Drogheda)	27	12	8	7	44	27	44	P
3.	Waterford United FC (Waterford)	27	12	8	7	41	28	44	PO
4.	Athlone Town AFC (Athlone)	27	10	7	10	40	39	37	
5.	Cobh Ramblers FC (Cobh)	27	9	8	10	34	28	35	
6.	Galway United FC (Galway)	27	9	8	10	33	38	35	
7.	Longford Town FC (Longford)	27	7	13	7	31	38	34	
8.	Monaghan United FC (Monaghan)	27	7	9	11	30	46	30	
9.	St. Francis FC (Dublin)	27	7	7	13	20	33	28	*
10	Limerick FC (Limerick)	27	4	8	13	23	55	20	
		270	92	86	92	352	352	362	

* St. James's Gate AFC (Dublin) were expelled from the league pre-season as they were unable to meet financial guarantees. Their place was awarded to St. Francis FC (Dublin).

FAI Cup Final   (Dalymount Park, Dublin – 04/05/1997)

SHELBOURNE FC (DUBLIN)   2-0   Derry City FC (Derry)

Campbell 81', S.Geoghegan 87'

Shelbourne: Gough, Neville, Campbell, Scully, D.Geoghegan, Vaudequin (Costello 88'), Sheridan, Flood, O'Rourke, Rutherford (Baker 89'), S.Geoghegan.

Derry City: Devine, Boyle (Semple 83'), Dyles, Curran, Dunne, Hargan Hutton, Hegarty, Keddy, Beckett, L.Coyle.

Semi-Finals

Bohemian FC (Dublin)	0-2	Derry City FC (Derry)
Waterford United FC (Waterford)	1-2	Shelbourne FC (Dublin)

Quarter-Finals

Bohemian FC (Dublin)	1-0	St. Patrick's Athletic FC (Dublin)
Bray Wanderers AFC (Bray)	0-1	Shelbourne FC (Dublin)
Derry City FC (Derry)	1-0	Cork City FC (Cork)
Waterford United FC (Waterford)	1-0	Drogheda United FC (Drogheda)

1997-98

League of Ireland Premier Division 1997-98	Bohemian FC	Cork City FC	Derry City FC	Drogheda United	Dundalk FC	Finn Harps FC	Kilkenny City FC	St. Patrick's Ath.	Shamrock Rovers	Shelbourne FC	Sligo Rovers FC	University College
Bohemian FC (Dublin)	■			2-1		1-0	4-3		0-1	0-1		2-0
	■	4-2	1-0	1-1	2-0	4-2	8-1	0-0	1-1	1-0	1-1	0-0
Cork City FC (Cork)	2-0	■	0-1		0-0			1-1				1-2
	1-1	■	2-0	1-1	3-0	3-1	1-0	0-1	2-1	4-4	1-1	1-0
Derry City FC (Derry)	1-0		■	3-0	0-0	0-0				1-2		0-3
	1-0	1-1	■	4-1	1-2	1-0	1-1	1-1	0-1	2-2	0-0	1-1
Drogheda United FC (Drogheda)		1-2		■			1-1	1-2	0-1		1-1	
	0-1	1-2	0-1	■	1-0	0-2	0-0	1-3	1-3	0-1	2-4	0-0
Dundalk FC (Dundalk)	3-3		0-2		■	2-1	1-0		2-1		1-2	
	2-2	1-0	0-1	1-1	■	2-0	3-0	0-0	0-0	0-1	5-0	1-1
Finn Harps FC (Ballybofey)		1-2		1-0		■		0-2		0-0		1-2
	3-2	2-1	1-0	2-0	0-1	■	2-1	1-2	2-1	3-1	1-1	1-0
Kilkenny City FC (Kilkenny)		1-2	1-0			2-2	■	1-2	1-1		2-1	
	1-1	0-2	0-5	2-1	1-2	2-3	■	0-2	1-2	1-3	0-1	1-1
St. Patrick's Athletic FC (Dublin)	0-2		1-0		4-2			■		0-0		1-0
	0-0	3-3	0-0	2-0	1-0	1-0	1-0	■	2-0	2-3	1-2	1-1
Shamrock Rovers FC (Dublin)		2-2	3-1		5-2	2-2		0-1	■		0-0	
	2-1	1-3	1-0	0-0	1-2	2-1	1-0	0-1	■	0-2	1-1	2-0
Shelbourne FC (Dublin)		1-1		1-0			3-0		2-1	■	2-0	
	0-1	3-1	1-0	5-0	2-0	3-2	2-1	0-2	1-1	■	3-0	3-1
Sligo Rovers FC (Sligo)	2-1	4-1	1-1		3-0	0-2		1-1			■	
	2-2	0-2	3-0	2-1	3-3	2-2	2-0	3-4	0-1	1-1	■	2-1
University College Dublin AFC (Dublin)			1-1		3-0		1-0		0-0	2-3	5-1	■
	2-1	0-0	1-2	3-0	1-3	0-0	1-2	1-1	0-3	2-1	1-1	■

	Premier Division	Pd	Wn	Dw	Ls	GF	GA	Pts	
1.	ST. PATRICK'S ATHLETIC FC (DUBLIN)	33	19	11	3	46	24	68	
2.	Shelbourne FC (Dublin)	33	20	7	6	58	32	67	
3.	Cork City FC (Cork)	33	14	11	8	50	40	53	
4.	Shamrock Rovers FC (Dublin)	33	14	10	9	41	32	52	
5.	Bohemian FC (Dublin)	33	13	11	9	50	36	50	
6.	Dundalk FC (Dundalk)	33	12	9	12	41	43	45	
7.	Sligo Rovers FC (Sligo)	33	10	14	9	46	49	44	
8.	Finn Harps FC (Ballybofey)	33	12	7	14	41	43	43	
9.	Derry City FC (Derry)	33	10	10	13	30	31	40	
10.	University College Dublin AFC (Dublin)	33	9	12	12	36	38	39	PO
11.	Kilkenny City FC (Kilkenny)	33	4	7	22	27	63	19	R
12.	Drogheda United FC (Drogheda)	33	2	9	22	20	55	15	R
		396	139	118	139	486	486	535	

Top goal-scorers 1997-98

1) Stephen GEOGHEGAN   (Shelbourne FC)   17
2) Tony COUSINS   (Shamrock Rovers FC)   15
3) Graham LAWLOR   (Bohemian FC)   13
4) Ian GILZEAN   (St. Patrick's Athletic FC)   12
   Jason SHERLOCK   (University College Dublin AFC) 12

Promotion/Relegation Play-off   (05/05/1998 – 08/05/1998)

University College Dublin AFC (Dublin)   2-1, 3-1   Limerick FC (Limerick)

League of Ireland Division One 1997-98	Athlone Town	Bray Wanderers	Cobh Ramblers	Galway United	Home Farm-Ev.	Limerick AFC	Longford Town	Monaghan Utd.	St. Francis FC	Waterford Utd/
Athlone Town AFC (Athlone)			2-4	2-0					1-1	0-1
		1-2	2-0	2-1	0-1	1-1	2-0	2-1	1-4	0-1
Bray Wanderers AFC (Bray)	1-1		0-0	0-1			1-0	2-1		
	2-1		7-0	2-1	2-0	3-2	4-0	4-0	1-0	0-1
Cobh Ramblers FC (Cobh)				1-1			2-0	2-1	1-3	0-1
	2-1	0-1		1-0	1-0	2-1	1-0	0-1	2-3	1-2
Galway United FC (Galway)		1-0				2-1		2-0	1-0	
	2-1	1-4	4-1		2-1	2-2	1-0	3-1	5-0	0-1
Home Farm-Everton FC (Dublin)	4-1		0-1	0-0			0-0	0-0		
	1-2	0-0	2-1	1-1		1-2	1-0	2-1	1-1	3-0
Limerick AFC (Limerick)	1-1	2-1	2-2				6-0			
	0-0	1-0	1-0	1-0	1-1		1-0	3-1	2-0	1-2
Longford Town FC (Longford)	1-2	1-3		0-2				0-4		0-2
	2-2	1-0	2-2	1-2	0-1	0-2		0-2	1-1	0-0
Monaghan United FC (Monaghan)	1-1				0-0	1-2				0-2
	0-2	0-2	2-1	2-1	3-3	1-2	1-3		1-2	1-2
St. Francis FC (Dublin)				0-2	0-2	2-0	0-0			
	1-0	4-3	1-3	1-2	1-1	1-2	0-0	0-1		1-4
Waterford United FC (Waterford)		1-3		2-1	1-1	0-0			0-0	
	2-0	0-3	1-1	1-0	1-0	3-0	1-0	2-0	1-1	

	Division One	**Pd**	**Wn**	**Dw**	**Ls**	**GF**	**GA**	**Pts**	
1.	Waterford United FC (Waterford)	27	18	6	3	35	17	60	P
2.	Bray Wanderers AFC (Bray)	27	17	3	7	51	21	54	P
3.	Limerick FC (Limerick)	27	14	8	5	41	25	50	PO
4.	Galway United FC (Galway)	27	13	4	10	38	29	43	
5.	Home Farm-Everton FC (Dublin)	27	9	11	7	28	22	38	
6.	Cobh Ramblers FC (Cobh)	27	10	5	12	32	41	35	
7.	Athlone Town AFC (Athlone)	27	8	7	12	31	37	31	
8.	St. Francis FC (Dublin)	27	7	8	12	29	40	29	
9.	Monaghan United FC (Monaghan)	27	6	4	17	26	44	22	
10	Longford Town FC (Longford)	27	2	6	19	12	47	12	
		270	104	62	104	323	323	374	

FAI Cup Final   (Dalymount Park, Dublin – 10/05/1998)

CORK CITY FC (CORK)　　　　　　　　0-0　　　　　　　　Shelbourne FC (Dublin)

Cork City: Mooney, Napier, Coughlan, Daly, Cronin, Flanagan, Freyne, Hill, Cahill, Glynn, Kabia (Caulfield 60').
Shelbourne: Gough, Costello (Smith 46'), McCarthy, Scully, D.Geoghegan, Baker, Fenlon, Fitzgerald, Rutherford, S.Geoghegan, Kelly.

Final Replay   (Dalymount Park, Dublin – 16/05/1998)

CORK CITY FC (CORK)　　　　　　　　1-0　　　　　　　　Shelbourne FC (Dublin)
Coughlan 75'

Shelbourne: Gough, Smith, Scully, McCarthy, D.Geoghegan, Kelly, Fitzgerald (Neville 85'), Fenlon, Rutherford (Sheridan 80'), Baker, S.Geoghegan (Morley 80').
Cork City: Mooney, O'Donoghue (Long 76'), Daly, Coughlan, Cronin, Hill, Flanagan, Freyne, Cahill, Caulfield, Hartigan (Glynn 55').

Semi-Finals

Athlone Town AFC (Athlone)	1-3	Cork City FC (Cork)
Finn harps FC (Ballybofey)	0-0, 0-1	Shelbourne FC (Dublin)

Quarter-Finals

Athlone Town AFC (Athlone)	1-1, 2-1	Longford Town FC (Longford)
Cork City FC (Cork)	2-0	Sligo Rovers FC (Sligo)
St. Patrick's Athletic FC (Dublin)	2-2, 1-1 (aet), 2-2 (aet)	Shelbourne FC (Dublin)
	(Shelbourne FC won 5-3 on penalties)	
University College Dublin AFC (Dublin)	0-1	Finn Harps FC (Ballybofey)

1998-99

League of Ireland Premier Division 1998-99	Bohemian FC	Bray Wanderers AFC	Cork City FC	Derry City FC	Dundalk FC	Finn Harps FC	St. Patrick's Athletic FC	Shamrock Rovers FC	Shelbourne FC	Sligo Rovers FC	University College Dublin	Waterford AFC
Bohemian FC (Dublin)	■	0-0	0-2		2-1	0-1						0-1
	■	1-2	0-2	0-1	1-0	2-3	1-1	1-1	2-0	0-1	3-0	0-1
Bray Wanderers AFC (Bray)		■	1-3		1-0				0-1	1-2		0-1
	0-1	■	0-1	0-1	0-0	0-0	1-4	3-4	1-0	1-1	0-0	6-0
Cork City FC (Cork)			■	0-1	2-0	2-1	--	3-0	2-1			0-4
	0-0	3-0	■	2-1	4-1	2-0	1-2	3-1	2-1	1-0	1-2	5-0
Derry City FC (Derry)	0-1	1-1		■		1-0	0-0		1-0			
	0-2	5-1	1-1	■	0-1	2-1	0-1	1-1	0-1	2-0	2-0	1-0
Dundalk FC (Dundalk)			0-1		■			1-1	1-2	3-2	0-2	
	0-1	0-1	1-1	2-2	■	0-0	2-0	1-1	1-2	0-2	2-0	2-0
Finn Harps FC (Ballybofey)		0-3		1-0		■	0-3	4-1		1-0	2-0	
	1-0	6-2	1-1	2-2	0-0	■	2-1	2-1	3-2	1-1	0-0	1-2
St. Patrick's Athletic FC (Dublin)	1-3	1-0	1-0		1-0		■		4-0	0-0		
	3-0	3-0	2-0	1-0	3-1	2-2	■	3-0	2-1	4-1	1-0	2-0
Shamrock Rovers FC (Dublin)	1-1	0-0		1-0		0-1		■		0-0		
	3-0	0-1	0-3	0-0	1-1	2-0	2-1	■	2-1	1-1	2-0	0-0
Shelbourne FC (Dublin)	1-2			2-0	1-1	1-0		1-0	■			0-2
	2-1	1-0	3-3	2-0	1-2	0-0	0-1	2-2	■	1-1	1-1	1-0
Sligo Rovers FC (Sligo)	2-1		2-5	2-0		2-0		1-0		■		2-1
	2-2	0-0	0-2	3-3	2-0	1-1	1-4	2-3	1-3	■	0-1	1-1
University College Dublin AFC (Dublin)	2-0	1-3	2-2	2-1				0-1	0-0		■	
	2-0	3-1	0-1	2-2	0-0	3-0	2-2	0-2	1-1	2-0	■	1-1
Waterford United FC (Waterford)			1-0	2-0		0-0	1-0			1-2		■
	0-0	1-0	0-2	1-2	1-0	0-3	0-2	1-1	0-0	1-1	1-0	■

	Premier Division	**Pd**	**Wn**	**Dw**	**Ls**	**GF**	**GA**	**Pts**	
1.	ST. PATRICK'S ATHLETIC FC (DUBLIN)	33	22	7	4	58	21	73	
2.	Cork City FC (Cork)	33	21	7	5	62	25	70	
3.	Shelbourne FC (Dublin)	33	13	8	12	37	35	47	
4.	Finn Harps FC (Ballybofey)	33	12	10	11	39	40	46	
5.	Derry City FC (Derry)	33	12	9	12	34	32	45	
6.	University College Dublin AFC (Dublin)	33	10	12	11	31	32	42	
7.	Waterford United FC (Waterford)	33	11	9	13	21	37	42	
8.	Shamrock Rovers FC (Dublin)	33	9	13	11	34	40	40	
9.	Sligo Rovers FC (Sligo)	33	9	11	13	37	50	38	
10.	Bohemian FC (Dublin)	33	10	7	16	28	37	37	PO
11.	Bray Wanderers AFC (Bray)	33	8	8	17	30	45	32	R
12.	Dundalk FC (Dundalk)	33	6	9	18	23	40	27	R
		396	143	110	143	434	434	539	

Top goal-scorers 1998-99

1) Trevor MOLLOY   (St. Patrick's Athletic FC)   15
2) Ian GILZEAN   (St. Patrick's Athletic FC)   12
3) Kevin FLANAGAN   (Cork City FC)   11
   Marcus HALLOWS   (Sligo Rovers FC)   11
   Derek SWANS   (Bohemian FC)   11

Promotion/Relegation Play-off   (05/05/1999 + 08/05/1999)

Cobh Ramblers FC (Cobh)   0-5, 0-2   Bohemian FC (Dublin)

League of Ireland Division One 1998-99	Athlone Town AFC	Cobh Ramblers FC	Drogheda United FC	Galway United FC	Home Farm-Everton FC	Kilkenny City FC	Limerick AFC	Longford Town FC	Monaghan United FC	St. Francis FC
Athlone Town AFC (Athlone)	■	2-3	0-1	1-1	1-1	2-0	1-1	1-1	4-1	1-1
	■	1-0	1-2	2-2	3-1	2-2	0-2	3-1	3-0	2-0
Cobh Ramblers FC (Cobh)	2-2	■	1-2	0-3	2-2	4-0	1-1	2-0	1-1	2-0
	4-0	■	2-0	3-0	2-1	3-1	1-0	0-2	3-0	4-1
Drogheda United FC (Drogheda)	1-1	4-1	■	0-2	3-2	1-0	1-1	1-0	1-1	2-2
	4-0	1-1	■	1-1	1-0	0-1	1-0	1-2	2-0	1-1
Galway United FC (Galway)	4-0	2-0	2-1	■	2-1	0-0	2-1	0-0	3-0	2-0
	2-0	0-2	2-2	■	2-1	1-0	0-0	0-0	1-1	1-1
Home Farm-Everton FC (Dublin)	2-1	0-1	0-2	2-3	■	1-2	1-2	1-3	1-1	2-0
	3-0	2-3	1-5	0-2	■	2-1	3-1	2-0	2-1	3-2
Kilkenny City FC (Kilkenny)	4-1	3-1	1-1	1-1	1-0	■	2-1	2-2	0-2	1-0
	1-2	0-2	2-2	4-2	1-0	■	1-1	3-1	3-3	2-2
Limerick AFC (Limerick)	3-1	1-1	1-0	1-1	0-1	1-1	■	0-0	1-1	2-1
	3-2	3-0	0-3	0-1	1-0	0-2	■	2-0	1-0	3-0
Longford Town FC (Longford)	0-1	0-1	1-1	1-1	1-0	1-0	0-1	■	2-1	2-0
	1-0	2-0	1-2	1-1	2-0	3-1	3-0	■	2-0	2-3
Monaghan United FC (Monaghan)	1-0	2-0	1-1	2-0	0-0	1-1	0-1	2-1	■	4-0
	5-1	1-0	0-0	3-3	1-1	0-1	1-1	0-1	■	3-1
St. Francis FC (Dublin)	0-2	2-2	0-3	0-1	0-1	0-1	0-0	0-0	1-1	■
	1-1	1-0	0-3	2-2	1-2	0-3	2-2	0-2	0-3	■

	Division One	Pd	Wn	Dw	Ls	GF	GA	Pts	
1.	Drogheda United FC (Drogheda)	36	17	13	6	57	32	64	P
2.	Galway United FC (Galway)	36	16	16	4	53	34	64	P
3.	Cobh Ramblers FC (Cobh)	36	17	7	12	55	43	58	PO
4.	Longford Town FC (Longford)	36	15	9	12	41	33	54	
5.	Kilkenny City FC (Kilkenny)	36	14	11	11	49	46	53	
6.	Limerick FC (Limerick)	36	13	13	10	39	35	52	
7.	Monaghan United FC (Monaghan)	36	10	14	12	44	44	44	
8.	Athlone Town AFC (Athlone)	36	10	10	16	45	61	40	
9.	Home Farm-Everton FC (Dublin)	36	11	5	20	42	54	38	*
10	St. Francis FC (Dublin)	36	2	12	22	25	68	18	
		360	125	110	125	450	450	485	

* Home Farm-Everton FC (Dublin) severed their link with English club Everton FC (Liverpool) and changed their name to Home Farm-Fingal FC (Dublin) for next season.

FAI Cup Final   (Tolka Park, Dublin – 10/05/1999)

BRAY WANDERERS AFC (BRAY)   0-0   Finn Harps FC (Ballybofey)

Bray Wanderers: Walsh, Doohan, Tresson, Lynch, Kenny, Tierney, Smyth, Farrell, Ryan (Brien 28'), Fox, Keogh.
Finn Harps: McKenna, Scanlon, D.Boyle, Dykes, Minnock, Mohan, Harkin, O'Brien, Kavanagh, Speak, Mulligan.

Final Replay   (Tolka Park, Dublin – 16/05/1999)

BRAY WANDERERS AFC (BRAY)   2-2   Finn Harps FC (Ballybofey)

O'Connor 87', O'Brien 120'   *Speak 60', Mohan 103'*

Finn Harps: McKenna, Scanlon, D.Boyle, Dykes, Minnock, Mohan (McGettigan 115'), O'Brien, Harkin (Bradley 108'), McGrenaghan, Speak (Sheridan 112'), Mulligan.
Bray Wanderers: Walsh, Lynch, Tresson, Doohan, Kenny, Tierney (Brien 27'), Smyth (Byrne 68'), Keogh, Farrell (O'Connor 40'), Fox, O'Brien.

Final 2nd Replay   (Tolka Park, Dublin – 20/05/1999)

BRAY WANDERERS AFC (BRAY)   2-1   Finn Harps FC (Ballybofey)

Byrne 38', 73'   *Speak 12'*

Bray Wanderers: Walsh, Kenny, Doohan, Lynch, Farrell (Smyth 87'), O'Connor, Tresson, Fox, Keogh, Byrne, O'Brien.
Finn Harps: McKenna, Scanlon (R.Boyle 65'), D.Boyle, Dykes, Minnock, Mohan (Bradley 83'), O'Brien, Harkin, McGrenaghan (Sheridan 77'), Mulligan, Speak.

Semi-Finals

Galway United FC (Galway)	1-2	Finn Harps FC (Ballybofey)
Shelbourne FC (Dublin)	1-2	Bray Wanderers AFC (Bray)

Quarter-Finals

Derry City FC (Derry)	0-2	Shelbourne FC (Dublin)
Galway United FC (Galway)	1-0	St. Patrick's Athletic FC (Dublin)
Kilkenny City FC (Kilkenny)	2-2, -:+	Finn Harps FC (Ballybofey)

(Kilkenny City FC forfeited the game after they refused to travel for the replay as they had only 2 fit players, both goalkeepers)

Sligo Rovers FC (Sligo)	1-1, 0-0, 0-1	Bray Wanderers AFC (Bray)

1999-2000

League of Ireland Premier Division 1999-2000	Bohemian FC	Cork City FC	Derry City FC	Drogheda United FC	Finn Harps FC	Galway United FC	St. Patrick's Athletic	Shamrock Rovers	Shelbourne FC	Sligo Rovers FC	University College	Waterford AFC
Bohemian FC (Dublin)	■	0-0				0-1	0-0	1-1	4-1	1-2		
	■	3-0	3-0	2-1	1-0	1-3	0-0	1-3	0-1	3-2	1-0	0-2
Cork City FC (Cork)	2-1	■		3-1			1-1			0-0	1-1	
	1-1	■	0-0	3-0	2-0	3-0	1-0	2-0	1-2	0-1	1-0	0-0
Derry City FC (Derry)		1-4	■	2-1			0-0		0-0	2-0	1-1	
	0-0	1-0	■	0-2	2-0	2-0	0-3	1-0	1-0	1-3	0-2	3-0
Drogheda United FC (Drogheda)	0-3			■	0-2		0-3	0-0		0-5	1-0	
	0-2	0-0	1-2	■	3-2	3-1	1-2	0-4	0-0	1-1	0-1	1-1
Finn Harps FC (Ballybofey)	0-0	1-1	1-2		■				2-3	2-1		
	0-1	1-2	1-1	0-0	■	1-2	1-1	1-0	0-1	2-1	0-0	4-0
Galway United FC (Galway)	0-1	0-2	2-1	2-2	0-4	■	1-0					
	1-2	1-4	0-2	1-1	1-3	■	1-2	0-3	0-0	5-0	2-1	0-0
St. Patrick's Athletic FC (Dublin)		1-1		1-0			■	0-0	1-2			0-0
	1-3	2-0	1-2	1-0	2-1	3-0	■	1-1	3-2	0-0		1-0
Shamrock Rovers FC (Dublin)		1-2			3-3	0-0		■	2-1	4-2		1-2
	0-1	1-3	3-0	4-1	3-1	2-1	2-1	■	1-1	4-1	0-0	1-0
Shelbourne FC (Dublin)		4-0	2-2	0-0		1-1			■	2-1		
	1-0	3-2	2-0	1-0	1-1	1-1	1-0	3-0	■	1-0	0-0	1-0
Sligo Rovers FC (Sligo)				0-0		1-1	2-2		0-4	■	0-1	
	0-0	0-5	2-0	1-1	1-1	1-0	0-1	3-5	2-4	■	1-2	1-0
University College Dublin AFC (Dublin)					1-1	1-1	2-1	1-1			■	2-1
	0-2	2-2	1-0	3-0	1-0	0-2	2-2	3-0	0-2	1-1	■	2-2
Waterford United FC (Waterford)	0-0	2-2			1-0	0-0			0-2	1-1		■
	0-2	1-3	2-2	1-0	2-3	1-2	3-1	0-0	0-0	1-0	0-2	■

	Premier Division	Pd	Wn	Dw	Ls	GF	GA	Pts	
1.	SHELBOURNE FC (DUBLIN)	33	19	12	2	49	20	69	
2.	Cork City FC (Cork)	33	16	10	7	53	32	58	
3.	Bohemian FC (Dublin)	33	16	9	8	40	23	57	
4.	University College Dublin AFC (Dublin)	33	13	12	8	40	29	51	
5.	Shamrock Rovers FC (Dublin)	33	13	11	9	49	36	50	
6.	St. Patrick's Athletic FC (Dublin)	33	13	11	9	40	31	50	
7.	Derry City FC (Derry)	33	12	10	11	32	38	46	
8.	Finn Harps FC (Ballybofey)	33	8	10	15	39	41	34	
9.	Galway United FC (Galway)	33	8	10	15	32	49	34	
10.	Waterford United FC (Waterford)	33	7	12	14	24	38	33	PO
11.	Sligo Rovers FC (Sligo)	33	5	10	18	31	60	25	R
12.	Drogheda United FC (Drogheda)	33	4	11	18	21	53	23	R
		396	134	128	134	450	450	530	

Top goal-scorers 1999-2000

1) Pat MORLEY (Cork City FC) 20
2) Stephen GEOGHEGAN (Shelbourne FC) 12
   James MULLIGAN (Finn Harps FC) 12
4) Padraig MORAN (Sligo Rovers FC) 11
5) Glen CROWE (Bohemian FC) 9

Promotion/Relegation Play-off (03/05/2000 + 06/05/2000)

Kilkenny City FC (Kilkenny)   1-0, 1-0   Waterford United FC (Waterford)

League of Ireland Division One 1999-2000

Team	Athlone Town AFC	Bray Wanderers AFC	Cobh Ramblers FC	Dundalk FC	Home Farm-Fingal FC	Kilkenny City FC	Limerick AFC	Longford Town FC	Monaghan United FC	St. Francis FC
Athlone Town AFC (Athlone)	—	1-1	1-0	0-0	1-0	0-1	3-0	1-1	2-0	0-0
	—	0-2	2-2	1-1	0-0	1-1	1-2	1-1	2-2	1-0
Bray Wanderers AFC (Bray)	3-1	—	2-2	0-1	5-1	1-0	2-1	1-1	5-2	2-0
	2-1	—	5-0	2-3	3-0	2-1	3-2	1-0	1-0	1-0
Cobh Ramblers FC (Cobh)	1-0	0-3	—	0-3	1-0	3-1	2-1	0-2	6-4	2-0
	1-0	2-0	—	0-1	0-1	2-3	2-1	1-6	1-0	2-2
Dundalk FC (Dundalk)	0-1	1-1	1-1	—	2-0	1-0	2-1	4-1	0-2	0-0
	1-0	1-2	2-1	—	2-0	2-1	2-0	0-1	0-1	1-2
Home Farm-Fingal FC (Dublin)	1-0	2-2	2-0	1-2	—	2-2	1-2	3-2	3-0	2-1
	1-0	0-3	2-2	0-1	—	0-1	2-2	1-2	2-2	0-1
Kilkenny City FC (Kilkenny)	4-1	1-0	0-1	2-0	2-2	—	1-0	2-1	2-2	1-0
	5-1	5-1	0-1	1-2	1-0	—	3-2	2-1	2-1	5-0
Limerick AFC (Limerick)	1-1	1-2	1-0	1-3	3-1	0-0	—	0-3	2-0	0-1
	1-1	0-0	3-3	2-1	1-1	0-3	—	0-2	2-2	1-1
Longford Town FC (Longford)	3-1	2-4	2-1	1-1	4-1	3-1	2-0	—	4-1	1-2
	1-0	2-2	2-1	1-0	2-2	1-1	2-1	—	3-1	2-1
Monaghan United FC (Monaghan)	0-1	3-1	1-2	3-2	2-2	1-3	5-2	0-1	—	0-0
	2-2	0-0	1-4	1-2	2-1	1-5	0-0	0-4	—	1-1
St. Francis FC (Dublin)	1-1	0-3	1-2	0-2	2-2	0-4	0-0	0-3	1-1	—
	0-1	1-1	1-1	0-3	2-4	0-0	2-1	2-1	2-2	—

Division One

	Team	Pd	Wn	Dw	Ls	GF	GA	Pts	
1.	Bray Wanderers AFC (Bray)	36	21	9	6	69	38	72	P
2.	Longford Town FC (Longford)	36	21	7	8	71	40	70	P
3.	Kilkenny City FC (Kilkenny)	36	20	7	9	65	34	67	PO
4.	Dundalk FC (Dundalk)	36	20	6	10	50	31	66	
5.	Cobh Ramblers FC (Cobh)	36	14	8	14	52	59	50	
6.	Athlone Town AFC (Athlone)	36	8	14	14	31	42	38	
7.	Home Farm-Fingal FC (Dublin)	36	8	11	17	43	60	35	
8.	Fingal-St. Francis FC (Dublin)	36	6	14	15	28	54	33	*
9.	Monaghan United FC (Monaghan)	36	6	12	18	46	73	30	
10.	Limerick FC (Limerick)	36	6	11	19	36	60	29	
		360	130	100	130	489	489	490	

Cobh Ramblers FC 0-0 Kilkenny City on 23/10/1999 was abandoned after 40 minutes due to floodlight failure. The match way replayed on 01/12/1999 finishing Cobh Ramblers FC 2-3 Kilkenny City.

After the Kilkenny City 3-2 Limerick match on 12/11/1999, the result was annulled as Kilkenny fielded an ineligible player. The match was replayed on 20/04/2000 ending 1-0 but this match was disputed and a civil judge ruled that it should never have been played. As a result, the scoreline of the original match was reinstated.

* St. Francis FC (Dublin) changed their name to Fingal-St. Francis FC (Dublin)

FAI Cup Final (Tolka Park, Dublin – 30/04/2000)

| SHELBOURNE FC (DUBLIN) | 0-0 | Bohemian FC (Dublin) |

Shelbourne: Williams, Heary, D.Geoghegan, McCarthy, Scully, D.Baker, Doolin, S.Geoghegan, Fenlon, Keddy, R.Baker.

Bohemian: Michael Dempsey, T.O'Connor, Brunton, Hunt (Doyle 61'), Maher, John, Byrne (Kelly 56'), Caffrey, Swan (Crowe 82'), G.O'Connor, Mark Dempsey.

Final Replay (Dalymount Park, Dublin – 05/05/2000 – 7,155)

| SHELBOURNE FC (DUBLIN) | 1-0 | Bohemian FC (Dublin) |

Fenlon 39'

Bohemian: Michael Dempsey, T.O'Connor, Brunton (Doyle 87'), Hunt, Maher, John, Byrne (Swan 51'), Caffrey, Kelly (Crowe 63'), G.O'Connor, Mark Dempsey.

Shelbourne: Williams, Heary, D.Geoghegan, McCarthy, Scully, D.Baker, Doolin (Campbell 90'), S.Geoghegan, Fenlon, Keddy, R.Baker.

Semi-Finals

| Bohemian FC (Dublin) | 2-1 | Bray Wanderers AFC (Bray) |
| Galway United FC (Galway) | 0-2 | Shelbourne FC (Dublin) |

Quarter-Finals

Bluebell United FC (Dublin)	0-0, 1-2	Shelbourne FC (Dublin)
Bohemian FC (Dublin)	2-0	St. Mochta's FC (Dublin)
Finn Harps FC (Ballybofey)	1-3	Galway United FC (Galway)
Kilkenny City FC (Kilkenny)	0-2	Bray Wanderers AFC (Bray)

2000-2001

League of Ireland Premier Division 2000-2001	Bohemian FC	Bray Wanderers	Cork City FC	Derry City FC	Finn Harps FC	Galway United FC	Kilkenny City FC	Longford Town	St. Patrick's Ath.	Shamrock Rovers	Shelbourne FC	University College
Bohemian FC (Dublin)	■	1-0	0-1		5-1	2-2		2-1				
	■	3-1	1-1	1-1	1-0	5-0	2-1	2-1	2-2	0-1	0-1	2-0
Bray Wanderers AFC (Bray)		■	2-1		2-1	5-0		4-1				1-0
	3-1	■	1-0	1-0	0-0	0-1	3-0	3-1	2-2	2-2	3-0	1-2
Cork City FC (Cork)		1-0	■	1-0		3-1		1-0	0-4			2-2
	0-0	0-0	■	0-2	1-0	2-0	3-1	0-0	1-0	1-2	1-1	2-1
Derry City FC (Derry)	0-2			■	2-0	0-1		0-0	1-1	3-3		
	1-0	1-1	1-1	■	3-1	0-1	1-0	0-1	1-1	2-0	1-1	0-1
Finn Harps FC (Ballybofey)		4-1	1-1		■		2-0	2-1		2-2		
	1-1	1-0	0-1	0-1	■	1-0	1-1	2-2	0-1	0-0	2-2	1-1
Galway United FC (Galway)				1-1		■	2-0		2-2	1-1	0-0	1-2
	0-2	2-2	0-2	1-0	5-2	■	1-2	1-0	1-1	1-0	1-1	1-4
Kilkenny City FC (Kilkenny)	0-5		1-4	0-1			■	1-1		0-4		
	0-0	2-2	0-0	0-2	0-1	0-1	■	0-1	0-2	1-1	0-3	0-1
Longford Town FC (Longford)	1-3	1-3			2-1			■		0-1	2-0	
	1-6	0-1	2-1	1-0	4-1	2-2	2-1	■	0-3	2-1	0-1	2-0
St. Patrick's Athletic FC (Dublin)					1-4		3-0	2-1	■		4-1	2-1
	2-1	1-1	1-1	1-0	2-1	3-0	3-0	2-4	■	0-1	0-2	1-1
Shamrock Rovers FC (Dublin)	4-6	1-2	1-2	2-3			3-1	1-1		■		
	0-0	1-1	4-1	2-0	2-0	0-0	2-1	3-2	1-2	■	1-3	1-1
Shelbourne FC (Dublin)	2-4	3-2	0-1		0-0		3-1		3-1		■	
	4-2	0-1	2-0	0-1	0-1	3-1	1-0	1-1	3-1	2-2	■	3-1
University College Dublin AFC (Dublin)	3-4			1-1	1-1		1-0		2-1	1-2		■
	0-1	1-1	0-0	0-1	3-2	0-1	2-1	0-2	1-1	2-2	0-1	■

	Premier Division	**Pd**	**Wn**	**Dw**	**Ls**	**GF**	**GA**	**Pts**	
1.	BOHEMIAN FC (DUBLIN)	33	18	8	7	66	35	62	
2.	Shelbourne FC (Dublin)	33	17	9	7	53	37	60	
3.	Cork City FC (Cork)	33	15	11	7	36	29	56	
4.	Bray Wanderers AFC (Bray)	33	15	10	8	52	35	55	
5.	St. Patrick's Athletic FC (Dublin)	33	14	11	8	54	41	53	
6.	Derry City FC (Derry)	33	12	9	12	31	28	45	
7.	Shamrock Rovers FC (Dublin)	33	10	12	11	50	47	42	
8.	Longford Town FC (Longford)	33	12	6	15	40	47	42	
9.	Galway United FC (Galway)	33	10	10	13	34	47	40	
10.	University College Dublin AFC (Dublin)	33	9	10	14	36	44	37	PO
11.	Finn Harps FC (Ballybofey)	33	8	12	13	36	46	36	R
12.	Kilkenny City FC (Kilkenny)	33	1	6	26	14	66	9	R
		396	141	114	141	502	502	537	

Top goal-scorers 2000-01

1) Glen CROWE   (Bohemian FC)   25
2) Sean FRANCIS   (Shamrock Rovers FC)   13
   Liam KELLY   (St. Patrick's Athletic FC)   13
   Colm TRESSON   (Bray Wanderers AFC)   13
5) Alex NESOVIC   (Finn Harps FC/Bohemian FC)   12

Promotion/Relegation Play-off

Athlone Town AFC (Athlone)   2-1, 1-2 (aet)   (4-2 on penalties)   University College Dublin AFC

League of Ireland Division One 2000-2001	Athlone Town	Cobh Ramblers	Drogheda United	Dundalk FC	Home Farm-Fingal	Limerick AFC	Monaghan United	St. Francis FC	Sligo Rovers FC	Waterford AFC
Athlone Town AFC (Athlone)	—	1-0	0-0	1-2	1-2	1-0	2-3	2-0	1-1	0-0
	—	2-0	2-1	1-1	5-2	2-2	2-1	3-0	0-0	1-0
Cobh Ramblers FC (Cobh)	2-0	—	2-2	2-0	6-1	1-3	2-2	1-0	0-2	1-1
	1-5	—	2-1	3-2	0-1	3-1	0-1	1-0	1-4	0-2
Drogheda United FC (Drogheda)	1-2	2-0	—	0-3	0-2	1-1	1-0	0-1	0-1	0-2
	1-4	3-1	—	0-3	1-1	2-1	2-4	1-1	1-3	0-2
Dundalk FC (Dundalk)	2-1	3-2	1-0	—	0-1	0-0	1-0	7-0	2-5	1-0
	3-0	2-2	1-0	—	3-1	1-1	2-0	2-0	3-1	1-0
Home Farm-Fingal FC (Dublin)	0-0	1-0	0-0	1-2	—	1-1	0-0	1-0	4-1	1-1
	1-2	2-2	3-2	2-1	—	1-5	2-4	2-2	3-2	3-3
Limerick AFC (Limerick)	0-1	1-0	1-0	0-2	1-0	—	0-2	1-0	2-0	1-1
	0-0	0-2	3-1	1-1	0-0	—	2-0	1-4	2-1	1-1
Monaghan United FC (Monaghan)	3-1	0-0	2-0	4-0	1-0	2-0	—	1-1	1-1	0-0
	1-2	2-1	1-0	1-1	2-2	3-1	—	3-1	0-3	1-2
St. Francis FC (Dublin)	0-1	3-0	1-1	1-1	1-1	2-1	3-5	—	0-3	0-2
	1-1	0-1	1-1	2-6	0-0	0-2	1-2	—	1-2	1-1
Sligo Rovers FC (Sligo)	4-2	3-2	2-0	1-1	1-0	1-0	1-2	1-0	—	1-3
	1-2	1-0	1-0	2-1	3-0	2-2	1-2	2-1	—	1-4
Waterford United FC (Waterford)	0-0	3-1	4-0	1-2	3-0	0-1	0-0	1-1	2-0	—
	1-2	3-1	3-1	1-1	2-0	0-1	2-2	2-0	3-2	—

	Division One	**Pd**	**Wn**	**Dw**	**Ls**	**GF**	**GA**	**Pts**	
1.	Dundalk FC (Dundalk)	36	20	9	7	65	38	69	P
2.	Monaghan United FC (Monaghan)	36	18	11	7	59	40	65	P
3.	Athlone Town AFC (Athlone)	36	18	10	8	53	37	64	PO
4.	Sligo Rovers FC (Sligo)	36	19	5	12	61	48	62	
5.	Waterford United FC (Waterford)	36	16	13	7	56	30	61	
6.	Limerick FC (Limerick)	36	13	11	12	40	39	50	
7.	Home Farm-Fingal FC (Dublin)	36	10	13	13	43	58	43	*
8.	Cobh Ramblers FC (Cobh)	36	10	6	20	43	60	36	
9.	Drogheda United FC (Drogheda)	36	4	9	23	27	62	21	
10.	Fingal-St. Francis FC (Dublin)	36	3	11	22	29	64	20	
		360	131	98	131	476	476	491	

* Home Farm-Fingal FC (Dublin) changed their club name to Dublin City FC (Dublin) for next season.

FAI Cup Final (Tolka Park, Dublin – 13/05/2001 – 9,500)

BOHEMIAN FC (DUBLIN)   1-0   Longford Town FC (Longford)

O'Connor 62'

Bohemian: Russell, O'Connor, Hill, Caffrey, Maher, Moloy, Fullam (Webb 26'), Hunt, Rutherfrod, Nesovic (Morrison 48'), Crowe.

Longford Town: O'Brien, Murphy, Smith (Perth 88'), McNally, W.Byrne, Gavin (Holt 59'), S.Byrne, Kelly, Prunty, O'Connor, Zeller (Notaro 46').

Semi-Finals

Bohemian FC (Dublin)	1-0	Shamrock Rovers FC (Dublin)
Waterford United FC (Waterford)	1-1, 0-1	Longford Town FC (Longford)

Quarter-Finals

Cobh Ramblers FC (Cobh)	0-1	Waterford United FC (Waterford)
Kilkenny City FC (Kilkenny)	2-7	Bohemian FC (Dublin)
Portmarnock FC (Portmarnock)	1-2	Longford Town FC (Longford)
Shelbourne FC (Dublin)	1-1, 0-3	Shamrock Rovers FC (Dublin)

2001-2002

League of Ireland Premier Division 2001-2002	Bohemian FC	Bray Wanderers	Cork City FC	Derry City FC	Dundalk FC	Galway United FC	Longford Town FC	Monaghan United	St. Patrick's Athletic	Shamrock Rovers	Shelbourne FC	University College
Bohemian FC (Dublin)			1-0			1-0	3-0		1-1	4-0	3-0	
		2-0	2-2	1-0	1-1	3-0	1-1	3-0	0-2	0-1	4-6	6-0
Bray Wanderers AFC (Bray)	2-2		0-2		1-2		4-1			2-1	0-0	
	0-0		2-2	0-0	5-1	2-0	5-1	5-0	0-2	1-1	0-3	1-1
Cork City FC (Cork)	0-3				0-0		5-1		0-2	0-1		
	0-1	2-2		1-0	0-1	4-0	2-1	2-0	2-1	2-1	1-0	0-2
Derry City FC (Derry)		1-2	1-0				6-1		3-0			1-1
	1-0	3-1	1-0		1-1	2-0	1-1	2-0	3-1	2-0	0-0	1-1
Dundalk FC (Dundalk)	1-1			4-2		1-1		0-1		1-2	1-1	
	3-1	0-3	1-3	1-0		1-1	1-1	3-0	0-2	0-0	1-1	1-1
Galway United FC (Galway)	1-5	3-5	0-3	2-3			0-0					
	1-5	0-2	1-2	0-1	0-1		1-1	8-0	0-4	0-2	0-1	1-0
Longford Town FC (Longford)			0-0	1-0	1-3			2-0	1-1	1-5		
	2-0	3-2	4-1	1-0	2-2	1-2		1-1	3-3	1-2	1-0	1-3
Monaghan United FC (Monaghan)		0-3			0-3	1-2			0-4		1-0	0-3
	1-1	1-1	2-2	1-2	1-0	0-0	0-2		1-2	2-3	0-1	1-4
St. Patrick's Athletic FC (Dublin)	2-0	2-1	3-2	3-0		3-1				1-0		
	1-1	2-0	1-3	1-0	2-0	3-0	3-2	1-1		2-1	3-2	1-2
Shamrock Rovers FC (Dublin)					4-1	3-0		3-2			0-2	0-1
	1-0	4-0	1-3	1-1	1-0	3-0	0-0	4-0	0-0		3-0	3-1
Shelbourne FC (Dublin)				0-1		2-0	3-0		2-1			0-0
	1-0	2-0	2-1	1-1	4-0	3-0	2-0	3-1	1-1	2-0		0-1
University College Dublin AFC (Dublin)		0-0	1-0			3-1	1-2		0-0			
	1-1	1-2	1-1	2-2	2-1	1-2	1-0	1-0	0-0	1-3	2-3	

	Premier Division	Pd	Wn	Dw	Ls	GF	GA	Pts	
1.	SHELBOURNE FC (DUBLIN)	33	19	6	8	50	28	63	
2.	Shamrock Rovers FC (Dublin)	33	17	6	10	54	32	57	
3.	St. Patrick's Athletic FC (Dublin)	33	20	8	5	59	29	53	*
4.	Bohemian FC (Dublin)	33	14	10	9	57	32	52	
5.	Derry City FC (Derry)	33	14	9	10	42	30	51	
6.	Cork City FC (Cork)	33	14	7	12	48	39	49	
7.	University College Dublin AFC (Dublin)	33	12	12	9	40	39	48	
8.	Bray Wanderers AFC (Bray)	33	12	10	11	54	45	46	
9.	Longford Town FC (Longford)	33	10	10	13	41	51	40	PO
10.	Dundalk FC (Dundalk)	33	9	12	12	37	46	39	R
11.	Galway United FC (Galway)	33	5	4	24	28	73	19	R
12.	Monaghan United FC (Monaghan)	33	2	6	25	19	85	12	R
		396	148	100	148	529	529	529	

Top goal-scorers 2001-02

1) Glen CROWE (Bohemian FC) 21
2) Jason BYRNE (Bray Wanderers AFC) 14
   Sean FRANCIS (Shamrock Rovers FC) 14
   Charles Mbabazi LIVINGSTONE (St. Patrick's Athletic FC) 14
5) Tony GRANT (Shamrock Rovers FC) 13

* St. Patrick's Athletic FC (Dublin) had 9 points deducted for fielding Paul Marney in the first 3 games of the season. This was later revoked after arbitration, however Shelbourne FC appealed against this decision which was taken to the High Court where the appeal was rejected. It was then discovered by the Shelbourne chief executive that Ugandan player Charles Mbabazi Livingstone had not been properly registered by St. Patrick's Athletic for the first 5 games of the season and so St. Patrick's Athletic FC had 15 points deducted.

Promotion/Relegation Play-off

Longford Town FC (Longford) 1-0, 2-3 (aet) Finn Harps FC (Ballybofey)
(Longford Town FC won 6-5 on penalties)

League of Ireland Division One 2001-2002	Athlone Town	Cobh Ramblers	Drogheda United	Dublin City FC	Finn Harps FC	Kilkenny City FC	Limerick AFC	Sligo Rovers FC	Waterford AFC
Athlone Town AFC (Athlone)		2-1	2-2	1-2	0-2	1-4	0-2	2-0	1-1
		1-1	0-0	0-2	2-1	0-0	4-1	3-3	0-1
Cobh Ramblers FC (Cobh)	4-2		0-0	1-2	1-2	0-1	0-2	1-1	0-0
	0-4		0-1	1-0	0-1	0-1	1-2	3-0	0-2
Drogheda United FC (Drogheda)	2-0	3-1		6-1	2-0	0-0	4-2	2-1	0-0
	2-2	1-0		1-3	1-1	1-0	2-0	5-0	2-2
Dublin City FC (Dublin)	2-1	1-2	2-2		3-1	2-1	4-0	1-2	1-2
	1-1	0-2	1-1		3-3	4-4	1-0	2-2	3-1
Finn Harps FC (Ballybofey)	3-1	3-1	1-1	0-1		3-3	1-0	1-1	2-0
	2-1	0-0	3-3	1-0		2-2	5-3	0-3	1-2
Kilkenny City FC (Kilkenny)	4-1	2-1	1-2	0-2	3-0		1-0	3-1	0-3
	4-1	1-2	1-0	3-2	2-3		4-1	0-2	0-0
Limerick AFC (Limerick)	1-2	0-1	0-0	1-1	0-1	1-0		2-1	3-4
	2-2	1-1	0-3	3-2	0-0	1-0		0-5	4-0
Sligo Rovers FC (Sligo)	1-1	2-1	0-1	0-1	0-1	1-0	0-0		1-2
	1-0	0-3	1-1	2-3	0-2	1-1	0-0		3-1
Waterford United FC (Waterford)	1-2	1-0	2-2	1-1	5-0	1-1	2-0	3-0	
	0-0	3-3	0-0	0-1	3-4	0-0	2-0	2-0	

	Division One	**Pd**	**Wn**	**Dw**	**Ls**	**GF**	**GA**	**Pts**	
1.	Drogheda United FC (Drogheda)	32	14	16	2	53	28	58	P
2.	Finn Harps FC (Ballybofey)	32	15	9	8	51	47	54	PO
3.	Dublin City FC (Dublin)	32	15	8	9	55	46	53	
4.	Waterford United FC (Waterford)	32	13	12	7	47	35	48	*
5.	Kilkenny City FC (Kilkenny)	32	12	9	11	47	39	45	
6.	Sligo Rovers FC (Sligo)	32	8	9	15	35	48	33	
7.	Athlone Town AFC (Athlone)	32	7	11	14	40	53	32	
8.	Cobh Ramblers FC (Cobh)	32	8	7	17	32	42	31	
9.	Limerick FC (Limerick)	32	8	7	17	32	54	31	
		288	100	88	100	392	392	355	

* Waterford United FC (Waterford) had 3 points deducted for fielding an ineligible player.

Fingal-St. Francis FC (Dublin) were taken over by and merged into St. Patrick's Athletic FC (Dublin) prior to the start of the season. This occurred too late to find a replacement club for the season.

Elected: Kildare County FC (Newbridge)

Premier Division reduced to 10 clubs and Division One extended to 12 clubs for next season

FAI Cup Final   (Tolka Park, Dublin – 07/04/2002)

DUNDALK FC (DUNDALK)   2-1   Bohemian FC (Dublin)

Haylock 44', 50'   *O'Connor 40'*

Dundalk: Connolly, Whyte, McGuinness, Broughan, Crawley, Hoey, Flanagan, Kavanagh, Lawless (McArdle 72'), Reilly, Haylock.

Bohemian: Russell, O'Connor, Caffrey, Hawkins, Webb, Harkin (Byrne 79'), Hunt, Morrison (Hill 72'), Rutherford, Molloy (O'Neill 86'), Crowe.

Semi-Finals

Bohemian FC (Dublin)	2-1	Derry City FC (Derry)
Dundalk FC (Dundalk)	4-0	Shamrock Rovers FC (Dublin)

Quarter-Finals

Bohemian FC (Dublin)	1-1, 4-0	Bray Wanderers AFC (Bray)
Dundalk FC (Dundalk)	1-1, 2-0	Finn Harps FC (Ballybofey)
Shamrock Rovers FC (Dublin)	2-0	Sligo Rovers FC (Sligo)
University College Dublin AFC (Dublin)	2-2, 0-1	Derry City FC (Derry)

2002-2003

League of Ireland Premier Division 2002-2003	Bohemian FC	Bray Wanderers	Cork City FC	Derry City FC	Drogheda United	Longford Town	St. Patrick's Ath.	Shamrock Rovers	Shelbourne FC	University College
Bohemian FC (Dublin)	■		2-0	2-2	1-1			3-2		1-1
	■	4-0	1-1	3-2	3-1	1-0	1-1	3-2	1-2	2-1
Bray Wanderers AFC (Bray)	1-3	■	1-2	0-2	2-0			1-2		
	1-1	■	2-3	3-3	3-2	2-2	0-0	1-1	1-5	0-0
Cork City FC (Cork)		3-1	■	2-1				1-1	2-1	0-1
	1-1	3-0	■	3-1	1-0	1-1	2-0	3-2	3-0	3-2
Derry City FC (Derry)				■		1-1	2-0	0-0	0-1	
	0-3	3-1	0-0	■	2-1	1-1	2-0	1-2	1-0	1-0
Drogheda United FC (Drogheda)			0-0	3-1	■		0-0	0-2		0-1
	0-2	2-1	1-0	2-1	■	0-1	1-2	3-2	0-3	1-0
Longford Town FC (Longford)	1-0		1-0		0-0	■				0-2
	1-2	1-0	3-2	1-1	2-1	■	0-1	0-0	0-2	1-1
St. Patrick's Athletic FC (Dublin)	2-0	1-4	1-0		0-2		■			
	1-1	1-2	4-1	1-0	1-1	2-2	■	1-2	2-2	2-2
Shamrock Rovers FC (Dublin)		3-1			3-2	2-1		■	0-1	0-1
	1-1	2-1	4-1	3-1	5-0	0-1	0-1	■	0-0	0-0
Shelbourne FC (Dublin)	0-1				0-1	1-1	2-0		■	
	1-2	3-1	2-1	2-0	3-3	3-0	1-2	0-1	■	2-1
University College Dublin AFC (Dublin)		0-0		1-0			0-0		0-2	■
	1-2	1-1	1-0	0-2	3-0	0-0	1-0	1-2	1-3	■

	Premier Division	**Pd**	**Wn**	**Dw**	**Ls**	**GF**	**GA**	**Pts**	
1.	BOHEMIAN FC (DUBLIN)	27	15	9	3	47	27	54	
2.	Shelbourne FC (Dublin)	27	15	4	8	44	26	49	
3.	Shamrock Rovers FC (Dublin)	27	12	7	8	42	29	43	
4.	Cork City FC (Cork)	27	11	6	10	37	34	39	
5.	Longford Town FC (Longford)	27	8	11	8	25	29	35	
6.	University College Dublin AFC (Dublin)	27	8	9	10	23	25	33	
7.	St. Patrick's Athletic FC (Dublin)	27	8	9	10	27	33	33	
8.	Derry City FC (Derry)	27	8	7	12	31	37	31	
9.	Drogheda United FC (Drogheda)	27	8	6	13	26	40	30	PO
10.	Bray Wanderers AFC (Bray)	27	4	8	15	31	53	20	R
		270	97	76	97	333	333	367	

Top goal-scorers 2002-03

1) Glen CROWE   (Bohemian FC)   18
2) John O'FLYNN   (Cork City FC)   14
3) Jason BYRNE   (Bray Wanderers AFC) 12
4) Noel HUNT   (Shamrock Rovers FC) 11

Longford Town FC (Longford) had 9 points deducted for fielding Avery John against Cork City FC, Bohemian FC and Bray Wanderers FC but this penalty was revoked on appeal.

Promotion/Relegation Play-offs   (29/01/2003 – 08/02/2003)

Galway United FC (Galway)	2-0, 0-3	Drogheda United FC (Drogheda)
Cobh Ramblers FC (Cobh)	2-2, 0-2	Drogheda United FC (Drogheda)
Galway United FC (Galway)	2-0, 0-1	Finn Harps FC (Ballybofey)

League of Ireland Division One 2002-2003	Athlone Town	Cobh Ramblers	Dublin City FC	Dundalk FC	Finn Harps FC	Galway United	Kildare County	Kilkenny City	Limerick AFC	Monaghan Utd.	Sligo Rovers	Waterford AFC
Athlone Town AFC	■	1-3	2-1	2-0	0-0	0-3	1-2	1-1	1-3	0-0	2-2	2-3
Cobh Ramblers FC	3-1	■	1-3	0-0	1-1	2-0	1-1	3-2	3-2	3-2	2-1	2-3
Dublin City FC	2-1	3-2	■	2-4	0-2	2-0	2-0	3-4	0-1	3-2	1-2	5-1
Dundalk FC	2-4	2-2	2-2	■	3-1	0-4	0-2	0-0	1-1	1-2	1-3	0-1
Finn Harps FC	4-0	1-2	2-0	2-1	■	1-3	1-2	2-0	3-0	3-1	3-1	4-1
Galway United FC	3-1	1-0	2-1	1-1	3-0	■	3-0	1-0	1-0	1-1	0-1	0-0
Kildare County FC	1-3	4-1	2-0	2-3	0-3	3-2	■	3-1	1-3	0-0	1-0	1-1
Kilkenny City FC	1-2	1-2	0-0	2-2	0-1	1-1	4-1	■	0-2	0-3	1-1	1-3
Limerick FC	0-0	2-3	1-3	1-2	2-5	1-1	0-0	1-3	■	1-0	3-2	1-3
Monaghan United FC	1-0	1-1	1-1	1-1	1-1	1-1	0-4	1-1	3-1	■	0-1	1-1
Sligo Rovers FC	3-0	3-2	1-1	0-2	1-1	4-2	0-0	1-0	0-0	0-2	■	1-2
Waterford United FC	2-2	2-0	2-1	1-0	0-0	1-0	2-2	4-0	1-0	2-2	1-0	■

	Division One	Pd	Wn	Dw	Ls	GF	GA	Pts	
1.	Waterford United FC (Waterford)	22	13	7	2	37	25	46	P
2.	Finn Harps FC (Ballybofey)	22	12	5	5	41	22	41	PO
3.	Galway United FC (Galway)	22	10	6	6	34	21	36	PO
4.	Cobh Ramblers FC (Cobh)	22	10	5	7	39	38	35	PO
5.	Kildare County FC (Newbridge)	22	9	6	7	32	31	33	
6.	Sligo Rovers FC (Sligo)	22	8	6	8	28	27	30	
7.	Dublin City FC (Dublin)	22	8	4	10	36	35	28	
8.	Monaghan United FC (Monaghan)	22	5	11	6	26	27	26	
9.	Dundalk FC (Dundalk)	22	5	8	9	28	36	23	
10	Limerick FC (Limerick)	22	6	5	11	26	36	23	
11.	Athlone Town AFC (Athlone)	22	5	6	11	26	40	21	
12.	Kilkenny City FC (Kilkenny)	22	3	7	12	23	38	16	
		264	94	76	94	376	376	358	

The season was changed to run from Spring to Autumn.

FAI Cup Final (Tolka Park, Dublin – 27/10/2002 – 9,000)

DERRY CITY FC (DERRY)　　　　　　1-0　　　　　　Shamrock Rovers FC (Dublin)

Coyle 47'

Derry City: Gough, Harkin, McLaughlin, E.McCallion, Hargan, Hutton, Martyn, Doherty, Friars (McCready 66'), Coyle (T.McCallion 57'), Kelly.

Shamrock Rovers: O'Dowd, Costello, Scully, Palmer, Byrne (Robinson 69'), S.Grant (Francis 73'), Colwell, Dimech, Keddy, Hunt, T.Grant.

Semi-Finals

Cork City FC (Cork)	0-1	Derry City FC (Derry)
Shamrock Rovers FC (Dublin)	2-0	Bohemian FC (Dublin)

Quarter-Finals

Bray Wanderers AFC (Bray)	0-4	Bohemian FC (Dublin)
Derry City FC (Derry)	3-1	St. Patrick's Athletic FC (Dublin)
Finn Harps FC (Ballybofey)	1-1, 0-2	Cork City FC (Cork)
Kilkenny City FC (Kilkenny)	0-1	Shamrock Rovers FC (Dublin)

2003

League of Ireland Premier Division 2003	Bohemian FC	Cork City FC	Derry City FC	Drogheda United FC	Longford Town FC	St. Patrick's Athletic FC	Shamrock Rovers FC	Shelbourne FC	University College Dublin	Waterford AFC
Bohemian FC (Dublin)		1-0	3-1	1-1	1-1	3-0	2-1	0-1	2-1	1-1
		1-1	1-1	1-0	1-1	1-2	1-1	1-0	1-0	5-1
Cork City FC (Cork)	1-2		1-0	1-0	0-0	0-2	2-2	1-1	0-0	2-2
	3-2		1-1	4-0	4-1	0-0	1-0	0-0	1-0	1-1
Derry City FC (Derry)	0-3	1-1		0-0	1-1	1-1	1-1	0-0	0-2	1-2
	0-3	1-0		0-1	2-3	2-2	1-1	2-0	1-0	4-1
Drogheda United FC (Drogheda)	2-0	0-1	1-1		0-5	2-2	0-1	0-1	0-0	3-0
	1-2	3-1	1-0		2-2	4-2	1-2	1-1	2-0	1-3
Longford Town FC (Longford)	2-4	0-1	0-1	0-2		2-0	1-2	2-1	2-1	0-1
	1-1	0-3	4-0	0-0		1-1	0-0	0-2	2-1	1-0
St. Patrick's Athletic FC (Dublin)	2-4	0-2	2-2	3-3	1-2		1-0	0-1	0-0	1-0
	1-0	1-1	4-1	3-1	1-1		1-1	0-0	2-0	4-1
Shamrock Rovers FC (Dublin)	0-0	0-2	1-1	3-2	0-1	3-5		1-1	2-0	1-1
	1-2	2-1	5-1	0-0	2-3	1-0		2-4	1-0	0-1
Shelbourne FC (Dublin)	1-3	2-0	3-1	2-0	2-1	2-0	0-2		0-0	3-1
	2-2	1-1	1-0	3-0	3-2	2-2	1-0		1-1	1-1
University College Dublin (Dublin)	0-1	1-1	2-0	2-1	2-0	0-0	1-1	0-1		3-0
	2-1	0-3	1-1	1-0	0-3	0-0	2-2	0-2		1-2
Waterford United FC (Waterford)	2-1	3-0	0-1	0-2	0-0	0-0	3-3	1-2	2-2	
	1-3	2-1	1-1	2-1	1-1	4-2	2-0	0-4	1-1	

	Premier Division	Pd	Wn	Dw	Ls	GF	GA	Pts	
1.	SHELBOURNE FC (DUBLIN)	36	19	12	5	52	28	69	
2.	Bohemian FC (Dublin)	36	18	10	8	58	37	64	
3.	Cork City FC (Cork)	36	13	14	9	43	33	53	
4.	Longford Town FC (Longford)	36	12	12	12	46	44	48	
5.	St. Patrick's Athletic FC (Dublin)	36	10	16	10	48	48	46	
6.	Waterford United FC (Waterford)	36	11	12	13	44	58	45	
7.	Shamrock Rovers FC (Dublin)	36	10	14	12	45	46	44	
8.	Drogheda United FC (Drogheda)	36	9	10	17	38	50	37	
9.	Derry City FC (Derry)	36	7	15	14	33	51	36	PO
10.	University College Dublin AFC (Dublin)	36	7	13	16	27	39	34	R
		360	116	128	116	434	434	476	

Top goal-scorers 2003

1) Jason BYRNE (Shelbourne FC) 21
2) Glen CROWE (Bohemian FC) 19
3) Tony BIRD (St. Patrick's Athletic FC) 14
   Andrew MYLER (Drogheda United FC) 14
   John O'FLYNN (Cork City FC) 14

Promotion/Relegation Play-offs (03/12/2003 – 13/12/2003)

Finn Harps FC (Ballybofey)	0-0, 1-2 (aet)	Derry City FC (Derry)
Finn Harps FC (Ballybofey)	1-0, 2-1	Bray Wanderers AFC (Bray)
Limerick FC (Limerick)	0-0, 0-4	Derry City FC (Derry)

League of Ireland Division One 2003	Athlone Town AFC	Bray Wanderers AFC	Cobh Ramblers FC	Dublin City FC	Dundalk FC	Finn Harps FC	Galway United FC	Kildare County FC	Kilkenny City FC	Limerick AFC	Monaghan United FC	Sligo Rovers FC
Athlone Town AFC (Athlone)		1-0	2-0	1-2		1-2						3-0
		2-0	0-1	0-1	0-1	1-2	0-0	2-3	2-1	2-0	1-0	1-1
Bray Wanderers AFC (Bray)			3-1		2-0	3-1		3-0		1-0		
	5-3		3-1	1-1	3-1	1-1	2-0	3-2	2-1	2-1	2-1	0-0
Cobh Ramblers FC (Cobh)						0-0	2-0	1-1	3-2	0-2		0-1
	2-0	1-2		1-3	2-1	1-0	0-5	1-2	0-0	0-2	6-1	1-1
Dublin City FC (Dublin)		1-1	0-0		1-0	1-0		2-2			2-1	
	1-1	1-1	0-0		1-0	0-3	2-0	0-1	2-1	3-1	1-1	1-0
Dundalk FC (Dundalk)	1-1		0-2			1-2		2-1		0-1		
	1-1	1-1	0-0	0-2		1-1	4-0	0-0	1-1	3-1	2-1	2-2
Finn Harps FC (Ballybofey)							3-1	2-1	1-0	0-1	2-0	0-1
	1-1	2-0	5-0	2-2	3-1		1-1	2-0	6-0	0-0	2-1	1-0
Galway United FC (Galway)	1-1	3-3		0-1	0-5							2-1
	2-2	2-2	1-0	2-2	1-1	2-2		0-1	4-1	4-3	4-1	1-1
Kildare County FC (Newbridge)	2-0	0-3					0-2			3-0		0-0
	1-1	0-1	3-1	1-0	3-2	0-0	5-3		1-0	1-1	3-1	2-1
Kilkenny City FC (Kilkenny)	0-1			0-1	0-0		0-1	2-3				1-2
	2-1	0-3	1-2	0-1	3-3	1-4	0-1	0-3		1-4	1-1	0-1
Limerick AFC (Limerick)	4-3	2-2		1-0			5-0	1-1	1-1		3-1	
	1-0	1-2	1-1	0-1	2-1	1-1	1-1	2-1	2-1		1-0	4-0
Monaghan United FC (Monaghan)	0-1		1-1		1-1		0-3		1-0			2-3
	3-0	0-0	1-1	0-2	0-0	1-2	0-0	1-1	5-2	2-3		2-3
Sligo Rovers FC (Sligo)		3-2		2-3	1-0				1-1	3-1		
	1-1	1-0	1-1	2-3	0-0	0-0	1-1	2-2	0-2	2-1	4-0	

Division One

		Pd	Wn	Dw	Ls	GF	GA	Pts	
1.	Dublin City FC (Dublin)	33	19	10	4	44	26	67	P
2.	Bray Wanderers AFC (Bray)	33	18	10	5	59	35	64	PO
3.	Finn harps FC (Ballybofey)	33	17	11	5	52	24	62	PO
4.	Limerick FC (Limerick)	33	16	9	8	55	38	57	PO
5.	Kildare County FC (Newbridge)	33	15	10	8	50	39	55	
6.	Sligo Rovers FC (Sligo)	33	11	13	9	39	39	46	
7.	Galway United FC (Galway)	33	10	13	10	48	53	43	
8.	Cobh Ramblers FC (Cobh)	33	9	11	13	33	45	38	
9.	Athlone Town AFC (Athlone)	33	9	10	14	37	42	37	
10	Dundalk FC (Dundalk)	33	6	14	13	36	40	32	
11.	Monaghan United FC (Monaghan)	33	3	9	21	28	60	15	*
12.	Kilkenny City FC (Kilkenny)	33	2	6	25	25	65	12	
		396	135	126	135	506	506	528	

* Monaghan United FC (Monaghan) had 3 points deducted for fielding an ineligible player in the Round 18 match versus Dublin City FC (which they lost 0-2).

FAI Cup Final (Lansdowne Road, Dublin – 26/10/2003 – 15,000)

LONGFORD TOWN FC (LONGFORD)   2-0   St. Patrick's Athletic FC (Dublin)

Francis 32', Barrett 90'

Longford Town: O'Brien, Murphy, Ferguson, McGovern, Dillon, Kirby (Lavine 83'), Perth, Keogh, Prunty, Barrett, Francis.

St. Patrick's Athletic: Adamson, Prenderville, Maguire, Foley, Delaney (Foy, 79), Dunne, Fahy, Byrne (Donnelly 31'), Osam, McPhee (Freeman 55'), Bird.

Semi-Finals

Bohemian FC (Dublin)	1-1, 3-4 (aet)	St. Patrick's Athletic FC (Dublin)
Longford Town FC (Longford)	1-0	Galway United FC (Galway)

Quarter-Finals

Drogheda United FC (Drogheda)	1-1, 0-3	Bohemian FC (Dublin)
Longford Town FC (Longford)	3-1	Waterford United FC (Waterford)
St. Patrick's Athletic FC (Dublin)	2-1	Kildare County FC (Newbridge)
Sligo Rovers FC (Sligo)	1-2	Galway United FC (Galway)

2004

League of Ireland Premier Division 2004	Bohemian FC	Cork City FC	Derry City FC	Drogheda United FC	Dublin City FC	Longford Town FC	St.Patrick's Athletic	Shamrock Rovers FC	Shelbourne FC	Waterford United FC
Bohemian FC (Dublin)	■	1-0	0-1	0-0	4-0	1-1	2-2	3-2	2-0	2-2
	■	2-3	3-0	0-1	2-4	0-0	3-1	2-2	1-1	2-2
Cork City FC (Cork)	1-1	■	1-1	3-2	1-1	2-0	3-0	1-0	0-1	2-0
	0-1	■	2-1	0-0	3-1	1-0	2-1	1-1	0-2	2-3
Derry City FC (Derry)	0-0	0-1	■	1-0	2-3	0-0	1-1	1-0	0-0	1-0
	0-0	1-1	■	0-2	2-1	0-0	0-0	1-0	0-2	0-1
Drogheda United FC (Drogheda)	0-3	1-3	4-0	■	2-1	0-1	0-2	3-0	2-5	1-2
	0-3	2-0	2-0	■	2-0	0-1	0-1	1-0	2-2	0-0
Dublin City FC (Dublin)	0-0	0-1	0-2	2-3	■	2-1	1-2	1-2	2-3	1-3
	2-1	0-1	0-2	1-1	■	0-1	1-1	0-4	1-3	3-1
Longford Town FC (Longford)	0-1	1-2	3-0	3-1	2-0	■	2-1	1-1	4-1	1-1
	0-2	1-1	1-0	0-0	0-0	■	1-3	1-0	0-2	0-2
St. Patrick's Athletic FC (Dublin)	1-2	0-3	0-1	1-1	2-2	1-0	■	2-0	0-0	2-1
	0-2	0-2	1-1	0-2	3-1	1-1	■	1-2	1-2	0-1
Shamrock Rovers FC (Dublin)	0-1	1-1	0-0	1-2	1-3	2-0	3-1	■	1-4	1-2
	2-1	2-1	1-0	1-2	0-0	1-1	1-2	■	3-0	4-0
Shelbourne FC (Dublin)	1-1	0-0	0-2	0-2	4-1	3-1	3-1	1-1	■	2-1
	0-0	2-2	1-0	3-0	2-1	1-1	2-0	1-0	■	1-0
Waterford United FC (Waterford)	1-1	1-4	1-0	1-3	3-2	0-1	0-2	2-0	3-1	■
	0-1	1-1	0-2	2-1	2-1	1-1	0-1	3-1	1-1	■

	Premier Division	Pd	Wn	Dw	Ls	GF	GA	Pts	
1.	SHELBOURNE FC (DUBLIN)	36	19	11	6	57	37	68	
2.	Cork City FC (Cork)	36	18	11	7	52	32	65	
3.	Bohemian FC (Dublin)	36	15	15	6	51	30	60	
4.	Drogheda United FC (Drogheda)	36	15	7	14	45	43	52	
5.	Waterford United FC (Waterford)	36	14	8	14	44	49	50	
6.	Longford Town FC (Longford)	36	11	13	12	32	34	46	
7.	Derry City FC (Derry)	36	11	11	14	23	32	44	
8.	St. Patrick's Athletic FC (Dublin)	36	11	9	16	38	49	42	
9.	Shamrock Rovers FC (Dublin)	36	10	8	18	41	47	38	
10.	Dublin City FC (Dublin)	36	6	7	23	39	69	25	R
		360	130	100	130	422	422	490	

Note: Derry City 0-1 Waterford United on 18/09/2004 was abandoned after 19 minutes due to a floodlight failure. The match was replayed on 02/11/2004 with the result 1-0.

The Premier Division was extended to 12 clubs for next season

Top goal-scorers 2004

1)	Jason BYRNE	(Shelbourne FC)	24
2)	Glen CROWE	(Bohemian FC)	17
3)	Daryl MURPHY	(Waterford United FC)	14
	Declan O'BRIEN	(Drogheda United FC)	14
5)	Kevin DOYLE	(Cork City FC)	12

League of Ireland Division One 2004	Athlone Town AFC	Bray Wanderers AFC	Cobh Ramblers FC	Dundalk FC	Finn Harps FC	Galway United FC	Kildare County FC	Kilkenny City FC	Limerick FC	Monaghan United FC	Sligo Rovers FC	University College Dublin
Athlone Town AFC (Athlone)	■		1-4		1-2	1-2	2-1	1-1	0-1			
	■	0-2	3-2	0-2	1-2	1-0	1-2	2-0	4-0	4-1	2-2	0-1
Bray Wanderers AFC (Bray)	5-3	■			1-1	0-0		0-0		2-0	2-2	
	2-1	■	3-0	5-1	0-0	1-0	1-1	3-1	2-0	4-2	4-0	0-2
Cobh Ramblers FC (Cobh)	1-0	1-2	■	2-1					8-1			0-1
	5-0	1-4	■		0-1	2-4	0-0	1-5	1-1	0-1	3-1	3-2	1-1
Dundalk FC (Dundalk)		3-2		■		1-1		3-1		1-2	3-2	1-3
	4-1	0-6	2-2	■	0-2	1-3	2-1	1-1	2-1	0-1	1-0	0-1
Finn Harps FC (Ballybofey)	6-0	2-0	1-0	3-0	■					1-0		0-1
	1-0	0-1	0-0	2-0	■	2-1	2-2	1-0	3-1	3-1	3-0	1-0
Galway United FC (Galway)		4-3		1-5		■	2-6	1-1	3-0	1-1		
	4-0	3-1	0-0	3-3	1-1	■	1-1	1-0	3-1	4-1	3-1	1-1
Kildare County FC (Newbridge)		2-0	2-0	0-2			■	3-1	2-0			1-2
	2-1	0-2	2-1	1-0	1-1	1-3	■	1-1	0-0	1-2	2-0	0-0
Kilkenny City FC (Kilkenny)		0-1	2-1		0-1			■	2-1	0-3		
	1-0	0-0	1-1	0-2	2-1	1-2	0-2	■	0-1	1-0	2-2	1-1
Limerick FC (Limerick)		1-3	1-2	1-4					■	1-1	1-0	
	1-2	1-0	1-1	1-2	1-2	0-3	0-2	0-0	■	0-0	0-1	0-3
Monaghan United FC (Monaghan)		1-4			0-0		0-1			■	1-0	0-0
	1-5	1-2	2-0	1-2	0-1	0-1	0-1	0-3	2-0	■	0-1	0-3
Sligo Rovers FC (Sligo)	1-2		1-1			3-1	3-1	4-2			■	
	2-0	0-0	2-2	2-0	1-2	3-1	2-3	4-1	1-0	4-0	■	1-2
University College Dublin AFC (Dublin)	3-0				3-0		3-0	1-1		2-0		■
	4-3	2-0	1-1	2-1	1-1	4-0	0-2	4-1	3-0	4-1	2-1	■

	Division 1	Pd	Wn	Dw	Ls	GF	GA	Pts	
1.	Finn Harps FC (Ballybofey)	33	23	7	3	60	19	76	P
2.	University College Dublin AFC (Dublin)	33	22	9	2	63	21	75	P
3.	Bray Wanderers AFC (Bray)	33	19	8	6	62	29	65	P
4.	Kildare County FC (Newbridge)	33	18	8	7	54	32	62	
5.	Galway United FC (Galway)	33	14	10	9	55	49	52	
6.	Dundalk FC (Dundalk)	33	14	4	15	46	57	46	
7.	Sligo Rovers FC (Sligo)	33	11	5	17	46	50	38	
8.	Cobh Ramblers FC (Cobh)	33	7	11	15	47	53	32	
9.	Kilkenny City FC (Kilkenny)	33	6	9	18	28	53	27	
10.	Athlone Town AFC (Athlone)	33	9	2	22	42	68	26	*
11.	Monaghan United FC (Monaghan)	33	8	5	20	28	63	26	*
12.	Limerick FC (Limerick)	33	4	8	21	18	55	20	
		396	155	86	155	549	549	545	

* Athlone Town AFC (Athlone) and Monaghan United FC (Monaghan) each had 3 points deducted for fielding an ineligible player.

FAI Cup Final (Lansdowne Road, Dublin – 24/10/2004 – 10,000)

LONGFORD TOWN FC (LONGFORD)　　　　2-1　　　　Waterford United FC (Waterford)
Kirby 86', Keegan 88'　　　　　　　　　　　　　　　　　　　　　　　　　　　　　　*Bruton 62'*

Longford: O'Brien, Murphy, Prunty, Dillon, Gartland, Martin (Keegan 70), Kirby, Fitzgerald, Barrett (Perth 90+4), Lavine, Baker.

Waterford: Connor, Whelehan, Frost, Breen, Purcell, Reynolds, Carey (Sullivan 61), Mulcahy, Quitongo (Waters 61), Bruton, Murphy.

Semi-Finals

Derry City FC (Derry)	1-2	Waterford United FC (Waterford)
Longford Town FC (Longford)	0-0, 2-1	Drogheda United FC (Drogheda)

Quarter-Finals

Derry City FC (Derry)	1-0	Kildare County FC (Newbridge)
Longford Town FC (Longford)	2-2, 3-0	Athlone Town AFC (Athlone)
University College Dublin AFC (Dublin)	0-0, 2-3	Drogheda United FC (Drogheda)
Waterford United FC (Waterford)	2-2, 2-1	Rockmount FC (Whitechurch)

2005

League of Ireland Premier Division 2005	Bohemian FC	Bray Wanderers	Cork City FC	Derry City FC	Drogheda United	Finn Harps FC	Longford Town	St. Patrick's Ath.	Shamrock Rovers	Shelbourne FC	U.C. Dublin	Waterford United
Bohemian FC (Dublin)	■	1-2	2-3		3-1	1-0		1-3	0-3			
	■	1-0	0-2	0-1	3-2	1-0	2-0	1-1	1-1	2-1	1-1	2-1
Bray Wanderers AFC (Bray)	3-1	■	0-3	0-2		1-0			0-1	1-0		
	1-2	■	1-2	0-1	2-2	2-1	1-1	2-1	2-3	2-2	1-0	2-1
Cork City FC (Cork)		3-0	■	2-0	1-0		0-1		1-0			
	2-1	1-1	■	2-0	0-1	2-0	0-0	3-1	3-0	1-0	0-0	1-1
Derry City FC (Derry)				■	3-0	3-1	2-0	2-0	2-1		0-1	
	3-1	2-2	3-1	■	3-0	3-2	1-0	2-2	2-3	0-0	3-0	1-0
Drogheda United FC (Drogheda)	3-2		1-1		■	2-0		1-1	0-0	0-2		
	2-2	3-0	0-1	0-2	■	1-0	1-1	1-1	2-1	0-0	1-2	1-0
Finn Harps FC (Ballybofey)		2-4	1-2	0-1		■	5-0		3-0		1-2	
	1-3	1-2	0-2	0-2	0-0	■	0-0	0-2	1-1	0-3	1-0	2-0
Longford Town FC (Longford)		1-1	0-0		0-1		■		0-2	1-0	3-0	
	1-0	2-1	0-1	0-0	1-1	1-0	■	1-0	2-1	0-2	1-0	1-2
St. Patrick's Athletic FC (Dublin)	0-1				0-0	1-3		■	3-1		0-0	
	0-0	2-0	0-2	1-1	0-2	2-0	0-1	■	1-1	0-1	3-2	1-0
Shamrock Rovers FC (Dublin)		0-1	0-2			4-2			■	0-2		1-2
	1-2	3-2	1-3	0-2	1-0	1-4	0-2	0-0	■	0-2	1-0	0-0
Shelbourne FC (Dublin)		5-0	0-0			1-0		1-0		■	4-2	5-0
	2-1	4-1	0-2	1-2	3-3	3-0	1-0	3-1	1-2	■	1-1	1-0
University College Dublin AFC (Dublin)	1-3		0-2	2-2			2-2				■	2-3
	1-1	3-2	1-5	1-0	0-2	1-1	0-0	1-0	0-0	1-1	■	1-0
Waterford United FC (Waterford)	2-0		2-2		1-0	2-2		1-1				■
	2-0	1-2	2-2	1-3	0-3	2-1	0-3	1-0	0-1	2-4	0-0	■

Premier Division

		Pd	Wn	Dw	Ls	GF	GA	Pts	
1.	CORK CITY FC (CORK)	33	22	8	3	53	18	74	
2.	Derry City FC (Derry)	33	22	6	5	56	25	72	
3.	Shelbourne FC (Dublin)	33	20	7	6	62	25	67	
4.	Drogheda United FC (Drogheda)	33	12	12	9	40	33	48	
5.	Longford Town FC (Longford)	33	12	9	12	29	32	45	
6.	Bohemian FC (Dublin)	33	13	6	14	42	47	45	
7.	Bray Wanderers AFC (Bray)	33	11	6	16	40	57	39	
8.	Waterford United FC (Waterford)	33	9	7	17	30	49	34	
9.	University College Dublin AFC (Dublin)	33	7	12	14	28	44	33	
10.	St. Patrick's Athletic FC (Dublin)	33	7	11	15	26	36	32	
11.	Shamrock Rovers FC (Dublin)	33	9	8	16	33	52	27	*PO
12.	Finn Harps FC (Ballybofey)	33	5	6	22	30	51	21	R
		396	149	98	149	469	469	537	

Note: Shamrock Rovers FC (Dublin) had 8 points deducted for "financial irregularities" in their license application.

Top goal-scorers 2005

1) Jason BYRNE   (Shelbourne FC)   22
2) Mark FARREN   (Derry City FC)   18
3) Kevin McHUGH   (Finn Harps FC)   13
4) Eamon ZAYED   (Bray Wanderers AFC)   12
5) John O'FLYNN   (Cork City FC)   11

Promotion/Relegation Play-Off (22/11/2005 + 25/11/2005)

Shamrock Rovers FC (Dublin)   1-2, 1-1   Dublin City FC (Dublin)

League of Ireland Division One 2005	Athlone Town	Cobh Ramblers	Dublin City	Dundalk	Galway United	Kildare County	Kilkenny City	Limerick	Monaghan United	Sligo Rovers
Athlone Town AFC (Athlone)	■	0-2	1-3	1-2	0-2	4-2	0-0	0-1	1-1	0-0
	■	0-3	0-2	0-0	2-0	0-2	0-1	3-1	1-1	0-0
Cobh Ramblers FC (Cobh)	2-2	■	0-3	1-1	1-1	1-0	0-2	2-1	4-1	0-2
	2-0	■	0-2	2-1	4-1	1-2	1-0	3-2	0-1	1-1
Dublin City FC (Dublin)	1-0	0-1	■	1-1	0-2	0-0	2-2	1-1	5-1	3-1
	1-0	2-0	■	2-3	4-1	1-0	0-0	0-2	4-0	1-1
Dundalk FC (Dundalk)	2-2	0-0	2-3	■	0-0	1-2	0-5	4-0	2-2	0-0
	0-1	2-2	0-0	■	0-3	1-2	2-1	1-0	5-0	1-2
Galway United FC (Galway)	2-1	1-1	3-1	0-3	■	1-1	2-0	5-2	0-1	1-1
	1-1	2-3	1-1	1-0	■	0-0	0-1	3-1	1-1	0-2
Kildare County FC (Newbridge)	2-1	2-1	1-1	1-1	0-1	■	1-1	0-1	0-0	0-0
	1-0	0-0	0-3	3-0	1-2	■	0-2	1-3	0-1	2-2
Kilkenny City FC (Kilkenny)	4-0	1-0	2-1	1-1	0-2	2-0	■	3-1	2-1	2-1
	0-2	1-2	2-2	0-1	0-0	1-2	■	0-2	1-3	2-0
Limerick FC (Limerick)	3-1	0-2	2-1	0-0	0-1	1-2	0-2	■	2-1	1-1
	0-0	1-1	1-1	0-1	2-1	1-1	2-1	■	1-1	1-2
Monaghan United FC (Monaghan)	2-1	0-2	1-1	1-2	2-0	2-1	1-4	1-2	■	0-4
	2-3	2-2	0-2	0-2	1-3	2-0	0-0	1-2	■	1-4
Sligo Rovers FC (Sligo)	0-0	1-1	1-1	0-2	1-1	1-0	2-0	1-1	2-0	■
	1-0	2-1	1-1	1-0	4-1	2-1	1-0	0-0	0-1	■

	Division 1	**Pd**	**Wn**	**Dw**	**Ls**	**GF**	**GA**	**Pts**	
1.	Sligo Rovers FC (Sligo)	36	15	16	5	45	27	61	P
2.	Dublin City FC (Dublin)	36	15	14	7	57	34	59	PO
3.	Cobh Ramblers FC (Cobh)	36	15	11	10	49	40	56	
4.	Kilkenny City FC (Kilkenny)	36	15	8	13	46	35	53	
5.	Galway United FC (Galway)	36	14	11	11	46	43	53	
6.	Dundalk FC (Dundalk)	36	12	13	11	44	40	49	
7.	Limerick FC (Limerick)	36	13	9	14	44	49	48	
8.	Kildare County FC (Newbridge)	36	10	11	15	33	42	41	
9.	Monaghan United FC (Monaghan)	36	9	9	18	36	66	36	
10.	Athlone Town AFC (Athlone)	36	6	10	20	28	52	28	
		360	124	112	124	428	428	484	

FAI Cup Final   (Lansdowne Road, Dublin – 04/12/2005 – 24,521)

DROGHEDA UNITED FC (DROGHEDA)   2-0   Cork City FC

Whelan 52', O'Brien 83'

Drogheda: Connor, Lynch, Webb, Gartland, Gray, Whelan, Robinson, Bradley (Keegan 73), Sandvliet, Ristila (Rooney 76), D. O'Brien (Bernard 90).

Cork: Devine, Horgan, O'Halloran (O'Brien 83), Murray, Bennett, Gamble, O'Callaghan, Woods, Kearney, O'Flynn, Fenn (Behan 72).

Semi-finals

Cork City FC (Cork)	1-0	Derry City FC (Derry)
Drogheda United FC (Drogheda)	2-1	Bray Wanderers AFC (Bray)

Quarter-finals

Bray Wanderers AFC (Bray)	3-2	University College Dublin AFC (Dublin)
Cork City FC (Cork)	3-1	Sligo Rovers FC (Sligo)
Derry City FC (Derry)	1-0	Shamrock Rovers FC (Dublin)
Drogheda United FC (Drogheda)	2-1	Bohemian FC (Dublin)

2006

League of Ireland Premier Division 2006	Bohemian	Bray Wanderers	Cork City	Derry City	Drogheda	Dublin City	Longford	St. Patrick's Ath.	Shelbourne	Sligo Rovers	U.C. Dublin	Waterford United
Bohemian FC (Dublin)	■	1-1			2-2		0-1			0-1		3-1
	■	3-0	0-0	1-2	0-1		0-1	0-0	2-1	0-2	2-1	4-2
Bray Wanderers AFC (Bray)		■	2-1				0-2		2-3	1-1		
	0-3	■	0-0	2-3	0-1	0-2	1-0	1-2	2-2	1-2	1-1	3-1
Cork City FC (Cork)	1-0		■				1-1		1-0	0-0		4-1
	1-0	6-0	■	1-1	1-0	1-0	2-1	0-0	2-1	2-0	1-0	2-0
Derry City FC (Derry)	1-1	0-0	1-0	■	0-0				4-0	0-0		
	1-0	3-0	2-0	■	1-2	3-0	1-0	3-1	2-0	3-1	2-0	4-0
Drogheda United FC (Drogheda)		1-1	0-0		■		2-0			1-0	1-0	
	1-0	1-0	0-0	3-1	■	2-2	1-0	2-1	1-3	2-2	1-0	4-0
Dublin City FC (Dublin)						■						
	1-2		0-4	1-0	0-1	■	0-2	0-2	1-2	0-0	2-1	
Longford Town FC (Longford)	3-0		0-2				■	0-0		0-2		
	3-1	1-0	0-2	0-1	0-0	1-1	■	2-0	0-0	0-0	0-0	3-0
St. Patrick's Athletic FC (Dublin)		5-1	0-1	0-1	3-0			■	1-3			0-1
	0-1	3-0	2-0	1-1	0-1		0-0	■	2-2	3-1	0-0	0-0
Shelbourne FC (Dublin)	2-1			2-2	2-2		2-0		■			
	2-0	4-1	2-2	1-0	2-1	1-0	0-0	3-0	■	3-0	6-0	5-1
Sligo Rovers FC (Sligo)	1-0				2-3		3-2	0-2		■		0-0
	1-0	2-0	0-3	3-1	0-0	2-0	3-1	1-1	1-1	■	0-1	3-1
University College Dublin AFC (Dublin)		4-0	1-1				3-1	0-0	0-2	1-0	■	
	0-1	4-1	0-0	0-0	0-0		2-2	0-1	1-2	3-0	■	2-1
Waterford United FC (Waterford)		3-0		0-1			1-2		0-1		0-0	■
	1-3	1-1	0-0	1-2	2-3	0-1	0-0	1-3	0-1	1-2	0-1	■

	Premier Division	Pd	Wn	Dw	Ls	GF	GA	Pts	
1.	SHELBOURNE FC (DUBLIN)	30	18	8	4	60	27	62	##
2.	Derry City FC (Derry)	30	18	8	4	46	20	62	
3.	Drogheda United FC (Drogheda)	30	16	10	4	37	23	58	
4.	Cork City FC (Cork)	30	15	11	4	37	15	56	
5.	Sligo Rovers FC (Sligo)	30	11	7	12	33	42	40	
6.	University College Dublin AFC (Dublin)	30	9	11	10	26	26	38	
7.	St. Patrick's Athletic FC (Dublin)	30	9	10	11	32	29	37	
8.	Longford Town FC (Longford)	30	8	10	12	23	27	34	
9.	Bohemian FC (Dublin)	30	9	5	16	29	34	29	-3
10.	Bray Wanderers AFC (Bray)	30	3	8	19	22	64	17	
11.	Waterford United FC (Waterford)	30	2	6	22	20	58	12	PO
12.	Dublin City FC (Dublin)	17	4	3	10	11	24	15	##
		330	118	94	118	365	365	445	-3

Dublin City FC resigned from the league on 19/07/2006 after 17 games and their results were deleted.

Bohemian FC 2-1 Shelbourne FC played on 18/08/2006 had the result annulled on 30/10/2006 as Bohemian FC had fielded ineligible player Jason McGuinness. However, this decision was reversed on 14/11/2006 and the result was allowed to stand with Bohemian FC having 3 points deducted instead.

The League of Ireland (LoI) merged into the Football Association of Ireland (FAI) and the League was re-structured for the 2007 season with clubs being assessed on their 4-year record, financial position etc., for admittance to the Premier Division.

Shelbourne FC were refused a Premier Division license for 2007 due to their financial situation and their inability to pay their players, some of whom were sold on or made free agents.

Top goal-scorers 2006

1)	Jason BYRNE	(Shelbourne FC)	15
2)	Glen CROWE	(Shelbourne FC)	12
3)	Declan O'BRIEN	(Drogheda United FC)	11
	Roy O'DONOVAN	(Cork City FC)	11
5)	Mark FARREN	(Derry City FC)	9

Promotion/Relegation Play-off

Dundalk FC (Dundalk)	1-1, 2-1	Waterford United FC (Waterford)

League of Ireland Division 1 2006	Athlone Town	Cobh Ramblers	Dundalk	Finn Harps	Galway United	Kildare County	Kilkenny City	Limerick	Monaghan	Shamrock Rovers
Athlone Town AFC (Athlone)		2-1	0-1	2-1	0-5	1-2	3-0	0-1	2-2	0-3
		0-2	2-0	1-0	1-0	0-0	0-0	0-1	0-4	0-2
Cobh Ramblers FC (Cobh)	2-0		2-3	3-0	0-1	1-1	2-0	1-0	2-1	1-1
	0-0		3-1	1-2	1-1	1-2	1-1	2-1	4-0	1-1
Dundalk FC (Dundalk)	4-0	1-1		1-1	1-0	2-0	2-1	1-0	3-1	1-1
	1-2	0-1		1-3	1-0	0-1	2-0	3-1	4-0	0-2
Finn Harps FC (Ballybofey)	2-0	1-2	0-1		0-1	3-1	2-1	0-0	4-0	0-1
	1-1	1-1	1-2		2-2	2-2	1-2	3-2	4-1	0-0
Galway United FC (Galway)	1-1	1-0	1-3	1-1		1-1	2-1	1-0	2-0	1-0
	0-0	2-1	0-0	1-1		1-1	1-1	2-0	6-2	1-0
Kildare County FC (Newbridge)	2-2	0-1	2-3	1-3	1-2		2-1	1-1	4-2	1-1
	1-0	0-4	0-3	2-5	0-2		1-0	0-1	2-0	0-3
Kilkenny City FC (Kilkenny)	2-2	2-3	0-1	0-2	1-5	1-2		2-2	0-4	0-1
	0-2	1-2	0-2	1-0	1-4	0-0		0-1	1-1	0-0
Limerick FC (Limerick)	0-2	0-1	1-2	2-1	1-5	1-2	4-1		1-1	0-2
	1-2	1-0	2-3	2-1	1-3	1-0	2-1		1-0	1-0
Monaghan United FC (Monaghan)	1-0	0-0	1-0	0-1	0-1	0-2	2-0	1-2		2-2
	0-1	3-1	1-3	0-0	0-0	1-1	1-3	0-1		0-0
Shamrock Rovers FC (Dublin)	2-0	1-0	0-0	4-0	1-0	3-0	2-0	1-1	2-0	
	2-0	1-1	2-1	2-0	0-0	2-0	1-0	3-1	4-0	

	Division 1	Pd	Wn	Dw	Ls	GF	GA	Pts	
1.	Shamrock Rovers FC (Dublin)	36	21	12	3	53	13	72	P -3
2.	Dundalk FC (Dundalk)	36	22	5	9	57	33	71	PO
3.	Galway United FC (Galway)	36	19	12	5	57	25	69	
4.	Cobh Ramblers FC (Cobh)	36	16	10	10	50	33	58	
5.	Limerick FC (Limerick)	36	14	5	17	38	48	47	##
6.	Finn Harps FC (Ballybofey)	36	12	10	14	49	45	46	
7.	Kildare County FC (Newbridge)	36	11	10	15	38	55	43	
8.	Athlone Town AFC (Athlone)	36	11	9	16	29	47	42	
9.	Monaghan United FC (Monaghan)	36	6	9	21	32	64	27	
10.	Kilkenny City FC (Kilkenny)	36	3	8	25	25	65	17	
		360	135	90	135	428	428	492	-3

Shamrock Rovers FC had 3 points deducted for fielding the ineligible player Paul Shiels on 23/07/2006 versus Dundalk.

Limerick FC (Limerick) were refused a license for the next season but a new club called Limerick '37 FC (Limerick) was formed and took their place in Division 1.

Elected: Limerick '37 FC (Limerick), Wexford Youths FC (Wexford)

FAI Cup Final   (Lansdowne Road, Dublin – 03/12/2006 – 16,022)

DERRY CITY FC (DERRY)   4-3 (aet)   St. Patrick's Athletic FC (Dublin)

Forde 25', Delaney 85', Hutton 107', Brennan 110' o.g.   *Mulcahy 20', Molloy 74' pen., O'Connor 103'*

Derry City: Forde, McCallion, Brennan, Hutton, Delaney, Deery, Higgins, Molloy, McCourt, Farren, Beckett.

St. Patrick's Athletic: Ryan, Quigley, C.Foley, Brennan, Frost, Murphy, M.Foley, Mulcahy, Rutherford, Keegan, Molloy.

Semi-finals

Sligo Rovers FC (Sligo)	0-0, 0-5	Derry City FC (Derry)
Shamrock Rovers FC (Dublin)	0-2	St. Patrick's Athletic FC (Dublin)

Quarter-finals

Athlone Town AFC (Athlone)	1-2	Shamrock Rovers FC (Dublin)
Derry City FC (Derry)	2-0	University College Dublin AFC (Dublin)
St. Patrick's Athletic FC (Dublin)	4-1	Longford Town FC (Longford)
Sligo Rovers FC (Sligo)	0-0, 4-3	Killester United FC (Killester)

2007

League of Ireland Premier Division 2007

Team	Boh	Bray	Cork	Derry	Drog	Gal	Long	St Pat	Sham	Sligo	UCD	Wat
Bohemian FC (Dublin)	■			1-1	2-0	0-0		0-2	3-0	2-0		
	■	2-0	2-1	0-0	0-0	1-1	5-0	2-0	2-1	1-0	0-0	1-0
Bray Wanderers AFC (Bray)	0-3	■	1-1		1-1			3-0	2-1			
	1-0	■	1-1	1-1	1-2	0-1	1-3	0-0	0-2	2-0	2-1	2-1
Cork City FC (Cork)	0-1		■			0-0	3-2	0-1	1-0			
	2-1	2-2	■	1-1	0-0	0-0	2-0	1-0	0-0	1-2	4-1	2-0
Derry City FC (Derry)	1-2	3-0	1-2	■			1-0	1-1		0-0		
	0-0	1-0	1-4	■	0-1	0-0	3-1	0-1	1-0	4-1	0-1	1-1
Drogheda United FC (Drogheda)		1-1	2-1	1-0	■					1-0	0-1	
	1-0	4-1	2-2	2-1	■	2-2	1-1	2-0	0-2	3-0	3-2	3-0
Galway United FC (Galway)			1-0	1-1		■	2-1	0-1		2-0	2-1	
	0-1	0-1	1-2	1-1	2-3	■	1-1	0-1	1-1	0-2	0-0	1-2
Longford Town FC (Longford)		0-1		3-1	1-2		■	2-1		1-1		1-1
	3-0	1-1	1-2	0-0	0-1	0-3	■	1-2	0-3	0-1	1-0	1-0
St. Patrick's Athletic FC (Dublin)	0-1	4-2			0-0			■	5-0			4-1
	0-0	3-1	1-1	2-1	1-0	1-2	4-2	■	2-1	3-1	1-1	3-0
Shamrock Rovers FC (Dublin)					0-2	4-0	0-1		■	0-0		0-0
	0-0	1-0	2-0	1-1	1-2	1-0	2-0	0-0	■	1-0	2-0	2-0
Sligo Rovers FC (Sligo)			0-1	0-0			2-3			■	2-1	1-2
	2-1	3-0	4-1	0-2	0-2	1-1	2-1	0-4	2-0	■	1-0	1-1
University College Dublin AFC (Dublin)		1-1	1-2			0-1	0-3	2-4			■	2-1
	1-0	2-0	0-1	1-1	0-1	2-2	2-2	2-2	0-0	0-2	■	3-0
Waterford United FC (Waterford)	0-0	0-0	0-3	2-1	1-1	0-0						■
	0-1	1-2	1-0	0-1	1-1	1-0	2-1	2-1	0-2	1-2	1-3	■

	Premier Division	Pd	Wn	Dw	Ls	GF	GA	Pts	
1.	DROGHEDA UNITED FC (DROGHEDA)	33	19	11	3	48	24	68	
2.	St. Patrick's Athletic FC (Dublin)	33	18	7	8	54	29	61	
3.	Bohemian FC (Dublin)	33	16	10	7	35	17	58	
4.	Cork City FC (City)	33	15	10	8	44	32	55	
5.	Shamrock Rovers FC (Dublin)	33	14	9	10	36	26	51	
6.	Sligo Rovers FC (Sligo)	33	12	5	16	34	45	41	
7.	Derry City FC (Derry)	33	8	13	12	30	31	37	
8.	Galway United FC (Galway)	33	7	14	12	28	35	35	
9.	Bray Wanderers AFC (Bray)	33	8	10	15	30	48	34	
10.	University College Dublin AFC (Dublin)	33	7	10	16	31	44	31	
11.	Waterford United FC (Waterford)	33	7	9	17	23	47	30	POR
12.	Longford Town FC (Longford)	33	9	8	16	34	49	29	P -6
		396	140	116	140	427	427	530	-6

Shamrock Rovers 1-1 Waterford United played on 18/05/2007 was abandoned after 52 minutes due to an unstable floodlight pylon. The match was replayed on 10/07/2007 and finished with a 2-0 scoreline.

Longford Town FC had 6 points deducted for a breach of the license agreement regulations.

Top goal-scorers 2007

1) Dave MOONEY   (Longford Town FC)   19
2) Mark QUIGLEY   (St. Patrick's Athletic FC) 15
3) Roy O'DONOVAN   (Cork City FC)   14
4) Tadhg PURCELL   (Shamrock Rovers FC)   12
5) Eamon ZAYED   (Drogheda United FC)   11

Promotion/Relegation Play-off

Finn Harps FC (Ballybofey)   3-0, 3-3   Waterford United FC (Waterford)

League of Ireland Division 1 2007	Athlone Town	Cobh Ramblers	Dundalk	Finn Harps	Kildare County	Kilkenny City	Limerick '37	Monaghan	Shelbourne	Wexford Youths
Athlone Town AFC (Athlone)		0-1	1-2	1-0	4-2	1-1	3-2	2-2	1-4	0-1
		0-0	0-2	2-2	0-2	3-0	0-1	0-0	1-0	3-0
Cobh Ramblers FC (Cobh)	2-0		2-1	0-0	1-0	4-1	2-1	2-1	1-1	2-2
	3-0		1-0	1-0	5-1	2-0	0-2	3-0	1-0	1-0
Dundalk FC (Dundalk)	3-0	0-0		1-1	4-3	4-0	0-2	1-0	1-0	2-0
	6-2	0-0		3-2	2-0	3-2	0-0	3-1	3-0	4-0
Finn Harps FC (Ballybofey)	1-1	1-0	1-0		3-1	6-0	2-0	3-0	1-0	1-0
	2-0	0-2	0-0		2-0	5-0	2-0	0-0	2-1	1-2
Kildare County FC (Newbridge)	1-2	1-2	3-1	0-3		2-2	3-0	1-1	1-4	2-1
	2-1	0-2	0-0	1-0		3-3	1-2	1-1	1-1	1-1
Kilkenny City FC (Kilkenny)	0-2	0-7	0-0	1-3	1-1		2-0	2-1	2-5	0-2
	2-3	0-0	1-2	0-1	3-3		0-1	2-2	1-1	0-1
Limerick '37 FC (Limerick)	4-1	0-0	4-1	1-3	0-0	1-2		0-2	1-1	5-0
	1-1	0-0	0-1	1-1	2-0	2-2		1-0	3-2	3-0
Monaghan United FC (Monaghan)	1-0	0-4	2-0	0-4	0-1	3-0	1-1		1-0	2-0
	0-2	1-2	1-1	0-2	1-3	0-2	0-1		4-0	2-2
Shelbourne FC (Dublin)	2-0	1-2	1-0	1-2	2-1	0-0	4-0	1-1		1-3
	1-0	2-2	0-2	0-1	2-2	2-0	1-1	1-1		1-0
Wexford Youths FC (Dublin)	1-1	0-0	0-0	0-1	1-2	3-0	1-1	2-3	1-2	
	1-2	1-0	0-3	0-1	2-2	0-1	1-1	2-3	1-1	

	Division 1	Pd	Wn	Dw	Ls	GF	GA	Pts	
1.	Cobh Ramblers FC (Cobh)	36	22	11	3	57	17	77	P
2.	Finn Harps FC (Ballybofey)	36	23	7	6	61	20	76	POP
3.	Dundalk FC (Dundalk)	36	19	9	8	56	30	66	
4.	Limerick '37 FC (Limerick)	36	13	12	11	45	41	51	
5.	Shelbourne FC (Dublin)	36	11	11	14	46	45	44	
6.	Athlone Town AFC (Athlone)	36	11	8	17	40	55	41	
7.	Kildare County FC (Newbridge)	36	9	12	15	48	62	39	
8.	Monaghan United FC (Monaghan)	36	9	11	16	38	52	38	
9.	Wexford Youths FC (Wexford)	36	7	10	19	32	55	31	
10.	Kilkenny City FC (Kilkenny)	36	5	11	20	33	79	26	##
		360	129	102	129	456	456	489	

Wexford Youths FC 1-1 Limerick '37 FC played on 31/07/2007 was abandoned after 76 minutes due to a power failure. The game was replayed on 16/09/2007 and finished with a 1-1 scoreline.

Promotion Play-Off

Finn Harps FC (Ballybofey)   2-0   Dundalk FC (Dundalk)

Kilkenny City FC (Kilkenny) resigned from the league at the end of the season.

Elected: Sporting Fingal FC (Dublin).

FAI Cup Final   (RDS Stadium, Dublin – 02/12/2007 – 10,000)

| CORK CITY FC (CORK) | 1-0 | Longford Town FC (Longford) |

Behan 60'

Cork City: Devine, Lordan, O'Callaghan, Murray, Woods (O'Brien 67'), McSweeney, Gamble, Healy, Kearney (Farrelly 85'), Behan, O'Flynn.

Longford Town: Kelly, Sullivan, Brennan, Doherty, Prunty, Duffy (Reilly 78'), Doyle, Rutherford, Martin, Mooney, Baker (Wexler 55').

Semi-finals

| Bohemian FC (Dublin) | 0-2 | Cork City FC (Cork) |
| University College Dublin AFC (Dublin) | 0-1 | Longford Town FC (Longford) |

Quarter-finals

Derry City FC (Derry)	0-1	University College Dublin AFC (Dublin)
Longford Town FC (Longford)	3-1	Limerick '37 FC (Limerick)
St. Patrick's Athletic FC (Dublin)	1-2	Bohemian FC (Dublin)
Waterford United FC (Waterford)	1-1, 0-4	Cork City FC (Cork)

2008

League of Ireland Premier Division 2008	Bohemian	Bray Wanderers	Cobh Ramblers	Cork City	Derry City	Drogheda	Finn Harps	Galway United	St. Patrick's Ath.	Shamrock Rovers	Sligo Rovers	U.C. Dublin
Bohemian FC (Dublin)	■	2-1		3-1	0-1		3-0		3-0			
		1-1	3-0	2-1	0-0	2-0	3-0	2-1	0-1	2-1	3-0	2-0
Bray Wanderers AFC (Bray)		■	3-2		2-1	4-3	0-1		0-1			2-1
	0-2		1-0	0-3	1-0	1-0	1-0	0-1	0-3	1-0	0-0	0-2
Cobh Ramblers AFC (Cobh)	0-2		■	1-1			4-1		1-0			2-0
	0-1	1-2		0-0	0-3	0-4	1-3	1-1	0-1	2-0	1-3	0-0
Cork City FC (Cork)		3-0		■	1-1	0-0	1-1			0-0	2-0	
	0-1	0-0	5-0		1-1	0-2	3-0	3-2	0-0	1-1	1-0	1-0
Derry City FC (Derry)		4-2			■	0-1	1-0	2-0		1-1		
	0-0	4-0	1-0	2-3		2-0	2-1	0-0	0-3	0-1	0-0	4-1
Drogheda United FC (Drogheda)	1-2		0-0			■	1-2	1-1	0-2	1-1		
	1-2	2-0	3-0	0-1	0-1		1-0	1-0	2-2	0-1	1-1	2-1
Finn Harps FC (Ballybofey)		2-2					■	0-1	2-0	0-2		2-0
	0-2	1-0	2-1	0-1	0-2	1-3		0-2	0-3	1-1	0-1	1-0
Galway United FC (Galway)	0-2	4-0		3-2		3-0		■		1-1		
	0-1	2-3	0-1	1-3	0-4	0-1	2-2		2-2	0-2	1-1	1-2
St. Patrick's Athletic FC (Dublin)		0-3	0-1	2-1			0-1		■		1-0	2-0
	0-1	1-1	1-0	3-2	0-1	0-1	5-1	1-0		1-1	3-1	0-0
Shamrock Rovers FC (Dublin)	1-2	2-2		3-0	1-1			1-3		■		1-1
	0-1	2-0	0-0	1-1	1-1	0-0	0-2	3-1	0-1		1-0	1-1
Sligo Rovers FC (Sligo)	0-1	2-0	4-0		3-3		1-1		2-1		■	
	1-2	3-0	3-1	0-1	0-0	0-0	4-1	3-0	1-2	3-2		0-0
University College Dublin AFC (Dublin)	0-1			1-2	1-0		0-1		0-1			■
	1-1	2-2	1-1	0-2	2-3	1-3	1-0	0-1	0-3	0-2	0-0	

	Premier Division	Pd	Wn	Dw	Ls	GF	GA	Pts	
1.	BOHEMIAN FC (DUBLIN)	33	27	4	2	55	13	85	
2.	St. Patrick's Athletic FC (Dublin)	33	20	6	7	48	24	66	
3.	Derry City FC (Derry)	33	16	10	7	46	25	58	
4.	Sligo Rovers FC (Sligo)	33	12	12	9	41	28	48	
5.	Cork City FC (Cork)	33	15	11	7	45	28	46	-10
6.	Drogheda United FC (Drogheda)	33	12	9	12	38	32	35	-10
7.	Bray Wanderers AFC (Bray)	33	11	6	16	28	52	39	
8.	Shamrock Rovers FC (Dublin)	33	8	13	12	33	35	37	
9.	Galway United FC (Galway)	33	8	8	17	34	49	32	
10.	Finn Harps FC (Ballybofey)	33	9	4	20	26	53	31	R
11.	Cobh Ramblers FC (Cobh)	33	6	8	19	27	55	26	R
12.	University College Dublin AFC (Dublin)	33	4	9	20	19	46	21	R
		396	148	100	148	440	440	524	-20

Cork City FC and Drogheda United FC each had 10 points deducted after entering administration.

The Premier Division was reduced to 10 clubs from the next season.

Top goal-scorers 2008

1)	Mark FARREN	(Derry City FC)	15
	Dave MOONEY	(Cork City FC)	15
	Mark QUIGLEY	(St. Patrick's Athletic FC)	15
4)	Killian BRENNAN	(Bohemian FC)	11
5)	Padraig AMOND	(Shamrock Rovers FC)	9
	Glen CROWE	(Bohemian FC)	9
	Ryan GUY	(St. Patrick's Athletic FC)	9

League of Ireland Division 1 2008	Athlone Town	Dundalk	Fingal	Kildare County	Limerick '37	Longford Town	Monaghan United	Shelbourne	Waterford United	Wexford Youths
Athlone Town AFC (Athlone)		2-2	0-1	3-0	0-3	0-0	1-0	0-1	1-1	1-0
		0-3	0-3	1-1	2-2	1-0	0-0	0-1	0-0	3-1
Dundalk FC (Dundalk)	7-0		2-1	4-1	0-1	1-2	3-0	2-1	2-1	1-0
	1-0		3-2	6-0	0-2	0-0	3-0	1-3	1-0	2-1
Sporting Fingal FC (Dublin)	1-0	0-0		2-0	2-0	0-0	0-1	2-1	3-1	2-3
	2-0	1-1		2-2	1-0	1-1	4-0	0-0	3-1	2-0
Kildare County FC (Newbridge)	1-0	1-6	1-1		0-2	0-2	1-2	1-2	1-2	1-2
	1-1	1-2	0-2		1-2	0-1	4-0	1-3	1-2	2-0
Limerick '37 FC (Limerick)	0-0	2-0	1-1	1-2		1-3	2-1	1-2	5-1	1-1
	0-0	1-2	1-3	4-0		2-1	2-2	0-3	0-3	2-0
Longford Town FC (Longford)	1-1	0-3	0-3	0-1	1-2		1-3	1-2	0-3	2-4
	3-0	1-2	5-1	0-0	1-2		3-0	2-0	0-2	0-1
Monaghan United FC (Monaghan)	3-0	2-2	0-2	3-3	0-2	5-1		2-0	2-0	1-2
	1-2	0-0	1-0	0-0	1-0	1-0		1-0	0-0	0-2
Shelbourne FC (Dublin)	3-3	0-0	0-0	3-1	1-1	5-0	1-0		0-0	1-0
	2-0	0-0	1-1	5-0	0-2	2-0	2-0		2-0	1-0
Waterford United FC (Waterford)	3-0	0-1	2-1	3-1	3-1	4-0	1-1	0-1		1-0
	1-1	1-0	2-0	3-2	3-1	1-1	5-0	1-1		1-0
Wexford Youths FC (Dublin)	0-0	3-1	2-2	0-1	3-0	0-2	1-3	0-3	1-1	
	2-0	0-5	0-1	1-1	1-0	1-1	1-2	2-2	1-2	

	Division 1	Pd	Wn	Dw	Ls	GF	GA	Pts	
1.	Dundalk FC (Dundalk)	36	21	8	7	69	30	71	P
2.	Shelbourne FC (Dublin)	36	20	10	6	55	25	70	
3.	Waterford United FC (Waterford)	36	18	9	9	55	35	63	
4.	Sporting Fingal FC (Dublin)	36	17	11	8	53	32	62	
5.	Limerick '37 FC (Limerick)	36	15	7	14	49	45	52	
6.	Monaghan United FC (Monaghan)	36	13	8	15	38	51	47	
7.	Wexford Youths FC (Wexford)	36	10	7	19	36	51	37	
8.	Longford Town FC (Longford)	36	9	8	19	36	55	35	
9.	Athlone Town AFC (Athlone)	36	6	14	16	23	51	32	
10.	Kildare County FC (Newbridge)	36	6	8	22	34	73	26	POR
		360	135	90	135	448	448	495	

Promotion/Relegation Play-off

Mervue United AFC (Galway) 2-2, 3-0 Kildare County FC (Newbridge)

FAI Cup Final (RDS Stadium, Dublin – 23/11/2008 – 10,281)

BOHEMIAN FC (DUBLIN) 2-2 (aet) Derry City FC (Derry)
Crowe 64', Byrne 70' pen *(4-2 penalties)* *Morrow 60', 76'*

Bohemian: Murphy, Heary, Rossiter, O'Donnell, Burns, Oman, Fenn (Kolonas 61'), Deegan (Cronin 105'), Crowe, Byrne (McGill 77'), Brennan.
Derry City: Doherty, McCallion, Delaney, Hutton, Gray, Morrow (McHugh 105'), McGlynn (Stewart 90'), Deery, Molloy (Higgins 90'), Farren, McGinn.

Semi-finals

Galway United FC (Galway) 0-1 Derry City FC (Derry)
St. Patrick's Athletic FC (Dublin) 1-3 Bohemian FC (Dublin)

Quarter-finals

Cork City FC (Cork) 1-1, 0-0 (aet) Derry City FC (Derry)
 (Derry City FC won 5-3 on penalties)
Sporting Fingal FC (Dublin) 3-3, 0-2 St. Patrick's Athletic FC (Dublin)
Galway United FC (Galway) 1-1, 2-0 Bray Wanderers AFC (Bray)
Wayside Celtic FC (Dublin) 1-6 Bohemian FC (Dublin)

2009

League of Ireland Premier Division 2009	Bohemian	Bray Wanderers	Cork City	Derry City	Drogheda United	Dundalk	Galway United	St. Patrick's Ath.	Shamrock Rovers	Sligo Rovers
Bohemian FC (Dublin)	■	1-2	1-0	1-0	4-0	3-2	5-0	3-1	0-0	3-1
	■	2-0	0-1	1-1	1-0	5-0	2-0	3-0	2-0	2-0
Bray Wanderers AFC (Bray)	1-1	■	3-2	0-1	1-2	1-1	1-2	0-1	1-2	2-2
	1-3	■	0-2	1-1	0-1	1-1	2-2	2-1	0-0	3-1
Cork City FC (Cork)	0-2	1-0	■	2-0	0-0	2-1	4-2	0-1	0-0	0-0
	0-1	2-1	■	1-0	1-0	1-2	1-0	0-1	0-0	1-0
Derry City FC (Derry)	0-1	3-0	1-1	■	0-1	3-0	1-3	1-0	0-1	1-2
	3-2	2-0	2-1	■	1-0	0-1	1-1	1-0	0-0	1-2
Drogheda United FC (Drogheda)	1-1	1-2	0-1	1-3	■	2-2	4-0	1-2	0-1	2-2
	0-1	0-0	2-1	0-3	■	1-1	0-1	1-0	2-2	0-0
Dundalk FC (Dundalk)	0-2	0-0	1-0	1-2	4-2	■	3-0	0-0	2-4	2-2
	0-1	3-0	1-2	1-0	3-0	■	1-0	0-1	0-1	0-2
Galway United FC (Galway)	0-2	3-1	2-2	3-1	0-2	0-3	■	2-1	0-1	1-0
	0-2	3-0	0-2	0-3	1-1	1-0	■	2-1	1-3	0-0
St. Patrick's Athletic FC (Dublin)	0-2	2-0	1-1	0-2	1-0	1-0	1-2	■	1-0	0-2
	3-1	1-1	0-3	0-3	2-1	2-0	0-3	■	1-2	2-2
Shamrock Rovers FC (Dublin)	1-0	3-1	1-2	2-1	2-0	2-2	1-1	1-0	■	3-1
	2-1	0-1	1-1	1-2	1-1	3-1	1-0	2-0	■	2-1
Sligo Rovers FC (Sligo)	1-0	1-0	0-3	0-4	3-1	3-4	2-0	2-0	1-2	■
	0-0	2-1	1-1	0-1	2-2	1-3	2-0	0-1	0-3	■

	Premier Division	**Pd**	**Wn**	**Dw**	**Ls**	**GF**	**GA**	**Pts**	
1.	BOHEMIAN FC (DUBLIN)	36	24	5	7	62	21	77	
2.	Shamrock Rovers FC (Dublin)	36	21	10	5	51	27	73	
3.	Cork City FC (Cork)	36	17	9	10	42	28	60	##
4.	Derry City FC (Derry)	36	18	5	13	49	31	59	##
5.	Dundalk FC (Dundalk)	36	12	8	16	46	51	44	
6.	Sligo Rovers FC (Sligo)	36	11	10	5	41	51	43	
7.	St. Patrick's Athletic FC (Dublin)	36	13	4	19	29	46	43	
8.	Galway United FC (Galway)	36	12	6	18	36	57	42	
9.	Drogheda United FC (Drogheda)	36	7	11	18	32	50	32	PO
10.	Bray Wanderers AFC (Bray)	36	6	10	20	30	56	28	PO
		360	141	78	141	418	418	501	

Derry City FC (Derry) were relegated at the end of the season for holding "dual contracts" with their players. Cork City FC (Cork) were dissolved at the end of the season after being refused a license for the 2010 season.

As a result of the above relegations, Bray Wanderers AFC retained their Premier Division status for the next season.

Top goal-scorers 2009

1) Gary TWIGG   (Shamrock Rovers FC)   24
2) Jason BYRNE   (Bohemian FC)   22
3) Rafael CRETARO   (Sligo Rovers FC)   15
4) Chris TURNER   (Dundalk FC)   12
5) Mark FARREN   (Derry City FC)   10

Promotion/Relegation Play-offs

Sporting Fingal FC (Dublin)	2-0, 2-2	Bray Wanderers AFC (Bray)
Drogheda United FC (Drogheda)	2-0	Bray Wanderers AFC (Bray)
Shelbourne FC (Dublin)	1-2	Sporting Fingal FC (Dublin)

Limerick FC (Limerick) changed their name during pre-season from Limerick '37 FC (Limerick)

League of Ireland Division 1 2009

Team	Athlone Town	Fingal	Finn Harps	Kildare County	Limerick	Longford Town	Mervue United	Monaghan	Shelbourne	U.C. Dublin	Waterford United	Wexford Youths
Athlone Town AFC (Athlone)	■		0-6	2-2				1-2		0-5	1-2	2-0
	■	1-2	2-2	3-1	0-2	2-5	2-2	2-3	2-2	0-1	1-2	0-1
Sporting Fingal FC (Dublin)	2-3	■	4-1		2-1			2-2	1-0			0-1
	2-0	■	1-0	1-0	1-1	3-0	2-0	4-0	1-0	0-1	1-4	2-0
Finn Harps FC (Ballybofey)			■			1-0		0-2	1-3	0-5	1-1	
	1-1	3-2	■	2-1	1-2	1-0	2-0	1-2	1-1	1-2	1-3	0-2
Kildare County FC (Newbridge)		2-3	0-2	■			0-1		1-5			1-2
	0-1	0-8	1-1	■	0-0	2-3	0-3	0-2	0-3	0-1	0-2	0-3
Limerick FC (Limerick)	6-1		3-0	2-3	■		2-1	3-3			2-1	
	0-0	1-4	1-1	3-0	■	1-4	4-1	0-0	0-1	0-0	0-2	2-0
Longford Town FC (Longford)	3-0	0-4			1-2	■	1-1		1-4			
	0-1	1-3	0-0	4-0	2-3	■	3-0	3-3	0-2	0-3	1-3	0-1
Mervue United AFC (Galway)	3-1	1-4	0-1			0-1	■		2-4	1-2		
	0-1	1-1	1-1	1-4	1-0	3-2	■	1-5	0-1	1-2	0-2	0-0
Monaghan United FC (Monaghan)		2-2		6-1			4-2	■	0-3			3-0
	0-0	0-3	1-0	5-1	1-0	2-0	1-2	■	0-1	2-3	0-0	0-0
Shelbourne FC (Dublin)	0-0				3-3	4-5			■	2-2		1-2
	2-0	1-0	2-1	2-0	1-0	2-2	7-0	2-1	■	1-3	1-0	2-1
University College Dublin AFC (Dublin)			5-0	2-1	2-1		3-0			■	2-3	2-0
	1-1	0-1	1-1	4-0	2-1	3-1	1-0	3-0	0-1	■	0-0	0-1
Waterford United FC (Waterford)		0-0		2-0		1-0	1-0	0-2	0-1		■	
	2-1	1-1	4-0	2-0	2-1	1-0	2-0	6-0	0-1	0-1	■	1-2
Wexford Youths FC (Dublin)		1-0		2-0	1-1	0-0			0-0			■
	1-0	0-1	2-1	0-3	0-2	2-1	1-0	0-2	1-2	0-1	0-1	■

	Division 1	Pd	Wn	Dw	Ls	GF	GA	Pts	
1.	University College Dublin AFC (Dublin)	33	23	5	5	63	21	74	P
2.	Shelbourne FC (Dublin)	33	22	7	4	66	31	73	PO
3.	Sporting Fingal FC (Dublin)	33	21	6	6	68	28	69	PO/P
4.	Waterford United FC (Waterford)	33	20	6	7	51	21	66	
5.	Monaghan United FC (Monaghan)	33	16	7	10	58	48	55	
6.	Wexford Youths FC (Wexford)	33	15	5	13	27	31	50	
7.	Limerick FC (Limerick)	33	11	9	13	48	43	42	**
8.	Finn Harps FC (Ballybofey)	33	8	9	16	35	51	33	
9.	Longford Town FC (Longford)	33	8	5	20	46	61	29	
10.	Athlone Town AFC (Athlone)	33	6	9	18	32	63	27	
11.	Mervue United AFC (Galway)	33	6	5	22	28	64	23	
12.	Kildare County FC (Newbridge)	33	4	3	26	25	85	15	PO
		396	160	76	160	547	547	556	

Promotion/Relegation Play-off

Kildare County FC (Newbridge)   walkover   Salthill Devon FC (Salthill)
(Kildare County FC withdrew so Salthill Devon FC were duly promoted)

Cobh Ramblers FC (Cobh), relegated from the Premier Division in 2007-08, did not play in Division 1 during this season. Therefore Kildare County FC, relegated from Division 1 in 2008, retained their Division 1 status.

Promoted: Cork City FORAS (Cork) **, Salthill Devon FC (Salthill)

** Cork City FORAS (Friends of the Rebel Army Society) were formed to replace the dissolved club Cork City FC and were awarded a place in Division 1 for the next season.

FAI Cup Final (Tallaght Stadium, Dublin – 22/11/2009)

SPORTING FINGAL FC (DUBLIN)   2-1   Sligo Rovers FC (Sligo)
James 84' pen., O'Neill 90'   *Doyle 57'*
Sporting Fingal: Quigley, James, Maher, Paisley, Fitzgerald, Williams, Bayly, McFaul, C.Byrne, O'Neill, Zayed.
Sligo Rovers: C.Kelly, Boco, Peers, Keane, Kendrick, Ventre, Cash (Morrison 55'), Ryan, Doyle, Blinkhorn, Cretaro (Meenan 70').

Semi-finals

Sporting Fingal FC (Dublin)	4-2	Bray Wanderers AFC (Bray)
Sligo Rovers FC (Sligo)	1-0	Waterford United FC (Waterford)

Quarter-finals

Bohemian FC (Dublin)	0-0, 1-2	Sligo Rovers FC (Sligo)
Sporting Fingal FC (Dublin)	2-2, 2-1 (aet)	Shamrock Rovers FC (Dublin)
Longford Town FC (Longford)	0-0, 1-2	Bray Wanderers FC (Bray)
Waterford United FC (Waterford)	1-1, 2-0	St. Patrick's Athletic FC (Dublin)

2010

League of Ireland Premier Division 2010	Bohemian	Bray Wanderers	Drogheda	Dundalk	Fingal	Galway United	St. Patrick's Ath.	Shamrock Rovers	Sligo Rovers	U.C. Dublin
Bohemian FC (Dublin)		0-0	2-0	3-1	1-1	0-2	1-1	1-0	2-0	3-1
		2-0	1-0	3-0	1-0	2-3	1-1	0-0	0-0	0--0
Bray Wanderers AFC (Bray)	0-3		1-1	2-0	0-3	4-0	3-2	2-2	1-3	2-2
	0-2		2-2	0-1	1-3	0-2	0-4	0-0	2-3	0-6
Drogheda United FC (Drogheda)	0-1	0-2		1-3	0-4	3-3	0-3	0-2	2-3	1-0
	2-4	0-0		1-3	1-1	0-1	2-1	0-2	2-2	0-3
Dundalk FC (Dundalk)	1-2	0-2	2-1		0-2	3-0	0-3	5-1	2-4	1-1
	1-0	2-3	2-2		1-2	0-0	0-0	2-1	1-0	3-0
Sporting Fingal FC (Dublin)	0-0	2-2	1-2	1-0		3-1	2-3	3-3	1-1	4-1
	0-2	1-0	4-1	2-1		2-0	2-2	1-1	1-1	1-2
Galway United FC (Galway)	3-2	2-2	2-1	1-1	0-1		1-1	0-1	2-2	1-4
	2-2	2-1	3-1	0-1	2-2		0-2	0-1	0-0	2-2
St. Patrick's Athletic FC (Dublin)	0-1	2-0	2-0	1-2	1-1	4-2		1-3	0-0	2-1
	3-1	3-0	0-1	1-0	0-0	2-0		1-2	1-0	3-0
Shamrock Rovers FC (Dublin)	3-0	4-1	2-0	4-0	1-2	3-0	2-1		1-0	4-1
	1-0	1-0	1-1	0-2	1-1	2-0	0-2		1-1	0-0
Sligo Rovers FC (Sligo)	1-1	2-1	2-1	1-0	4-3	3-0	1-0	1-2		4-0
	1-2	5-1	6-0	2-2	0-1	1-0	0-0	1-1		2-1
University College Dublin AFC (Dublin)	0-2	4-0	1-1	0-2	1-2	0-1	3-2	3-2	1-2	
	1-2	1-0	2-0	3-1	0-0	0-0	1-0	1-2	0-2	

	Premier Division	**Pd**	**Wn**	**Dw**	**Ls**	**GF**	**GA**	**Pts**	
1.	SHAMROCK ROVERS FC (DUBLIN)	36	19	10	7	57	34	67	
2.	Bohemian FC (Dublin)	36	19	10	7	50	29	67	
3.	Sligo Rovers FC (Sligo)	36	17	12	7	61	36	63	
4.	Sporting Fingal FC (Dublin)	36	16	14	6	60	38	62	
5.	St. Patrick's Athletic FC (Dublin)	36	16	9	11	55	33	57	
6.	Dundalk FC (Dundalk)	36	14	6	16	46	50	48	
7.	University College Dublin AFC (Dublin)	36	11	8	17	47	54	41	
8.	Galway United FC (Galway)	36	9	11	16	38	59	38	PO
9.	Bray Wanderers AFC (Bray)	36	6	9	21	35	72	27	PO
10.	Drogheda United FC (Drogheda)	36	4	9	23	30	74	21	##
		360	131	98	131	479	479	491	

Drogheda United FC were initially relegated after finishing bottom of the Premier Division. However, they were spared from relegation when Sporting Fingal FC withdrew their licence application for the 2011 season on 10th February 2011 before folding a day later.

Top goal-scorers 2010

1) Gary TWIGG   (Shamrock Rovers FC)   20
2) Padraig AMOND   (Sligo Rovers FC)   17
3) Ciaran KILDUFF   (University College Dublin AFC) 15
4) Jake KELLY   (Bray Wanderers AFC)   14
5) Jason BYRNE   (Bohemian FC)   12
   Fahrudin KUDOZOVIC   (Dundalk FC)   12

Relegation Play-Off

Galway United FC (Galway)   1-0   Bray Wanderers AFC (Bray)

Promotion/Relegation Play-off

Monaghan United FC (Monaghan)   0-0, 1-1 (aet)   Bray Wanderers AFC (Bray)
(Bray Wanderers AFC won 7-6 on penalties)

Promotion Play-Off

Waterford United FC (Waterford)   1-3   Monaghan United FC (Monaghan)

League of Ireland Division 1 2010	Athlone Town	Cork City	Derry City	Finn Harps	Limerick	Longford Town	Mervue United	Monaghan United	Salthill Devon	Shelbourne	Waterford United	Wexford Youth
Athlone Town AFC (Athlone)		0-1			1-5	0-0	1-0			0-2		
		1-1	1-3	0-1	1-3	2-0	1-0	4-4	2-2	0-0	1-1	1-0
Cork City FORAS (Cork)					1-0	2-1	1-0	1-2		0-1		
	0-1		1-1	2-1	1-2	1-0	4-2	0-1	1-0	0-1	0-2	1-0
Derry City FC (Derry)	2-2	0-1		2-2			6-0			3-0		
	1-0	1-1		2-0	0-0	0-0	4-1	2-3	1-0	1-0	2-0	3-1
Finn Harps FC (Ballybofey)	2-2	1-0			1-1		4-0		3-2			1-1
	0-0	0-0	1-1		0-3	2-0	2-3	0-0	2-0	1-1	1-1	2-1
Limerick FC (Limerick)		1-3	0-1			3-1				0-1		1-0
	3-2	1-3	0-1	2-1		2-0	2-0	1-1	5-0	1-0	0-0	2-0
Longford Town FC (Longford)			1-1	1-0			2-2			1-2	0-2	1-2
	2-1	1-1	1-3	3-2	1-0		2-1	0-3	2-2	3-5	2-1	0-1
Mervue United AFC (Galway)					0-1			2-1	2-1		1-6	2-5
	1-0	2-4	1-2	1-3	1-1	4-3		1-1	2-2	0-1	2-3	0-1
Monaghan United FC (Monaghan)	2-0		0-1	2-0	0-0	2-0					4-2	
	0-0	1-0	0-1	0-1	2-1	2-2	4-0		3-0	0-2	1-0	4-2
Salthill Devon FC (Salthill)	1-1		1-5		1-3	1-4		1-3			1-1	
	0-1	1-3	0-7	0-1	2-3	0-3	2-0	1-6		0-2	0-1	0-0
Shelbourne FC (Dublin)		2-0		3-1			3-0	2-1	5-0		1-2	
	6-2	1-1	1-2	1-0	0-4	1-1	4-0	1-1	3-0		0-1	1-2
Waterford United FC (Waterford)	3-2		2-0	3-1	3-0							1-0
	0-0	1-1	1-0	2-0	2-1	2-0	3-0	1-2	8-0	0-3		3-0
Wexford Youth FC (Dublin)	1-3	2-1	1-1				1-4	2-1	1-1	0-3		
	2-1	0-2	1-5	3-0	5-3	1-2	3-2	0-1	0-3	1-1	1-0	

	Division 1	Pd	Wn	Dw	Ls	GF	GA	Pts	
1.	Derry City FC (Derry)	33	20	9	4	65	24	69	P
2.	Waterford United FC (Waterford)	33	20	6	7	59	27	66	PO
3.	Monaghan United FC (Monaghan)	33	18	8	7	59	29	62	PO
4.	Shelbourne FC (Dublin)	33	18	7	8	57	31	61	
5.	Limerick FC (Limerick)	33	17	6	10	55	35	57	
6.	Cork City FORAS (Cork)	33	15	7	11	39	31	52	
7.	Wexford Youth FC (Dublin)	33	12	6	15	42	54	42	
8.	Finn Harps FC (Ballybofey)	33	10	10	13	37	43	40	
9.	Longford Town FC (Longford)	33	9	8	16	39	53	35	
10.	Athlone Town AFC (Athlone)	33	6	13	14	35	50	31	
11.	Mervue United AFC (Galway)	33	5	4	24	34	84	19	
12.	Salthill Devon FC (Salthill)	33	3	6	24	26	86	15	PO
		396	153	90	153	547	547	549	

Promotion/Relegation Play-off

Cobh Ramblers FC (Cobh)   0-1, 1-2   Salthill Devon FC (Salthill)

FAI Cup Final   (Aviva Stadium, Dublin – 14/11/2010 – 36,101)

SLIGO ROVERS FC (SLIGO)   0-0 (aet)   Shamrock Rovers FC (Dublin)
(2-0 penalties)

Sligo Rovers: Kelly, Keane, Peers, Lauchlan, Davoran, Boco, Ndo, Ventre (O'Grady 118'), McCabe, Russell, Doyle.
Shamrock Rovers: Mannus, Rice, Sives, Flynn, Stevens, Dennehy, Bradley, Turner, Chambers (Baker 69', Price 113'), Stewart (Kavanagh 102'), Twigg.

Semi-finals

Bohemian FC (Dublin)	0-1	Sligo Rovers FC (Sligo)
Shamrock Rovers FC (Dublin)	2-2, 1-0	St. Patrick's Athletic FC (Dublin)

Quarter-finals

Bohemian FC (Dublin)	3-0	Bray Wanderers AFC (Bray)
St. Patrick's Athletic FC (Dublin)	3-1	Sporting Fingal FC (Dublin)
Shamrock Rovers FC (Dublin)	6-0	Galway United FC (Galway)
Sligo Rovers FC (Sligo)	3-0	Monaghan United FC (Monaghan)

2011

League of Ireland Premier Division 2011	Bohemian	Bray Wanderers	Derry City	Drogheda United	Dundalk	Galway United	Shamrock Rovers	Sligo Rovers	St. Patrick's Ath.	U.C. Dublin
Bohemian FC (Dublin)		1–1	0–2	1–0	0–1	0–1	1–1	0–0	0–1	1–0
		2–1	0–1	2–0	3–1	2–0	0–1	0–3	0–0	2–0
Bray Wanderers AFC (Bray)	1–3		1–2	2–1	1–5	2–0	1–0	0–0	0–1	2–1
	1–2		1–2	1–2	1–0	4–0	1–2	0–3	0–3	4–0
Derry City FC (Derry)	3–0	1–1		2–0	2–0	6–0	0–0	0–1	1–1	7–0
	0–0	1–1		2–2	0–0	4–0	1–0	0–0	2–0	2–1
Drogheda United FC (Drogheda)	0–1	0–1	2–2		1–2	1–1	0–4	0–3	1–4	0–1
	0–2	1–4	0–3		2–2	1–0	0–1	0–3	4–3	3–1
Dundalk FC (Dundalk)	0–0	0–0	1–0	1–2		3–2	1–1	1–1	1–2	3–1
	1–3	2–2	0–2	1–0		6–1	1–2	1–1	0–2	2–0
Galway United FC (Galway)	0–2	0–3	1–4	1–2	0–3		0–1	0–3	0–0	
	0–3	0–6	0–3	1–2	2–2		2–3	0–8	0–2	3–4
St. Patrick's Athletic FC (Dublin)	1–0	0–1	1–1	3–0	3–1	4–0		1–0	2–0	3–1
	1–1	5–2	1–0	4–0	2–2	4–0		1–2	1–0	6–0
Shamrock Rovers FC (Dublin)	1–2	3–1	3–0	2–0	1–0	3–0	0–1		2–0	4–0
	1–2	3–0	1–1	2–0	5–0	7–1	2–0		0–0	4–2
Sligo Rovers FC (Sligo)	0–0	2–3	1–1	3–0	3–2	5–2	0–0	2–1		1–1
	1–1	1–0	1–1	4–0	2–2	6–1	1–1	1–0		2–2
University College Dublin AFC (Dublin)	0–2	0–1	0–2	2–1	0–2	3–0	1–6	2–1	1–3	
	2–0	1–2	2–2	5–4	3–0	2–1	1–2	0–1	2–1	

	Premier Division	Pd	Wn	Dw	Ls	GF	GA	Pts	
1.	SHAMROCK ROVERS FC (DUBLIN)	36	23	8	5	69	24	77	
2.	Sligo Rovers FC (Sligo)	36	22	7	7	73	19	73	
3.	Derry City FC (Derry)	36	18	14	4	63	23	68	
4.	St. Patrick's Athletic FC (Dublin)	36	17	12	7	62	35	63	
5.	Bohemian FC (Dublin)	36	17	9	10	39	27	60	
6.	Bray Wanderers FC (Bray)	36	15	6	15	53	50	51	
7.	Dundalk FC (Dundalk)	36	11	11	14	50	53	44	
8.	University College Dublin AFC (Dublin)	36	10	4	22	42	80	34	
9.	Drogheda United FC (Drogheda)	36	7	4	25	32	77	25	
10.	Galway United FC (Galway)	36	1	3	32	20	115	6	POR
		360	141	78	141	503	503	501	

Top goalscorers

1) Eamon ZAYED (Derry City FC) 22
2) Eoin DOYLE (Sligo Rovers FC) 20
3) Danny NORTH (St. Patrick's Athletic FC) 15
   Gary TWIGG (Shamrock Rovers FC) 15
5) Mark QUIGLEY (Dundalk FC) 13

Promotion/Relegation Play-off (1/11/2011 + 4/11/2011)

Monaghan United FC (Monaghan)   2-0, 3-1   Galway United FC (Galway)

League of Ireland Division 1 2011

	Athlone Town	Cork City	Finn Harps Ath.	Limerick	Longford Town	Mervue United	Monaghan United	Salthill Devon	Shelbourne	Waterford United	Wexford Youths
Athlone Town FC (Athlone)	■	0-0	1-0	0-1	1-1	1-0	0-3	2-0	0-4	0-3	2-0
	■	0-7	0-1			4-1	0-5		0-2		
Cork City FORAS (Cork)	2-0	■	5-0	1-0	1-1	3-0	2-2	1-0	4-1	2-3	1-0
		■	5-2	3-3	3-1		3-1				2-2
Finn Harps FC (Ballybofey)	1-0	0-2	■	2-2	1-2	2-0	2-2	0-0	0-3	1-0	0-1
			■		1-2	1-2		0-3	2-0		4-1
Limerick FC (Limerick)	3-0	0-0	1-0	■	1-0	2-0	0-2	3-0	0-3	1-0	0-1
	3-1			■	1-0			1-1		3-0	6-0
Longford Town FC (Longford)	2-0	1-3	3-2	1-2	■	2-1	1-3	2-0	1-2	1-0	2-1
	0-2				■	2-2		1-1	1-3	2-1	
Mervue United AFC (Galway)	1-2	1-1	2-1	0-2	2-1	■	3-1	0-0	1-2	1-1	3-0
		1-2	1-0	0-1		■		0-1		0-2	
Monaghan United FC (Monaghan)	1-0	1-1	1-0	1-1	1-0	1-2	■	3-0	0-1	2-0	2-1
				0-1	3-2		■	3-0		3-1	2-0
Salthill Devon FC (Salthill)	1-1	1-5	0-4	0-1	0-1	1-2	2-5	■	0-1	0-2	2-1
	1-3	0-4				0-5		■		1-4	1-3
Shelbourne FC (Dublin)	2-0	1-1	1-0	1-1	1-0	4-0	2-3	4-1	■	2-1	4-2
		1-2	4-0	1-2			1-2		■		3-0
Waterford United FC (Waterford)	0-0	1-2	1-0	1-2	1-0	1-0	0-1	4-0	0-1	■	0-1
	5-1	1-3	0-0		2-0			1-0		■	
Wexford Youth FC (Dublin)	0-1	1-2	0-2	2-3	0-2	3-5	1-2	1-3	0-1	1-2	■
	3-3			1-3	0-3		5-2		0-2		■

	Division 1	**Pd**	**Wn**	**Dw**	**Ls**	**GF**	**GA**	**Pts**	
1.	Cork City FORAS (Cork)	30	20	9	1	73	26	69	P
2.	Shelbourne FC (Dublin)	30	22	2	6	62	24	68	P
3.	Monaghan United FC (Monaghan)	30	21	4	5	60	27	67	POP
4.	Limerick FC (Limerick)	30	20	6	4	49	22	66	
5.	Waterford United FC (Waterford)	30	13	3	14	37	31	42	
6.	Longford Town FC (Longford)	30	12	4	14	38	41	40	
7.	Mervue United AFC (Galway)	30	10	4	16	37	45	34	
8.	Athlone Town FC (Athlone)	30	9	5	16	25	53	32	
9.	Finn Harps FC (Ballybofey)	30	8	4	18	29	45	28	
10.	Wexford Youths FC (Dublin)	30	4	2	24	29	69	14	
11.	Salthill Devon FC (Salthill)	30	2	5	23	18	74	11	
		330	141	48	141	457	457	471	

The Premier League was extended to 12 clubs from the next season. Cork City FORAS (Cork) and Shelbourne FC (Dublin) were therefore automatically promoted and Monaghan United FC (Monaghan) entered the Promotion/Relegation Play-off where they beat Galway United FC (Galway) to win promotion.

In December 2011, it was announced that Galway United FC would not be applying for a licence for the 2012 season following the announcement that the Galway United Supporters' Trust, who had kept the club afloat during the 2011 season in the absence of the directors, would be applying for league membership as Galway United Supporters Trust FC.

The directors of Galway United claimed that they hoped to return to the League of Ireland for the start of the 2013 season and the GUST were subsequently refused the opportunity to have their application to the League of Ireland assessed by the FAI. The FAI instead insisted upon merger negotiations between GUST and one of Mervue United AFC and Salthill Devon FC. GUST members voted unanimously against the proposals of both clubs, preferring to remain as an independent entity.

Following the refusal of the FAI to accept GUST's late application for a license and there being no club genuinely representative club for Galway city and county competing in the league for 2012, Salthill Devon FC re-branded their League team to "SD Galway FC", changing their colours, adopting the maroon and white worn by Galway United and switching their matches from their home at Drom to Eamonn Deacy Park, the home of Galway United FC.

FAI Cup Final   (Aviva Stadium, Dublin – 06/11/2011 – 21,662)

Shelbourne FC (Dublin)	1-1 (aet)	SLIGO ROVERS FC (SLIGO)
Hughes 33'	*(1-4 penalties)*	*Davoren 48'*

Shelbourne: Delany, Boyle, S. Byrne, Paisley, I. Ryan, Cassidy (James 117'), Clancy, Dawson, McGill (Bermingham 120'), Sullivan (C. Byrne 59'), Hughes.

Sligo Rovers: Clarke (Kelly 120'), Davoren, Keane, McGuinness, Peers, Dillon (Blinkhorn 60'), Russell (Cretaro 78'), R. Ryan, Ventre, Doyle, Greene.

Semi-finals

Shelbourne FC (Dublin)	1-1, 3-1	St Patrick's Athletic FC (Dublin)
Bohemian FC (Dublin)	0-1	Sligo Rovers FC (Sligo)

Quarter-finals

Cork City FORAS (Cork)	0-1	St. Patrick's Athletic FC (Dublin)
Dundalk FC (Dundalk)	0-0, 0-1 (aet)	Bohemian FC (Dublin)
Sligo Rovers FC (Sligo)	1-0	Shamrock Rovers FC (Dublin)
Shelbourne FC (Dublin)	4-3	Limerick FC (Limerick)

2012

League of Ireland Premier Division 2012	Bohemian	Bray Wanderers	Cork City	Derry City	Drogheda United	Dundalk	Monaghan United	Shamrock Rovers	Shelbourne	Sligo Rovers	St. Patrick's Ath.	U.C. Dublin
Bohemian FC (Dublin)	■	0–0	1–0	1–2	1–1	2–1		4–0	0–2	0–0	0–0	1–0
		1–1		1–4					2–2		2–3	
Bray Wanderers FC (Bray)	2–1	■	0–3	0–4	2–4	1–1		2–2	2–3	1–2	3–3	3–1
	1–4			0–0	1–3			1–3		0–0		
Cork City FORAS (Cork)	1–1	1–1	■		2–2	2–3	3–2		1–1	0–0	0–1	0–1	4–2
		2–0			3–2	3–0		1–2		0–0		
Derry City FC (Derry)	1–0	3–2	2–0	■	0–3	1–2		0–1	0–1	1–2	0–2	0–0
	2–0		0–1			4–0				2–1	1–2	
Drogheda United FC (Drogheda)	1–0	3–1	1–1	2–0	■	0–0		1–2	3–1	1–3	0–0	1–0
			2–1			3–2		0–2	2–1	2–1	0–0	
Dundalk FC (Dundalk)	0–2	0–2	1–1	1–1	1–2	■		1–1	0–0	1–2	0–2	2–1
	2–2	2–1							0–1		0–1	1–2
Monaghan United FC (Monaghan)							■					
Shamrock Rovers FC (Dublin)	2–0	0–0	1–1	1–1	3–1	6–0		■	4–0	1–1	1–1	2–2
	0–1		1–3		7–0				2–2			2–1
Shelbourne FC (Dublin)	1–2	2–1	1–2	1–0	1–2	4–0		2–3	■	1–1	1–1	1–2
		0–0	3–2	0–2						1–3	0–2	
Sligo Rovers FC (Sligo)	1–0	1–1	2–2	1–1	4–1	3–0		3–0	3–0	■	1–1	2–1
	3–1			4–1		3–0		0–2			3–2	3–0
St Patrick's Athletic FC (Dublin)	2–1	1–0	0–0	3–0	0–2	1–2		5–1	1–0	0–0	■	2–0
		0–1	1–0					2–1				5–0
University College Dublin AFC (Dublin)	1–2	2–3	1–0	0–1	1–1	1–1		0–2	0–2	1–0	1–1	■
	2–2	3–1	3–2		1–0			1–1				

	Premier Division	**Pd**	**Wn**	**Dw**	**Ls**	**GF**	**GA**	**Pts**	
1.	SLIGO ROVERS FC (SLIGO)	30	17	10	3	53	23	61	
2.	Drogheda United FC (Drogheda)	30	17	6	7	51	36	57	
3.	St. Patrick's Athletic FC (Dublin)	30	15	10	5	44	22	55	
4.	Shamrock Rovers FC (Dublin)	30	14	10	6	56	37	52	
5.	Derry City FC (Derry)	30	11	6	13	36	36	39	
6.	Cork City FORAS (Cork)	30	8	12	10	38	36	36	
7.	Bohemian FC (Dublin)	30	9	9	12	35	38	36	
8.	Shelbourne FC (Dublin)	30	9	8	13	35	43	35	
9.	University College Dublin AFC (Dublin)	30	8	7	15	32	48	31	
10.	Bray Wanderers FC (Bray)	30	5	10	15	33	54	25	
11.	Dundalk FC (Dundalk)	30	4	8	18	23	63	20	
12.	Monaghan United FC (Monaghan)	0	0	0	0	0	0	0	##
		330	117	96	117	436	436	447	

Monaghan United FC (Monaghan) announced their withdrawal from the League of Ireland on 18th June 2012 after 14 games had been played. Their record was subsequently expunged.

Top goalscorers

1) Gary TWIGG   (Shamrock Rovers FC)   22
2) Danny NORTH   (Sligo Rovers FC)   15
3) Jason BYRNE   (Bray Wanderers FC)   14
4) Declan O'BRIEN   (Drogheda United FC)   12
5) Chris FAGAN   (St. Patrick's Athletic FC) 12
   Philip HUGHES   (Shelbourne FC)   10
   Vincent SULLIVAN   (Cork City FC)   12

League of Ireland Division 1 2012	Athlone Town	Finn Harps	Limerick	Longford Town	Mervue United	SD Galway FC	Waterford United	Wexford Youths
Athlone Town FC (Athlone)	■	2–0	0–1	1–2	2–1	2–1	1–4	0–1
	■	1–1	0–1	1–1	0–3	2–0	2–3	0–3
Finn Harps FC (Ballybofey)	1–2	■	1–3	1–3	4–3	3–0	0–1	0–1
	2–0	■	1–1	1–0	3–2	2–0	1–2	3–3
Limerick FC (Limerick)	2–1	2–1	■	1–2	2–0	3–0	0–1	4–0
	1–0	3–0	■	0–0	4–0	1–0	0–1	1–3
Longford Town FC (Longford)	2–1	1–3	0–2	■	4–2	1–0	3–2	1–0
	0–0	0–1	0–2	■	2–0	1–2	0–1	2–0
Mervue United AFC (Galway)	0–1	3–0	1–2	0–1	■	1–2	0–0	3–0
	2–0	1–1	0–3	4–5	■	0–0	0–2	0–0
SD Galway FC (Galway)	0–1	1–5	2–5	1–1	2–2	■	0–2	1–1
	3–0	2–0	0–1	1–3	2–1	■	0–1	2–2
Waterford United FC (Waterford)	1–1	0–2	3–1	0–2	3–1	1–0	■	4–0
	0–0	1–1	2–1	4–2	1–2	3–0	■	1–2
Wexford Youths FC (Dublin)	1–2	3–0	0–1	1–2	2–0	2–0	6–0	■
	4–2	2–2	1–3	1–1	1–2	4–1	1–2	■

	Division 1	Pd	Wn	Dw	Ls	GF	GA	Pts	
1.	Limerick FC (Limerick)	28	20	2	6	51	20	62	P
2.	Waterford United FC (Waterford)	28	18	4	6	46	29	58	
3.	Longford Town FC (Longford)	28	15	5	8	42	33	50	
4.	Wexford Youths FC (Dublin)	28	11	6	11	45	40	39	
5.	Finn Harps FC (Ballybofey)	28	10	6	12	40	43	36	
6.	Athlone Town FC (Athlone)	28	8	5	15	25	41	29	
7.	Mervue United AFC (Galway)	28	6	5	17	34	49	23	
8.	SD Galway FC (Galway)	28	5	5	18	23	51	20	
		224	93	38	93	306	306	317	

FAI Cup Final (Aviva Stadium, Dublin – 04/11/2012 – 16,117)

DERRY CITY FC (DERRY) 3-2 (aet) St. Patrick's Athletic FC (Dublin)

Greacen 55', Patterson 69' pen, 105' *O'Connor 53', Fagan 87'*

Derry City: Doherty, McEleney, McCaffrey, Madden, Greacen (McBride 98'), Molloy, McNamee (Higgins 81'), McLaughlin, McEleney (Patterson 59'), Deery, McDaid.

St Patrick's Athletic: Clarke, Browne, Bermingham, Kenna, O'Brien (Flynn 105'), Forrester, Chambers, Carroll (Russell 24'), Kelly (Faherty 45'), O'Connor, Fagan.

Semi-finals

Derry City FC (Derry)	1-1, 3-0	Shelbourne FC (Dublin)
Dundalk FC (Dundalk)	0-3	St. Patrick's Athletic FC (Dublin)

Quarter-finals

Shelbourne FC (Dublin)	2-1	Shamrock Rovers FC (Dublin)
Bohemian FC (Dublin)	0-1	Dundalk FC (Dundalk)
St. Patrick's Athletic FC (Dublin)	0-0, 1-1 (aet)	Drogheda United FC (Drogheda)
	Drogheda United won 3-2 on penalties	
Derry City FC (Derry)	7-1	Mervue United AFC (Galway)

2013

League of Ireland Premier Division 2013	Bohemian	Bray Wanderers	Cork City	Derry City	Drogheda United	Dundalk	Limerick	Shamrock Rovers	Shelbourne	Sligo Rovers	St. Patrick's Athletic	U.C. Dublin
Bohemian FC (Dublin)		3-2	1-2	0-4	1-1	0-2	0-1	0-0	0-3	0-3	0-2	2-1
		0-1		2-0		1-1		1-0		0-2		1-3
Bray Wanderers FC (Bray)	1-3		1-2	2-3	3-2	0-1	0-4	0-0	1-0	0-0	0-1	2-2
			1-2			0-2	1-0		1-1		1-3	1-1
Cork City FC (Cork)	2-1	1-3		0-1	1-0	2-2	2-3	1-2	1-1	3-1	0-2	2-1
	1-0			4-1					5-3		4-2	2-0
Derry City FC (Derry)	2-1	2-0	1-1		1-1	0-1	2-1	2-1	4-0	0-1	0-1	2-4
		2-0			0-2		6-0	0-0	3-1	1-2		
Drogheda United FC (Drogheda)	2-2	2-1	1-1	2-3		0-1	2-2	0-3	0-0	1-1	1-2	3-2
	1-0	2-0	2-3				3-0					1-0
Dundalk FC (Dundalk)	3-0	1-0	2-0	1-3	2-2		2-2	0-0	1-0	1-3	2-1	2-3
			4-0	3-0	1-0		1-2	3-1		2-0		
Limerick FC (Limerick)	2-1	4-4	0-0	0-1	0-1	3-2		1-1	0-0	0-0	0-1	3-1
	1-0		2-1					2-0	1-0		0-0	1-3
Shamrock Rovers FC (Dublin)	1-1	7-0	1-1	2-1	1-1	1-0	1-0		1-0	1-1	3-0	1-1
		3-0	2-1		3-1					1-2	0-4	
Shelbourne FC (Dublin)	0-1	1-2	2-1	0-1	1-3	1-3	2-1	0-0		0-2	0-3	2-0
	0-3				2-2	1-2		1-2				1-2
Sligo Rovers FC (Sligo)	0-0	3-0	2-0	3-0	2-2	0-1	2-1	0-0	2-0		1-1	5-2
		2-0	0-0		3-1		2-0		2-0			
St. Patrick's Athletic FC (Dublin)	1-1	2-0	2-1	1-1	1-0	1-2	3-0	0-0	4-0	2-0		5-0
	1-1			1-1	0-0	2-0			1-0	2-0		
University College Dublin AFC (Dublin)	1-0	4-5	3-0	0-6	2-2	1-2	1-1	2-0	1-2	0-3	0-1	
				1-3		0-2	1-4		0-3	1-3		

	Premier Division	Pd	Wn	Dw	Ls	GF	GA	Pts	
1)	ST. PATRICK'S ATHLETIC FC (DUBLIN)	33	21	8	4	56	20	71	
2)	Dundalk FC (Dundalk)	33	21	5	7	55	30	68	
3)	Sligo Rovers FC (Sligo)	33	19	9	5	53	22	66	
4)	Derry City FC (Derry)	33	17	5	11	57	39	56	
5)	Shamrock Rovers FC (Dublin)	33	13	13	7	43	28	52	
6)	Cork City FC (Cork)	33	13	7	13	47	50	46	
7)	Limerick FC (Limerick)	33	11	9	13	38	46	42	
8)	Drogheda United FC (Drogheda)	33	8	14	11	44	46	38	
9)	University College Dublin AFC (Dublin)	33	8	6	19	45	73	30	
10)	Bohemian FC (Dublin)	33	7	8	18	27	47	29	
11)	Bray Wanderers FC (Bray)	33	7	6	20	33	66	27	PO
12)	Shelbourne FC (Dublin)	33	5	6	22	25	56	21	R
		396	150	96	150	523	523	546	

Top goalscorers

1) Rory PATTERSON   (Derry City FC)   18
2) Declan O'BRIEN   (Drogheda United FC)   14
3) Ciarán KILDUFF   (Cork City FC)   13
   Patrick HOBAN   (Dundalk FC)   13
   David McMILLAN   (Sligo Rovers FC)   13

Promotion/Relegation Play-offs

Mervue United AFC (Galway)   1-0, 2-3 (aet)   Longford Town FC (Longford)
Aggregate 3-3. Longford Town FC won 3-0 on penalties.

Bray Wanderers FC (Bray)   2-2, 3-2   Longford Town FC (Longford)

League of Ireland Division 1 2013	Athlone Town	Cobh Ramblers	Finn Harps	Longford Town	Mervue United	Salthill Devon	Waterford United	Wexford Youths
Athlone Town FC (Athlone)		1-1	1-0	2-0	0-0	3-3	0-1	4-0
		0-0	1-0	1-2	3-0	1-0	1-0	1-0
Cobh Ramblers FC (Cobh)	1-1		2-2	3-4	5-3	1-2	3-0	5-0
	0-1		3-2	4-3	3-2	1-0	2-1	3-0
Finn Harps FC (Ballybofey)	2-3	4-1		1-0	1-0	1-0	0-1	0-0
	3-2	2-2		0-0	0-2	2-0	0-2	1-0
Longford Town FC (Longford)	2-1	5-1	2-3		1-1	2-1	2-1	3-1
	0-1	7-2	3-1		1-3	4-0	2-1	2-1
Mervue United AFC (Galway)	2-2	1-0	2-2	1-2		2-1	2-1	4-1
	2-4	2-0	4-0	1-0		2-1	1-0	0-0
Salthill Devon FC (Galway)	1-2	1-1	2-1	0-5	0-0		1-2	1-2
	0-1	1-0	0-0	1-1	0-1		1-4	3-2
Waterford United FC (Waterford)	1-0	0-0	1-1	1-1	0-4	3-2		0-1
	1-1	1-0	3-0	1-0	0-0	5-0		4-0
Wexford Youths FC (Dublin)	0-2	3-0	2-1	0-1	2-0	3-0	2-1	
	0-2	3-1	3-1	0-0	1-4	2-1	0-2	

Division 1	Pd	Wn	Dw	Ls	GF	GA	Pts	
1) Athlone Town FC (Athlone)	28	16	7	5	42	22	55	P
2) Longford Town FC (Longford)	28	15	5	8	55	34	50	PO
3) Mervue United AFC (Galway)	28	14	7	7	46	31	49	
4) Waterford United FC (Waterford)	28	14	5	9	40	24	47	
5) Wexford Youths FC (Dublin)	28	10	3	15	29	47	33	
6) Finn Harps FC (Ballybofey)	28	8	7	13	31	42	31	
7) Cobh Ramblers FC (Cobh)	28	8	7	13	42	54	31	
8) Salthill Devon FC (Galway)	28	4	5	19	23	54	17	
	224	89	46	89	308	308	313	

Mervue United AFC and Salthill Devon FC withdrew from the league to make way for Galway FC after the FAI decided that Galway City and County Galway should be represented in the League of Ireland by a single club. Cobh Ramblers FC replaced Monaghan United FC as members of the League of Ireland.

FAI Cup Final   (Aviva Stadium, Dublin – 03/11/2013 – 17,573)

Drogheda United FC (Drogheda) 2-3 SLIGO ROVERS FC (SLIGO)
O'Conor 13', R. Brennan 90+2' *North 78', 85', Elding 90+4'*

Drogheda United: Schlingermann, Daly, Prendergast, McNally, Grimes, Byrne (Hynes 90'), Cassidy, O'Conor (Rusk 77'), R. Brennan, G. Brennan, O'Brien.

Sligo Rovers: Rogers, Keane, Peers, Henderson (McMillan 65'), Davoren, Ndo, Ventre, Cretaro (North 70'), Djilali, Greene (Gaynor 84'), Elding.

Semi-finals

Drogheda United FC (Drogheda)	1-0	Dundalk FC (Dundalk)
Sligo Rovers FC (Sligo)	3-0	Shamrock Rovers FC (Dublin)

Quarter-finals

St. Patrick's Athletic FC (Dublin)	0-2	Shamrock Rovers FC (Dublin)
Shelbourne FC (Dublin)	1-5	Dundalk FC (Dundalk)
Finn Harps FC (Ballybofey)	1-1, 0-2	Drogheda United FC (Drogheda)
Sligo Rovers FC (Sligo)	1-0	Derry City FC (Derry)

2014

League of Ireland Premier Division 2014

Team	Athlone Town	Bohemian	Bray Wanderers	Cork City	Derry City	Drogheda United	Dundalk	Limerick	Shamrock Rovers	Sligo Rovers	St. Patrick's Athletic	University College Dublin
Athlone Town FC (Athlone)	—	1-3 / 0-0	0-0 / 1-1	0-3 / 0-2	0-1	6-0 / 0-3	0-1	3-0 / 1-1	1-4	0-2	0-2	2-0
Bohemian FC (Dublin)	2-2	—	1-1 / 2-1	0-2 / 2-1	1-1 / 2-1	2-2	0-2 / 2-0	0-1 / 1-1	1-3 / 2-2	0-2	1-1	0-0
Bray Wanderers FC (Bray)	1-1	0-5	—	0-2	0-0 / 1-1	1-3 / 1-1	1-0	1-0	0-3 / 0-1	1-0 / 2-4	1-3	3-5 / 2-0
Cork City FC (Cork)	1-0	1-1 / 1-0	3-1 / 1-1	—	2-0	3-1 / 2-1	1-2	3-0 / 1-0	3-0 / 2-1	1-1 / 1-0	1-1	2-1
Derry City FC (Derry)	3-2 / 1-1	4-0	5-0 / 0-1	0-1	—	2-0	2-2 / 1-2	0-0 / 2-1	0-1	1-0 / 0-1	0-0	1-1 / 0-1
Drogheda United FC (Drogheda)	3-2 / 1-1	1-0	0-2 / 1-1	0-1 / 1-0	1-1	—	4-1 / 1-1	1-4 / 0-2	2-3	1-2 / 2-3	0-4	4-0
Dundalk FC (Dundalk)	2-0	1-1 / 3-2	5-1	4-0 / 2-0	3-0 / 5-0	7-0	—	2-1 / 1-0	2-2 / 0-0	3-0	0-0	5-2
Limerick FC (Limerick)	2-1 / 4-2	1-2	0-0 / 4-1	1-2 / 0-1	0-4	0-1 / 0-3	1-2	—	4-1 / 1-0	0-3	2-0	2-1
Shamrock Rovers FC (Dublin)	1-0	0-0	2-1 / 1-0	0-2 / 2-0	1-1	0-1 / 1-0	0-1	1-1 / 1-0	—	1-0	2-1	2-0 / 3-0
Sligo Rovers FC (Sligo)	2-1 / 3-1	3-2	3-0	0-0	2-2	1-1 / 0-2	0-1	2-0	0-1	—	2-2 / 1-4	5-0 / 4-0
St. Patrick's Athletic FC (Dublin)	4-0 / 0-2	3-1 / 3-1	3-2	3-2	5-2	6-0	1-4 / 1-0	1-1 / 0-1	1-0 / 1-1	1-0	—	3-2 / 3-2
University College Dublin AFC (Dublin)	2-1 / 1-1	0-3 / 0-0	0-0	0-1 / 0-4	1-6	2-1 / 1-0	1-4 / 0-2	1-1 / 1-3	0-2	1-0	1-1	—

Premier Division

	Team	Pd	Wn	Dw	Ls	GF	GA	Pts	
1)	DUNDALK FC (DUNDALK)	33	22	8	3	73	24	74	
2)	Cork City FC (Cork)	33	22	6	5	51	25	72	
3)	St. Patrick's Athletic FC (Dublin)	33	19	8	6	66	37	65	
4)	Shamrock Rovers FC (Dublin)	33	18	8	7	43	26	62	
5)	Sligo Rovers FC (Sligo)	33	12	7	14	44	36	43	
6)	Limerick FC (Limerick)	33	12	5	16	37	45	41	
7)	Bohemian FC (Dublin)	33	9	13	11	40	41	40	
8)	Derry City FC (Derry)	33	9	11	13	42	41	38	
9)	Drogheda United FC (Drogheda)	33	10	6	17	40	63	36	
10)	Bray Wanderers FC (Bray)	33	5	11	17	28	61	26	
11)	University College Dublin AFC (Dublin)	33	6	7	20	27	71	25	POR
12)	Athlone Town FC (Athlone)	33	4	10	19	35	56	22	R
		396	148	100	148	526	526	544	

Top goalscorers

1) Christy FAGAN		(St. Patrick's Athletic FC)	20
   Patrick HOBAN		(Dundalk FC)			20
3) Conan BYRNE		(St. Patrick's Athletic FC)	18
4) Rory GAFFNEY		(Limerick FC)			14
5) Billy DENNEHY		(Cork City FC)			13
   Daniel CORCORAN	(Bohemian FC)			13

Promotion/Relegation Play-offs

Galway FC (Galway)					2-0, 2-1			Shelbourne FC (Dublin)

University College Dublin AFC (Dublin)	1-2, 0-3			Galway FC (Galway)

Galway FC won 5-1 on aggregate and were promoted. University College Dublin AFC were relegated.

Note: Galway FC changed their name to Galway United FC before the start of the 2015 season.

League of Ireland Division 1 2014	Cobh Ramblers	Finn Harps	Galway	Longford Town	Shamrock Rovers B	Shelbourne	Waterford United	Wexford Youths
Cobh Ramblers FC (Cobh)		0-2	1-5	0-0	1-1	2-2	0-0	0-1
		1-0	1-2	0-3	3-0	3-3	2-2	2-2
Finn Harps FC (Ballybofey)	5-0		1-1	0-1	0-1	1-1	0-0	1-1
	0-0		0-0	0-2	0-1	3-2	1-0	1-1
Galway FC (Galway)	4-0	1-1		0-1	0-0	0-1	2-0	1-0
	4-1	3-0		0-3	5-0	0-1	1-0	2-2
Longford Town FC (Longford)	2-0	1-0	2-2		6-0	0-1	0-0	3-3
	4-2	0-0	1-2		5-0	3-0	3-1	2-2
Shamrock Rovers B FC (Dublin)	3-1	0-3	1-1	2-1		1-1	0-1	0-2
	6-0	0-1	0-3	0-3		0-2	3-0	0-2
Shelbourne FC (Dublin)	2-0	2-0	2-4	3-2	1-1		3-3	2-0
	2-0	1-1	1-1	0-0	3-2		3-1	3-0
Waterford United FC (Waterford)	4-0	2-0	0-0	2-3	1-0	0-1		1-2
	2-1	0-2	1-1	0-2	0-2	1-3		0-3
Wexford Youths FC (Dublin)	3-2	2-2	0-1	0-1	3-2	1-0	1-3	
	2-1	3-0	2-1	0-2	2-0	1-1	4-0	

	Division 1	Pd	Wn	Dw	Ls	GF	GA	Pts	
1)	Longford Town FC (Longford)	28	18	6	4	56	19	60	P
2)	Shelbourne FC (Dublin)	28	14	10	4	46	30	52	PO
3)	Galway FC (Galway)	28	13	10	5	47	23	49	POP
4)	Wexford Youths FC (Dublin)	28	13	7	8	45	35	46	
5)	Finn Harps FC (Ballybofey)	28	7	11	10	26	28	32	
6)	Shamrock Rovers B FC (Dublin)	28	7	5	16	25	50	26	
7)	Waterford United FC (Waterford)	28	6	7	15	25	43	25	
8)	Cobh Ramblers FC (Cobh)	28	2	8	18	24	66	14	
		224	80	64	80	294	294	304	

FAI Cup Final   (Aviva Stadium, Dublin – 02/11/2014 – 17,038)

Derry City FC (Derry)　　　　　　　　　0-2　　　ST. PATRICK'S ATHLETIC FC (DUBLIN)

Fagan 52', 90+4'

Derry City: Doherty, Ventre, McBride (McNamee 65'), Barry, Jarvis, Dooley, Lowry, Molloy, McEleney (Houston 90+2'), Duffy, Patterson

St. Patrick's Athletic: Clarke, O'Brien (McCormack 80'), Hoare, Browne, Bermingham, Byrne, Fahey (Chambers 90+4'), Bolger, Brennan, Forrester (Fitzgerald 90+2'), Fagan.

Semi-finals

St. Patrick's Athletic FC (Dublin)	6-1	Finn Harps FC (Ballybofey)
Shamrock Rovers FC (Dublin)	1-1, 0-2	Derry City FC (Derry)

Quarter-finals

Shamrock Rovers FC (Dublin)	0-0, 2-1	Dundalk FC (Dundalk)
Drogheda United FC (Drogheda)	2-2, 0-5	Derry City FC (Derry)
St. Patrick's Athletic FC (Dublin)	3-2	Bohemian FC (Dublin)
Avondale United FC (Cork)	1-1, 1-4	Finn Harps FC (Ballybofey)

2015

League of Ireland Premier Division 2015

	Bohemian	Bray Wanderers	Cork City	Derry City	Drogheda United	Dundalk	Galway United	Limerick	Longford Town	Shamrock Rovers	Sligo Rovers	St. Patrick's Athletic
Bohemian FC (Dublin)	—	0-0 / 0-1	1-1	4-2	0-1 / 2-2	0-3 / 3-0	2-0	2-1 / 1-1	2-0	3-1	1-0	0-1 / 2-0
Bray Wanderers FC (Bray)	0-1 / 3-1	—	0-1 / 0-0	1-0	0-1 / 1-0	0-1	0-5 / 1-1	4-0 / 2-2	0-1	0-3 / 2-2	1-0	1-0
Cork City FC (Cork)	4-0	1-0	—	3-0 / 0-0	4-1	1-2 / 2-2	2-0 / 1-0	5-0 / 2-3	2-0 / 2-3	0-0	3-2	3-1
Derry City FC (Derry)	1-2 / 2-3	0-0 / 3-1	0-2	—	3-0 / 0-2	0-1 / 0-2	0-2	0-0	3-0 / 1-0	0-0	1-1	0-3
Drogheda United FC (Drogheda)	0-1 / 2-2	4-2	1-2 / 1-1	1-1	—	1-2	2-0	1-1 / 1-4	0-3 / 0-3	0-1	3-2 / 0-4	0-2
Dundalk FC (Dundalk)	1-2	8-1 / 4-0	1-1	1-0 / 6-0	1-0	—	3-0 / 0-0	6-2	1-0 / 0-0	2-0	3-0 / 2-2	3-0 / 4-1
Galway United FC (Galway)	5-3	0-1	1-3 / 0-4	1-2 / 1-1	1-0	2-4	—	3-2 / 1-3	1-2 / 4-2	1-2	0-1 / 2-1	1-4 / 0-1
Limerick FC (Limerick)	0-3 / 4-3	0-1	0-1 / 0-2	0-2	1-2 / 1-3	1-1	2-4	—	2-2 / 3-3	1-1 / 0-2	3-2	1-2 / 3-1
Longford Town FC (Longford)	2-1	2-0 / 1-0	1-4	0-0 / 4-2	1-1	0-2	0-1	1-0	—	0-2 / 1-3	1-1 / 1-1	2-2 / 0-3
Shamrock Rovers FC (Dublin)	0-0 / 1-1	1-0	0-0 / 3-0	4-1	1-0 / 5-3	2-2 / 1-1	3-0 / 2-0	4-1	3-2	—	5-1	1-0 / 0-2
Sligo Rovers FC (Sligo)	0-0 / 0-2	1-3 / 3-2	1-1 / 0-2	1-1 / 1-0	2-0	1-2	1-1 / 2-3	1-1	3-2 / 1-1	1-2	—	0-3
St. Patrick's Athletic FC (Dublin)	3-1	3-0 / 1-0	0-0 / 1-2	2-0 / 0-1	2-2 / 2-1	0-2	3-1	3-1	3-0	0-0	3-0 / 0-2	—

	Premier Division	Pd	Wn	Dw	Ls	GF	GA	Pts	
1)	DUNDALK FC (DUNDALK)	33	23	9	1	78	23	78	
2)	Cork City FC (Cork)	33	19	10	4	57	25	67	
3)	Shamrock Rovers FC (Dublin)	33	18	11	4	56	27	65	
4)	St. Patrick's Athletic FC (Dublin)	33	18	4	11	52	34	58	
5)	Bohemian FC (Dublin)	33	15	8	10	49	42	53	
6)	Longford Town FC (Longford)	33	10	9	14	41	53	39	
7)	Derry City FC (Derry)	33	9	8	16	32	42	35	
8)	Bray Wanderers FC (Bray)	33	9	6	18	27	51	33	
9)	Sligo Rovers FC (Sligo)	33	7	10	16	39	55	31	
10)	Galway United FC (Galway)	33	9	4	20	39	61	31	
11)	Limerick FC (Limerick)	33	7	8	18	46	73	29	POR
12)	Drogheda United FC (Drogheda)	33	7	7	19	32	62	28	R
		396	151	94	151	548	548	547	

Top goalscorers

1) Richie TOWELL   (Dundalk FC)   25
2) Karl SHEPPARD   (Cork City FC)   13
3) Vinny FAHERTY   (Limerick FC)   12
   Jake KEEGAN   (Galway United FC)   12
   Enda CURRAN   (Galway United FC)   12
   Michael DRENNAN   (Shamrock Rovers FC)   12
   David McMILLAN   (Dundalk FC)   12
   Daniel CORCORAN   (Sligo Rovers FC)   12

Promotion/relegation Play-offs

University College Dublin AFC (Dublin)   0-1, 1-2   Finn Harps FC (Ballybofey)
           Finn Harps FC (Ballybofey) won 3-1 on aggregate

Limerick FC (Limerick)   1-0, 0-2 (aet) Finn Harps FC (Ballybofey)
           Finn Harps FC won 2-1 on aggregate and were promoted. Limerick FC were relegated.

League of Ireland Division 1 2015	Athlone Town	Cabinteely	Cobh Ramblers	Finn Harps	Shelbourne	University College Dublin	Waterford United	Wexford Youths
Athlone Town FC (Athlone)		2-2	4-0	1-0	2-3	1-1	1-0	0-1
		0-1	1-4	1-1	2-1	2-2	3-4	3-1
Cabinteely FC (Cabinteely)	2-0		2-2	1-1	0-1	0-2	1-0	1-0
	1-3		1-0	2-3	0-1	0-3	1-1	2-3
Cobh Ramblers FC (Cobh)	1-0	1-0		2-3	1-0	0-3	1-0	1-4
	2-1	2-1		0-1	2-2	1-1	0-2	0-3
Finn Harps FC (Ballybofey)	1-0	2-0	2-0		1-0	2-2	3-2	1-3
	0-0	1-0	2-0		1-0	3-0	0-0	4-1
Shelbourne FC (Dublin)	1-3	1-0	1-1	0-0		0-2	1-0	2-4
	3-1	0-0	2-0	3-2		2-1	3-0	0-0
University College Dublin AFC (Dublin)	1-2	6-1	1-1	2-2	0-1		3-0	4-1
	3-1	1-0	3-0	1-0	2-1		5-1	1-2
Waterford United FC (Waterford)	1-1	3-1	1-1	0-2	2-2	0-0		1-4
	0-1	1-0	1-3	0-3	1-2	0-1		2-3
Wexford Youths FC (Dublin)	2-0	7-0	1-0	0-1	2-3	1-0	1-2	
	3-0	3-2	2-1	2-0	4-1	1-0	4-0	

Cabinteely FC fielded an ineligible player in their game against University College Dublin AFC on 31st July 2015. Although they originally lost the game 3-1, the FAI subsequently awarded the match to University College Dublin AFC as a 3-0 win and fined Cabinteely FC €2,500.

	Division 1	Pd	Wn	Dw	Ls	GF	GA	Pts	
1)	Wexford Youths FC (Dublin)	28	20	1	7	63	32	61	P
2)	Finn Harps FC (Ballybofey)	28	16	7	5	42	23	55	POP
3)	University College Dublin AFC (Dublin)	28	14	7	7	51	26	49	PO
4)	Shelbourne FC (Dublin)	28	13	6	9	37	34	45	
5)	Athlone Town FC (Athlone)	28	9	6	13	36	42	33	
6)	Cobh Ramblers FC (Cobh)	28	8	6	14	27	45	30	
7)	Waterford United FC (Waterford)	28	5	6	17	25	51	21	
8)	Cabinteely FC (Cabinteely)	28	5	5	18	22	50	20	
		224	90	44	90	303	303	314	

FAI Cup Final   (Aviva Stadium, Dublin – 08/11/2015 – 25,103)

Cork City FC (Cork)　　　　　　　0-1 (aet)　　　　　　　DUNDALK FC (DUNDALK)

Towell 107'

Cork City: McNulty, Bennett, D. Dennehy, Gaynor, Buckley, B. Dennehy, Dunleavy, Miller (Healy 60'), O'Connor, O'Sullivan (Morrissey 80'), Sheppard (Murray 101').

Dundalk: Rogers, Massey, Gartland, Boyle, Gannon (O'Donnell 44'), Towell, Shields, Meenan (Mountney 78'), Horgan, Finn, McMillan (Kilduff 71').

Semi-finals

Dundalk FC (Dundalk)	2-0	Longford Town FC (Longford)
Bray Wanderers FC (Bray)	0-1	Cork City FC (Cork)

Quarter-finals

Bray Wanderers FC (Bray)	2-0	Killester United
Derry City FC (Derry)	1-1	Cork City FC (Cork)
Longford Town FC (Longford)	3-1	Sheriff Y.C. (Dublin)
Dundalk FC (Dundalk)	4-0	Sligo Rovers FC (Sligo)

2016

League of Ireland Premier Division 2016	Bohemian	Bray Wanderers	Cork City	Derry City	Dundalk	Finn Harps	Galway United	Longford Town	Shamrock Rov.	Sligo Rovers	St. Patrick's Ath.	Wexford Youths
Bohemian FC (Dublin)	■	0-0	0-1	0-1	0-2	2-0	1-1	2-0	0-4	1-0	5-1	3-3
	■				1-2		1-0	1-0	3-2		1-0	
Bray Wanderers FC (Bray)	0-2	■	0-2	0-3	1-3	1-0	1-2	0-0	1-1	4-0	1-0	3-0
	2-1	■	4-1	2-2	2-1					4-0	2-1	
Cork City FC (Cork)	2-0	4-0	■	2-1	1-0	3-1	5-3	6-0	2-0	1-2	1-0	1-1
	0-0		■		2-0		5-2	3-0			3-1	5-0
Derry City FC (Derry)	1-0	2-0	1-0	■	0-5	2-2	2-1	4-0	3-0	0-2	1-1	1-0
	2-1		0-0	■			0-0		2-2	2-1		
Dundalk FC (Dundalk)	2-1	1-0	0-1	1-1	■	3-0	2-1	4-3	1-1	1-0	2-0	3-2
			2-1	3-1	■	2-0	4-1			0-3		
Finn Harps FC (Ballybofey)	0-0	1-0	0-1	2-1	0-7	■	1-0	1-0	0-1	3-0	1-2	0-1
	1-0	2-1		0-5		■		0-1	0-2		1-1	
Galway United FC (Galway)	1-0	4-0	2-2	0-0	1-0	1-0	■	2-2	0-1	1-2	0-3	4-2
	2-0	0-2	0-5			3-2	■		0-0			
Longford Town FC (Longford)	0-1	1-1	0-3	1-1	0-4	0-2	1-1	■	0-2	2-2	0-1	2-4
		0-2		2-3	0-3			■	2-4		0-1	
Shamrock Rovers FC (Dublin)	3-1	2-0	0-0	0-1	0-2	1-1	2-0	2-1	■	3-0	0-2	2-0
		0-0			0-3	4-2			■	0-0	3-1	
Sligo Rovers FC (Sligo)	1-0	0-0	0-0	0-0	0-1	1-1	1-1	3-0	0-2	■	1-0	4-1
			0-0			0-0	2-1	1-0	3-2	■		5-0
St. Patrick's Athletic FC (Dublin)	3-0	1-2	3-1	0-1	0-4	4-0	1-3	3-3	0-2	1-1	■	4-0
	0-1			0-2	5-2		1-0			0-0	■	4-1
Wexford Youths FC (Dublin)	0-1	2-0	0-1	1-2	1-2	1-1	0-2	0-2	2-0	0-5	0-1	■
		1-3		0-0	0-1	0-0	5-4	2-0				■

Sligo Rovers FC vs Finn Harps FC was abandoned due to floodlight failure but it was ruled that the 1-1 scoreline should stand.

	Premier Division	**Pd**	**Wn**	**Dw**	**Ls**	**GF**	**GA**	**Pts**	
1)	DUNDALK FC (DUNDALK)	33	25	2	6	73	28	77	
2)	Cork City FC (Cork)	33	21	7	5	65	23	70	
3)	Derry City FC (Derry)	33	17	11	5	48	29	62	
4)	Shamrock Rovers FC (Dublin)	33	16	7	10	46	34	55	
5)	Sligo Rovers FC (Sligo)	33	13	10	10	42	35	49	
6)	Bray Wanderers FC (Bray)	33	13	7	13	39	40	46	
7)	St. Patrick's Athletic FC (Dublin)	33	13	6	14	45	41	45	
8)	Bohemian FC (Dublin)	33	12	5	16	30	37	41	
9)	Galway United FC (Galway)	33	10	8	15	44	54	38	
10)	Finn Harps FC (Ballybofey)	33	8	8	17	23	49	32	
11)	Wexford Youths FC (Dublin)	33	6	5	22	31	70	23	POR
12)	Longford Town FC (Longford)	33	2	8	23	25	71	14	R
		396	156	84	156	511	511	552	

Top goalscorers

1) Sean MAGUIRE   (Cork City FC)   18
2) Rory PATTERSON   (Derry City FC)   17
3) David McMILLAN   (Dundalk FC)   16
4) Vincent FAHERTY   (Galway United FC)   12
5) Conan BYRNE   (St. Patrick's Athletic FC) 11

Promotion/Relegation Play-offs

Cobh Ramblers FC (Cobh)   0-2, 2-1   Drogheda United FC (Drogheda)

Wexford Youths FC (Dublin)   2-0, 0-3   Drogheda United FC (Drogheda)
    Drogheda United FC won 3-2 on aggregate and were promoted. Wexford Youths FC were relegated.

Note: Wexford Youths FC changed their name to Wexford FC at the end of the season.

League of Ireland Division 1 2016	Athlone Town	Cabinteely	Cobh Ramblers	Drogheda United	Limerick	Shelbourne	University College Dublin	Waterford United
Athlone Town FC (Athlone)	■	3-1	0-2	1-2	0-5	1-3	1-2	3-3
	■	4-0	0-2	0-1	0-2	1-0	1-1	*1-3*
Cabinteely FC (Cabinteely)	2-1	■	1-2	0-0	0-2	0-4	0-0	0-2
	5-1	■	1-3	1-0	0-1	1-2	0-2	2-0
Cobh Ramblers FC (Cobh)	2-2	2-0	■	1-1	0-3	1-0	0-2	4-0
	2-1	3-0	■	2-1	2-0	0-0	1-1	3-1
Drogheda United FC (Drogheda)	2-2	4-0	1-0	■	0-3	1-0	1-2	2-1
	1-0	1-0	2-0	■	3-3	2-0	1-2	2-0
Limerick FC (Limerick)	3-0	3-0	6-1	2-2	■	5-1	4-1	7-2
	1-0	2-0	2-0	2-1	■	2-0	4-3	4-0
Shelbourne FC (Dublin)	2-1	1-1	0-1	3-0	3-4	■	1-2	0-2
	3-0	2-1	2-0	0-2	1-1	■	1-2	0-1
University College Dublin AFC (Dublin)	1-1	2-1	3-1	2-2	1-2	2-0	■	1-3
	5-1	4-1	0-1	1-1	2-3	3-2	■	2-1
Waterford United FC (Waterford)	*3-0*	3-1	1-2	1-2	2-5	1-4	3-1	■
	3-0	0-0	2-2	1-3	1-5	2-1	1-8	■

Athlone Town FC failed to field a team for their fixture against Waterford United FC on 3rd June 2016. Waterford were therefore awarded a 3-0 result for the match, with Athlone forfeiting the fixture. As further punishment, Athlone Town were also fined €1,000 and stripped of home advantage for their August clash with Waterford United.

	Division 1	Pd	Wn	Dw	Ls	GF	GA	Pts	
1)	Limerick FC (Limerick)	28	24	3	1	86	26	75	P
2)	Drogheda United FC (Drogheda)	28	15	7	6	42	29	52	POP
3)	Cobh Ramblers FC (Cobh)	28	15	5	8	40	33	50	PO
4)	University College Dublin AFC (Dublin)	28	14	6	8	57	40	48	
5)	Waterford United FC (Waterford)	28	10	3	15	43	65	33	
6)	Shelbourne FC (Dublin)	28	9	3	16	36	40	30	
7)	Cabinteely FC (Cabinteely)	28	4	4	20	19	54	16	
8)	Athlone Town FC (Athlone)	28	3	5	20	26	62	14	
		224	94	36	94	349	349	318	

Note: Waterford United FC (Waterford) changed their name to Waterford FC (Waterford) at the end of the season.

FAI Cup Final   (Aviva Stadium, Dublin – 06/11/2016 – 26,400)

CORK CITY FC (CORK)   1-0 (aet)   Dundalk FC (Dundalk)

Maguire 120'

Cork City: McNulty, Bennett, Browne, Beattie, O'Connor, Dooley, Bolger (O'Sullivan 96'), Morrissey (Healy 100'), Buckley, Sheppard (Ogbene 78'), Maguire.

Dundalk: Rogers, Gartland, Massey, Boyle, Gannon, O'Donnell, Finn, Shields (Mountney 55'), McEleney (Shiels 77'), McMillan (Kilduff 79'), Horgan.

Semi-finals

Dundalk FC (Dundalk)	2-2	Derry City FC (Derry)
St. Patrick's Athletic FC (Dublin)	1-3	Cork City FC (Cork)

Quarter-finals

Shamrock Rovers FC (Dublin)	0-5	Cork City FC (Cork)
University College Dublin AFC (Dublin)	0-1	Dundalk FC (Dundalk)
Wexford Youths FC (Dublin)	1-3	Derry City FC (Derry)
St. Patrick's Athletic FC (Dublin)	3-2	Cobh Ramblers FC (Cobh)

2017

League of Ireland Premier Division 2017	Bohemian	Bray Wanderers	Cork City	Derry City	Drogheda United	Dundalk	Finn Harps	Galway United	Limerick	St. Patrick's Athletic	Shamrock Rovers	Sligo Rovers
Bohemian FC (Dublin)		3-2	0-2	1-4	0-0	0-1	2-0	1-1	1-2	0-4	0-2	2-0
		0-1	0-0	0-1			3-1	1-1		3-2		
Bray Wanderers FC (Bray)	1-2		0-2	3-2	2-1	0-3	5-3	1-0	0-1	1-1	4-2	2-2
					2-1		2-3	3-3	1-1		1-0	
Cork City FC (Cork)	0-1	2-1		3-0	5-0	2-1	5-0	4-0	4-1	1-0	4-1	2-1
		1-0		0-0		1-1		2-1				0-1
Derry City FC (Derry)	2-0	2-3	1-2		4-0	3-1	0-2	2-1	1-1	2-2	3-1	4-0
		0-5			2-1	0-4	3-0		3-0	1-1		
Drogheda United FC (Drogheda)	0-1	0-0	1-4	0-0		0-6	0-2	2-2	0-2	2-0	2-1	1-1
	1-4		0-1						0-1	0-2	0-0	
Dundalk FC (Dundalk)	2-0	1-3	0-3	0-0	3-1		4-0	2-0	1-0	3-0	2-1	4-0
	0-1	1-0		3-0				3-0	6-0	0-1		
Finn Harps FC (Ballybofey)	2-1	0-3	0-1	0-2	0-2	0-2		1-1	3-2	3-1	0-1	2-1
		0-1		2-3	0-2			1-3				1-2
Galway United FC (Galway)	1-2	1-2	1-1	0-0	0-1	2-1	2-1		3-1	1-1	1-2	1-1
			2-1	4-1	3-4				1-1	1-2	3-1	
Limerick FC (Limerick)	0-1	5-3	0-3	1-1	3-0	0-3	1-1	1-1		2-2	0-2	5-1
	1-0		2-1		1-0		0-2	2-2				0-0
St. Patrick's Athletic FC (Dublin)	1-3	1-2	0-3	2-1	2-0	0-2	1-2	1-1	0-2		2-1	1-1
	3-1	4-2					4-0	2-2			2-0	
Shamrock Rovers FC (Dublin)	2-1	2-0	1-2	0-1	4-1	2-1	3-2	2-0	1-1	1-1		1-0
	1-2		3-1	0-2			4-1		2-1			1-1
Sligo Rovers FC (Sligo)	2-0	3-2	1-2	1-1	1-1	0-4	0-0	1-1	3-0	1-1	1-0	
	1-0	0-0		3-0		1-1			1-1			

	Premier Division	Pd	Wn	Dw	Ls	GF	GA	Pts	
1)	CORK CITY FC (CORK)	33	24	4	5	67	23	76	
2)	Dundalk FC (Dundalk)	33	22	3	8	72	24	69	
3)	Shamrock Rovers FC (Dublin)	33	17	3	13	49	41	54	
4)	Derry City FC (Derry)	33	14	9	10	49	40	51	
5)	Bohemian FC (Dublin)	33	14	5	14	36	40	47	
6)	Bray Wanderers FC (Bray)	33	13	7	13	55	52	46	
7)	Limerick FC (Limerick)	33	10	10	13	41	51	40	
8)	St. Patrick's Athletic FC (Dublin)	33	9	12	12	45	52	39	
9)	Sligo Rovers FC (Sligo)	33	8	15	10	33	44	39	
10)	Galway United FC (Galway)	33	7	14	12	45	50	35	R
11)	Finn Harps FC (Ballybofey)	33	9	3	21	35	67	30	R
12)	Drogheda United FC (Drogheda)	33	5	7	21	22	65	22	R
		396	152	92	152	549	549	548	

Top goalscorers

1)	Sean MAGUIRE	(Cork City FC)	20
2)	David McMILLAN	(Dundalk FC)	16
3)	Danny CORCORAN	(Bohemian FC)	15
	Gary McCABE	(Bray Wanderers FC)	15
5)	Rodrigo TOSI	(Limerick FC)	14
6)	Ronan MURRAY	(Galway United FC)	13

At the end of the season, the League was restructured into two 10-team divisions. This meant that there were no promotion/relegation play-offs this season. Three teams were relegated from the Premier Division with just the champions of the First Division promoted in return.

League of Ireland Division 1 2017	Athlone Town	Cabinteely	Cobh Ramblers	Longford Town	Shelbourne	University College Dublin	Waterford	Wexford
Athlone Town FC (Athlone)	■	3-3	2-1	0-3	1-4	0-2	1-0	1-0
		1-1	0-1	2-2	1-3	0-4	1-6	1-1
Cabinteely FC (Cabinteely)	2-0	■	4-1	0-0	0-1	0-1	0-0	2-0
	6-2		2-1	0-2	1-0	3-3	1-1	0-1
Cobh Ramblers FC (Cobh)	5-1	2-0	■	2-0	1-1	1-0	0-0	1-1
	3-1	0-3		2-0	0-1	1-0	2-1	1-0
Longford Town FC (Longford)	3-1	0-2	1-3	■	3-1	0-1	0-0	5-0
	7-1	1-0	2-1		1-3	1-1	0-1	1-0
Shelbourne FC (Dublin)	2-1	1-4	0-1	0-0	■	0-1	2-2	2-0
	4-1	3-1	0-1	0-0		1-1	1-1	1-2
University College Dublin AFC (Dublin)	4-1	2-2	0-1	2-0	4-0	■	0-2	2-0
	4-0	2-3	1-0	0-0	1-2		3-2	1-0
Waterford FC (Waterford)	2-1	3-0	2-1	1-0	1-0	1-1	■	2-0
	3-1	3-0	4-0	1-0	1-1	1-0		2-1
Wexford FC (Crossabeg)	1-2	1-1	1-2	0-0	1-0	1-1	0-1	■
	2-2	2-0	0-2	1-2	0-3	0-0	0-3	

Note: During September 2017 the FAI banned two Athlone Town players for 12 months after a UEFA investigation found clear betting evidence that they had conspired to fix the result of the 3-1 away defeat at Longford Town played on 29th April 2017.

	Division 1	Pd	Wn	Dw	Ls	GF	GA	Pts	
1)	Waterford FC (Waterford)	28	17	8	3	47	17	59	P
2)	Cobh Ramblers FC (Cobh)	28	16	3	9	37	28	51	
3)	University College Dublin AFC (Dublin)	28	13	8	7	42	23	47	
4)	Shelbourne FC (Dublin)	28	11	7	10	37	32	40	
5)	Longford Town FC (Longford)	28	10	8	10	34	26	38	
6)	Cabinteely FC (Cabinteely)	28	10	8	10	41	37	38	
7)	Wexford FC (Crossabeg)	28	4	7	17	16	41	19	
8)	Athlone Town FC (Athlone)	28	4	5	19	29	79	17	
		224	85	54	85	283	283	309	

FAI Cup Final   (Aviva Stadium, Dublin – 05/11/2017 – 24,210)

Dundalk FC (Dundalk)　　　　　1-1 (aet)　　　　　CORK CITY FC (CORK)

N. Vemmelund 95'　　　*Cork City won 5-3 on penalties*　　　*A. Campion 111'*

Dundalk: Rogers, Gartland (Hoare 91'), Massey, Vemmelund, Gannon, O'Donnell, Benson, McEleney (Mountney 108'), McGrath (Connolly 71'), McMillan, Duffy.

Cork City: McNulty, Bennett, Beattie, Griffin, Delaney, Dooley, Keohane (Sadlier 57'), McCormack, Morrissey (Bolger 98'), Buckley (Campion 98'), Sheppard.

Semi-finals

| Cork City FC (Cork) | 1-0 | Limerick FC (Limerick) |
| Dundalk FC (Dundalk) | 1-1, 4-2 (aet) | Shamrock Rovers FC (Dublin) |

Quarter-finals

Bluebell United (Dublin)	2-4	Shamrock Rovers FC (Dublin)
Galway United FC (Galway)	1-2	Limerick FC (Limerick)
Dundalk FC (Dundalk)	4-0	Drogheda United FC (Drogheda)
Longford Town FC (Longford)	1-4	Cork City FC (Cork)

2018

League of Ireland Premier Division 2018	Bohemian	Bray Wanderers	Cork City	Derry City	Dundalk	Limerick	St. Patrick's Athletic	Shamrock Rovers	Sligo Rovers	Waterford
Bohemian FC (Dublin)		2-1	0-2	0-1	0-2	0-0	0-1	3-1	2-2	0-1
		6-0	4-2	1-2	1-1	5-0	1-0	1-1	0-3	1-3
Bray Wanderers FC (Bray)	1-3		0-4	2-1	0-2	0-1	1-2	1-0	1-2	2-2
	0-5		1-3	2-1	1-3	0-2	3-1	0-3	2-1	0-0
Cork City FC (Cork)	3-0	4-0		4-2	1-0	2-1	1-0	1-0	1-0	2-0
	1-0	5-1		5-0	0-1	3-0	1-1	0-0	1-2	3-0
Derry City FC (Derry)	3-1	5-1	0-0		1-4	5-0	2-1	0-0	0-2	1-0
	0-2	2-0	0-3		0-4	2-1	2-1	0-1	1-2	1-2
Dundalk FC (Dundalk)	3-0	0-0	1-0	2-2		8-0	5-0	2-1	2-1	1-0
	2-0	5-0	2-1	3-2		4-0	1-1	1-2	5-0	2-0
Limerick FC (Limerick)	1-1	1-0	1-1	0-3	0-3		0-1	0-1	1-2	0-2
	1-1	2-1	0-2	0-1	0-1		0-4	0-2	1-3	2-1
St. Patrick's Athletic FC (Dublin)	2-2	5-0	2-3	5-2	0-0	1-0		2-0	2-0	1-0
	1-3	3-0	1-3	5-0	1-3	2-1		0-1	0-3	3-0
Shamrock Rovers FC (Dublin)	1-2	6-0	3-0	6-1	0-0	1-1	1-0		1-0	1-1
	0-1	5-0	0-0	2-0	2-5	5-0	3-0		2-0	3-1
Sligo Rovers FC (Sligo)	0-2	2-1	1-4	2-1	0-2	0-1	0-0	0-0		1-2
	1-1	2-1	0-2	0-2	0-2	0-0	1-2	2-0		2-3
Waterford FC (Waterford)	1-0	3-0	2-1	2-1	2-1	3-6	2-0	2-1	1-1	
	1-1	2-0	1-2	4-0	1-2	4-1	2-0	0-1	1-0	

	Premier Division	Pd	Wn	Dw	Ls	GF	GA	Pts	
1)	DUNDALK FC (DUNDALK)	36	27	6	3	85	20	87	
2)	Cork City FC (Cork)	36	24	5	7	71	27	77	
3)	Shamrock Rovers FC (Dublin)	36	18	8	10	57	27	62	
4)	Waterford FC (Waterford)	36	18	5	13	52	44	59	
5)	St. Patrick's Athletic FC (Dublin)	36	15	5	16	51	47	50	
6)	Bohemian FC (Dublin)	36	13	9	14	52	45	48	
7)	Sligo Rovers FC (Sligo)	36	12	6	18	38	50	42	
8)	Derry City FC (Derry)	36	13	3	20	47	70	42	
9)	Limerick FC (Limerick)	36	7	6	23	25	75	27	POR
10)	Bray Wanderers FC (Bray)	36	5	3	28	23	96	18	R
		360	152	56	152	501	501	512	

Top goalscorers

1) Patrick HOBAN   (Dundalk FC)   29
2) Kieran SADLIER   (Cork City FC)   16
3) Graham CUMMINS   (Cork City FC)   15
4) Graham BURKE   (Shamrock Rovers FC) 13
   Michael DUFFY   (Dundalk FC)   13
6) Daniel CARR   (Shamrock Rovers FC) 11
   Daniel CORCORAN   (Bohemian FC)   11

Promotion/Relegation Play-offs

Drogheda United FC (Drogheda)   0-1, 2-1   Shelbourne FC (Dublin)
   Aggregate 2-2. Drogheda United FC won 4-2 on penalties.

Drogheda United FC (Drogheda)   1-1, 0-2   Finn Harps FC (Ballybofey)

Finn Harps FC (Ballybofey)   1-0, 2-0   Limerick FC (Limerick)
   Finn Harps FC won 3-0 on aggregate and were promoted. Limerick FC were relegated.

League of Ireland Division 1 2018

	Athlone Town	Cabinteely	Cobh Ramblers	Drogheda United	Finn Harps	Galway United	Longford Town	Shelbourne	University College Dublin	Wexford
Athlone Town FC (Athlone)	■	1-2	1-4	0-1	1-1	0-3	1-1	0-5	1-3	3-0
	■	1-3	0-0		1-3				0-1	
Cabinteely FC (Cabinteely)	4-0	■	0-1	3-2	0-1	1-2	1-0	2-0	2-0	0-1
		■	2-0	2-2				1-1		1-2
Cobh Ramblers FC (Cobh)	1-0	1-0	■	1-5	0-2	0-0	0-1	0-3	0-2	2-1
			■	0-2	0-1	1-2			2-2	
Drogheda United FC (Drogheda)	6-0	2-0	2-1	■	2-1	2-2	1-1	1-1	2-0	2-0
	2-1			■	0-1	2-2	2-1		0-3	
Finn Harps FC (Ballybofey)	4-0	1-0	0-1	2-1	■	1-0	2-4	1-1	1-3	1-0
	7-1				■	2-0	3-0	0-0		3-0
Galway United FC (Galway)	4-1	3-1	3-0	0-1	1-2	■	0-0	1-2	2-0	4-1
	4-1	3-2				■	1-4			1-1
Longford Town FC (Longford)	5-1	3-0	2-2	1-0	1-2	3-2	■	1-1	0-2	3-0
	3-0	4-1	1-2				■		2-2	3-0
Shelbourne FC (Dublin)	7-0	0-0	1-0	1-1	0-0	2-0	3-2	■	1-1	4-1
	2-2		3-1	0-1		3-0	6-1	■		
University College Dublin AFC (Dublin)	3-0	3-1	3-1	2-0	3-2	1-1	1-5	2-1	■	3-2
		4-1			1-1	2-0		1-1	■	
Wexford FC (Crossabeg)	7-0	0-1	1-1	1-8	1-1	0-0	0-2	0-1	0-8	■
	2-0		0-2	0-0				1-2	0-3	■

	Division 1	Pd	Wn	Dw	Ls	GF	GA	Pts	
1)	University College Dublin AFC (Dublin)	27	17	6	4	59	29	57	P
2)	Finn Harps FC (Ballybofey)	27	16	6	5	46	22	54	POP
3)	Shelbourne FC (Dublin)	27	13	11	3	52	21	50	PO
4)	Drogheda United FC (Drogheda)	27	14	7	6	50	27	49	PO
5)	Longford Town FC (Longford)	27	13	6	8	54	36	45	
6)	Galway United FC (Galway)	27	10	7	10	41	36	37	
7)	Cabinteely FC (Cabinteely)	27	9	3	15	32	45	30	
8)	Cobh Ramblers FC (Cobh)	27	8	5	14	24	41	29	
9)	Wexford FC (Crossabeg)	27	4	5	18	23	59	17	
10)	Athlone Town FC (Athlone)	27	1	4	22	16	81	7	
		270	105	60	105	397	397	375	

FAI Cup Final   (Aviva Stadium, Dublin – 04/11/2018 – 30,412)

Cork City FC (Cork) 1-2 DUNDALK FC (DUNDALK)
Sadlier 21' (pen) *Hoare 19', McEleney 73'*

Cork City: McNulty, Bennett, Griffin, McCarthy, McLoughlin, Keohane (Cummins 75'), McCormack (Murphy 85'), Morrissey (McNamee 67'), Sadlier, Buckley, Sheppard.

Dundalk: Rogers, Gartland, Massey, Gannon (Cleary 86'), Hoare, Shields, Benson (Jarvis 90'), McEleney, Mountney (McGrath 58'), Hoban, Duffy.

Semi-finals

Dundalk FC (Dundalk)	1-0	University College Dublin AFC (Dublin)
Bohemian FC (Dublin)	1-1, 1-2	Cork City FC (Cork)

Quarter-finals

University College Dublin AFC (Dublin)	2-1	Waterford FC (Waterford)
Limerick FC (Limerick)	0-4	Dundalk FC (Dundalk)
Longford Town FC (Longford)	0-7	Cork City FC (Cork)
Derry City FC (Derry)	1-3	Bohemian FC (Dublin)

2019

League of Ireland Premier Division 2019	Bohemian	Cork City	Derry City	Dundalk	Finn Harps	St. Patrick's Athletic	Shamrock Rovers	Sligo Rovers	University College Dublin	Waterford
Bohemian FC (Dublin)	■	0-1	1-1	0-2	1-0	1-0	1-0	1-2	3-0	0-0
	■	1-0	0-0	2-1	5-3	3-0	2-1	2-1	10-1	1-2
Cork City FC (Cork)	2-0	■	0-0	0-2	1-1	1-1	1-3	0-0	2-0	0-2
	0-0	■	1-4	1-0	0-0	0-1	1-1	2-4	3-2	1-2
Derry City FC (Derry)	0-2	2-0	■	0-2	4-0	1-1	0-1	2-0	3-0	3-2
	0-0	4-0	■	2-2	4-0	1-3	0-2	3-0	0-0	2-0
Dundalk FC (Dundalk)	1-0	1-0	2-2	■	3-0	1-0	2-1	1-1	2-1	4-0
	2-1	1-0	1-0	■	5-0	4-0	3-2	4-0	3-0	3-0
Finn Harps FC (Ballybofey)	0-1	3-4	2-3	1-1	■	0-2	0-1	1-2	3-0	3-2
	1-0	0-0	1-0	0-3	■	1-2	0-3	2-0	0-0	1-0
St. Patrick's Athletic FC (Dublin)	1-1	1-0	1-3	1-0	0-0	■	0-1	2-1	2-0	0-3
	0-0	1-1	1-0	0-1	1-0	■	0-2	2-1	0-0	0-2
Shamrock Rovers FC (Dublin)	0-1	2-0	2-0	0-0	3-0	1-0	■	3-0	3-1	2-1
	1-0	3-0	2-2	0-1	1-0	0-0	■	0-0	7-0	2-1
Sligo Rovers FC (Sligo)	0-2	1-2	0-0	2-1	1-1	0-1	2-1	■	1-0	0-0
	1-1	1-1	1-2	0-2	3-1	1-1	0-0	■	5-1	0-0
University College Dublin AFC (Dublin)	0-2	2-1	0-2	1-3	3-0	1-1	0-1	0-2	■	4-1
	3-0	0-1	1-3	0-5	1-0	0-1	0-3	0-2	■	1-2
Waterford FC (Waterford)	0-0	2-0	2-2	0-3	4-0	2-0	1-2	3-3	1-0	■
	1-2	1-2	1-1	0-1	0-1	1-2	1-5	2-0	4-2	■

	Premier Division	Pd	Wn	Dw	Ls	GF	GA	Pts	
1)	DUNDALK FC (DUNDALK)	36	27	5	4	73	18	86	
2)	Shamrock Rovers FC (Dublin)	36	23	6	7	62	21	75	
3)	Bohemian FC (Dublin)	36	17	9	10	47	28	60	
4)	Derry City FC (Derry)	36	15	12	9	56	34	57	
5)	St. Patrick's Athletic FC (Dublin)	36	14	10	12	29	35	52	
6)	Waterford FC (Waterford)	36	12	7	17	46	53	43	
7)	Sligo Rovers FC (Sligo)	36	10	12	14	38	47	42	
8)	Cork City FC (Cork)	36	9	10	17	29	49	37	
9)	Finn Harps FC (Ballybofey)	36	7	7	22	26	64	28	
10)	University College Dublin AFC (Dublin)	36	5	4	27	25	82	19	R
		360	139	82	139	431	431	499	

Top goalscorers

1) Junior OGEDI-UZOKWE   (Derry City FC)   14
2) Patrick HOBAN   (Dundalk FC)   13
3) Michael DUFFY   (Dundalk FC)   12
4) Danny MANDROIU   (Bohemian FC)   11
   David PARKHOUSE   (Derry City FC)   11
   Aaron GREENE   (Shamrock Rovers FC) 11
   Romeo PARKES   (Sligo Rovers FC)   11

Promotion/Relegation Play-offs

Cabinteely FC (Cabinteely)   0-0, 1-1   Longford Town FC (Longford)
    Aggregate 1-1. Cabinteely FC won 3-1 on penalties.

Cabinteely FC (Cabinteely)   1-1, 1-5   Drogheda United FC (Drogheda)

Drogheda United FC (Drogheda)   1-0, 0-2   Finn Harps FC (Ballybofey)

League of Ireland Division 1 2019

Team	Athlone Town	Bray Wanderers	Cabinteely	Cobh Ramblers	Drogheda United	Galway United	Limerick	Longford Town	Shelbourne	Wexford
Athlone Town FC (Athlone)	■	0-5	2-2	1-1	3-5	0-4	1-1	0-1	0-2	4-2
	■				0-2			1-5	1-2	3-1
Bray Wanderers FC (Bray)	0-1	■	1-1	1-0	3-1	2-1	2-0	3-2	0-1	2-1
	3-0	■		3-3			1-0			
Cabinteely FC (Cabinteely)	3-2	0-3	■	2-2	0-5	1-0	1-2	1-1	1-0	2-0
	3-1	2-1	■		0-1	3-0	2-0			
Cobh Ramblers FC (Cobh)	0-1	1-0	0-1	■	1-4	2-1	2-3	0-0	2-1	6-1
	2-1		1-1	■					1-0	1-1
Drogheda United FC (Drogheda)	4-2	1-0	1-4	4-0	■	3-0	3-2	0-1	0-0	2-1
			0-0	4-2	■				1-3	6-0
Galway United FC (Galway)	1-1	0-1	0-0	1-2	0-1	■	0-1	2-1	2-3	2-0
			2-2	7-1	1-3	■			0-3	
Limerick FC (Limerick)	2-0	1-0	1-0	3-1	0-0	2-1	■	0-0	0-1	1-1
	1-1			3-4	1-4		■	3-1		4-1
Longford Town FC (Longford)	3-1	2-0	0-1	1-0	3-0	2-1	1-0	■	2-0	1-0
		1-2			2-1	4-0		■	0-2	
Shelbourne FC (Dublin)	2-1	1-0	2-3	1-0	2-1	3-0	2-0	1-0	■	3-0
			0-0	1-1					■	5-2
Wexford FC (Crossabeg)	2-0	2-0	0-2	2-2	1-2	0-4	0-0	1-2	1-2	■
		1-5	1-2			0-0		0-2		■

	Division 1	Pd	Wn	Dw	Ls	GF	GA	Pts	
1)	Shelbourne FC (Dublin)	27	19	3	5	50	19	60	P
2)	Drogheda United FC (Drogheda)	27	16	3	8	59	36	51	PO
3)	Longford Town FC (Longford)	27	16	3	8	41	23	51	PO
4)	Cabinteely FC (Cabinteely)	27	14	8	5	39	28	50	PO
5)	Bray Wanderers FC (Bray)	27	14	4	9	44	26	46	
6)	Cobh Ramblers FC (Cobh)	27	8	7	12	38	51	31	
7)	Galway United FC (Galway)	27	7	5	15	36	42	26	
8)	Athlone Town FC (Athlone)	27	4	6	17	30	61	18	
9)	Wexford FC (Crossabeg)	27	2	5	20	22	65	11	
10)	Limerick FC (Limerick)	27	10	6	11	33	41	10	
		270	110	50	110	392	392	354	

Limerick FC (Limerick) had 26 points deducted after failing to comply with the League of Ireland profitability and sustainability rules.

FAI Cup Final (Aviva Stadium, Dublin – 03/11/2019 – 33,111)

Dundalk FC (Dundalk)   1-1 (aet)   SHAMROCK ROVERS FC (DUBLIN)
Duffy 90+3'   *Shamrock Rovers won 4-2 on penalties.*   *McEneff 89' pen.*

Dundalk: Rogers, Gartland, Massey, Gannon, Hoare (Kelly 90+1'), Cleary, Benson (Mountney 112'), Murray (Kelly 61'), McGrath, Hoban (Flores 99'), M. Duffy.

Shamrock Rovers: Mannus, O'Brien, Kavanagh (Farrugia 68'), Lopes, Grace, Finn, McEneff, Byrne, O'Neill, Greene (Lafferty 111'), Burke (Bolger 90+1').

Semi-finals

Bohemian FC (Dublin)	0-2	Shamrock Rovers FC (Dublin)
Sligo Rovers FC (Sligo)	0-1	Dundalk FC (Dundalk)

Quarter-finals

Galway United FC (Galway)	1-2	Shamrock Rovers FC (Dublin)
Sligo Rovers FC (Sligo)	4-0	University College Dublin AFC (Dublin)
Waterford FC (Waterford)	1-3	Dundalk FC (Dundalk)
Crumlin United FC (Dublin)	0-2	Bohemian FC (Dublin)

2020

Play was halted in mid-March due to the effects of the COVID-19 pandemic. The FAI subsequently announced a contingency plan with the aim of completing the domestic season at a later date with a reduced number of games to play. The competition resumed on 31th July and was played to completion with each club facing the others in home and away matches.

League of Ireland Premier Division 2020	Bohemian	Cork City	Derry City	Dundalk	Finn Harps	St. Patrick's Athletic	Shamrock Rovers	Shelbourne	Sligo Rovers	Waterford
Bohemian FC (Dublin)	■	3-0	2-1	2-1	0-2	2-0	0-1	2-0	2-0	0-2
Cork City FC (Cork)	0-1	■	1-1	0-2	1-0	1-2	0-3	0-1	3-0	0-0
Derry City FC (Derry)	2-0	3-1	■	1-2	1-1	0-0	1-2	2-0	0-2	2-0
Dundalk FC (Dundalk)	0-0	3-0	1-0	■	0-0	1-1	0-4	3-2	0-2	2-2
Finn Harps FC (Ballybofey)	0-1	1-1	0-0	0-4	■	3-2	0-2	0-1	1-0	1-0
St. Patrick's Athletic FC (Dublin)	1-2	1-0	0-2	1-1	2-0	■	0-0	2-0	0-0	0-1
Shamrock Rovers FC (Dublin)	1-0	6-0	2-0	3-2	3-1	0-0	■	0-0	4-0	6-1
Shelbourne FC (Dublin)	1-3	1-1	1-1	1-2	1-1	1-0	0-2	■	1-0	0-1
Sligo Rovers FC (Sligo)	0-1	2-1	1-0	3-1	3-1	0-2	2-3	2-1	■	2-1
Waterford FC (Waterford)	0-2	0-0	2-1	1-0	2-3	3-0	0-2	0-1	1-0	■

	Premier Division	**Pd**	**Wn**	**Dw**	**Ls**	**GF**	**GA**	**Pts**	
1)	SHAMROCK ROVERS FC (DUBLIN)	18	15	3	0	44	7	48	
2)	Bohemian FC (Dublin)	18	12	1	5	23	12	37	
3)	Dundalk FC (Dundalk)	18	7	5	6	25	23	26	
4)	Sligo Rovers FC (Sligo)	18	8	1	9	19	23	25	
5)	Waterford FC (Waterford)	18	7	3	8	17	22	24	
6)	St. Patrick's Athletic FC (Dublin)	18	5	6	7	14	17	21	
7)	Derry City FC (Derry)	18	5	5	8	18	18	20	
8)	Finn Harps FC (Ballybofey)	18	5	5	8	15	24	20	
9)	Shelbourne FC (Dublin)	18	5	4	9	13	22	19	POR
10)	Cork City FC (Cork)	18	2	5	11	10	30	11	R
		180	71	38	71	198	198	251	

Top goalscorers

1)	Patrick HOBAN	(Dundalk FC)	10
2)	Jack BYRNE	(Shamrock Rovers FC)	9
3)	Graham BURKE	(Shamrock Rovers FC)	8
	Andre WRIGHT	(Bohemian FC)	8
5	Daniel GRANT	(Bohemian FC)	7
	Aaron GREENE	(Shamrock Rovers FC)	7

Promotion/Relegation Play-offs

Bray Wanderers FC (Bray)	0-1	Galway United FC (Galway)
University College Dublin AFC (Dublin)	2-3 (aet)	Longford Town FC (Longford)
Galway United FC (Galway)	1-2	Longford Town FC (Longford)
Shelbourne FC (Dublin)	0-1	Longford Town FC (Longford)

Longford Town FC were promoted and Shelbourne FC were relegated.

League of Ireland Division 1 2020

	Athlone Town	Bray Wanderers	Cabinteely	Cobh Ramblers	Drogheda United	Galway United	Longford Town	Shamrock Rovers	University College Dublin	Wexford
Athlone Town FC (Athlone)		0-1	1-3	2-1	3-3	1-4	0-4	0-4	2-4	1-3
Bray Wanderers FC (Bray)	3-1		3-0	0-0	0-1	0-1	3-0	1-0	2-0	2-0
Cabinteely FC (Cabinteely)	1-1	4-2		1-0	0-2	0-1	0-3	1-0	0-3	1-5
Cobh Ramblers FC (Cobh)	3-2	1-2	1-2		0-2	2-2	2-0	0-0	0-6	4-0
Drogheda United FC (Drogheda)	0-2	3-1	5-1	0-1		1-0	0-1	3-2	5-1	2-0
Galway United FC (Galway)	2-2	0-0	0-2	0-1	1-3		0-1	2-1	2-2	1-0
Longford Town FC (Longford)	2-0	0-2	1-3	0-1	1-1	2-6		2-0	3-1	3-1
Shamrock Rovers II FC (Dublin)	3-1	0-2	0-2	0-1	2-2	1-1	1-2		2-5	2-0
University College Dublin AFC	2-1	1-3	5-1	1-0	1-3	0-3	0-0	3-1		8-0
Wexford FC (Crossabeg)	0-1	1-3	0-0	0-4	0-3	0-0	2-1	0-2	1-1	

Division 1

		Pd	Wn	Dw	Ls	GF	GA	Pts	
1)	Drogheda United FC (Drogheda)	18	12	3	3	39	17	39	P
2)	Bray Wanderers FC (Bray)	18	12	2	4	30	13	38	PO
3)	University College Dublin AFC (Dublin)	18	9	3	6	44	29	30	PO
4)	Longford Town FC (Longford)	18	9	2	7	26	23	29	POP
5)	Galway United FC (Galway)	18	7	6	5	26	19	27	
6)	Cobh Ramblers FC (Cobh)	18	8	3	7	22	20	27	
7)	Cabinteely FC (Cabinteely)	18	8	2	8	22	33	26	
8)	Shamrock Rovers II FC (Dublin)	18	4	3	11	22	28	15	
9)	Athlone Town FC (Athlone)	18	3	3	12	21	43	12	
10)	Wexford FC (Crossabeg)	18	3	3	12	13	39	12	
		180	75	30	75	265	264	255	

FAI Cup Final (Aviva Stadium, Dublin – 06/12/2020 – Behind closed doors)

Shamrock Rovers FC (Dublin)   2-4 (aet)   DUNDALK FC (DUNDALK)
Greene 49', Lopes 74'   *McMillan 69', 72' pen., 117', Hoare 111'*

Shamrock Rovers: Mannus, O'Brien (Grace 45+3'), Kavanagh (Lafferty 84'), Lopes, Scales, Finn (Marshall 83'), McEneff, Byrne, Watts (Bolger 83'), Greene (Williams 106'), Burke.

Dundalk: Rogers, Gartland (Hoare 106'), Boyle, Gannon (Leahy 95'), Cleary, Dummigan, Shields, McEleney (Mountney 95'), Sloggett (Flores 87'), McMillan, Duffy (Kelly 111').

Semi-finals

Shamrock Rovers FC (Dublin)	2-0	Sligo Rovers FC (Sligo)
Athlone Town FC (Athlone)	0-11	Dundalk FC (Dundalk)

Quarter-finals

Athlone Town FC (Athlone)	4-1	Shelbourne FC (Dublin)
Finn Harps FC (Ballybofey)	2-3	Shamrock Rovers FC (Dublin)
Bohemian FC (Dublin)	1-4	Dundalk FC (Dundalk)
Sligo Rovers FC (Sligo)	0-0 (aet)	Derry City FC (Derry)

Sligo Rovers FC won 3-1 on penalties.

2021

League of Ireland Premier Division 2021	Bohemian	Derry City	Drogheda United	Dundalk	Finn Harps	Longford Town	Shamrock Rovers	Sligo Rovers	St. Patrick's Athletic	Waterford
Bohemian FC (Dublin)		1-2	5-0	5-1	4-0	2-2	1-0	1-3	0-1	3-0
		3-3	2-1	1-1	1-2	1-1	3-1	1-0	3-2	1-2
Derry City FC (Derry)	1-1		1-1	1-1	1-2	1-1	0-2	1-1	2-2	1-2
	1-1		3-0	1-0	2-2	3-0	2-4	2-0	1-0	2-0
Drogheda United FC (Drogheda)	1-1	1-2		0-1	1-1	4-1	0-1	1-1	3-1	1-0
	3-2	1-0		0-1	3-1	2-0	0-1	0-0	0-1	1-2
Dundalk FC (Dundalk)	0-1	2-1	2-1		1-2	1-1	2-1	0-1	1-1	1-3
	2-1	1-2	1-2		1-0	2-0	1-0	4-1	1-4	1-0
Finn Harps FC (Ballybofey)	1-0	1-2	0-1	1-1		1-1	0-2	1-2	0-2	2-1
	1-2	1-1	0-0	2-2		5-0	2-1	2-2	3-1	0-1
Longford Town FC (Longford)	0-2	2-0	0-4	2-2	0-0		0-1	0-1	1-3	1-2
	1-4	0-2	1-1	1-0	0-3		0-1	0-1	1-4	1-1
Shamrock Rovers FC (Dublin)	2-1	1-1	1-1	2-1	1-1	2-1		0-1	1-1	3-0
	1-1	2-1	2-1	3-1	3-0	1-0		2-0	3-1	2-0
Sligo Rovers FC (Sligo)	4-0	0-1	1-2	1-1	1-0	2-0	1-1		1-1	*3-0*
	1-1	1-2	2-0	2-1	0-1	1-0	0-1		2-0	1-1
St. Patrick's Athletic FC (Dublin)	2-1	2-0	2-1	0-2	4-1	3-0	1-2	2-0		1-0
	2-2	1-0	2-0	1-0	2-2	3-2	0-1	0-3		2-1
Waterford FC (Waterford)	0-1	0-1	0-7	0-3	1-2	1-0	1-4	1-2	1-1	
	1-0	2-2	1-0	1-1	4-1	4-1	1-3	1-0	0-0	

Sligo Rovers were awarded a 3-0 victory after Waterford failed to appear for the scheduled game on 15th May 2021 due to COVID-19 cases in their squad.

	Premier Division	**Pd**	**Wn**	**Dw**	**Ls**	**GF**	**GA**	**Pts**	
1)	SHAMROCK ROVERS FC (DUBLIN)	36	24	6	6	59	28	78	
2)	St. Patrick's Athletic FC (Dublin)	36	18	8	10	56	42	62	
3)	Sligo Rovers FC (Sligo)	36	16	9	11	43	32	57	
4)	Derry City FC (Derry)	36	14	12	10	49	42	54	
5)	Bohemian FC (Dublin)	36	14	10	12	60	46	52	
6)	Dundalk FC (Dundalk)	36	13	9	14	44	46	48	
7)	Drogheda United FC (Drogheda)	36	12	8	16	45	43	44	
8)	Finn Harps FC (Ballybofey)	36	11	11	14	44	52	44	
9)	Waterford FC (Waterford)	36	12	6	18	36	56	42	POR
10)	Longford Town FC (Longford)	36	2	9	25	22	71	15	R
		360	136	88	136	458	458	496	

Top goalscorers

1) Georgie KELLY   (Bohemian FC)   21
2) Danny MANDROIU   (Shamrock Rovers FC)   15
3) Mark DOYLE   (Drogheda United FC)   13
4) Patrick HOBAN   (Dundalk FC)   12
5) Matty SMITH   (St. Patrick's Athletic FC)   11
   Johnny KENNY   (Sligo Rovers FC)   11
   Graham BURKE   (Shamrock Rovers FC)   11

Promotion/Relegation Play-offs

Bray Wanderers FC (Bray)	0-0, 1-0	Galway United FC (Galway)
Treaty United FC (Limerick)	0-3, 2-1	University College Dublin AFC (Dublin)
Bray Wanderers FC (Bray)	0-2	University College Dublin AFC (Dublin)
Waterford FC (Waterford)	1-2	University College Dublin AFC (Dublin)

University College Dublin AFC were promoted and Waterford FC were relegated.

League of Ireland Division 1 2021	Athlone Town	Bray Wanderers	Cabinteely	Cobh Ramblers	Cork City	Galway United	Shelbourne	Treaty United	University College Dublin	Wexford
Athlone Town FC (Athlone)		0-0	1-2	2-1	0-2	3-1	1-3	1-4	2-3	3-0
		2-1	1-2		1-0				0-2	
Bray Wanderers FC (Bray)	1-2		3-0	2-1	0-0	0-0	1-4	0-0	4-0	3-1
	0-1		1-2		0-0		1-0			
Cabinteely FC (Cabinteely)	0-1	0-3		1-0	1-0	0-3	1-3	2-1	1-2	0-2
				1-2	2-2	0-1	0-2	0-2		
Cobh Ramblers FC (Cobh)	0-0	1-1	1-0		1-0	0-4	1-2	0-2	0-4	3-2
		1-2			0-1	2-0		0-2		
Cork City FC (Cork)	0-1	2-2	0-2	2-1		1-1	1-3	2-3	1-1	5-0
	3-1		4-0			3-0	0-2			4-0
Galway United FC (Galway)	2-1	1-2	1-0	2-0	2-3		0-0	1-1	2-2	1-0
	1-0						3-1	0-0	4-1	2-1
Shelbourne FC (Dublin)	1-0	3-3	1-0	2-2	2-1	4-0		2-2	3-1	1-0
	1-1	1-1						1-0	1-1	4-0
Treaty United FC (Limerick)	1-0	2-0	1-4	1-1	2-1	0-1	1-1		2-1	1-0
	1-1			3-0	0-0					1-1
University College Dublin AFC (Dublin)	2-2	0-0	4-1	1-2	0-0	0-2	0-0	3-2		2-1
	6-0	4-3	5-2		1-0		2-1			
Wexford FC (Crossabeg)	4-4	0-1	2-3	1-2	0-0	1-3	0-1	1-2	0-6	
		4-2	2-1	3-1				2-1		

Cabinteely FC vs Galway United FC was postponed. The FAI subsequently awarded the result to Galway United FC by a 3-0 scoreline.

	Division 1	Pd	Wn	Dw	Ls	GF	GA	Pts	
1)	Shelbourne FC (Dublin)	27	16	9	2	49	23	57	P
2)	Galway United FC (Galway)	27	15	6	6	39	25	51	PO
3)	University College Dublin AFC (Dublin)	27	13	7	7	55	38	46	POP
4)	Treaty United FC (Limerick)	27	11	9	7	36	27	42	PO
5)	Bray Wanderers FC (Bray)	27	9	10	8	36	31	37	PO
6)	Cork City FC (Cork)	27	8	9	10	37	28	33	
7)	Athlone Town FC (Athlone)	27	9	6	12	32	43	33	
8)	Cobh Ramblers FC (Cobh)	27	8	4	15	25	46	28	
9)	Cabinteely FC (Cabinteely)	27	8	1	18	26	47	25	
10)	Wexford FC (Crossabeg)	27	6	3	18	29	56	21	
		270	103	64	103	364	364	373	

FAI Cup Final   (Aviva Stadium, Dublin – 28th November 2021 – 37,126)

ST. PATRICK'S ATHLETIC FC (DUBLIN)   1-1 (aet)   Bohemian FC (Dublin)
Forrester 115'   *St. Patrick's Athletic won 4-3 on penalties*   *Feely 117'*

St. Patrick's Athletic: Jaros, Bone (Hickman 90+5'), Barrett (Abankwah 81'), Desmond, Bermingham, Lennon (King 60'), Lewis (Coughlan 96'), Smith (McClelland 75'), Burns, Forrester, Benson.

Bohemian: Talbot, Lyons, Cornwall, Kelly (Feely 75'), Wilson, Buckley (Levingston 105'), Devoy, Coote (Mallon 85'), Tierney, Burt (Ward 102'), Kelly.

Semi-finals

| Bohemian FC (Dublin) | 1-0 | Waterford FC (Waterford) |
| St. Patrick's Athletic FC (Dublin) | 3-1 | Dundalk FC (Dundalk) |

Quarter-finals

Bohemian FC (Dublin)	4-0	Maynooth University Town FC (Maynooth)
St. Patrick's Athletic FC (Dublin)	3-0	Wexford FC (Crossabeg)
University College Dublin AFC (Dublin)	2-3	Waterford FC (Waterford)
Finn Harps FC (Ballybofey)	3-3, 1-3 (aet)	Dundalk FC (Dundalk)